THE STATE OF ECONOMIC AND SOCIAL HUMAN RIGHTS

This edited volume offers original scholarship on economic and social human rights from leading and new cutting-edge scholars in the fields of economics, law, political science, sociology, and anthropology. It analyzes the core economic and social rights and the crucial topic of nondiscrimination, and includes an innovative section on "meta" rights. The main chapters answer important questions about economic and social rights performance around the world by emphasizing the obstacles that prevent governments from fulfilling their obligations. The book's introductory and concluding chapters address conceptual issues and correct mistakes often made by critics of economic and social rights. All together the interdisciplinary analysis offers a detailed and up-to-date discussion to help scholars and policy makers find the best ways to instantiate economic and social rights.

Lanse Minkler is an Associate Professor of Economics at the University of Connecticut, and former Director of Socio-Economic Rights and Co-Founder of the Economic and Social Right Research Group at the university's Human Rights Institute. His earlier research concerned worker knowledge contributions and worker motivations and the intersection between ethics and economics, which resulted in his book *Integrity and Agreement: Economics When Principles Also Matter* (2008). His current research interests center on human rights, particularly on the right to work, and constitutionalizing economic and social rights. He coedited *Economic Rights: Conceptual, Measurement, and Policy Issues* (with Shareen Hertel, 2007), and has published in top human rights journals.

The State of Economic and Social Human Rights

A GLOBAL OVERVIEW

Edited by

Lanse Minkler

University of Connecticut

CAMBRIDGE UNIVERSITY PRESS
Cambridge, New York, Melbourne, Madrid, Cape Town,
Singapore, São Paulo, Delhi, Mexico City

Cambridge University Press
32 Avenue of the Americas, New York, NY 10013-2473, USA

www.cambridge.org
Information on this title: www.cambridge.org/9781107609136

© Cambridge University Press 2013

First published 2013

Printed in the United States of America

A catalog record for this publication is available from the British Library.

Library of Congress Cataloging in Publication data
The state of economic and social human rights : a global overview / [edited by] Lanse
Minkler, University of Connecticut.
   pages cm
Includes bibliographical references and index.
ISBN 978-1-107-02802-9 – ISBN 978-1-107-60913-6 (pbk.)
1. Human rights – Economic aspects.   2. Human rights – Social aspects.   I. Minkler,
Lanse, editor of compilation.
JC571.S7855   2013
330–dc23   2012036773

ISBN 978-1-107-02802-9 Hardback
ISBN 978-1-107-60913-6 Paperback

Contents

Contributors

Cathy Albisa, Executive Director, National Economic and Social Rights Initiative

Kristy A. Belton, Ph.D. Candidate in Political Science, University of Connecticut

Salil D. Benegal, Ph.D. Candidate in Political Science, University of Connecticut

Catherine Buerger, Ph.D. Candidate in Anthropology, University of Connecticut

Audrey R. Chapman, Healey Professor of Medical Humanities and Ethics, University of Connecticut Health Center

Michael Freeman, Professor of Government, University of Essex

Mark Gibney, Carol G. Belk Distinguished Professor of Political Science, University of North Carolina – Asheville

Philip Harvey, Professor of Law and Economics, Rutgers School of Law – Camden

Shareen Hertel, Associate Professor of Political Science and Human Rights, University of Connecticut

Christopher Jeffords, Assistant Professor in Economics, Indiana University of Pennsylvania; Visiting Assistant Professor in Economics, Eastern Connecticut State University

Kathryn Libal, Assistant Professor of Social Work, University of Connecticut

Gillian MacNaughton, Executive Director of the Program on Human Rights and the Global Economy, Northeastern University School of Law

Lanse Minkler, Associate Professor of Economics, University of Connecticut

Ken Neubeck, Emeritus Professor of Sociology, University of Connecticut

Flavia Piovesan, Professor of Constitutional Law and Human Rights, Catholic University of São Paulo

Susan Randolph, Associate Professor of Economics, University of Connecticut

Brittany Scott, Campaign Coordinator, Human Right to Housing Program, National Economic and Social Rights Initiative

Lyle Scruggs, Associate Professor of Political Science, University of Connecticut

Kate Tissington, Research and Advocacy Officer at the Socio-Economic Rights Institute of South Africa

Christian Zimmermann, Assistant Vice President, Federal Reserve Bank of St. Louis

Acknowledgments

Most of the chapters in this volume originated from the annual workshop of the Economic and Social Rights Research Group (ESRG) at the University of Connecticut (UCONN) in April 2011. Comprised of UCONN faculty, students, and affiliated faculty from around the country and sponsored by UCONN's Human Rights Institute, the ESRG is devoted to the interdisciplinary study of economic and social human rights. I feel lucky to be part of such an unusual and interesting intellectual community. I especially thank my colleague and co-organizer Shareen Hertel, not only for her help on this project, but also for her vision and energy in co-founding and guiding the ESRG.

I thank all of the authors of this volume, both ESRG members and not, for their careful development of each chapter. All chapters went through a significant revision process; some were revised many times. I am grateful that all of the authors approached the editing process in a cooperative spirit and seriously entertained suggestions, even when they disagreed.

Richard Wilson is the Director of the Human Rights Institute and I appreciate his ongoing support of the ESRG. I also thank Davita Silfen Glasberg, Fe Delos-Santos, Michael Freeman, and Kristy A. Belton for their help and suggestions. Finally, I am grateful to Cambridge University Press editor John Berger not only for his support of this project, but also for his support of economic and social human rights more generally.

Introduction: Why Economic and Social Human Rights?

Lanse Minkler

To begin to appreciate the magnitude of suffering endured by those living in poverty, consider this: measured head to toe, a traveler condemned to walk on the backs of Earth's population subsisting on $2 per day or less would cover the same distance as four roundtrip voyages to the moon.[1] Such a journey would take fifty-four years of nonstop walking.[2] That option, however, would be better than being forced to say the names of each so afflicted, which would take 195 years of nonstop talking.[3] Moreover, income poverty representations understate the true magnitude of human suffering. Even those with higher incomes may suffer hardships associated with poor health, housing, and education. Their sources of income may be precarious; they may lack clean water and sanitation or otherwise live in a spoiled environment. As always, these maladies disproportionately affect women, children, minorities, and the persecuted and dispossessed.

Although good development and growth policies are necessary, they have not been remotely sufficient to reach those most in need. For instance, researchers have concluded that neither current nor conceivable economic growth rates would be sufficient to achieve the Millennium Development Goal (MDG) of halving even the lower global poverty rate of $1 per day or less from 1990 by 2015 (Besley and Burgess 2003;

---

[1] The World Bank estimates that there were 2.564 billion people living in extreme poverty in 2005, virtually unchanged from the 1981 number (World Bank 2008, table 3). For a comprehensive criticism of how the World Bank calculates its poverty headcount figures and its political and moral implications, see Pogge (2010).

[2] The distance arrived at assumes an average height of 4 feet, and an average distance to the moon of 238,900 miles. The walking speed was assumed to be a brisk 4 miles an hour.

[3] Assuming 2.4 seconds per name.

Kimenyi 2007).[4] Furthermore, policy goals such as those embodied in the MDGs are just that, goals, or desirable objectives. Contrast that approach with the human rights approach. Specifically, economic and social (ES) human rights – the rights to the goods, services, and means to an adequate standard of living – are universal moral entitlements whose power is (or should be) legally ensured. ES rights enable each and every individual to claim sufficient resources to live a dignified life no matter what a country's average income or income distribution might be.

ES rights are becoming increasingly recognized in the law. For example, South Africa's 1996 postapartheid constitution innovatively includes rights of access to housing, food, water, and social security. In 2005, India's parliament adopted the National Rural Employment Guarantee Act, which gives rural head of households the statutory right to paid employment for 100 days per year.[5] More comprehensively, researchers associated with the Toronto Initiative for Economic and Social Rights have surprisingly identified at least one ES right provision in 95% of the world's developing country constitutions.[6]

Of course, even if laws are on the books (de jure protections), it does not mean they are implemented in practice (de facto implementation). We need to carefully examine the obstacles to de facto implementation. To do that we must be very clear about what ES rights are; when they are relevant; the extent of obligations; what laws, legal strategies, and policies are most suited for the realization of ES rights, and in what contexts.

The interdisciplinary analysis offered in this volume attempts to help scholars and policy makers find the best ways to instantiate ES rights. The authors in this volume provide a detailed, up-to-date discussion of ES rights. They also examine the role of the associated obligations, especially the obstacles to respecting, protecting, and fulfilling those obligations. For instance, we will see that not only can globalization, discrimination, and states' failures to recognize their extraterritorial obligations to other

---

4   The notable exception is China, which has seen the numbers of its population subsisting on $2/day or less drop from 972 million in 1981 to 474 million in 2005, despite its population growing by 311 million during that time (World Bank 2008, table 3).

5   Also, in the summer of 2010, the United Nations (UN) General Assembly officially confirmed the rights to clean water and sanitation as human rights. Even states in the United States have recently passed ES rights legislation. New York became the first state to pass legislation giving domestic workers modest protections against exploitative conditions, and Vermont enacted a single-payer health insurance system.

6   Access http://www.tiesr.org/data.html. As we will see, contributors to this volume further detail the widespread legalization of social security and environmental human rights.

states hamper ES rights fulfillment, but also, more subtly, that things like growing meat consumption and even Keynesian economics are obstacles as well.

1. WHAT ARE ECONOMIC AND SOCIAL HUMAN RIGHTS?

Most fundamentally, human rights are based on and meant to assure the realization of human dignity.[7] ES rights, like all human rights, are moral entitlements everyone has just because they are human. ES rights are therefore not contingent on one's virtue, behavior, attributes, or failings; nor, as moral entitlements, are they contingent on external circumstances such as political and economic systems or a society's wealth.

The Universal Declaration of Human Rights (UDHR), adopted by the UN General Assembly in 1948, famously enshrines the full catalog of human rights – that is, moral entitlements.[8] Of its thirty articles, Articles 22–26 have come to be identified with ES rights. Those articles cover entitlements to work, social security, education, and an adequate standard of living, which includes food, clothing, housing, and medical care. Although often ignored, we also include Article 28 because it reads, "Everyone is entitled to a social and international order in which the rights and freedoms set forth in this Declaration can be fully realized." Human rights are consistent with many different policies and institutions, but this Article imposes additional constraints on the rules of the game. Among other things, Article 28 obligates foreign governments from also violating the ES rights of domestic citizens.

Although moral entitlements are nice, they may be of little comfort to those who experience real-life violations. That recognition led to two additional covenants, the International Covenant on Civil and Political Rights (ICCPR) and the International Covenant on Economic, Social, and Cultural Rights (ICESCR), which were adopted by the UN General Assembly in 1976. Together, the UDHR, ICCPR, and ICESCR are referred to as the International Bill of Human Rights.[9] While separating the rights into two covenants contributes to the perception that the nature

---

[7] I will further touch upon foundational arguments; Michael Freeman will take up possible objections in his concluding chapter.

[8] For a good account of the history of the Declaration, see Lauren (1998). He argues that the Declaration is a Western articulation of universal principles that can be found in the best of the world's cultural and social values.

[9] Other international covenants that include some ES rights include the Convention on the Elimination of All Forms of Discrimination (see especially part II) and the Convention on the Rights of the Child. ES rights are also included in The African Charter of Human and

and value of human rights differ by category, the intent was to provide legal protections and support for the moral entitlements embodied in the UDHR. By signing and, more importantly, ratifying these covenants, countries are expected to align their laws and policies with the principles articulated in the UDHR and then detailed in the covenants. The covenants convert moral rights into ostensibly enforceable legal rights. However, enforceability further requires an enforcement agency and sufficient political and legal institutions in countries.

Once a country has ratified the ICESCR, often with reservations or exclusions, the Committee on Economic, Social and Cultural Rights (CESCR) is tasked with monitoring the implementation of the covenant. State parties are required to submit reports about their implementation efforts to the committee within two years of adopting the ICESCR, and then every five years thereafter. The committee uses the reports to assess and comment on a country's progress. To further clarify its interpretation of the ICESCR's provisions, the CESCR issues general comments; to date, it has published twenty-one.

However, the CESCR has very limited tools to compel countries to respect their ES rights obligations. The committee lacks the power to levy fines or to imprison violators, but it can try to work constructively with noncompliant governments. What it does have is the bully pulpit; it can reveal egregious violators to the international community, the so-called name-and-shame game. Often, of course, that is not enough.[10]

I now close this section with a brief discussion of what ES rights are not. Human rights are not entitlements to all things good or important.

Peoples' Rights, The Cairo Declaration on Human Rights in Islam, and the American Declaration of the Rights and Duties of Man.

[10] Even if it had better enforcement mechanisms, the CESCR still requires reliable, accurate information on which to base its analyses. Government policy makers themselves need accurate information about their own ES rights performance as well as alternative policy options. For some time now, human rights nongovernment organizations (NGOs), policy makers, and scholars have used cross-national databases to assess civil and political human rights performance, such as the Political Terror Scale, the CIRI Human Rights Data Project, Polity IV Project, and the World Bank's Worldwide Governance Indicators. Similarly scholars have recently been using data sources such as the Physical Quality of Life Indicator, Human Development Indicator, and Human Poverty Index in order to assess ES rights performance. Myriad theoretical and empirical issues remain, perhaps the most important of which is the continuing need for comprehensive disaggregated data, but early pioneering efforts attempted to assess and rank country ES rights performance. These works include the "residual" approaches of Kimenyi (2007), Cingranelli and Richards (2007), and Richards and Clay (2009) and the "frontier" approach of Fukuda-Parr, Lawson-Remer, and Randolph (2009) and Randolph, Fukuda-Parr, and Lawson-Remer (2010).

As Jack Donnelly notes, we do not have human rights to love, charity, or compassion (Donnelly 2003). ES rights do not entitle us to things that are often the objectives of economic and social justice. In particular, we are not entitled to any income equality beyond what is necessary to assure an adequate standard of living for human dignity. ES rights fulfillment is consistent with wealth, consumption, and social status disparities, perhaps significant ones. The extent of permitted disparities remains an interesting and somewhat contentious issue.[11]

Finally, ES rights doctrine does not constitute a comprehensive social, political, or economic theory. For instance, neoclassical economics theorizes about individual behavior, exchange, institutions (firms, markets, government, social), and macroeconomic processes and outcomes. Marxism has a systematic analysis of economic systems and individual behavior (from material conditions) that focuses on class (property relationships), alienation, and the process of social change (historical materialism). Human rights doctrine is far less comprehensive than either of the aforementioned, and is fairly agnostic on individual behavior and institutions beyond what is necessary to assure respect for human rights. The advantage of this lack of grand theorizing is that human rights doctrine is consistent with a wide variety of theories, and it is likely that the best of existing cultural, social, and economic institutions could be made to conform with human rights doctrine. The disadvantage is that there is no internal map in human rights doctrine that explicates necessary institutional reform, nor does it provide the expansive social justice that many seem to desire.

---

[11] The CESCR employs the core obligation approach, which sets the minimal essential levels of food, education, shelter, water, sanitation, and health facilities a state is obligated to guarantee its citizens. The minimal essential levels are meant to assure universal human dignity, but the exact requirements could vary in time and place depending on local circumstances (e.g., the minimal shelter needs of one living in Bangkok differ significantly from one living in the Yukon Territory). The primary virtue of this approach is that it bounds human rights claims and state obligations, which in turn can enhance political feasibility. In contrast, proponents for a more expansive approach argue that the requirements for human dignity entail more than the minimal basket of the core obligations approach (Bilchitz 2007; MacNaughton in this volume). If the moral rights included in the UDHR only require minimal essential levels of goods and services for human dignity, why didn't the framers refer to a minimum standard of living instead of an adequate standard of living? This approach calls for more equality of income, wealth, consumption, and social status than the core obligation approach. The primary counter might ask how this upper bound is determined; how exactly are state obligations bounded in a human flourishing approach?

2. SOME CONTEMPORARY ISSUES

The purpose of this book is to shed light on the status of ES rights. Necessarily, many important issues are only partly addressed or are left unaddressed altogether. Those issues include the foundations of ES rights, their costs, and the relevance of the notion of the interdependence and indivisibility of all human rights. This section touches on each of those issues.

a. Foundations

As expressed in human rights doctrine and the International Bill of Human Rights, the central foundation for all human rights is human dignity. Human dignity in turn is perhaps best defined as *intrinsic worth* – that is, a noncontingent worth each human possesses simply by virtue of our humanity (Gewirth 1992).[12] Everyone matters, but why do humans – as opposed to, say, frogs – uniquely possess this kind of worth, and do the explanations differ for different kinds of human rights?

Many foundational arguments insist that humans are unique in some important way. For instance, Alan Gewirth argues that each person has a justified sense of worth by virtue of his or her purposeful actions, and that each of us must also rationally attribute that same worth to other persons (Gewirth 1992, 1996). While differing in some important details, arguments pointing to human agency and autonomy are related. David Copp (1992) argues that for human autonomy and rationality to be realized, certain needs have to be fulfilled. That need fulfillment in turn provides the rationale for certain human rights, particularly the right to an adequate standard of living. Amartya Sen (1999, 2004) and James Griffin (2001) focus on *human agency*, the ability of humans to choose our own goals or life plans, and then the ability to pursue them. Humans can only realize their agency if they enjoy substantial freedoms, freedoms necessarily guaranteed by the entire catalog of human rights. Sen in particular is sensitive to the possible objection that justice accounts should include personal responsibility, not just entitlements. Based on agency, however, he argues that personal responsibility requires social responsibility because people cannot be truly responsible unless they have the kinds of choices that health, nutrition, literacy, and participation provide (Sen 1999).

---

[12] For an argument that the concept of dignity is too elastic to provide a proper foundation for human rights, see Bagaric and Allan (2006).

There are other kinds of justifications for human rights. For instance, Henry Shue (1996) argues that if everyone has a right to something, then basic subsistence and security are both required for the enjoyment of that right, and therefore everyone also has basic rights to subsistence and security. That argument justifies a minimal basket of both civil and political rights on the one hand and economic and social rights on the other. Finally, Jack Donnelly (2003), a skeptic of foundational justifications, argues that human rights exist because the international community has agreed that they are fundamentally important, and that governments can only enjoy legitimacy if they fulfill their human rights obligations. Similar to all of the preceding arguments, Donnelly's analysis applies to all human rights. Furthermore, Donnelly has gone to great lengths to try to dispel the "myth" that Western governments were ever hostile to economic and social rights (Donnelly 2007).

The brevity of this description is not meant to imply that any disputes over either the origins of human rights or their purported differences have been decisively settled.[13] Such a standard would be impossible; certainly there is no universal agreement about any one moral or political philosophy. However, I do mean to suggest that as a body of rights, ES rights are on similar footing to all other human rights because they share the same foundations and justifications, however strong those may be. ES rights may possess special features that imply implementation difficulties, which in turn could weaken their initial justifications, but those kinds of objections require close scrutiny. I address one such objection next; Michael Freeman will provide a more detailed analysis in his concluding chapter.

b. Costs

A central objection to ES rights aims at costs. Simple intuition suggests that many, perhaps all, countries do not have the resources to provide the goods and services required by ES rights. Maurice Cranston famously discusses the issue when questioning the very validity of ES rights with the

---

[13] Osiatynski (2007) offers a most interesting difference between ES rights and civil and political rights. He suggests that governments typically provide the services underlying civil and political rights, whereas individuals usually provide the goods and services underlying ES rights for themselves. Therefore, he suggests that ES rights should only be legally binding for those unable to provide for themselves or for wards of the state. Perhaps not anticipated by Osiatynski, I think his argument provides further justification for the central ES right of employment, and when coupled with a conditional income guarantee for those unable to engage in paid work (young, old, severely disabled), goes a long way to assure the right to an adequate standard of living.

test of practicality: if something is impossible to do, it cannot constitute a right (or duty) (Cranston 1967). Even the drafters of the ICESCR gave special attention to the anticipated cost considerations by including the infamous "progressive realization" clause.[14] Are overwhelming costs the obstacle that simple intuition suggests?

First, it is important to note that all human rights impose costly obligations. Eide (1989) argues that human rights impose three different kinds of obligations on governments: the obligation to (1) respect through noninterference, (2) protect from interference by others, and (3) fulfill the right for those otherwise unable.[15] That refinement of obligations implies, for instance, that it is quite costly for governments to protect us from harm by others (i.e., protect our civil rights) or to organize electoral processes (i.e., fulfill our political rights).

Second, some evidence suggests that economic rights, conceived of as conditional social security support plus guaranteed government employment for all of those unable to find jobs, may not be as costly as often assumed, at least for higher-income countries. Phil Harvey has estimated the financial costs of a guaranteed employment program in the United States from 1977 to 1986, a period in which the official unemployment rate ranged from a low of 5.8% to a high of 9.7% (Harvey 1989). After netting out the additional taxes paid by program workers and subtracting redundant social security expenditures (that would have been paid to the unemployed), Harvey estimates that the government employment program would have added, on average, 3.2% to the federal budget over the time period. That average includes a low figure of a .36% surplus in 1979 and a high of a 7.4% increase in the federal budget in 1982. With significantly different assumptions, I found similar results (Minkler 2011). In 2006, when the official unemployment rate was 4.7%, I estimate that a government employment program that generated 3.7 million new jobs would have cost $123 billion, an increase of 4.6% to the federal budget. For 2009, when official unemployment stood at 9.7%, the program would have cost $308 billion, added 10.7% to the federal budget,

---

[14]   The clause basically obligates governments to fulfill economic and social rights only to their (resource) ability. That ability should increase over time as resources grow, and those richer countries that are in a position to do so are obligated to provide aid. Unfortunately, some governments have hidden behind the clause in an attempt to excuse their poor performance, and richer countries largely fail to meet their (imperfect) obligations.

[15]   Shue provided an earlier, similar three-part delineation with his avoid/protect/aid framework in the 1980 first edition of his book (Shue 1996), but Eide's framework has become the standard in human rights doctrine.

and generated 9.3 million new jobs.[16] Although these kinds of estimates beg for scrutiny from economists, they do cast doubt about commonly held assumptions on the feasibility of ES rights.

What about poorer countries? It is certainly true that respecting, protecting, and fulfilling ES rights obligations will be more burdensome for governments in poorer countries, just as it is for civil and political human rights, but even that differential burden may not be as insurmountable as it appears. First, as Sen reminds us, the relative cost of labor is lower in poorer countries (Sen 1999). That means the labor services provided by teachers and medical technicians, to name just a few ES rights providers, cost relatively less than highly skilled or capital-intensive goods and services (which are relatively scarce). It also means that jobs programs of the type discussed previously will be relatively cheap. Moreover, and as also pointed out by Sen, it is not only how rich a country is that matters, it is also how it spends its resources. Throughout his seminal book, Sen documents how well the relatively poor Indian state of Kerala does in meeting literacy and longevity goals precisely because it spends an unusual share of its scarce resources on education and medical services. None of this suggests that the quantity of available resources or economic growth is not important, indeed – and obviously – they are, but it does suggest that even poorer governments can go a significant way toward meeting their ES rights obligations right now.

Additionally, these poorer countries should receive assistance from richer ones. Thomas Pogge provides perhaps the strongest moral argument for why rich countries are obligated to transfer resources to poorer ones. He argues that the current international world order (e.g., trade regime, power relationships based on colonial heritage) privileges rich countries while actively harming poorer ones. Because there are feasible alternative economic arrangements, rich countries are violating the negative rights of interference of the poorer ones by inflicting harm (Pogge 2005). Even if one is not persuaded by that philosophical argument, one needs to look no further than the International Bill of Human Rights for justification. Article 2 of the International Covenant on Economic, Social, and Cultural Rights states that governments are obligated to realize ES rights "through international assistance and cooperation, especially

---

[16] Similarly, Harvey (2011) estimates that a federal government program that generated 8.2 million jobs in 2010 would have had a net cost of $235 billion. Harvey argues there, as he does in his chapter in this volume, that a federal employment program would be a lot cheaper than standard macroeconomic stimulus policies to create new jobs for the unemployed.

economic and technical." This places a direct ES obligation on wealthy states to support poor ones in achieving these rights. Perhaps even more interestingly, and as noted earlier, Article 28 in the UDHR provides an entitlement "to a social and international order in which the rights and freedoms set forth in this Declaration can be fully realized." This under-appreciated article is the subject of both extraterritorial obligations – especially of rich states to poorer ones – and Mark Gibney's chapter in this book.

If fulfilling ES rights obligations is indeed feasible, as the preceding suggests, then why do they so often go unfulfilled? In his concluding chapter, Michael Freeman addresses this topic, but the answer may ulti-mately prove to be found in human psychology as much as standard economics. The fields of moral psychology and behavioral economics have attempted to find the factors behind moral behavior, such as fulfill-ing one's moral obligations. The answers range from rational deliberation to selfish genes.[17] Whatever the underlying cause proves to be, it would hardly be surprising if the more proximate cause points to the perceived social distance between the obligatory party and the rights holder; in other words, between the rich and the poor.[18]

Finally, it is important to note that there exists a glaring need for cost-benefit analyses of the institutional and policy options confronting policy makers. Governments are accountable not only for ES rights out-comes but their conduct as well. For instance, should a country try to constitutionalize ES rights?[19] How important is democracy in effecting ES rights outcomes? What patent protections should a country enforce? How beneficial is development aid and what is its best use? What is the role for the market in the provision of health care? What is the best design for government employment programs? These sorts of questions can only be answered after careful qualitative and quantitative study, the kind that can be provided by social scientists such as political scientists and, importantly, economists.

To date, too few economists have waded into ES rights data or insti-tutional and policy analysis. It is not for the lack of ability. Economists may have so far ignored the subject because of methodological differences

---

[17] For instance, for the former, see the work of cognitive development theorist Lawrence Kohlberg (Colby and Kohlberg 1987); for the latter, see the work of behavioral economist Nick Wilkinson (2008).

[18] For instance, a recent study by psychologists suggests that individuals in higher social classes act more unethically than those in lower social classes, including being more likely to take valued goods from others (Piff et al. 2011).

[19] On this, see Minkler (2009).

with human rights doctrine (Reddy 2011). Economists emphasize individual preferences and utility, and mostly focus on consequentialist welfare standards such as *Pareto optimality*, in which no one person can be made better off without making at least one person worse off. In contrast, human rights doctrine emphasizes human dignity and is nonconsequentialist in that everyone is entitled to certain rights irrespective of utility valuations. Nevertheless, there is virtually no reason why economists could not bring their impressive tool kits to bear on the costs and benefits of different policies and institutions to reach specific human rights objectives. For a long time now economists have analyzed political institutions, the civil rights necessary for free market exchanges, and property rights, so the subject of rights is certainly not foreign to their discipline.

c. On the Interdependence and Indivisibility of All Human Rights

The idea that all human rights are dependent upon one another and must be taken together as a unified package originated in UN circles in the 1950s, and has increasingly gained common currency ever since (Whelan 2006).[20] This notion of Interdependence and Indivisibility (I/I) is especially attractive to those who must either defend ES rights on the one hand, or civil and political rights on the other. The first group can use I/I to defend ES rights against the types of criticisms offered by Cranston (1967), discussed previously. The second group can use I/I to defend their favored rights against the criticisms of those espousing cultural relativist ideas such as "Asian Values," which de-emphasize or dismiss altogether civil and political rights.[21] Moreover, the notion of universality in the UDHR itself seems to provide the foundation for I/I. The UDHR preamble concludes with:

> Now, therefore, The General Assembly Proclaims this Universal Declaration of Human Rights as a common standard of achievement for all peoples and all nations, to the end that every individual and every organ of society, keeping this Declaration constantly in mind, shall strive by teaching and education to promote respect for these rights and freedoms and by

[20] The concept of Interdependence and Indivisibility was a central topic in both the first and second World Conferences on Human Rights (in 1968 and 1993, respectively), and to the drafting of the 1986 Declaration on the Right to Development (Whelan 2006).

[21] On the Asian Values argument, see Donnelly (2003, ch. 7). Also see Whelan (2006), who notes that the 1968 Proclamation of Teheran at the First World Conference on Human Rights provides a good example of the idea that ES rights are functionally prior to civil and political rights.

progressive measures, national and international, *to secure their univer-sal and effective recognition and observance*, both among the peoples of Member States themselves and among the peoples of territories under their jurisdiction. (Emphasis added.)

Nothing in the preamble, or the rest of the Declaration for that matter, indicates that a member state may pick and choose which human rights it likes best and ignore the rest. Tellingly, there are no subsections in the UDHR entitled "economic and social rights" or "civil and political rights."

Nevertheless, there are both conceptual and empirical challenges to I/I. James Nickel (2008) argues that the degree to which any one right can support another depends on the quality of its implementation, defined as the ability to stop threats to rights bearers. Because developing countries necessarily have difficulty providing high-quality implementation across all rights due to resource and institutional constraints, the concept of indivisibility is somewhat untenable. At an empirical level, that insight receives some support. Minkler and Sweeney (2011) examine 151 devel-oping countries from 1998 to 2005 to see if the people in them enjoy basic rights (subsistence and security) simultaneously. The authors found only a modest correlation coefficient of .15 over all countries and time periods, which indicates that I/I is indeed difficult to achieve in practice.[22] In a somewhat different vein, Laplante (2007) demonstrates the hazards involved of not achieving I/I. She claims that truth commissions provide rich data on simultaneous violations of ES rights and civil and political rights. For instance, Peru's Truth and Reconciliation Commission find-ings show how economic and social inequalities contributed to political violence in the 1980s and 1990s, in which an estimated 70,000 people were killed and 12,000 "disappeared."

3. SECTIONS AND CHAPTERS

This book is organized into three sections. The chapters in the first section each consider one of five core ES rights (food, health, housing, social secu-rity, and work) specified in the International Bill of Human Rights. The

---

[22] Minkler and Sweeney (2011) use the Physical Integrity Index from the CIRI database to measure security, and the Human Poverty Index from the United Nations Development Programme to measure subsistence. Perhaps more importantly, the authors find that, after constructing an I/I dependent variable, regression analysis suggests that a country's income, degree of trade openness, democratic political institutions, population size, and degree of internal conflict are all important correlates of I/I.

second section focuses on the equal rights clause, or nondiscrimination principle, central to human rights doctrine, including chapters that consider the special problems confronted by women, children, and stateless people in realizing their ES rights. The third section considers *meta rights*, by which we mean rights that have collective dimensions grounded not only in the joint and shared nature of their enjoyment but also in the need for parties beyond a single nation-state to contribute to their fulfillment. The first two chapters of the section on meta rights consider the right to a social order within which all human rights can be realized. The next two chapters look at *emergent rights*, or rights that emerge to address new threats, such as environmental crises or widening gaps of global poverty. The following gives a very brief description of the chapters. Michael Freeman provides longer summaries to accompany his expert analysis in the concluding chapter.

a. Core Rights

Articles 23–26 of the UDHR establish the core ES rights. The rights to adequate food, health, housing, education, social security, and work define and support the fundamental ES right to an adequate standard of living. Although we do not have a chapter on the right to education, this section covers all other core rights.[23]

The first chapter in this section, by Susan Randolph and Shareen Hertel, provides a comprehensive overview and analysis of the right to food by examining international law, the drivers of hunger, and implementation and monitoring efforts. The authors reveal both novel and well-worn reasons for why governments do not, or cannot, meet their obligations to respect, protect, and fulfill their citizens' rights to food. For instance, they discuss new challenges posed by climate change, increased meat consumption on the part of a growing global middle class, and the shift toward biofuel production.

The next chapter, by Audrey Chapman and Salil Benegal, provides a sweeping critique of the negative consequences of globalization on the

---

[23] For more on the right to education, see the work of the late Katarina Tomasevski, who was perhaps the right's most ardent proponent. As special rapporteur of the UN Commission for Human Rights from 1998 to 2004, she considered it her job "to transform the luck of the few into the right of all" (Tomasevski 2006, 4). Among many other things, she identified fifty-eight countries where primary education is not free and/or compulsory. For a good review of Tomasevski's work, see Klees and Thapliyal (2007).

right to health. Among other things, their detailed and evidence-based account scrutinizes the roles of the World Bank and International Monetary Fund on the right to health, especially as outlined by the CESCR's General Comment 14.

The chapter by Cathy Albisa, Brittany Scott, and Kate Tissington examines the right to housing from a unique perspective. The authors compare the housing situations in Mumbai, Chicago, and Johannesburg to show not only how governments have violated their obligations to provide additional housing, but also how they have been complicit in the reduction of housing.

In Lyle Scruggs, Christian Zimmermann, and Chris Jeffords's chapter, they employ a unique data set to empirically examine the trends in the legal provision of social security for up to 173 countries from 1969 to 2010. Their novel analysis finds an increasing trend in social protection laws, and also that national income and being a party to the ICESCR are positively related with the legal institutionalization of ES rights.

Phil Harvey concludes this section with a fascinating historical account of U.S. government employment programs from the New Deal to the present time, and analyzes the surprising factors that account for why the United States has not been able to secure the right to employment.

b. Nondiscrimination

Because many people attain the goods and services that underlie ES rights with minimal legal protection, sometimes we overlook the necessity of a full range of legal rights and obligations in order to assure that all people can attain those things. Some people suffer from persistent and systematic violations of their ES rights, so their plight merits special attention. As emphasized in the first two articles of the UDHR, the right to be free from discrimination in the application of all human rights is the most basic human right of all.

Kathryn Libal and Ken Neubeck begin this section by noting that the near universal ratification of the Convention on the Rights of the Child means that children should possess the same ES rights as adults. The authors then document a different reality by examining child poverty and discrimination even in rich countries such as the United States.

Catherine Buerger then considers the plight of women, and particularly how de jure legal protections often fail to secure their ES rights not only because of the historical prioritization of civil and political rights, but also because of context-specific barriers. She illustrates these issues by examining women's employment protections and property rights in Ghana.

The section closes with Kristy Belton's analysis of the understudied problem of statelessness, which affects millions of people who suffer multiple types of discrimination simultaneously. Belton uses the ICESCR to show how the international community is failing to respect, protect, and fulfill the ES rights of the stateless, and concludes with practical suggestions for how these violations might be remedied.

c. Meta Rights

The final chapters examine meta rights. Two chapters explicitly reference Article 28 of the UDHR, while another two examine the important emergent rights to development, and to a clean environment.

In his chapter on Article 28, Mark Gibney first briefly explores the ethical underpinnings of the Article, and then examines why international human rights law has generally failed to ensure that states meet their international obligations. He closes by noting that some recent developments may signal positive change.

Gibney focuses on the international aspect of Article 28; Gillian MacNaughton takes a different approach by focusing on the national aspect in her chapter. She contends that human rights scholars and policymakers alike have failed to recognize the evidence of the adverse impacts of social inequality. MacNaughton argues that the right to a national social order, in which the rights in the UDHR may be fully realized, implies a right to social equality just as it implies a right to civil and political equality.

Next, Flavia Piovesan deciphers and advocates for the controversial right to development, which can be thought of as a right to an enabling environment that allows people to realize the full range of human rights. She argues that the right adds the principle of solidarity, which is necessary to generate the international cooperation called for in the UDHR and underlies international obligations.

Finally, Chris Jeffords closes the section by systematically examining 198 national constitutions of the world to find all environmental rights provisions in them. Surprisingly, he finds that 125 constitutions include at least one provision. Jeffords's unique data set allows him to categorize constitutions by provision number, type, and (approximate) age, all of which will be quite valuable to researchers and policymakers for years to come.

Taken as a whole, the chapters in this volume advance our understanding of economic rights across issue areas and at multiple levels of analysis. Individually, each chapter aims to provide a comprehensive analysis of the literature, key debates, and practical challenges to fulfilling specific ES rights. In a world of growing wealth but also unfathomable poverty and deepening inequality, understanding these issues and motivating action to address them are all the more urgent.

BIBLIOGRAPHY

Bagaric, Mirko and James Allan, 2006. "The Vacuous Concept of Dignity," *Journal of Human Rights* 5(2): 257–270.

Besley, Timothy and Robin Burgess, 2003. "Halving Global Poverty," *Journal of Economic Perspectives* 17: 3–22.

Bilchitz, David, 2007. *Poverty and Fundamental Rights: The Justification and Enforcement of Socio-Economic Rights*, Oxford: Oxford University Press.

Cingranelli, David and David L. Richards, 2007. "Measuring Government Effort to Respect Economic and Social Human Rights: A Peer Benchmark," in Shareen Hertel and Lanse Minkler (Eds.) *Economic Rights: Conceptual, Measurement, and Policy Issues*, 56–75, Cambridge: Cambridge University Press.

Colby, Ann and Lawrence Kohlberg, 1987. *The Measurement of Moral Judgment V.1*, Cambridge: Cambridge University Press.

Copp, David, 1992. "The Right to an Adequate Standard of Living: Justice, Autonomy, and the Basic Needs," *Social Philosophy and Society* 9: 231–261.

Cranston, Maurice, 1967. "Human Rights, Real and Supposed," in D.D. Raphael (Ed.) *Political Theory and the Rights of Man*, 43–53, Bloomington: Indiana University Press.

Donnelly, Jack, 2003. *Universal HR in Theory & Practice*, Ithaca, NY: Cornell University Press.

Donnelly, Jack, 2007. "The West and Economic Rights," in Shareen Hertel and Lanse Minkler (Eds.) *Economic Rights: Conceptual, Measurement, and Policy Issues*, 37–55, Cambridge: Cambridge University Press.

Eide, Asbjorn, 1989. "Realization of Social and Economic Rights: The Minimum Threshold Approach," *International Commission of Jurists Review* 43: 40–52.

Fukuda-Parr, Sakiko, Terra Lawson-Remer, and Susan Randolph, 2009. "An Index of Economic and Social Rights Fulfillment: Concept and Methodology," *Journal of Human Rights* 8(1): 195–221.

Gewirth, Alan, 1992. "Human Dignity as a Basis of Rights," in M. Meyer and W. Parent (Eds.) *The Constitution of Rights*, 10–28, Chicago: University of Chicago Press.

Gewirth, Alan, 1996. *The Community of Rights*, Chicago: University of Chicago Press.

Griffin, James, 2001. "Discrepancies between the Best Philosophical Account of Human Rights and the International Law of Human Rights," *Proceedings of the Aristotelian Society for the Systematic Study of Philosophy*, 101: 1–28.

Harvey, Philip, 1989. *Securing the Right to Employment: Social Welfare Policy and the Unemployed in the United States*, Princeton, NJ: Princeton University Press.

Harvey, Philip, 2011. "Back to Work: A Public Jobs Proposal for Economic Recovery." New York: Demos. Retrieved from http://www.demos.org/sites/default/files/publications/Back_To_Work_Demos.pdf.

Kimenyi, Mwangi S., 2007. "Economic Rights, Human Development Effort, and Institutions," in Shareen Hertel and Lanse Minkler (Eds.) *Economic Rights: Conceptual, Measurement, and Policy Issues*, 182–213, Cambridge: Cambridge University Press.

Klees, Steven and Nisha Thapliyal, 2007. "The Right to Education: The Work of Katarina Tomasevski," *Comparative Education Review* 51(4): 497–510.

Laplante, Lisa, 2007. "On the Indivisibility of Rights: Truth Commissions, Reparations, and the Right to Development," *Yale Human Rights and Development Law Journal* 10: 141–177.

Lauren, Paul, 1998. *The Evolution of International Human Rights*, Philadelphia: University of Pennsylvania Press.

Minkler, Lanse, 2009. "Economic Rights and Political Decision-making," *Human Rights Quarterly* 31(2): 368–393.

Minkler, Lanse. 2011. "On the Cost of Economic Rights in the U.S.," *Journal of Human Rights* 10(1): 34–54.

Minkler, Lanse and Shawna Sweeney, 2011. "On the Indivisibility and Interdependence of Basic Rights in Developing Countries," *Human Rights Quarterly* 33(2): 351–396.

Nickel, James, 2008. "Rethinking Indivisibility: Towards a Theory of Supporting Relations between Human Rights," *Human Rights Quarterly* 30: 984–1001.

Osiatynski, Wiktor, 2007. "Needs-Based Approach to Social and Economic Rights," in Shareen Hertel and Lanse Minkler (Eds.) *Economic Rights: Conceptual, Measurement, and Policy Issues*, 56–75, Cambridge: Cambridge University Press.

Piff, Paul, Daniel Stancato, Stephane Cote, Rodolfo Mendoza-Denton, and Dacher Keltner, 2011. "Higher Social Class Predicts Increased Unethical Behavior," *Proceedings of the National Academy of Sciences*. Retrieved from http://www.pnas.org/content/early/2012/02/21/1118373109.full.pdf+html?with-ds=yes.

Pogge, Thomas, 2005. "Severe Poverty as a Violation of Negative Duties," *Ethics and International Affairs*, 19: 1–8, 55–84.

Pogge, Thomas, 2007. "Severe Poverty as a Human Rights Violation," in Thomas Pogge (Ed.) *Freedom from Poverty as a Human Right: Who Owes What to the Very Poor?* Oxford 11–54: Oxford University Press.

Pogge, Thomas, 2010. *Politics as Usual*, Cambridge: Polity Press.

Randolph, Susan, Sakiko Fukuda-Parr, and Terra Lawson-Remer, 2010. "Economic and Social Rights Fulfillment Index: Country Scores and Rankings," *Journal of Human Rights* 9(3): 230–261.

Reddy, Sanjay, 2011. "Economics and Human Rights: A Non-Conversation," *Journal of Human Development and Capabilities* 12: 1, 63–72.

Richards, David and K. Chad Clay, 2009. "Measuring Government Effort to Respect Economic, Social, and Cultural Rights," Working Paper #13, Economic Rights Working Paper Series, Human Rights Institute, University of Connecticut.

Sen, Amartya, 1999. *Development as Freedom*, New York: Anchor Books/ Random House.

Sen, Amartya, 2004. "Elements of a Theory of Human Rights," *Philosophy and Public Affairs* 32: 315–356.

Shue, Henry, 1996. *Basic Rights: Subsistence, Affluence, and U.S. Foreign Policy*, 2nd edition, Princeton, NJ: Princeton University Press.

Tomasevski, Katarina, 2006. *Human Rights Obligations in Education: The 4-A Scheme*, Nijmegen, The Netherlands: Wolf Legal Publishers.

Whelan, Daniel, 2006. Interdependent, Indivisible, and Interrelated Human Rights: A Political and Historical Investigation, Unpublished Ph.D. Dissertation, University of Denver.

Wilkinson, Nick, 2008. *An Introduction to Behavioral Economics*, Hampshire: Palgrave MacMillan.

World Bank, 2008. *World Development Indicators: Poverty Data – A Supplement to World Development Indicators*.

I

Core Rights

2

The Right to Food: A Global Perspective

Susan Randolph and Shareen Hertel

I. INTRODUCTION

Global per capita food production has risen to unprecedented levels, yet the number of hungry people has increased. Hunger remains a pervasive reality in the world today: 925 million of the world's nearly 7 billion people are undernourished, an increase of more than 135 million hungry people since 1995, according to the United Nations (UN) Food & Agriculture Organization (FAO) (2010; FAO, Hunger Statistics). Today, someone in the world is dying of hunger or its complications every several minutes of every day (FAO 2010). Yet there are adequate food stocks available to feed the world's population (Paarlberg 2010), and the right to food is recognized formally under international law as well as informally by popular demand as a fundamental human right.

Indeed, realization of the right to food is essential to the fulfillment of other human rights. The right to life and the right to health are inextricably linked to the right to food. Hunger and undernourishment directly or indirectly account for more than half of the deaths in the world according to the United Nations Development Programme (UNDP) (2000). Malnutrition turns common childhood diseases into killers; roughly half of the deaths due to diarrhea, malaria, pneumonia, and measles can be attributed to malnutrition (Black, Morris, and Bryce 2003; Bryce et al. 2005). Enjoyment of the right to food is contingent, in turn, upon the realization of the right to education and the right to work. Malnutrition impedes learning and psychosocial development (Pridmore 2007; Alaimo, Olson, and Frangillo 2001). Poor health and low education and

but d... be under ICESCR

We gratefully acknowledge the support of NSF grant # 1061457.

21

skill development limit access to decent work that provides incomes above the poverty level.

Why, then, has so little progress been made in eliminating hunger, given the centrality of food to achieving multiple other rights? Considerable academic scholarship already exists on the politics of famine (most famously, Sen 1981); the economic underpinnings of food shortages (for example, Ghosh 2010); and the epidemiology of hunger, as cited previously. The broader human rights historical narrative, however, has tended to overlook the place of food-rights advocacy in particular, and economic-rights advocacy in general (Moyn 2010; see Chong 2010 as an exception). In this chapter, we explore the paradox of persistent global hunger, grounding our analysis in an assessment of the extent to which contemporary states are meeting various aspects of their commitments under international law to respect, protect, and fulfill the right to food.

We are mindful of the fact that the right to food can be mapped on two levels: on one, as a formal, legal obligation of states under international law; and on another, as a popular demand for access to food as a means of survival. We are also aware that proponents in the modern "food sovereignty" movement argue that hunger is perpetuated not only by neoliberal globalization but also by the system of state sovereignty, which the modern human rights regime reinscribes. Analyzing contemporary food-rights advocacy exposes a central paradox: an embrace of the rhetoric of rights by advocates but a rejection of the formal UN system by the most radical activists among them, who favor a discourse of food sovereignty instead (Shiva 2000; Uzondu 2010). Although mindful of this critique, we have chosen to frame the right to food in this chapter both in terms of food security and with reference to countries' individual and collective obligations under UN treaty law. We do so because the concrete benchmarks available to evaluate fulfillment of the right to food are, as of yet, calibrated around those benchmarks.

Taking Sen's perspective as a point of departure, we offer an integrated analysis of the politics and economics of hunger, starting from the premise that access to food is a human right that states have a normative obligation to fulfill and that people have a right to demand be met to the maximum extent states are capable. We introduce a new methodology for analyzing shortfalls in states' responsibility to respect, protect, and fulfill the right to food and present a range of contemporary examples of individual state practice. Our goal is to advance scholarship, while at the same time offering a tool for popular advocacy around hunger issues: a framework for holding individual states accountable for fulfilling the right to food.

II. THE RIGHT TO FOOD UNDER INTERNATIONAL LAW

In legal terms, the concept of food as a human right emerged along with the rest of contemporary international law in the aftermath of World War II. The right to food was initially codified in the UN Declaration of Human Rights (UDHR), Article 25 (UN General Assembly Resolution 217 A, III) and was reaffirmed in Article 11 of the International Covenant on Economic, Social and Cultural Rights (ICESCR). The monitoring committee for the ICESCR, the Committee on Economic, Social and Cultural Rights (CESCR), has since written General Comment # 3 on "The nature of States parties obligations" (in 1990) and General Comment #12 on "The right to adequate food" (in 1999) (UN CESCR 1990; UN CESCR 1999). The full scope of the right to food has evolved under international law not only in response to global efforts to combat hunger and malnutrition but also as a function of growth in our understanding of the factors that contribute to hunger and malnutrition.

Article 25, paragraph 1 of the UDHR refers to the right to food as one aspect of the right to a standard of living adequate to ensure the health and well-being of each person. The right to food is thus explicitly linked to individuals' health and well-being. Article 11 of the ICESCR goes beyond identifying the right to food as an aspect of the right to an adequate standard of living and articulates two separate but related entitlements: the right to adequate food (Art. 11, para. 1) and the "fundamental" right to be free from hunger (Art. 11, para. 2). Article 11 obligates state parties to the covenant to take specific measures individually and through international cooperation to ensure the right to adequate food and to eliminate hunger.

The right to adequate food is a *relative standard*, in that it is subject to progressive realization. That is, states that are party to the covenant are required to put in place measures, policies, and programs that lead to its full realization over time and to devote the "maximum of [their] available resources" to this end (see Art. 2 of the ICESCR). However, the right to freedom from discrimination in accessing adequate food is an *absolute standard*, meaning it is immediately actionable and universally applied equally (see Art. 2, para. 2 of the ICESCR). States party to the ICESCR must implement nondiscriminatory food policies immediately, even if the general level of fulfillment of access to adequate food is less in some countries than others (given the relative nature of progressive realization). Similarly, the right to be free from hunger is also an absolute standard, and must be fulfilled with immediate effect because freedom from hunger constitutes the minimum core content of the right to food.[1] As specified in General Comment 3 of the CESCR, states are obligated to uphold the minimum core content of each economic, social, and cultural right, if necessary, by drawing on assistance from the international community (UN CESCR 1990).

Article 11 of the ICESCR lays out a three-part rubric for fulfilling these rights, based on the following policy measures:

- First, increasing food **availability** nationally and internationally by increasing production, specifically by harnessing and disseminating technical and scientific knowledge to improve "methods of production, conservation and distribution of food" (Art. 11, para. 2a);
- Second, enhancing **access** to food at the country level by "ensuring an equitable distribution of world food supplies in relation to need" (Art. 11, para. 2b);
- Third, targeting food **utilization** by identifying good nutrition as a crucial link between food access and health outcomes at the individual level. Article 11, paragraph 2 thus instructs countries to disseminate "knowledge of the principles of nutrition" to ensure adequate utilization of food.

Yet other than these measures, the right to food remains relatively opaque in Article 11 of the ICESCR, as do the obligations of states party to the ICESCR acting individually and collectively.

Sparked in part by a request from member states during the 1996 World Food Summit, General Comment 12 was issued by the CESCR in 1999. General Comment 12 provides the most comprehensive definition of the substantive content of the right to food under international law, and expands on the three core dimensions of the right – food availability, food access, and food use. The aim was to provide guidance on the sorts of information that state parties to the ICESCR would need to monitor

---

[1] General Comment No. 3 of the CESCR specifies that the minimum core obligation of a state is to "ensure the satisfaction of, at the very least, minimum essential levels of each of the rights" (CESCR, 1990, para. 10). Freedom from hunger is widely viewed as the minimum essential level of the right to food (see for example, Alston, 1984; Kunnemann and Epal-Ratien 2004; Kent 2010, and Chopra 2009). In addition to the ICESCR's characterization of freedom from hunger as "fundamental," the CESCR's General Comment No. 12 singles out hunger and malnutrition as more urgent problems than inadequate food itself, and specifies that states are obligated to ensure "at the very least, the minimum essential level [of food] to be free from hunger" (UNCESCR 1999, para. 17). That being said, the question of what precisely defines freedom from hunger is not without some debate.

implementation of Article 11 of the covenant and to further delineate other core elements of the right to food beyond food security. It thus offers a detailed interpretation of the nature and scope of the right to food included in the ICESCR, drawing both on the Committee's analysis of country reports submitted by state parties to that treaty since 1979, and on the accumulation of knowledge to date regarding the economic, social, political, environmental, and other factors that influence the fulfillment of the right to food.

As elaborated in General Comment 12, the right to food encompasses "physical and economic access...to adequate food" that is produced or procured in a sustainable manner (UN CESCR 1999, para. 6 & 9). Physical accessibility requires that adequate food be available to every man, woman, and child, including those with medical problems, and physical or mental limitations (para. 13b). Economic accessibility requires that the financial cost of acquiring adequate food not be so high as to jeopardize the realization of other rights (para. 13a). This extends from the individual to the national level.

General Comment 12 defines "adequate food" more broadly than simply meeting the caloric needs of typical men, women, and children. Adequacy has several dimensions. First, it requires that the food contain sufficient macronutrients and micronutrients for optimal physical and mental development and maintenance, and to support desired activity levels (para. 9). Second, food adequacy requires that food be "free from adverse substances." Hence, protective measures must be put in place to prevent contamination or adulteration of food stuffs and to destroy any toxins (para. 10). Finally, food adequacy requires that access to food be ensured in a way that meets cultural or consumer acceptability standards and does not violate social norms (para. 11).

Beyond providing the legal substantive scope of the right to food, General Comment 12 also sets forth the procedural elements of the right and corresponding state obligations with regard to fulfilling the right. As is the case for other economic, social, and cultural rights, the nature of state obligations is threefold – to respect, protect, and fulfill – and entails both obligations of conduct and obligations of result. Respecting the right to food requires the state to restrain itself from taking measures that restrict access to food, while protecting the right entails ensuring that third parties (individuals or corporations) do not deprive people of access to food. Fulfilling the right to food (para. 15) imposes a twofold obligation on states: an obligation to facilitate and an obligation to provide. The former entails taking proactive measures (including legislative, administrative, budgetary, and judicial measures) that strengthen people's access to adequate food and their ability to utilize it to enhance their health. The latter entails directly providing food and complementary resources when it is not feasible for people to access adequate food or the complementary resources necessary to utilize it effectively. States are not required to ensure full realization of the right to food with immediate effect; rather, states are obligated to "take steps to achieve *progressively* the full realization of the right to adequate food" (para. 14) and are required to ensure "at the very least, the minimum essential level [of food] to be free from hunger" (para. 17).

General Comment 12 also confirms that the procedural rights of participation, nondiscrimination, accountability, and remedy apply with equal force to the right to food. It also imposes obligations on each state with regard to other states. Specifically, states are obligated to refrain from taking measures that endanger the realization of the right to food in other countries. States are also obliged to take proactive measures to facilitate the realization of the right to food in other countries. States must act collectively to fulfill the right to food – including by meeting the commitments for the Rome Declaration of the World Food Summit (para. 36). General Comment 3 of the CESCR more fully specifies the obligations of states under the covenant. The approach throughout is state-centric.

Yet this state-centric approach is increasingly problematic on several grounds. First, it fails to address the responsibilities of key global actors such as transnational corporations and international financial institutions that are not themselves states but can influence human rights outcomes significantly.[2] Second, the current state-centric approach adopts far too narrow a view of state responsibilities – unduly limiting them to the responsibilities of states to their "own" citizens, rather than extending such responsibilities to include "extra-territorial obligations" to prevent harm to people affected by the state's economic or other policy actions, who happen to live in other states. Only by taking such extraterritorial obligations seriously, Skogly and Gibney argue (2007), will states meaningfully engage in the "international cooperation" they are obliged to carry out both under the UN Charter (Article 1) and the ICESCR (Article 2, para. 1). Third, the current state-centric approach does not

---

[2]   As Narula notes (2006, 691): "[i]mplicit in this state-centric approach is the rationale that human rights are the by-product of relationships between governments and the individuals they govern, rather than relationships between global actors and individuals worldwide whose rights are affected by their actions."

acknowledge the individual complicity of comparably well-off people, worldwide, who benefit from maintaining an unjust global economic order (Pogge 2008; Gibney, in this volume).

III. GLOBAL AND NATIONAL LEVEL DRIVERS OF HUNGER

The full scope of the right to food has evolved under international law, not only in response to national and global efforts to combat hunger and malnutrition, but also as a function of growth in our understanding of the factors that contribute to hunger and malnutrition. We now first discuss global drivers of hunger, and then national drivers of hunger.

A. Global Drivers of Hunger

In recent years, a number of global forces have converged that have undermined national and cooperative global efforts to ensure the right to food. Here, we discuss several of the immediate causes, and several of the less proximate but no less significant ones.

In the immediate run, the combined effect of the dramatic increase in global food prices in 2007 and 2008 and the global financial crisis eroded food security for many of the world's poorest and most at-risk people. A confluence of shocks during this period sent food prices soaring, including: extreme weather incidents in major food-producing countries; increased fertilizer prices and other increased food production costs in the face of a spike in oil prices; and speculative investments in grain futures markets. Measures to stem rising food prices by some countries (specifically, the imposition of food export restrictions in some food-exporting countries) and increased grain purchases in some food-importing countries only amplified the rise in global prices (FAO, *Food Price Index Data Set*; UN High Level Task Force on the Global Food Security Crisis 2008).

The High Level Conference on Food Security sponsored by the UN in 2008 identified long-term supply and demand dynamics that deepened the impact of the crisis. On the supply side, these included a long-run decline in agricultural investment; the conversion of farmland to nonagricultural uses in the face of rapid urbanization; the shift to higher return crops instead of food crops; and land degradation, soil erosion, nutrient depletion, and water scarcity. On the demand side, population growth and dietary diversification – in particular, increased meat consumption, which accompanies rising incomes in large developing countries (especially

China) – have induced a secular increase in the demand for food.[3] The diversion of food crops for biofuels production has also served to amplify the increase in demand (Brown 2011).

These longer-term causes of the food crisis include the growing consolidation of the food chain over the past four decades – specifically in food distribution and retailing (Anderson 2008; Paarlberg 2010; Fielding 2011; Patel 2007) – along with the monopolization of key parts of the supply chain by a small number of large corporations, including seed producers.[4] Such consolidation has been fueled at the global level by the World Trade Organization's (WTO) member states' unwillingness not only to regulate agricultural subsidies but also to address the potentially negative impact that the patenting of seeds and other life forms may have on food security. At the national level, uneven enforcement of national antitrust regulation in countries such as the United States (Anderson 2008, 597) has accelerated the consolidation of key segments of the global food chain, and deregulation of the financial services sector nationally and internationally has allowed for intensified financial speculation on commodities futures (Ghosh 2010), which, in turn, has increased global food insecurity.

UN Special Rapporteur on the Right to Food Jean Ziegler argues that the combined effects of trade liberalization under the auspices of the WTO and recent bilateral trade agreements, along with agricultural liberalization and austerity programs under stabilization and structural adjustment agreements, have exacerbated hunger and food insecurity (UN Economic and Social Council 2001). In many cases, government accountability to international financial institutions has taken precedence over government accountability to a country's citizens to uphold its human rights commitments under the ICESCR; for example, when a state's repayment of multilateral debt has come ahead of ensuring the right to food. Further, structural adjustment programs have often undermined social safety nets, reducing social exchange and production entitlements by reducing wages and employment opportunities for those with fewer skills; increasing the price of basic foodstuffs, water, health care, and education; and increasing the price of agricultural inputs.

---

[3] According to Richard Fielding (2011), feedlot-raised meat production involves highly inefficient use of water and 66% of the world's supply of grain. http://www.rsis.edu.sg/publications/commentaries.html.

[4] William D. Schanbacher reports that "the top three seed companies (Monsanto, Dupont, and Syngenta) account for 47 percent of the global proprietary seed market" (2010, 58).

In the face of agricultural and trade liberalization, cash crop production for export has replaced subsistence food crop production for domestic use in many countries, further undermining food security – particularly when local regulatory environments in developing countries are weak. To a significant degree, the apparent comparative advantage of nonfood cash crops in developing countries is artificial. Developing country food producers cannot compete in the face of the extensive subsidies provided to agricultural producers of foodstuffs in developed countries. Beyond reducing locally produced food supplies, as noted by Narula (2006), the shift to cash crop production all too often damages local ecosystems due to heavy use of pesticides and the extensive tracts put under monoculture. Monoculture reduces biodiversity, and excessive pesticide use introduces new pesticide-resistant pests and viruses, damaging food crop production. In some countries, agricultural and trade liberalization have resulted in deforestation and consequent soil erosion in semiarid regions.

B. National Drivers of Hunger

Global forces and cooperative global efforts to promote the right to food certainly influence its enjoyment at the national level; however, national policy choices and constraints are equally as significant. As discussed previously, Article 11 of the ICESCR defines three central elements of securing the right to food – increasing availability, improving access, and enhancing utilization. Each of the three elements of food security is influenced by a tangle of interconnected factors. Measures for monitoring each of the three elements include indicators for tracking these underlying factors. Table 2.1 lists primary determinants of each of the three elements along with a selection of related process indicators that can be used to monitor the outcome of efforts to protect and promote the right to food.

Food availability constitutes the supply side of food security. Ensuring sufficient food production at the national and global levels is a prerequisite to fulfilling the right to food. At the national level, a number of policies can foster increased food availability, including: public investment or policies encouraging private investment in research to increase the efficiency and sustainability of food production; extension of improved processes and investment in agricultural infrastructure (such as irrigation, rural road networks, storage and processing facilities); policies aimed at enhancing access to productive inputs (e.g., improved seed varieties, fertilizer); and credit. Foreign aid can be instrumental here, as well. Countries that do

TABLE 2.1. *Determinants & measures of the right to food*

Increasing availability

Determinants	Measures
• Land devoted to food production→agricultural & trade policies • Amount irrigated land, extensiveness rural road networks, extensiveness crop storage/processing facilities→public expenditure on infrastructure for food production, storage, processing, and marketing • Technology for sustainable food production/ Yield Food Crops→public expenditure on food crop research, production & extension services & access to foreign technology on food crop production • Food Stocks • Climate/Season • Access to Food Aid	• Food Balance Sheets • Food Production Index • Food Grain Stocks • Food Aid (quantity, value, or share of consumption) • Cereal Yields • Share Agriculture investment in govt. budget • ODA to Agriculture • FAO Food Price Index • Ratio of food import value to total export value

Improving access

Determinants	Measures
• Income/Poverty Status • Access to land • Access to irrigation & other production inputs (improved seed varieties, fertilizer, etc.) • Knowledge food production technologies→access to extension services for food production • Access to credit • Household Food Stores • Food Prices • Social food entitlements→access to social welfare and nutrition safety nets (public or private) • Civil strife • Adult literacy & educational status • Degree gender equality	• Number or % poor people • Gini Coefficient of Income Distribution • Gini Coefficient of Land Distribution • Small-holder fertilizer usage rate per acre • Small-holder share land planted to improved varieties • Small-holder cereal yields • Domestic staple food prices • Conflict-related deaths • School completion rates • Ratio male to female school enrollment rates • Number or % Undernourished/Hungry

TABLE 2.1. *Determinants & measures of the right to food, continued*

Enhancing utilization

Determinants	Measures
• Access to Health Care • Access to Clean Water • Sanitation Facilities • Quality of food safety systems in place • Age • Disease prevalence • Nutrition, sanitation, and health knowledge	• % with access to primary health care • Vaccination Rates • % with access to Clean Water • % with access to Improved Sanitation Facilities • Disease Prevalence Rates • Child malnutrition rates • Mortality rates

not produce sufficient food to meet their population's needs must rely more heavily on foreign aid and/or global markets to ensure sufficient food is available to enable the realization of the right to food. Here, global food prices play a crucial role, as do the price countries can command for their exports and their export capacity. Food availability is jeopardized if countries do not earn enough export earnings to cover not only the cost of sufficient imported food and other critical imports – such as capital goods and intermediate inputs for domestic industry – but also foreign exchange obligations (e.g., debt service obligations). In the absence of sufficient food or financial aid, food availability will fall short of food needs.

Given sufficient food availability at the national, regional, and local levels, household entitlements – production, exchange, and social – determine access to sufficient food at the household level. Given sufficient access, household allocation determines the adequacy of a given person's access. Access to productive land along with knowledge of production techniques, access to extension services, productive inputs, and credit – as well as the cost of inputs and the sale price of output – all determine production entitlements. Inequality in the distribution of land is a major source of food insecurity in rural areas. Households with limited access to land and productive inputs or insufficient knowledge to make effective use of available land will need to rely on exchange and/or social entitlements to ensure their access to food. The same will be true should the farm gate price of crop production be insufficient to cover input costs.

Urban households must necessarily rely on exchange and social entitlements. When employment opportunities are limited and/or wages are low relative to the price of food, exchange entitlements will not be sufficient to ensure access to food. Global food prices closely track domestic food prices, but domestic trade policies play a role as well, as do policies directly or indirectly subsidizing or taxing basic food. Poverty is the primary cause of food insecurity, and policies increasing inequality drive up poverty rates at any given per capita income level. Social entitlements (both customary and state sponsored) enable households facing a collapse in production and exchange entitlements to maintain access to food, but are seldom sufficient to ensure access alone or over the long term.

Ill health and limited education are both a cause and a result of hunger and malnutrition, and are intimately related to food utilization. Hunger and malnutrition increase susceptibility to disease but tend to reduce food absorption, thus creating a vicious cycle. Impure water and inadequate sanitation initiate and intensify the downward spiral by reducing food utilization and increasing disease risk. Education increases knowledge of good sanitation and nutritional practices, but hunger and malnutrition reduce concentration and can lead to permanently reduced mental functioning, mental health problems, and compromised psychosocial functioning. These factors, in turn, limit the benefits of education and cut education short. Inadequate access to food and poor food utilization result in poor growth in children and excess mortality among all age groups, but especially children.

The implementation of national-level policies and measures that mediate competing claims on national resources is key to securing the right to food. Civil strife disrupts food supply chains, immediately undermining exchange entitlements in affected regions. The effect of civil strife, however, especially if prolonged, also extends to reducing availability (i.e., by reducing production and confiscating food stores in affected areas) and utilization (i.e., by destroying water and sanitation infrastructure as well as disrupting access to health care and food safety systems).

IV. MONITORING COMPLIANCE WITH GLOBAL AND NATIONAL LEVEL OBLIGATIONS TO RESPECT, PROTECT, AND FULFILL THE RIGHT TO FOOD

To assess state compliance with their obligations, we adopt the conceptual and methodological framework recommended by the Office of the High Commissioner for Human Rights (OHCHR) and associate structural, process, and outcome indicators with the obligations to respect, protect, and fulfill, respectively, the right to food (UN OHCHR, 2008). As specified by OHCHR:

- *Structural indicators* reflect commitments. At the global level, this includes global declarations, treaties, the adoption of global action plans, and the setting of goals. At the country level, it includes signing onto declarations, ratifying treaties, and putting in place the institutional structures and strategies necessary to secure the right to food.
- *Process indicators* reflect the accumulation of state efforts toward the realization of the right (i.e., the impact of multiple state-level factors that affect realization of the right to food). So for example, at the global level, this would include the magnitude of aid (financial or technical) provided in support of the right to food, and measures taken to ensure the international architecture better supports the right to food. At the national level, it would include indicators of the results of measures taken to increase food availability (e.g., food production per capita), food access (e.g., the poverty rate), and food utilization (e.g., population with access to improved water source).
- *Outcome indicators* focus directly on the extent to which the right to food is realized. In the case of the right to food, at the global level, this would include indicators such as the number of hungry people and the number of underweight children aged 0–5.

Although the structural-process-outcome configuration does not precisely mirror the trifold obligation to respect, protect, and fulfill human rights, as OHCHR argues, it makes it possible "to bring to the fore an assessment of steps taken by the States parties in meeting their human rights obligations" (UN OHCHR 2008, para. 8).

Data and space constraints prevent us from undertaking a fully comprehensive assessment of states' compliance with their obligations under the ICESCR regarding the right to food. Absent from our assessment is a discussion of specific instances where states have restricted peoples' access to food or have failed to restrain third parties from depriving people of access to food. Such a violations approach to monitoring compliance would usefully supplement the analysis here. Also absent from our assessment is a focus on whether the crosscutting principles of participation and nondiscrimination are being upheld. These issues can better be addressed in country case studies that can take advantage of the richer (but frequently not cross-nationally comparable) country-level data available.

A. Commitments to Uphold the Right to Food

The responsibility to respect not only requires that states refrain from restricting peoples' access to food but also obliges states to make specific global and national commitments to do so. The structural indicators we analyze capture these commitments. Notably, this is an area where states appear to be making progress – namely, in outlining specific commitments at the global and national level for safeguarding the right to food. Skeptics would argue that talk is cheap, however, so we analyze the nature, quality, and effectiveness of mechanisms for national implementation, as well.

World Commitments

The first World Food Conference took place in 1974, two years before the ICESCR came into force, and proclaimed the willingness of governments to engage in international cooperation toward the realization of the right to food by all people in all countries. The representatives of 135 countries issued the Universal Declaration on the Eradication of Hunger and Malnutrition, formally affirming that "every man, woman and child has the inalienable right to be free from hunger and malnutrition in order to develop their physical and mental faculties" (para. 1), and acknowledging that governments have the responsibility, in addition to working individually, "to work together for higher food production and more equitable and efficient distribution of food between countries and within countries" (para. 2). The specific measures enumerated and resolutions adopted to promote the right to food focused on increasing food availability – globally, by country, and by region within countries. The commitment of countries to act collectively to ensure the right to food has strengthened over time, and the focus of commitments to this end has shifted and evolved as increased consciousness of globalization, global warming, and other factors impinging on the right has taken hold.

The FAO, together with the World Health Organization (WHO), sponsored the first International Conference on Nutrition (ICN) in December of 1992. Delegates shared their expertise on the factors influencing hunger and malnutrition and discussed ways to eliminate them. Coming a decade after Amartya Sen's book *Poverty and Famines: An Essay on Entitlement and Deprivation* (1981) – in which he demonstrated that famines were the result of a lack of access to food rather than inadequate food production – the International Conference on Nutrition: World Declaration and Plan of Action for Nutrition (FAO and WHO,

1992) recognized that "globally there is enough food for all and that inequitable access is the main problem" (para. 1). The issues of food access and utilization dominated the conference; food availability was not entirely dismissed, but was taken up instead within the context of promoting environmentally sound and socially sustainable agricultural practices and reducing micronutrient deficiencies.

The World Food Summit of 1996 marked a watershed in international cooperation to end hunger. It led to the enunciation of the Rome Declaration on World Food Security and the adoption of the World Food Summit Plan of Action (FAO 1996). Representatives of the 182 countries involved pledged "political will and [their] common and national commitment to achieving food security for all and to an ongoing effort to eradicate hunger in all countries, with an immediate view to reducing the number of undernourished people to half their present level no later than 2015" (para. 2).

The World Food Summit articulated a commitment to ensure food security at all levels by committing states to support and implement the World Food Summit Plan of Action (FAO 1996). The plan included six broad commitments, encompassing efforts to address factors impeding the realization of the right to food (such as poverty, inequality, civil strife, and gender inequality) as well as efforts to directly increase food availability, access, and utilization at the individual, household, national, regional, and global levels. A seventh commitment obliged states to monitor progress toward realizing the right to food. As noted previously, the World Food Summit also requested guidance from the CESCR, which subsequently clarified the content of the right by issuing its General Comment 12.

Heads of states have met repeatedly since the issuance of General Comment 12 to collectively renew their commitment to working toward fulfilling the right to food and assess progress toward that end. The Millennium Development Goals (MDG) issued at the Millennium Summit of the UN member states in 2000 specified halving the percentage of hungry people relative to its 1990 value by 2015 as part of Millennium Development Goal One (UN General Assembly 2000, Res. #, Section 3, para. 19), and set up a monitoring framework to track progress to that end. Although the goal of halving the percentage of hungry people is not as ambitious as halving the number of hungry people (Pogge 2010), it was deemed a more realistic goal and remains the stated priority. In June 2002, the FAO held a follow-up World Food Summit (commonly referred to as the World Food Summit: Five Years Later) to assess progress made since the 1996 summit and discuss measures to accelerate it.

The dramatic increase in global food prices in 2007 and 2008 – along with the global financial crisis – eroded food security for many of the world's poorest and most at-risk people. These twin factors reversed progress toward the goal of halving the percentage of hungry people by 2015. The reversal precipitated the establishment by the UN secretary general of a High Level Task Force (HLTF) on the Global Food Security Crisis. The HLTF brought together experts from international agencies to craft a coordinated response to the crisis. Following this, a High-Level Conference on World Food Security was convened by the FAO in 2008. Those attending issued a declaration (i.e., the *Declaration of the High-Level Conference on World Food Security: The Challenges of Climate Change and Bioenergy*) that outlined both immediate/short-term measures and more intermediate/long-term measures that its signatories committed to undertake in order to overcome the crisis and ensure the realization of the goals of the 1996 World Food Summit. One month later, in July 2008, members of the High Level Conference issued a detailed analysis of the drivers of the global food crisis and a corresponding detailed set of measures, the Comprehensive Framework for Action (UN HLTF 2008) to catalyze action at all levels – civil society, government, regional, and international.

Measures to increase and stabilize food production and thus food availability reemerged as essential elements of the solution to the crisis (UN HLTF 2008). The 2009 World Summit on Food Security renewed commitments to eradicate global hunger, as did the 2010 MDG Follow-up Summit. Both summits adopted agendas for action to promote the right to food. Next, we analyze the substance of these and other policy commitments on hunger by focusing on the nature, quality, and effectiveness of mechanisms for national implementation; we also introduce indicators for assessing the extent of efforts made.

State Level Commitments

Designing the national policy framework necessary to implement the right to food is an intrinsically political process. If a state intends to ratify a treaty, it must ensure that its domestic legal regime is in conformance with the principles central to the treaty. This can entail amending or revoking existing laws if they conflict with the central purposes and obligations of the treaty. Ratification also obliges a state to create a policy framework for ensuring that the central purposes of the treaty can be achieved. In the case of the right to food, this means creating a policy framework to ensure access to adequate food at progressively more comprehensive levels over time.

The state can play a variety of different roles in fulfilling human rights and can use various forms of domestic law and social policy to do so (Gauri and Brinks 2010). A state may opt to constitutionalize the right to food, for example, and/or it may employ statutory law to ensure provision of this right. Even when the right to food is entirely absent from the constitution, there may be a broader social commitment to it – what legal scholar Cass Sunstein has termed a "constituitive commitment" (Sunstein 2004; Albisa 2011) – manifested through policies and programs.

Social policy design, in turn, can vary widely. Some states opt for a robust set of social welfare guarantees in the constitution and a correspondingly dense network of institutions, policies, and programs aimed at undergirding state-sponsored social welfare delivery. Other states emphasize a minimalist approach, in which the market principally determines the allocation of food and only the most marginalized people are directly provided for by government. Writing on economic rights fulfillment more generally, legal scholar Wiktor Osiatynski notes that the state can carry out a protective role; a regulatory role; a role of direct provisioning; or may opt to craft "values and directives that can at best be the goal for social policy but they are to be implemented by non-state actors or through international measures" (2007, 56–57). The choice depends upon local political culture, institutional legacies, and economic constraints, among other factors.

Constitutional Provisions and National Implementation Legislation. The FAO has urged states to create strong legal guarantees for the right to food: "If the law is truly to support the progressive realization of the right to food, there is a strong case for this orientation to be explicitly affirmed, whether in the constitution or a bill of rights or in specific laws" (FAO 2006, 14). If a state chooses to constitutionalize the right to food, it can either render the right justiciable or nonjusticiable. In the former case, the state creates a firm legal basis for entitlement by explicitly stating that citizens can take legal action to ensure fulfillment of the right. There is typically some form of provision for judicial review included in a constitution of this type, and individual citizens have access to the review process.[5] In the latter case, there is

---

[5] Legal scholars David S. Law and Mila Versteeg (2010; 2011) have conducted one of the first large-N studies of comparative constitutional evolution worldwide, and find an overarching trend toward inclusion of an increasing number of rights over time, and a growing proportion of constitutions that include similar types of rights and forms of

no comparable legal basis for enforcement. As Osiatynski observes, the desire to constitutionalize economic rights (including the right to food) stems from the goal of safeguarding those rights against political pressure (2007).

According to FAO researchers, twenty countries worldwide include the right to food in their constitutions: Bangladesh, Brazil, Colombia, Congo, Cuba, Ecuador, Ethiopia, Guatemala, Haiti, India, Islamic Republic of Iran, Malawi, Nicaragua, Nigeria, Pakistan, Paraguay, South Africa, Sri Lanka, Uganda, and Ukraine (FAO 1998). How robust are these rights? A cursory review of the language in the twenty constitutions cited by FAO as including the right to food reveals that only two of them included what could be judged as strongly justiciable provisions on the right to food (i.e, Guatemala, South Africa). Another two (i.e., Cuba and Pakistan) included somewhat less strongly worded but still justiciable provisions.[6] The remaining constitutions in that sample of twenty included the right to food, but in nonjusticiable language. These findings parallel those by Goderis and Versteeg (2011), whose analysis of trends in global constitutionalism reveals that only 15% of the world's 188 constitutions include provisions on the right to food. Although this number has increased steadily over the past six decades – from no constitutions including the right to food in 1946 to 4% a decade later to 6% by 1976 (the year the ICESCR came into force globally) to 15% by 2006 – the percentage of constitutions that include provisions on the right to food is still dwarfed by the number that include more conventional civil and political rights.

Osiatynski (2007), Guari and Brinks (2010), and others note that courts play a vital role in interpreting constitutional provisions on economic and social rights. In some states such as India, despite the fact that the right to food is included in the constitution only as a directive principle of state policy, it has nevertheless been judicially interpreted as

---

legal guarantee (including judicial review). There is, however, a simultaneous widening in the ideological orientation of constitutions – namely, a divergence between statist and libertarian constitutions. Economic rights provisions are increasingly included in statist, not libertarian, constitutions.

[6] Scholars Courtney Jung (2011) and Lanse Minkler (2009) have developed parallel research projects aimed at distinguishing between the different types of constitutional protections for economic rights. The core elements of their coding systems are similar, relying on the distinction between "justiciable" rights versus "directive principles" versus the entire absence of economic rights from the constitution. We employ Minkler's coding rubric here; we are grateful to Shaznene Hussein for related data analysis, and to Christopher Jeffords for insights on both the Minkler and Jung coding criteria.

being intrinsic to justiciable rights such as the right to life (FAO 2006; Gonsalves et al. 2004).

Although there is currently little uniformity in how states implement right to food legislation, the FAO nevertheless argues that each state should:

> [Review] all [of its] relevant legislation and institutions [to assess] the degree in which, in addition to achieving their own sectoral objectives, they contribute to an adequate regulatory and enabling framework for the realization of the right to food.... [N]ational legislation can also establish the framework within which the review and practical measures take place by: establishing general principles for the implementation of the right to adequate food; setting targets and deadlines; and establishing the institutional framework for policy-making and the monitoring of progress (1998, 45).[7]

Legislation can "clarify the roles and responsibilities of different agencies, define entitlements and recourse and monitoring mechanisms, and in general give direction to policy and underscore the prime importance of the right to food" (FAO 2006, 15). In some states, people whose right to food is violated can appeal to a national ombudsperson or national human rights commission for redress of right to food violations. Redress may include "restitution, satisfaction or guarantees of non-repetition" (FAO 2006, 16). In other states, victims can appeal to lower courts and, eventually, the constitutional court. In some states, there are specially mandated institutions created to foster stakeholder dialogue around food security issues, such as Brazil and Bolivia's national food security council's or Sierra Leone's Right to Food Secretariat (FAO 2006). These and similar institutions play a key role in monitoring national progress on progressive implementation of the right to food. They often provide data not only to the national legislature and executive but also to international treaty monitoring bodies.

B. Efforts Toward the Realization of the Right to Food

Having discussed structural indicators at some length (i.e., the commitments states make to protect the right to food), we turn now to the process indicators in order to evaluate states' efforts to protect and promote

---

[7] See related work on assessing macroeconomic policymaking and national budgeting from a human rights perspective: Balakrishnan (2005); Balakrishnan, Elson and Patel (2009); and Balakrishnan and Elson (2011).

this right in practice. Commitments to uphold the right to food mean little unless they are backed by concrete actions to protect and promote the right to food.

Global Efforts

In transforming commitments into effort, it is relevant to ask whether words have been backed up by monetary expenditures. Thus, we begin our assessment of global efforts to ensure the right to food by examining trends in foreign aid flows. However, changes in the policies of international organizations or changes in the international architecture can have an even greater impact on the ability of countries to ensure the right to food, so we conclude our examination of global efforts with a consideration of these factors.

Trends in Foreign Aid to Enhance Food Security. The pattern of foreign aid has shifted in response to the evolving understanding of the most critical factors affecting food security at any given time. This in turn has effected change in dominant views regarding the best means to influence food security. The total amount of aid to agriculture increased 2.2 fold from 1973–1975 to 1982–1984; decreased slightly until 1988–1990; fell precipitously to less than half its 1988–1990 value by 2003–2005; and then began to rise again.[8] The substantial increase in assistance to agriculture during the 1970s and early 1980s is consistent with the consensus view of the time that increasing food production offered the best prospect for ending hunger, and reflects the seriousness of the commitments made by the global community during the first World Food Conference.

The decline in aid to agriculture during the 1990s and early 2000s reflects both a decrease in total aid to all sectors during the 1990s and the recognition that a lack of access to food – rather than a lack of food availability – was the driving force of hunger and malnutrition at the time. In line with this shift, foreign assistance priorities were redirected toward poverty alleviation, as well, including support for expanding access to basic education (including adult literacy); basic health care (including maternal and child health care and nutrition supplementation); and investment in physical and economic infrastructure (including water supply and sanitation).

---

[8] The data available reflect aid commitments rather than disbursals. Commitments made in a given year are often disbursed over the life of a project lasting several years, and as a result, aid flows fluctuate substantially. By considering three-year averages, fluctuations in aid flows are reduced and more closely track average annual disbursals.

Table 2.2 shows the total level of foreign aid since 1995, and the share going to sectors deemed critical to ensuring food security. The share of total aid allocated to social infrastructure and services increases by thirteen percentage points, with substantial increases observed for the education, health, and population policies/programs and reproductive health subsectors. Within the education and health sectors, aid was increasingly targeted to basic services. Aid targeted to basic health services increased from 15% to 25% of total aid for health between 1996 and 2005; aid targeted to primary education increased from 15% percent to nearly 50% of total aid for education over the same period (OECD 2004). Beginning with the last period for which data are available (2006–2008), there is some evidence of a reversal in the downward trend in aid to the agricultural sector, perhaps in response to the Comprehensive Framework for Action's call for increasing aid to boost small-holder food production.

Despite the global community's expressed commitment to end hunger, direct Commodity Food Aid and Food Security Assistance has fallen sharply from 19.7% of total bilateral aid in 1970 to 1.2% of total bilateral aid in 2008, with only modest reversals of the trend in 1985–1987 and 2000–2002 (Islam, 2011, Table 2.1, 2). As a result, the number of countries where food aid provides a substantial portion of calories has fallen dramatically. As Table 2.3 shows, the number of countries where food aid provides more than 5% of total calories has fallen from forty-five to sixteen, and the number of countries where food aid provides more than 15% of total calories has fallen from thirteen to three. However, these figures do not include food aid provided in the context of humanitarian assistance.

The FAO (2010, 4) characterizes twenty-two states as being in "protracted crisis," and within them, 40% of the population is undernourished – representing one-fifth of all undernourished people globally. The most basic governing institutions are often imperiled in these states and social protection institutions are frayed to nonexistent. Food aid thus plays a critical role in human survival. Humanitarian aid constitutes an increasing share of total bilateral aid; its share in total bilateral aid increased from 1% in 1970–1972 to 7.4% in 2006–2008, with the sharpest increase taking place at the beginning of the 1990s (Islam, 2011, Table 2.1, 3). In 2009, it accounted for 44% of the Humanitarian Appeal (FAO 2010). According to the FAO (2010), food aid and other forms of food assistance (such as the provision of cash or vouchers enabling recipients to purchase food) are the best-funded sectors of humanitarian aid. They comprise a substantial portion of total aid for countries in

TABLE 2.2. *Distribution of total aid: Percentage allocated to selected sectors or activities*[1]

Sector or activity[2]	Period				
	1995– 1996	1997– 1999	2000– 2002	2003– 2005	2006– 2008
Social Infrastructure & Services	27.4	30.3	34.8	36.6	40.7
Education	5.7	7.4	7.5	7.7	7.9
Health	4.5	4.9	4.9	5.0	5.8
Population Programs/ Reproductive Health	1.8	2.5	3.3	4.0	6.2
Water & Sanitation	7.5	6.1	5.2	4.6	4.1
Government & Civil Society	5.7	5.9	8.4	10.9	11.7
Production Sectors	12.3	10.4	8.9	7.2	7.1
Agriculture, Forestry, Fishing	9.8	7.7	5.9	4.3	4.7
Commodity Aid/General Program Assistance	9.4	8.6	8.1	5.1	5.2
Development Food Aid/Food Security Assistance	1.7	2.7	3.2	1.4	1.1
Action Relating to Debt	6.0	6.4	8.2	16.5	10.2
Humanitarian Aid	4.9	8.1	6.1	8.0	6.7
Emergency Response	4.4	7.5	5.4	6.5	5.7
Refugees in Donor Countries	0.5	0.4	1.2	1.5	1.5

[1] Percentage is calculated as total of bilateral plus multilateral aid to sector over period concerned divided by total bilateral and multilateral aid over period.

[2] Main sectors/activities are left justified; subsectors and activity components are indented. Neither main nor subcategories are exhaustive.

Source: Islam 2011, table 2.2.

TABLE 2.3. *Food aid countries where food aid provides more than 5% (15% in bold) of calories*

1990–1992 (45/13)	1995–1997 (33/8)	2000–2002 (23/5)	2004–2006 (16/3)
Albania	Angola	Angola	Burundi
Angola	Antigua & Barbuda	Armenia	**Cape Verde**
Armenia	**Armenia**	Bosnia & Herzegovina	**Dem. Rep. Korea**
Azerbaijan	Azerbaijan	**Cape Verde**	Djibouti
Bolivia	Bolivia	**Dem. Rep. Korea**	**Eritrea**
Cape Verde	**Cape Verde**	Djibouti	Ethiopia
Comoros	Dem. Rep. Korea	**Eritrea**	Haiti
Djibouti	Djibouti	Ethiopia	Jordan
Dominica	Dominica	Georgia	Liberia
Egypt	Eritrea	**Guyana**	Maldives
El Salvador	**Georgia**	Haiti	Mauritania
Eritrea	Grenada	**Jordan**	Mongolia
Estonia	**Guyana**	Lebanon	Occupied Palestine
Ethiopia	Haiti	Liberia	Sao Tome & Principe
Gambia	Jamaica	Mongolia	Sudan
Georgia	Jordan	Mozambique	Tajikistan
Guatemala	Kyrgyzstan	Nicaragua	
Guyana	Lesotho	Occupied Palestine	
Haiti	**Liberia**	Rwanda	
Honduras	Maldives	Sao Tome & Principe	
Jamaica	Mozambique	**Serbia & Montenegro**	
Jordan	Nicaragua	**Sierra Leone**	
Kyrgyzstan	Occupied Palestine	Tajikistan	
Latvia	Moldova		
Lesotho	**Rwanda**		
Liberia	St. Kitts & Nevis		
Lithuania	St. Lucia		
Malawi	St. Vincent & Grenadines		
Maldives	**São Tome & Principe**		
Mauritania	Serbia & Montenegro		
Mongolia	Sierra Leone		
Mozambique	**Suriname**		
Nicaragua	Tajikistan		
Peru			
Moldova			
Romania			
Sao Tome & Principe			
Sri Lanka			
Sudan			
Suriname			
Tajikistan			
Tunisia			
Zambia			
Zimbabwe			

Data Source: FAO Statistical Office.

protracted crises: from a low of 10% in Uganda to a high of 64% in Somalia over the 2000–2008 period. Indeed, food aid and other forms of food assistance comprise a crucial means of reducing hunger for countries in protracted crises. During the acute phase of a crisis, they are lifesaving.

Unfortunately, as Table 2.2 reveals, there has been a substantial decline in the share of aid directly targeted to reducing hunger in the short-term. As a share of total aid (bilateral plus multilateral), it has fallen from 6.2% in 1997–1999 to 4.1% in 2006–2008.[9] Given the substantial increase in total aid commitments since the late 1990s, the absolute amount of aid targeted to reducing hunger in the short run increased slightly over the same period – although not nearly to the extent called for in international forums.

Global Policy and Rule Changes. By the early 1990s, the devastating impact of debt burdens on poor countries as well as the adverse impact of classic stabilization and structural adjustment programs was widely acknowledged, even by the International Monetary Fund (IMF) and World Bank (WB). In 1996, the Heavily Indebted Poor Country (HIPC) Initiative was launched to reduce debt to sustainable levels in poor countries and release funds for social service provision, in particular, poverty reduction (International Monetary Fund, 2011). In 1999, the IMF and WB began requiring countries to develop a Poverty Reduction Strategy Paper, mapping out their strategy to reduce poverty as a condition for debt relief through the HIPC Initiative. Conditionality for IMF stabilization and especially WB structural adjustment loans has also been reformed to better facilitate attainment of the Millennium Development Goals (World Bank 2004). Agreements increasingly protect continued spending on social services comprising a safety net for vulnerable groups. However, many claim these reforms do not go far enough and several case studies find evidence that stabilization and structural adjustment programs continue to contribute to hunger (UNDP 2001).[10]

The Doha Round of trade negotiations launched by the WTO in November 2001 proclaimed the goal of reforming the global trading system in order to redress past imbalances and thereby reduce global poverty

---

[9] Using food aid's share in the Humanitarian Appeal in 2009 as an estimate of food aid's share in humanitarian aid, the share of aid directly targeted to reducing hunger in the short-term is calculated from Table 2.2 as the sum of the amount specified as Development Food Aid/ Food Security Assistance (under commodity Aid /General Program Assistance) plus 44% of the amount specified as Humanitarian Aid.

[10] The 2005 Nigerian famine is a case in point.

by fostering the development of poor countries. Among other imbalances remaining at the conclusion of the Uruguay Round of trade negotiations, agricultural producers in developing countries could not compete globally in the face of high farm subsidies in high-income countries. As noted by Stiglitz and Charlton (2005, 50), "After implementation of Uruguay commitments, at more than US$300 billion, [farm subsidies in high income countries] . . . accounted for 48 per cent [of the value] of all [OECD] farm production," severely distorting trade against developing country agricultural production in general and food production in particular.

Since then, agricultural subsidies in high-income countries as a percentage of the value of farm production have hardly budged, although there has been some change in the form of the subsidies. Meanwhile, high-income countries have benefited at the expense of developing countries from further liberalization of trade in services under the WTO's General Agreement on Trade in Services. Bilateral trade agreements between the European Union (EU) and United States and various developing countries have further liberalized the laws governing the provision of formerly public services by transnational corporations (TNCs), including water crucial to food security.

The UN launched the Global Compact in 2000 with the goal of increasing TNCs' respect for international human rights, including the right to food.[11] Participation is, unfortunately, voluntary. In his 2003 report, the UN Special Rapporteur on the Right to Food Jean Zigler argued that states have extraterritorial obligations including a duty to prevent their own TNCs from violating human rights abroad (UN Economic and Social Council [ECOSOC] 2001). In 2005, UN Secretary General Kofi Annan appointed Special Representative John Ruggie to define more clearly the responsibilities of companies and build consensus between TNCs' home and host countries with regard to human rights. Ruggie's six-year effort yielded a set of guiding principles for business and human rights that the United Nations Human Rights Council endorsed in 2011 (UN Human Rights Council 2011). If adhered to, the standards integral to these guiding principles would address the potentially adverse impacts of business activity on human rights – including the right to food. It is, however, still too early to assess their impact.

---

[11] For an overview of the Global Compact, see the UN Web site on the compact at http://www.unglobalcompact.org/COP/index.html.

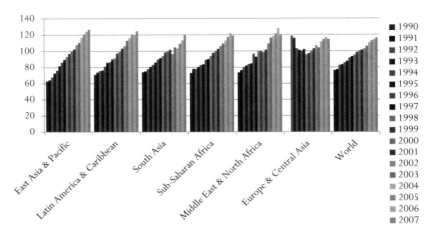

FIGURE 2.1. Food Production Index (1999–2001 = 100) Developing Countries Only *Source:* World Development Indicators (2011).

National Efforts

State expenditures are no doubt integral to food security; expenditures on social safety nets, agricultural investments, and so on contribute to enhancing food availability, access, and utilization. Country-level efforts to protect and promote the right to food for all people within their borders, however, involve more than directly providing food. The effectiveness of public expenditures, the set of incentives shaping the direction and nature of private-sector activity, the enforcement of relevant legal provisions, and the enlistment of foreign resources are also crucial. In this section, we thus consider these types of direct indicators of national trends in food availability, access, and utilization.

Food Availability. The adoption of effective measures to increase food production is a key means of increasing food availability. Figure 2.1 shows regional trends in FAO's food production index.[12] As can be seen, there has been a dramatic increase in food production in developing countries in every region except Europe and Central Asia. The gains were

---

[12]   The food production index is the sum of price-weighted volume of net food production (i.e., production minus the amount used for feed and seed) excluding coffee and tea, relative to the same value in a base year, multiplied by 100. The price weights used are the international prices prevailing in the base year. The food production index shows amount of food produced and available for consumption relative to the base year. Values greater than 100 indicate an increase in domestic food production relative to the base year; those less than 100 show a decrease. (FAO, *FAOSTATS*, 2011).

particularly pronounced in East Asia and the Pacific. The decline in the food production index in Europe and Central Asia reflects the dislocations in the wake of the transition from planned to market economies. These countries have now nearly regained the food production levels achieved at the outset of that transition.

The trend in the food production index reflects the success of measures undertaken to increase food production, such as: public expenditures on infrastructure for food production, storage, processing, and marketing; the adoption of trade and other policies fostering private-sector food production; and the successful extension of improved food-production technologies. It does not necessarily ensure improved access to food, however.

Food Access. Poverty is among the more important factors that affect food access, and may well be the most important factor. Poor households have limited access to land, productive inputs, food production technologies, and credit. They are also likely to have limited education and be the most vulnerable to civil strife. The global increase in food prices discussed earlier has depressed exchange entitlements, and this has the greatest adverse impact on poor households' access to food. Poor households spend a much higher proportion of their income on food than wealthier households. Countries implementing pro-poor policies can offset the adverse impact of rising food prices, at least to some degree.

Here, we consider whether countries are doing as much as they could to reduce poverty. A given level of inequality in the distribution of income results in a lower absolute poverty rate as per capita income rises. Accordingly, it is feasible to reduce poverty rates to a greater extent in countries with a higher per capita income. Thus, a comparison of poverty rates across countries reveals more about a country's per capita income level than its success in implementing pro-poor policies. One indicator that takes into account the feasibility of reducing poverty at a given per capita income level is the right to work component of the Social and Economic Rights Fulfillment (SERF) Index (Randolph, Fukuda-Parr, and Lawson-Remer 2010; Fukuda-Parr, Lawson-Remer, and Randolph 2009; Fukuda-Parr, Lawson-Remer, and Randolph 2011). This component right index assesses a country's performance as the proportion of the population that is not poor (using a \$2 per capita per day poverty line measured in 2005 PPP\$) relative to what is feasible given the country's per capita income level. Table 2.4 identifies those countries that are doing extremely well (i.e., achieving 90% of what is reasonably feasible); those doing extremely poorly (achieving less than 50% of what is

TABLE 2.4. *Percentage not-poor relative to feasible rate given best practice*

Percentage of feasible achievement

90% plus (47 countries)		75%–89% (28 countries)		50%–74% (12)		Less than 50% (28)	
Belarus,	Estonia	Mongolia	Egypt, Arab Rep.	Algeria	Nepal	St. Lucia	Angola
Ukraine	Latvia	Cuba	Ghana	Comoros	Sri Lanka	Papua New Guinea	Uzbekistan
Serbia	Lithuania	Turkey	Trinidad and Tobago	Cote d'Ivoire	Yemen, Rep.	Burkina Faso	India
Kazakhstan	Seychelles	Mexico	Bolivia	Honduras	Vietnam	South Africa	Congo, Rep.
Russian Federation	Slovenia	Morocco	Mauritania	Georgia	Haiti	Pakistan	Nigeria
Liberia	Bulgaria	Thailand	Peru	Suriname	Philippines	Indonesia	Swaziland
Togo	Chile	Paraguay	Armenia	Gabon	Cambodia	Bangladesh	Tanzania
Azerbaijan	Jordan	Tunisia	Uganda	Lesotho	Mali	Benin	Equatorial Guinea
Congo, Dem. Rep.	Kenya	Venezuela, RB	Nicaragua	Cape Verde	Senegal	Botswana	Singapore
Malawi	Moldova	Dominican Republic	Guatemala	Turkmenistan	Cameroon	Zambia	Mauritius
Burundi	Romania	Sao Tome and Principe	Djibouti	Colombia	Bhutan	Namibia	Saudi Arabia
Timor-Leste	Costa Rica	El Salvador	Tajikistan	China	Chad	Lao PDR	Oman
Rwanda	Uruguay	Ecuador	Belize			Madagascar	Lebanon
Sierra Leone	Macedonia, FYR	Brazil	Panama				Bahrain
Mozambique	Jamaica						
Guinea-Bissau	Gambia, The						
Ethiopia	Guyana						
Niger	Albania						
Montenegro	Argentina						
Bosnia and Herzegovina	Iran, Islamic Rep.						
Central African Republic	Kyrgyz Republic						
Croatia	Malaysia						

Data Source: Economic and Social Rights Empowerment Initiative (2011) www.serfindex.org/data.

48

reasonably feasible); as well as countries falling somewhere in between the extremes.[13] Although 47 of the 115 countries for which the index could be computed are doing an admirable job of holding down absolute poverty, absolute poverty rates in 28 of the 115 countries are dramatically higher than need be.

Food Utilization. Ensuring access to clean water and sanitation is critically important to ensuring food utilization. In their absence, water-borne diseases proliferate, reducing food absorption. Here again we turn to the SERF Index to learn whether countries are doing as much as they can in the face of their resource constraints to provide their citizens and residents with access to clean water and sanitation. The right to housing component of the SERF Index has two components: the proportion of the population with access to improved water sources and improved sanitation. Table 2.5 classifies countries according to their percentage achievement relative to best practice on this indicator. The results show the majority of countries could be doing considerably more to facilitate better food utilization. Although 31% of the 144 countries for which this index can be computed achieve a score of 90% or better, 21% achieve a score between 75% and 89.9%; 33% achieve a score between 50% and 74.9%; and 15% achieve a score below 50%.

C. Securing the Right to Food

Two issues are of concern here: whether countries' collective and individual commitments and efforts are sufficient to meet their obligations under international law, and the extent to which all people enjoy the right to food. As discussed in Section II, the right to food encompasses multiple dimensions. Here we consider only outcome measures reflecting the most fundamental aspects of the right to food – specifically, the right to be free from hunger and malnutrition.

We are farther from reaching the 1996 World Food Summit's goal of reducing the number of hungry people by half by 2015 than we were in 1996. Despite the extensive commitments made by the global community and individual countries, global and national efforts have been insufficient to stem the rise in the number of hungry people. Not all regions have fared equally, as Table 2.6 shows. Southern Asia and sub-Saharan Africa account for the bulk of the increase in hungry people. The number

[13] The resultant indicator is the same as the Right to Work Index, one of the five components of the SERF Index. See also www.serfindex.org.

TABLE 2.5. *Percentage with access to improved water and sanitation relative to feasible rate given best practice*

Percentage of feasible achievement							
90% plus (45 countries)		75%–89% (30 countries)		50%–74% (47 countries)		Less than 50% (22)	
Uruguay		Dominican Republic		Yemen, Rep.		Cambodia	
Bulgaria	Singapore	El Salvador	Suriname	Zambia	Fiji	Eritrea	Kiribati
Ukraine	United Arab Emirates	Iran, Islamic Rep.	Chile	Lao PDR	Central African Republic	Benin	Bolivia
Barbados	Cyprus	Rwanda	Mexico	Venezuela, RB	Peru	Haiti	Papua New Guinea
Guyana	Uzbekistan	Argentina	Latvia	Swaziland	Namibia	Angola	Congo, Dem. Rep.
Israel	Malta	Bhutan	Honduras	Cameroon	Solomon Islands	Tanzania	Nigeria
Malawi	Grenada	Libya	Comoros	Cote d'Ivoire	Guinea-Bissau	Mauritania	Togo
Qatar	Slovenia	Moldova		Pakistan			
Belize	Belarus	Turkey	Ecuador	Uganda	Nepal		
Lebanon	Tonga	Cuba	Antigua and Barbuda	Cape Verde	Saudi Arabia		
Maldives	Vietnam	Philippines	Guatemala	South Africa	Paraguay		
Albania	Serbia	Algeria	Tajikistan	Oman	Iraq		
Kyrgyz Republic	Estonia	Dominica	Trinidad and Tobago	Colombia	Vanuatu		
		Bangladesh	Jamaica	Nicaragua	Sao Tome and Principe		

Georgia	Mauritius	Tunisia		Lesotho	Liberia	Congo, Rep.
Gambia, The	Syrian Arab Republic	Timor-Leste		Morocco	Mali	Niger
Egypt, Arab Rep.	Macedonia, FYR	Russian Federation		China	Mongolia	Chad
Croatia	Kazakhstan		Brazil	Panama	Ghana	Mozambique
Burundi	Armenia			Indonesia	Guinea	Sierra Leone
Thailand	Montenegro			Romania	Burkina Faso	Madagascar
Malaysia	Sri Lanka			Micronesia, Fed. Sts.	Afghanistan	Ethiopia
St. Kitts and Nevis	St. Lucia			Botswana	Kenya	Gabon
Bosnia and Herzegovina	Costa Rica			Djibouti	Azerbaijan	Equatorial Guinea
Samoa				Senegal	Sudan	
				India		

Data Source: Economic and Social Rights Empowerment Initiative (2011) www.serfindex.org/data.

TABLE 2.6. *Trends in the percentage and number of hungry people*

Country Groups	1990–1992 %	1990–1992 million	1995–1997 %	1995–1997 million	2000–2002 %	2000–2002 million	2005–2007 %	2005–2007 million
World	16	843.4	14	787.5	14	833.0	13	847.5
Developing Regions	20	817.2	17	760.8	16	805.2	16	829.4
Northern Africa	–	5.0	–	5.4	–	5.6	–	6.1
Sub-Saharan Africa	31	166.3	31	189.0	30	203.2	26	202.5
Latin America & the Caribbean	12	54.3	11	53.3	10	50.7	8	47.1
Eastern Asia	18	215.6	12	149.8	10	142.2	10	139.5
Eastern Asia without China	8	5.5	11	8.0	13	9.1	12	9.1
Southern Asia	21	262.9	19	264.7	20	300.3	21	343.9
Southern Asia without India	26	90.5	26	102.0	23	99.7	23	106.2
Western Asia	5	7.2	8	12.2	8	13.4	7	13.5
Commonwealth of Independent States	6	16.7	6	17.9	7	19.0	–	9.6
Commonwealth of Independent States, Asia	16	10.9	13	9.2	17	12.4	9	7.1
Commonwealth of Independent States, Europe	–	5.8	–	8.8	–	6.6	–	2.6
Developed Regions	–	7.2	–	6.7	–	6.3	–	6.5
Transition countries of Southeastern Asia	–	2.3	–	2.0	5	2.5	–	1.9

Data Source: FAO Hunger Statistics (2011).

of hungry people has decreased in Latin America and the Caribbean, Eastern Asia, the Commonwealth of Independent States, and the transition countries of Southeastern Asia, but nowhere has it fallen anywhere close to half its 1996 value. An urgent question is why so little progress has been made by so many states in fulfilling their obligations to ensure the right to food. Why have the commitments made failed to yield more progress?

Clearly, global efforts have not matched global commitments. The dramatic increase in food prices from 2007 to 2008 was reversed, but only temporarily, as the long-run trend in FAO's Food Price Index shows

(FAO, *Food Price Index Data Set*).[14,15] Pronouncements that the crisis had abated, however, were premature. In August of 2010, food prices soared again: the FAO's Food Price Index peaked at 238, the highest level ever, in February of 2011. It has remained above 200 since then. Demand factors continue to put upward pressure on prices, and global efforts to attenuate these have been inadequate. Progress in building food stocks to mediate food price swings has been limited. Immediately after the 2007–2008 price surge, global efforts and accommodating weather enabled cereal stocks to be increased by 25%. At the end of 2009, cereal stocks fell again, and only began to recover in 2011. The forecast for 2012 is that stocks will recover to modestly exceed their peak 2009 value by the end of the end of the year (FAO, *Cereal Supply and Demand Data Set*).

The global increase in per capita meat consumption continues unabated, and simultaneously reflects growing food security for some and reduced food security for others. Globally, per capita meat consumption increased 20% between 1990 and 2007, fueled by income gains among some in developing countries (FAO, *FAOSTATS*, 2011). In China, per capita meat consumption increased by more than 100% (FAO, *FAOSTATS*, 2011). Given China's huge population and persistent growth, in the absence of dramatic increases in global grain production and declines in per capita meat consumption in high-income countries, this force is likely to relentlessly increase food prices, making the need to protect vulnerable populations both more urgent and more difficult.

As our examination of country efforts has shown, countries are not doing all they can in this regard, by any means. This insufficiency in effort observed in the majority of countries translates into poor outcomes, especially for vulnerable populations such as young children. Children who are malnourished over the long-term become stunted; that is, their height for age is below normal.[16] The right to food component of the SERF Index

---

[14] FAO's Food Price Index is a weighted average of five underlying indices: the FAO's Cereal Price Index, Dairy Price Index, Oils/Fat Price Index, Meats Price Index, and Sugar Price Index. Each of these indices compares prices of a basket of foods within the category concerned with the prices prevailing in 2002–2004. The weights are the average export share of each food group in 2002–2004. The base period 2002–2004 value of the index is set at 100, so a value of 200 implies food prices have doubled since the base year (FAO, *Food Price Index Data Set*).

[15] The spike in global food prices ensuing in January of 2007 reached a peak indexed value of 184.7 in June of 2008 and then declined to 121.4 by February of 2009.

[16] Low height for age (stunting) reflects insufficient nutrient absorption over the long-term and is officially defined as the percentage of children under the age of five whose height is more than two standard deviations below WHO height for age norms.

is the ratio of the percentage of children who are not malnourished (as assessed by the child stunting rate) to the attainable level given the country's per capita income level (Randolph, Fukuda-Parr, and Lawson-Remer 2010; Fukuda-Parr, Lawson-Remer, and Randolph 2011). As Table 2.7 shows, only 19 of the 123 countries for which the index can be computed achieve 90% or more of the feasible level. Of the 123 countries, 74 achieve less than 75% of the feasible level, surely an unacceptable outcome reflecting serious violation of their commitment to ensure the right to food.

V. CONCLUSION

There is no doubt that the global community and nation-states individually have articulated a strong commitment to ensuring fulfillment of the right to food, as demonstrated by the evolution of international law; the alignment of domestic constitutions and laws to accord with international law regarding the right to food; and repeated international conferences and corresponding action plans signed by the majority of nations. Law makes little difference, however, unless it can be implemented in practice, and conference documents remain mere rhetoric unless undergirded by political will.

There is enough food on the planet to adequately feed everyone alive today. However, the rules governing national agricultural policy and international trade, along with the economic incentives in the global food-production system, do not currently result in fulfillment of access to adequate food for all. In this chapter, we have analyzed the interplay of local, national, regional, and international factors that combine to make realizing the right to food an ongoing challenge. We have shown that states have been far more effective at putting normative commitments in place (i.e., structural indicators of progress) than they have been at affecting policy that would change the reality of pervasive and increasing hunger (i.e., measured using process and outcome indicators). We have also argued that the state-centric discourse on obligations to ensure adequate access to food underplays both the nature of states' own extraterritorial obligations and the crucial role of non-state actors with the power to significantly affect food policy.

We take seriously Pogge's injunction (2010) that each of us bears personal responsibility for transforming the systems that give rise to gross inequality. By framing hunger in human rights terms, we have sought to marshal the best existing indicators of progress to demonstrate how far

TABLE 2.7. *Score on right to food component of the SERF index*

SCORE ON RIGHT TO FOOD INDEX				
90%–100%	75%–89%	50%–74%	25%–49%	1%–24%
19 Countries	30 Countries	44 Countries	25 Countries	5 Countries
Moldova, Kyrgyz Republic, Chile, Togo, Senegal, Jamaica, Cuba, Jordan, Belarus, Uzbekistan, Nicaragua, Trinidad & Tobago, Georgia, Singapore, Tunisia, Brazil, Guyana, China, Liberia	Montenegro, Serbia, The Gambia, Bulgaria, Argentina, Dominican Republic, Haiti, Suriname, Ghana, Bosnia & Herzegovina, Sri Lanka, Paraguay, Sao Tome & Principe, Armenia, FYR Macedonia, Romania, Mauritius, Saudi Arabia, Turkmenistan, Algeria, Uruguay, Thailand, Colombia, Morocco, Mauritania, Ukraine, Russian Federation, Malaysia, Turkey, Oman	Venezuela, Lebanon, Mongolia, Dem. Rep. Congo, Mexico, Kazakhstan, Iran, Tajikistan, Bahrain, Iraq, Belize, Philippines, Panama, El Salvador, Kenya, Uganda, Mali, Syrian Arab Republic, Honduras, Guinea, Azerbaijan, Albania, Rep. Congo, Swaziland, Maldives, Libya, Central African Republic, Bolivia, Cameroon, Namibia, Ecuador, Vietnam, Egypt, Sudan, Eritrea, Peru, Cote d'Ivoire, Djibouti, Cambodia, Botswana, Guinea-Bissau, Gabon, Mozambique, Bangladesh	Sierra Leone, Tanzania, Burkina Faso, Pakistan, Nigeria, Chad, Benin, Lesotho, Indonesia, Zambia, Papua New Guinea, United Arab Emirates, Ethiopia, Nepal, Lao PDR, Comoros, Rwanda, India, Bhutan, Malawi, Kuwait, Madagascar, Niger, Equatorial Guinea, Angola	Timor-Leste, Burundi, Guatemala, Rep. Yemen, Afghanistan

Data Source: Economic and Social Rights Empowerment Initiative (2011) http://www.serfindex.org/data/.

we are collectively from respecting, protecting, and fulfilling this right. We have also sought to marshal public shame at the dying that happens each minute – needlessly given the availability of food, but constantly given ongoing problems of access and utilization.

REFERENCES

Alaimo, Katherine, Christine M. Olson, and Edward A. Frangillo Jr., 2001. "Food Insufficiency and American School-Aged Children's Cognitive, Academic, and Psychosocial Development," *Pediatrics*, 108(1): 44–53.

Albisa, Cathy, 2011. "Drawing Lines in the Sand: Building Economic and Social Rights Norms in the United States," in Shareen Hertel and Kathryn Libal (Eds.) *Human Rights in the United States: Beyond Exceptionalism*, 68–88, New York: Cambridge University Press.

Alston, Philip, 1984. "International Law and the Human Right to Food," in Philip Alston and Katarina Tomasevski (Eds.) *The Right to Food*, 9–68, The Netherlands, Martinus Nijkoff Publishers.

Anderson, Molly, 2008. "Rights-based Food Systems and the Goals of Food Systems Reform," *Agriculture and Human Values* 25(4): 593–608.

Balakrishnan, Radhika, 2005. *Why MES with Human Rights? Integrating Macro Economic Strategies with Human Rights*, New York: Marymount Manhattan College.

Balakrishnan, Radhika and Diane Elson (Eds.), 2011. *Economic Policy and Human Rights: Holding Governments to Account*, London: Zed Press.

Balakrishnan, Radhika, Diane Elson, and Raj Patel (Eds.), 2009. *Rethinking Macro Economic Strategies from a Human Rights Perspective (Why MES with Human Rights II)*, New York: Marymount Manhattan College.

Black, R.E., S.S. Morris, and J. Bryce, 2003. "Where and why are 10 million children dying every year?" *Lancet* 361(9376): 2226–2234.

Brown, Lester R., 2011. "The new geopolitics of food," *Foreign Policy* 186.

Bryce, Jennifer, Cynthia Boschi-Pinto, Kenji Shibuya, Robert E. Black, and the WHO Child Health Epidemiology Reference Group, 2005. "WHO estimates of the causes of death in children," *Lancet* 365: 1147–1152.

Chong, Daniel, 2010. *Freedom from Poverty: NGOs and Human Rights Praxis*, Philadelphia: University of Pennsylvania Press.

Chopra, Surabhi, 2009. "Holding the State Accountable for Hunger," *Economic and Political Weekly* XLIV(33): 8–12.

Economic and Social Rights Empowerment Initiative, 2011. Social and Economic Rights Fulfillment (SERF) Index Database. Retrieved from www.serfindex.org/data.

FAO (Food and Agriculture Organization of the United Nations), 1996. *Rome Declaration on World Food Security and World Food Summit Plan of Action*, 13–17, Rome. Retrieved from http://www.fao.org/docrep/003/w3613e/w3613e00.HTM.

FAO, 1998. "The Right to Food in National Constitutions," in *The Right to Food in Theory and Practice*, Rome. Retrieved from http://www.bvsde.paho.org/texcom/nutricion/booklet.pdf.

FAO, 2001. *Food Balance Sheets: A Handbook*, Rome. Retrieved from http://www.fao.org/docrep/003/x9892e/x9892e00.htm.

FAO, 2006. *(The) Right to Food in Practice: Implementation at the National Level*, Rome. Retrieved from http://www.fao.org/docs/eims/upload/214719/AH189_en.pdf

FAO, 2008. *Declaration of the High-Level Conference on World Food Security: The Challenges of Climate Change and Bioenergy*, Rome. Retrieved from http://www.un.org/issues/food/taskforce/declaration-E.pdf.

FAO, 2009. Declaration of the World Summit on Food Security, Rome. Retrieved from ftp://ftp.fao.org/docrep/fao/Meeting/018/k6050e.pdf.

FAO, 2010. *(The) State of Food Insecurity in the World: Addressing food insecurity in protracted crisis*, Rome. Retrieved from http:fao.org/docrep/013/i1683e/i1683e.pdf.

FAO, *Cereal Supply and Demand Data Set*. Retrieved from http://www.fao.org/worldfoodsituation/wfs-home/csdb/en/.

FAO, *FAOSTATS*. 2011. Retrieved from http://www.faostat.fao.org.

FAO, *Food Price Index Data Set*. Retrieved from http://www.fao.org/worldfoodsituation/wfs-home/foodpricesindex/en/.

FAO, Hunger Statistics. Retrieved from http://www.fao.org/hunger/en/.

FAO and WHO, 1992. International Conference on Nutrition: World Declaration and Plan of Action for Nutrition, Rome. Retrieved from www.who.int/nutrition/publications/policies/icn_worlddeclaration_planofaction1992/en/index.html.

Fielding, Richard, 2011. "Asia's Food Security Conundrum: More Apparent than Real?" S. Rajaratnam School of International Studies (RSIS) Commentaries 90/2011 of June 13, 2011. Retrieved from http://www.rsis.edu.sg/publications/commentaries.html.

Fukuda-Parr, Sakiko, Terra Lawson-Remer, and Susan Randolph, 2009. "An Index of Economic and Social Rights Fulfillment: Concept and Methodology," *Journal of Human Rights* 8(3): 195–221.

Fukuda-Parr, Sakiko, Terra Lawson-Remer, and Susan Randolph, 2011. SERF Index Methodology: Version 2011.1, Technical Note http://www.serfindex.org/data/.

Gauri, Varun and Daniel Brinks (Eds.), 2010. *Courting Social Justice: Judicial Enforcement of Social and Economic Rights in the Developing World*, New York: Cambridge University Press.

Ghosh, Jayati, 2010. "The Unnatural Coupling: Food and Global Finance," *Journal of Agrarian Change* 10(1): 72–86.

Goderis, Benedikt and Mila Versteeg, 2011. "The Transnational Origins of Constitutions: An Empirical Investigation." Paper presented for the Sixth Annual Conference on Empirical Legal Studies (November 4–5, 2011). Retrieved from http://papers.ssrn.com/sol3/papers.cfm?abstract_id=1865724.

Gonsalves, Colin, Vinay Naidoo, P. Ramesh Kumar, and Aparna Bhat (Eds.), 2004. Right to Food: Commissioners Reports, Supreme Court Orders, NHRC Reports, Articles, New Delhi: Socio-Legal Information Centre.

IMF (International Monetary Fund), 2011. Debt Relief Under the Heavily Indebted Poor Counties (HIPC) Initiative, 2011 Factsheet. Retrieved from http://www.imf.org/external/np/exr/facts/hipc.htm.

Islam, Nurul, 2011."Foreign Aid to Agriculture: Review of Facts and Analysis," International Food Policy Research Institute Discussion Paper 01053, January 2011.

Jung, Courtney, 2011. "Coding Manual: A description of the methods and decisions used to build a cross-national dataset of economic and social rights in developing country constitutions," Retrieved from http://www.tiesr.org/TIESR%20Coding%20Manual%208%20March%202011.pdf.

Kent, George, 2010. "The Global Hunger for Food and Justice," American Bar Association's *Human Rights Magazine* 37(1): Retrieved from http:www.americanbar.org/publications/human_rights_magazine_home/human_rights_vol37_2010/winter2010/the_human_right_to_food_and_dignity.html.

Kunnemann, Rolf and Sandra Epal-Ratien, 2004. "Using International Law to Respect, Protect, and Fulfill the Right to Food," chapter 5 in Rolf Kunnemann and Sandra Epal-Ratien, *The Right to Food: A Resource Manual for NGOs*. Retrieved from www.fao.org/righttofood/kc/downloads/vl/docs/AH291.pdf.

Law, David S. and Mila Versteeg, 2010. "The Evolution of Global Constitutionalism," Washington University St. Louis School of Law, Legal Studies Research Paper Series No. 10–10-01.

Law, David S. and Mila S. Versteeg, 2011. "The Evolution and Ideology of Global Constitutionalism," *California Law Review* 99, 5: 1164–1257.

Minkler, Lanse, 2009. "Economic Rights and Political Decisionmaking," *Human Rights Quarterly* 31(2): 368–393.

Moyn, Samuel, 2010. *The Last Utopia: Human Rights in History*, Cambridge, MA: Belknap Press of Harvard University.

Narula, Smita, 2006. "The Right to Food: Holding Global Actors Accountable Under International Law," *Columbia Journal of Transnational Law* 44(3): 691–800.

Olson, Christine M., 1999. "Nutrition and Health Outcomes Associated with Food Insecurity and Hunger," *Journal of Nutrition* 129(2): 521S–524S.

OECD (Organization for Economic Cooperation and Development), 2004. Development Cooperation Report.

Osiatynski, Wiktor, 2007. "Needs-Based Approach to Social and Economic Rights," in Shareen Hertel and Lanse Minkler (Eds.) *Economic Rights: Conceptual, Measurement, and Policy Issues, 56–75* New York: Cambridge University Press.

Paarlberg, Robert, 2010. *Food Politics: What Everyone Needs to Know*, New York: Oxford University Press.

Patel, Raj, 2007. *Stuffed and Starved: The Hidden Battle for the World Food System*, London: Portobello Books, Ltd.

Pogge, Thomas, 2008. *World Poverty and Human Rights*, 2nd edition, London: Polity Press.

Pogge, Thomas, 2010. *Politics as Usual: What Lies Behind the Pro-Poor Rhetoric*, Cambridge, UK: Polity Press.

Pridmore, P., 2007. *The Impact of Health on Education Access and Attainment: A Cross National Review of the Research Evidence*, CREATE Pathways to Access Research Monograph no. 2.

Randolph, Susan, Sakiko Fukuda-Parr, and Terra Lawson-Remer, 2010. "Economic and Social Rights Fulfillment Index: Country Scores and Rankings," *Journal of Human Rights* 9: 230–261.

Rodney, Walter, 2002. "How Europe Underdeveloped Africa," excerpted in Robin Broad (Ed.) *Global Backlash: Citizen Initiatives for a Just World Economy*, 77–79, Lanham, MA: Roman & Littlefield.

Schanbacher, William D., 2010. *The Politics of Food: The Global Conflict Between Food Security and Food Sovereignty*, Santa Barbara, CA: Praeger Security International/ABC-CLIO, LLC.

Sen, Amartya, 1981. *Poverty and Famines: An Essay on Entitlement and Deprivation*, Oxford: Oxford University Press.

Shiva, Vandana, 2000. *Stolen Harvest: The Hijacking of the Global Food Supply*, Brooklyn, NY: South End Press.

Skogly, Sigrun I. and Mark Gibney, 2007. "Economic Rights and Extraterritorial Obligations," in Shareen Hertel and Lanse Minkler (Eds.) *Economic Rights: Conceptual, Measurement, and Policy Issues*, 267–283, New York: Cambridge University Press.

Stiglitz, Joseph E. and Andrew Charlton, 2005. *Fair Trade for All*, Oxford: Oxford University Press.

Sunstein, Cass, 2004. *The Second Bill of Rights: FDR's Unfinished Revolution and Why We Need It More Than Ever*, New York: Basic Books.

UN (United Nations), 1975. *Report of the World Food Conference*, Rome, November 5–16, New York: United Nations.

UN, 2010. *Millennium Development Goals Report*, New York: United Nations. Retrieved from http://unstats.un.org/unsd/mdg/Resources/Static/Products/Progress2010/MDG_Report_2010_En_low%20res.pdf.

UN CESCR (UN Committee on Economic, Social and Cultural Rights), 1990. "The nature of States parties obligations (Art. 2. Para. 1): 12/14/1990 CESCR General Comment 3," Fifth Session. Retrieved from http://www.unhchr.ch/tbs/doc.nsf/%28Symbol%29/94bdbaf59b43a424c12563 ed0052b664?Opendocument.

UN CESCR, 1999. "The right to adequate food (Art. 11): 05/12/1999 E/C.12/1119/5. (General Comments)," Twentieth Session, Geneva, April 26–May 14, Agenda item 7. Retrieved from http://www.unhchr.ch/tbs/doc.nsf/o/3d02758c707031d58025677f003b73b9.

UNDP (UN Development Programme), 2000. *Human Development Report 2000*, New York: Oxford University Press.

UNDP, 2001. *Review of the Poverty Reduction Strategy Paper 5*. Retrieved from http://www.bb.undp.org/uploads/file/pdfs/poverty/Library/PRSP%20Library/UNDP%20%20Review%20of%20the%20PRSP.pdf.

UN ECOSOC (UN Economic and Social Council), 2001a. *The Highly Indebted Countries (HIPC) Initiative: A Human Rights Assessment of the Poverty Reduction Strategy Papers (PRSP)*, UN CHR, UN Doc. E/CN.4/2011/56. Prepared by Fantu Cheru.

UN ECOSOC, 2001b. *The Right to Food*, UN CHR, I/M/ Dpc/ A56210. Prepared by Jean Ziegler. Retrieved from www.righttofood.org/new/PDF/A56210.pdf.

UN ECOSOC, 2003. *The Right to Food*, 59th Sess., UN CHR, UN doc. E/CN.4/2003/54 Prepared by Jean Ziegler.

UN High Level Task Force on the Global Food Security Crisis, 2008. *Comprehensive Framework for Action.* Retrieved from http://www.un.org/issues/food/taskforce/Documentation/CFA Web.pdf.

UN Human Rights Council, 2011. *Report of the Special Representative of the Secretary General on the Issue of Human Rights and Transnational Corporations and Other Business Enterprises*, John Ruggie, UN doc. A/HRC/17/31. Retrieved from http://www.ohchr.org/documents/issues/business/A.HRC.17.31.pdf.

UN OHCHR (UN Office of the High Commissioner for Human Rights), 2008. *Report on Indicators for Promoting and Monitoring the Implementation of Human Rights*, HRI/MC/2008/3. Retrieved from http://www2.ohchr.org/english/issues/indicators/docs/HRI.MC.2008.3_en.pdf.

UN Statistical Office, *Series Metadata: Population undernourished, percentage.* Retrieved from http://unstats.unorog/unsd/mdg/Metadata.aspx?IndicatorId=0&SeriesId=566.

Uzondu, Chaka, 2010. "The Imperial Relations of Food: Food Sovereignty and Self-Determination," Unpublished dissertation, University of Connecticut.

World Bank, World Development Indicators. Retrieved from http://data.worldbank.org/data-catalog/world-development-indicators.

World Bank, 2004. "OP 8.60 Development Policy Lending." Retrieved from http://web.worldbank.org/WBSITE/EXTERNAL/PROJECTS/EXTPOLICIES/EXTOPMANUAL/0,,contentMDK:20471192~pagePK:64141683~piPK:64141620~theSitePK:502184,00.html.

3

Globalization and the Right to Health

Audrey R. Chapman and Salil D. Benegal

INTRODUCTION

Like many other economic and social rights, the recognition of a right related to health or health care is a relatively recent development. The Universal Declaration of Human Rights enumerates a right to a standard of living adequate for health and well-being that includes medical care (1948, Article 25). Article 12 of the International Covenant on Economic, Social and Cultural Rights (ICESCR; 1966) expands the conception of the right "to the highest attainable standard of physical and mental health" (referred to subsequently as the right to health). The broad brush strokes of Article 12 direct state parties to provide for maternal and child health; improve environmental and industrial hygiene; ensure prevention, treatment, and control of epidemic, endemic, occupational, and other diseases; and create conditions that would assure medical service and medical attention in the event of sickness to all.

There was considerable uncertainty about the precise requirements of the right and scope of state party responsibilities until 2000, when the United Nations Committee on Economic, Social and Cultural Rights (CESCR) adopted a general comment with its interpretation. According to the text of General Comment No.14 (GC 14), the right to health is an inclusive right that goes well beyond the four original provisions outlined in the ICESCR, which it characterizes as merely illustrative. The right to health is not understood as a right to be healthy (para. 8), but as the right to a variety of facilities, goods, services, and conditions necessary for the realization of the highest attainable standard of health (para. 9). These extend not only to the availability of timely and appropriate health care, but also incorporate the underlying determinants of health such as access to safe and potable water, adequate sanitation, an adequate supply of safe and nutritious food, healthy occupational and environmental conditions, and access to health-related education and information, including on sexual and reproductive health (para. 11). GC 14 emphasizes the special obligations of the state to provide for the satisfaction of the health needs of those whose poverty, disabilities, or background makes them more vulnerable (CESCR 2000, paras. 20–27). Like other general comments, GC 14 specifies three types of state responsibilities: the obligations to respect, protect, and fulfill the right (paras. 33–37). It also identifies parallel violations for each of the categories of obligations (paras. 46–52). There is an extensive list of core obligations whose realization is not subject to the availability of resources (paras. 43–44). The general comment also includes a section on the extraterritorial obligations of the state to provide international assistance and cooperation, to respect the enjoyment of the right to health in other countries, to cooperate in providing disaster relief and humanitarian assistance, and to refrain from imposing embargoes or similar measures restricting the supply of adequate medicines and medical equipment in another state (paras. 38–42).

Like the ICESCR itself, GC 14 takes for granted the post–World War II international order built on the sovereignty of nation-states and the relatively unconstrained ability of governments to determine their public policies. By 2000, however, globalization was transforming the economic and policy landscape for the right to health as well as affecting the implementation of other economic and social rights. *Globalization*, a process characterized by the growing interdependence of the world's people, involves the integration of economies, cultures, technologies, and governance. Although globalization is not a new phenomenon, the rapidity and degree to which states are being drawn into a global polity, economy, and culture are new developments. Also new is that the hegemony of the market economy constitutes the characteristic feature of contemporary globalization. As Rhoda Howard-Hassmann comments, "Although globalization includes political, social, and cultural aspects, the chief impetus and beneficiary of globalization is capitalism" (2010, 7). Over the past few decades, most countries have been integrated into a global marketplace characterized by reduced trade barriers and the reorganization of production across multiple national borders. This has placed all countries in an economically competitive environment in which powerful economic actors and international investors demand the elimination of onerous regulations, reduced labor protection measures to lower costs, and trade liberalization policies that open the country to foreign investors, all of which have implications for the protection and promotion of economic and social rights.

To date, globalization has disproportionately benefited the countries and economic entities with the resources and power to shape the rules under which the international economic system functions. Economic inequalities have risen significantly since the early 1990s, reflecting the increasing concentrations of income, resources, and wealth both between and within countries (Birdsall 2005). *Neoliberalism*, sometimes referred to as neoliberal globalization or market fundamentalism, the dominant economic doctrine under which globalization is taking place, presumes that markets and market principles are the appropriate basis for organizing most areas of economic and social life regardless of the ethical, human rights, and distributional consequences. As Paul O'Connell points out, the age of globalization is better understood as being an age of market hegemony during which all of the governments of the world, whether through ideological commitment or under externally imposed pressures of market discipline, embraced and implemented neoliberal policy prescriptions (2007). Concomitantly, neoliberalism favors a reduction in the role of the state in favor of giving the market free rein. To promote a business-friendly environment, neoliberalism's policy agenda advocates minimizing economic regulation, tightening fiscal discipline, enabling freer flows of capital across national boundaries, rolling back welfare, reducing expenditures on public goods, imposing strict controls on organized labor, and reducing tax reductions. Its policy prescriptions also include the privatization of public sector institutions, a decrease in state budgets, and the transfer of social services formerly provided by the state, such as health care, education, and basic social services, to the private sector (Gómez Isa 2005). All of these policies have had a detrimental impact on economic and social rights. Richard Falk uses the term "predatory globalization" to refer to the cumulative adverse effects of these policies on human well-being (1999, 2).

The orientation and principles of neoliberalism contravene the human rights ethos in fundamental ways. In contrast with neoliberalism's focus on the market, human rights are based on the recognition of the inherent dignity and worth of the human person and the commitment to the protection and promotion of human welfare. The human rights paradigm treats access to health and essential inputs such as water, sanitation, and adequate nutrition as entitlements and public goods, and not as commodities as in the neoliberal economic model. Human rights confer priority on the fulfillment of the needs of the most disadvantaged and vulnerable, the very groups neoliberal economic policies tend to harm the most (Chapman 2009). The fulfillment of economic and social rights depends on the existence of an effective and activist state, something that is anathema to neoliberalism.

Although some human rights analysts identify both negative and positive features in globalization, most are basically critical. Rhoda Howard-Hassman is an exception. She views globalization as the "second great transformation," which involves the transformation of the entire world from agricultural to industrial societies (2010). Recognizing that globalization often has short-term deleterious impacts on human rights, at the same time she argues that it brings about "human rights leapfrogging," enabling the concept and law of human rights to enhance the world's capacity to confront the negative aspects of industrialization. She acknowledges globalization's exacerbation of economic inequality across and within countries but balances it against globalization's reputed reduction in world poverty levels. Although she cautions that it is premature to draw conclusions as to whether globalization will benefit or harm human rights, she is basically optimistic (Howard-Hassman 2005, 2010). In contrast, Paul O'Connell argues that it is not possible to be committed to the protection of human rights and at the same time acquiescent in the dominant model of globalization. According to O'Connell, the conditions for the violation of human rights are structurally embedded in the neoliberal globalization program (O'Connell 2007). Many others are primarily critical as well, on both normative and policy grounds (Chapman 2009; Schrecker et al. 2010; Schrecker 2011). According to Margaret Somers, neoliberal globalization challenges not only the existence of particular economic and social entitlements apart from market relations, but also the extent to which a "right-to-have rights" is recognized (2008).

The focus of this chapter will be an exploration of the manner in which neoliberal globalization has affected the realization of the right to health. Arguably, the right to health is one of the economic and social rights most affected by the globalization process. As this chapter will show, globalization has considerably constrained the ability of states to respect, protect, and fulfill the requirements of the right to health.

IMPLICATIONS OF GLOBALIZATION FOR RIGHT TO HEALTH

Impact on Health Trends

Over the past thirty years of intensified market integration, prior trends of health improvement have slowed or reversed, particularly in poor countries, with growing health inequalities and reduced access to health care (Labonté et al. 2007). The health gap between the worst-off and best-off groups is growing: affluent populations are increasingly healthier and living longer; poorer populations have higher rates of illness and are dying at a younger age (Gostin and Hodge 2007). Econometric analysis using data on 136 countries suggests that on a global level, the effects of market-oriented economic policies between 1980 and 2000 canceled out much of the progress toward better health (as measured by life expectancy at birth) that would have resulted from medical progress if social and economic trends had continued on their 1960–1980 trajectory. In two regions – sub-Saharan Africa and the transitional economies exposed to the full rigors of the global marketplace after the fall of the Soviet Union – neoliberal policies contributed to a substantial decline in life expectancy. In the case of sub-Saharan Africa, only half of the loss was explained by the HIV epidemic, itself not unconnected to globalization (Cornia, Rosignoli, and Tiberti 2009). Rick Rowden makes the point that, historically, decreases in life expectancy of these magnitudes have been associated with plagues, famines, or natural catastrophes. However, Rowden attributes the decreases during the past two decades as primarily the result of policy changes (2009).

Impact on Health Access and Health Systems

The World Health Organization's (WHO) 2007 report opens with the observation that, "Health outcomes are unacceptably low across much of the developing world, and the persistence of deep inequalities in health status is a problem from which no country in world is exempt. At the centre of this human crisis is a failure of health systems" (1). Years of low financing of health systems have significantly weakened public health institutions in these countries. This is partly as a result of the pressures to defund and privatize health services imposed by international financial institutions, partly due to the crushing debt burden on many poor countries, and partly due to lower government revenues resulting from trade liberalization measures. It seems questionable, therefore, at this point in time whether most governments, particularly in poor- and middle-income states, have the institutional and infrastructure capabilities and medical and health staff to meet the requirements imposed by the right to health.

Policies advocated by international financial institutions (IFIs) have been a major contributor to this situation. A 1985 World Bank policy paper, *Paying for Health Services in Developing Countries: An Overview*, advocated focusing on prices and markets as the best strategy to improve the efficiency of health care. The paper also promoted the privatization of health care. It suggested that user fees are better for the poor because they provide improvements on the supply side, dismissing concerns about the ability and willingness of poor people to pay user fees (Rowden 2009). By 1987, the Bank was committed to a neoliberal approach to health care. This market approach became a key part of its structural adjustment programs, particularly during the 1990s (Rowden 2009). The World Bank's influential 1993 report, *Investing in Health*, reiterated the neoliberal agenda. The World Bank's 2004 *World Development Report*: *Making Services Work for Poor People* continued to endorse the basic neoliberal approach, advising that governments should decrease their role as public service providers and instead encourage private health care providers to sell services to their wealthier citizens and contract out with for-profit private companies and not-for-profit private providers to deliver health services for poorer citizens (Rowden 2009).

If the history of health care in Europe and other parts of the world in the first seven decades of the twentieth century can be depicted in terms of an ever-extending state involvement (Maarse 2006), the trend in the past thirty-five years is for health systems to move toward greater privatization. *Privatization* has been characterized as the transfer of ownership of an institution or service from a public to a private actor or alternatively as the removal of public authorities from the operation of an institution or service despite the state retaining ownership (De Feyter and Gómez Isa 2005). Privatization fragments the provision of health services and complicates planning and the rational allocation of health services. In many situations, it also makes health services more expensive, thus reducing access for the poor.

The imposition of user fees has been a central component of market prescriptions for health care. By 1998, about 40% of the World Bank's health, nutrition, and population projects, nearly 75% of which were in Africa, required the introduction or increased application of user fees. A 2006 survey of thirty-two African countries found twenty-seven imposing fees (Lister and Labonté 2009). Importantly, user fees and other cost-recovery mechanisms have decreased access to health care for the poor (Katz 2005; Oxfam International 2009; UNICEF 2008). A 2004 UK Department for International Development (DfID) report shows that user fees are often associated with reduced use of service, especially by the poor and vulnerable; there is a higher failure to complete treatments and delays in seeking treatment. The report recommends that the removal of user fees be accompanied by investments in health and a range of other actions designed to make health services more accessible to the poor (Rowden 2009). The WHO's 2008 *World Health Report* supports the position taken by DfID against user fees.

These reforms not only created exclusionary barriers that reduce access and marginalize vulnerable groups; they also led to a diffusion of responsibility, as neither the state nor private sector will provide essential services to those who cannot afford services such as basic primary care but still have a legitimate claim for them as a necessary aspect of their right to health. Kamat (2004) suggests that as states privatize such services in an attempt to integrate into a global economy, private investors may still be reluctant to enter into the market or replace them adequately due to a perceived lack of profitability. Hence, basic needs are often not met, and coverage is often limited to only those capable of payment rather than being accessible throughout the country. Poorer, older, and more vulnerable members of society suffer the most as a result of these transitions, as they often face a greater financial burden as a result of commercialized health services (Waitzkin, Jasso-Aguilar, and Iriart 2007).

The commercialization of health care and implementation of user fees without cross-subsidization or other measures to make these services more accessible to poor and other vulnerable groups can further exacerbate poverty traps and lead to vicious cycles where families are forced to bear significant financial burdens in order to obtain medical care. The case of 5% of Bolivian households incurring catastrophic health expenditure is not an anomaly (Silva et al. 2011), but part of a wider and concerning trend where the poor have been disproportionately affected by the burden of paying for health. Similar studies in rural China (Huong et al. 2007) or throughout sub-Saharan Africa (Leive and Xu 2008) show the extent to which lower-income groups are affected, with frequent cases of high medical costs forcing families to sell assets or enter heavy, prolonged debt. Leive and Xu show cross-national trends in Africa of poorer families frequently selling livestock or borrowing heavily in order to cope with medical payments, and these financial pressures are even worse for people in informal sectors who have little or no access to credit in order to bear costs.

Impact on the Social Determinants of Health

In many regions of the world the most valuable steps toward improvement of health are not the provision of medical services, but improvements in the social determinants of health. Briefly, the *social determinants* of health are the conditions in which people grow, live, work, and age that affect their opportunities to lead healthy lives. The right to health has always been broader than the right to health care. As interpreted in the 2000 General Comment on the Right to Health, the right to health not only extends to the availability of timely and appropriate health care but also incorporates what are termed the "underlying determinants of health," such as access to safe and potable water and adequate sanitation, an adequate supply of safe food, and healthy occupational and environmental conditions (CESCR 2000, para. 11). With the exception of healthy occupational and environmental conditions, these underlying determinants are also identified as core health obligations of the state whose realization is not subject to resource constraints (CESCR 2000, para. 43). In addition, the Committee has addressed the important link between health and water in a separate general comment (CESCR 2002).

In 2008, the WHO Commission on the Social Determinants of Health published its report, *Closing the Gap in a Generation: Health Equity Through Action on the Social Determinants of Health*. The report integrates extensive data from a wide variety of sources on the significant role of the social determinants of health in shaping health outcomes and generating inequalities in health status within and among countries. This analysis is juxtaposed with a compelling justice ethic. The report is unequivocal in its condemnation of the disparities in life opportunities and health status between rich and poor countries and between the rich and poor within countries. The Commission ascribes these differentials to "a toxic combination of poor social policies and programmes, unfair economic arrangements, and bad politics" (Commission on the Social Determinants of Health 2008, 26). Many of the poor social policies, unfair economic arrangements, and bad politics that the Commission criticizes reflect neoliberal policies.

Research conducted by the Globalization Knowledge Network for the Commission on the Social Determinants of Health identifies several, often interacting, pathways leading from globalization to changes in the social determinants of health, with detrimental consequences for health equity (Labonté et al. 2007):[1]

- Perhaps most importantly, given the strong and pervasive link between poverty and health (Braveman and Gruskin 2003), globalization has

---

[1]   The text on the impact of globalization on the social determinants of health is based on Chapman (2009).

rendered many poor people in low-income countries even poorer (Birdsall 2005). According to the WHO, "Poverty wields its destructive influence at every stage of human life, from the moment of conception to the grave. It conspires with the most deadly and painful diseases to bring a wretched existence to all those who suffer from it" (2001). Trade liberalization, the lowering of barriers to imports, and the global reorganization of production also tend to increase the economic vulnerability of large numbers of poor people (Labonté et al. 2007).

- Globalization is gradually leading to the emergence of a global labor market characterized by growing inequalities between skilled and unskilled workers both within and across national borders. Global economic integration and the development of a global labor force are generating increased pressures for labor market "flexibility" with detrimental effects on economic security for many workers. As countries compete for foreign investment and outsourced production, the need to appear "business friendly" affects their ability to adopt and implement labor standards, protecting workers' interests, strict health and safety regulations, and redistributive social policies (Labonté et al. 2007).

- Lack of access to safe water is linked with poverty and economic insecurity as well as being detrimental to health outcomes, particularly through diarrheal diseases caused by unclean water. Like health services, the neoliberal model treats water as a commodity. During the past two decades, transnational corporations have emerged as major actors in the water sector. International Monetary Fund (IMF) loan agreements with many of the smallest, poorest, and most debt-ridden countries have included conditions requiring water privatization or full-cost recovery policies. Private provision of services to meet basic needs, such as water and sanitation, invariably leads to escalating costs and inequitable access (Katz 2005). A market-based approach also makes it difficult to expand water-service delivery to previously unserved or underserved areas and to set affordable rates (Labonté et al. 2007).

- Trade reforms that lower trade barriers, as neoliberal ideology advocates, can be damaging to food security in the short- and medium-term unless countered by policies designed to offset the negative effects (Labonté et al. 2007). Evidence suggests that diets have been influenced by three important changes in the food system: the growth of transnational food companies, including supermarkets; liberalization of international food trade and foreign direct investment; and global food advertising and promotion. All three affect diets by altering the availability, prices, and desirability of different foods (Hawkes, Chopra, and Friel 2009). Increased global trade in food products appears to be associated with changes in diet and nutrition in many low- and middle-income countries away from traditional foods grown locally to store-bought foods, many of which are processed and high in sugars and carbohydrates. However, the manner in which global food trade is affecting different segments of the population in poor- and middle-income countries is not well researched (Hawkes et al. 2009).

Declines in public revenues from tariff reductions, the growing burden of public debt, and public policies promoted by multilateral organizations and increasingly adopted by governments all constrain the ability of many developing countries to meet basic needs related to the social determinants of health (Labonté et al. 2007).[2]

Impact of Globalization on the Availability of Health Personnel in Poor Countries

The availability of sufficient numbers of trained health personnel is essential to the provision of adequate and accessible health services. Currently, there is a critical global shortage of trained health care workers. In 2006, the WHO estimated there were 2.4 million too few physicians, nurses, and midwives to provide essential health interventions. As might be anticipated, the problem is most severe in poor countries. There is often an inverse correlation between need and the availability of health workers. Countries with the greatest burden of disease have the fewest workers; those with the lowest relative need, such as the United States, Canada, and the European countries, have the highest numbers. According to the WHO, fifty-seven countries, mostly in sub-Saharan Africa – but also a few in Asia, including India, Indonesia, and Bangladesh – face crippling health workforce shortages (WHO 2006).

---

[2]   There are extensive debates over globalization's impact on wealth and resource distribution both within and among countries. Although a thorough analysis of these arguments is beyond the scope of this chapter, in *Globalization and Its Discontents*, Stiglitz argues that the link between global economic integration and economic growth is overstated, highlighting several cases where Structural Adjustment Programs and trade liberalization have slowed growth, reduced the "size of the economic pie," and exacerbated income inequality. Other literature from Rodrik, Goldberg, and Pavnick and Birdsall examines these issues in more depth.

The development of a global health labor market has intensified the problem. Not only do many low-income countries face a shortage of health care workers, but when governments try to rectify the situation by investing in training, many of their best-trained health care personnel decide to leave the country to accept positions elsewhere, usually in wealthier countries. Hospitals, governments, and health institutions in developed countries attempt to fill vacancies by recruiting well-trained doctors and nurses from poor countries. Health professionals in poor countries are attracted by the higher salaries, better working conditions, greater opportunities for postgraduate training, and better prospects for advancement in affluent countries. In some developing countries – Ghana, for example – about 70% of doctors leave the country within three years of qualifying (Rowden 2009).

These factors have resulted in a brain drain from developing to developed countries. When poor countries with limited resources invest in the education of health care workers only to have them leave to practice in developed countries, these poor countries are, in effect, subsidizing wealthier countries. The International Organization for Migration estimates that developing nations spend US$500 million each year to educate health workers who then leave to work in North America, Western Europe, and South Asia (Kuehn 2007). This loss imposes a severe burden on health systems already weakened by epidemics, insufficient resources, and shortages of health workers.

There are also significant disparities within countries. Private health service providers often offer higher salaries than the public sector, thereby luring away well-qualified professionals. The proliferation of single disease initiatives, often programs sponsored by overseas health funders with parallel chains of command and funding mechanisms, has exacerbated the competition for staff. Discrepancies in salaries between regular public sector jobs and better-funded programs and projects have further aggravated the human resource crisis in fragile health systems (WHO 2008).

IMPACT OF TRANSNATIONAL ACTORS ON THE RIGHT TO HEALTH

World Bank and Structural Adjustment

Structural Adjustment Programs (SAPs) are the conditions imposed by the World Bank and IMF on developing countries as the prerequisite for obtaining a new loan or having the interest rates lowered on existing loans. Under structural adjustment, the economic model current from the early 1980s until the late 1990s, the IMF and World Bank imposed austerity policies on borrowers, ostensibly to end their fiscal imbalances, and required states to adopt a market orientation as well as to open their borders to foreign investment. More recently, the World Bank has moved from structural adjustment to a nominal focus on poverty reduction, but there is often little practical change. Rigid ceilings on public health and other social services expenditures imposed by the Bank's Medium-Term Expenditure Frameworks continue to restrict adequate funding for the realization of economic, social, and cultural rights. Almost all of the Poverty Reduction Strategy Papers (PRSPs), the national planning frameworks that are now a precondition for Bank concessional lending, include or refer to an existing Medium-Term Expenditure Framework. Once included in a PRSP, countries cannot adapt the limits on funding, even if a new essential need arises (Ooms and Hammonds 2008). Moreover, the PRSP process generally fails to take obligations related to the right to health into account (Chapman 2009).

SAPs have affected health-related policies and inhibited progressive realization of the right to health in three main ways. First, in many cases, structural adjustment and privatization have fragmented public health systems as wealthier demographics have opted out of state-provided health care and turned to the private sector (Barrientos 2000). This has led to increasingly fragmented health care systems with little coordination and declining coverage in terms of meeting essential needs or providing for a majority of the population. Second, there has been a larger-scale ontological and policy shift in governments' approach to health care services, with the focus shifting away from goals of universal access and greater emphasis being placed on cost-recovery mechanisms such as user fees that have often acted as exclusionary barriers, reducing equity and limiting coverage to only those able to afford it.

Third, SAPs have had an indirect impact on health care policies and outcomes by worsening the distribution of economic gains as well as reducing the size of the overall economic pie in many cases (Stiglitz 2003; Abouharb and Cingranelli 2007), hindering the abilities of people in much of the developing world to pay for their own health needs. Actions targeting price subsidies or worsening protections for other economic rights such as the right to work in developing countries such as Mozambique, Nigeria, and Nicaragua (Abouharb and Cingranelli 2007) have increased the cost burden on the poor for basic goods such as fuels, transportation, and food. States have also often been pressured to privatize and commodify essential social determinants of health such as water and sanitation services, and prevented from cross-subsidizing basic needs such as water, even though such actions impede equitable distribution of these goods (Alexander 2005).[3]

Large-scale panel data confirm this. In an analysis of 131 developing countries, Abouharb and Cingranelli (2007) found that implementation of World Bank and IMF structural agreements reduce government respect for the economic and social welfare of their citizens, contributing to a deterioration of the situation for the majority of the population in these countries. Specifically, user fees when privatizing water, health care, and education led to a greater marginalization of poor and vulnerable groups and only hindered realization of basic economic rights. SAPs and shifts toward investor-friendly, globally integrated economies led to reduced subsidies, as states were forced to reduce public spending, and the transfers of enterprises such as water and sanitation utilities to private investors. Both increased inequity and created monopolistic markets that saw reduced efficiency and responsiveness.

A multi-country review by the Structural Adjustment Participatory Review International Network (SAPRIN) reached similar conclusions. The study (SAPRIN 2004) found that a number of major problems were either caused or exacerbated by adjustment programs. According to the study: (1) adjustment policies contributed to the impoverishment and marginalization of local populations and increasing economic inequality; (2) trade liberalization, financial-sector liberalization, and the weakening of state support and demand for local goods and services devastated local industries, particularly the small- and medium-sized enterprises that provide the bulk of national employment; (3) neoliberal structural and sectoral policy reforms in the agricultural and mining sectors undermined the viability of small farms, weakened food security, and damaged the natural environment; and (4) the privatization of public utilities and services usually resulted in significant price increases for the public. Of particular relevance to economic and social rights, the SAPRIN review concluded that the quality of education and health care has generally declined as a result of pressure to reduce public expenditures and that cost-sharing

---

[3] Cross-subsidizing is the approach of charging different prices for different demographic groups of consumers, frequently having higher income groups pay larger amounts in order to subsidize lower wage earners. World Trade Organization rules have made this illegal (Alexander 2005).

schemes have imposed serious constraints on access to health care and education by poor people.

Case studies in Bolivia, El Salvador, and Argentina in the past decade highlight some of the destructive and fragmenting impacts that SAPs have had upon health care systems (Silva et al. 2011; Homedes et al. 2000; Barrientos 2000). Fragmented health care systems are marked by the development of parallel subsystems or entities of delivery that function separately without coordination, and by increased segmentation as different systems of health care deliver services only to certain economic groups stratified by income. Fragmentation and segmentation reduce standardization of services, ensure that essential curative or preventive treatments may only be available to certain socioeconomic groups, and increase overall transaction costs and reduce total coverage (Levcovitz 2007).

Silva et al. (2011) show that comprehensive implementation of SAP policies in Bolivia during the 1980s and 1990s had a destructive impact upon an already segmented health care system, worsening coverage and quality of care. The introduction of user fees in Bolivia excluded large segments of the population from basic health care and led to increases in out-of-pocket expenditures to such an extent that 5% of Bolivian households incurred catastrophic health expenditure (Aguilar Rivera, Xu, and Carrin 2006) and faced poverty.[4] Homedes et al. (2000) discuss similar outcomes in El Salvador, where privatization and increased commercialization of health care led to fragmentation as high-income groups left state-provided health care services, leading to a lack of funding and a rapid decline in the quality of the state-provided service that was mainly used by the poor.

World Trade Organization, TRIPS Agreement, and Access to Essential Medicines

Just as raw materials and labor were key resources in the first industrial revolution, intellectual property is a central asset in the twenty-first century knowledge-based economy. Economic globalization in recent decades has been accompanied by the internationalization of intellectual property institutions and standards. Not only have intellectual property

---

[4]   Although there is no consensus on what amount defines catastrophic health expenditure, the WHO defines it as expenditure that consumes 40% or more of a household's income, drastically increasing the likelihood of poverty or rapid debt accumulation (WHO 2007).

regimes become globalized, but the scope of the subject matter subject to intellectual property claims has also been expanded, and standards have become more rigorous. These trends were accelerated by the establishment of the WTO in 1994 and the adoption of the international Agreement on Trade-Related Aspects of Intellectual Property Rights (TRIPS) in 1995. The minimum standards of intellectual property protection stipulated by the TRIPS agreement have made it far more difficult for individual countries to tailor levels of intellectual property protection to fit their development needs and protect human rights.

The TRIPS agreement affects access to medicines, a key component of the right to health, in several ways. It obligates WTO members to grant patents in all fields of technology, including extending patent protection to pharmaceuticals – something few poor countries had previously done – and requires all countries to permit foreign entities to patent their products and processes. When large pharmaceutical corporations acquire patent rights globally, including in poor countries, it allows them to charge prices substantially higher than marginal costs. Although patent protection is often justified as providing a stimulus for research and development, this is rarely the case in countries lacking capital and the required scientific and technological infrastructure for pharmaceutical research (Correa 2009). TRIPS also restricts the right of governments to grant compulsory licenses to allow local manufacturers to produce patented products or processes without the consent of the patent owner. By requiring pharmaceutical patents it also cuts off the exports of cheap generic drugs from countries such as India to other poor countries. The implications can be shown in figures on the prices of patented antiretrovirals (ARVs) to treat AIDS. In 2000, the cost per patient per year often exceeded US $10,000. Indian generic firms made the same ARV treatment available in 2001 for less than US $400, and competition lowered the originator and generic drug prices thereafter. Indian generic manufacturers were able to make the ARVs cheaply because India did not then recognize pharmaceutical product patents, but TRIPS required India to do so after January 1, 2005 (Correa 2009).

Concerns with the impact of the TRIPS agreement on access to medicines and more broadly on public health are reflected in the Doha Ministerial Declaration on TRIPS and Public Health (WTO 2001). The Doha Declaration recognized the gravity of the public health problems afflicting many developing countries and least-developed countries, especially from HIV/AIDS, tuberculosis, malaria, and other epidemics (para. 1), and agreed that the TRIPS agreement should not prevent members from taking measures to protect public health (para. 4). The main solution it proposes is to affirm the flexibilities of the TRIPS agreement, particularly the right of countries to grant compulsory licenses in national emergencies. It did not resolve the even more knotty issue of WTO members with insufficient or no manufacturing capacity to be able to take advantage of the flexibilities. Although a subsequent WTO decision sought to address this issue, the mechanism is so cumbersome that it makes its provisions very difficult to use (Correa 2009).

International Aid Donors

The implementation of most economic and social rights, particularly the right to health, requires the investment of resources. By definition, poor countries generally lack sufficient resources. Over the past ten to fifteen years, developing countries' budget allocations for health have been supplemented by an unprecedented rise in public foreign aid and private philanthropic giving, resulting in billions of additional dollars being directed to addressing the health needs of middle-income and poor countries. It is estimated that total foreign assistance for health programs rose from $5.6 billion in 1990 to $21.8 billion in 2007 (Gates 2010). The revolution in global health funding has been paralleled by the proliferation of global health funding mechanisms and donors, including multilateral organizations such as the Global Fund to Fight AIDS, Tuberculosis and Malaria, the World Bank's Multi-Country AIDS Program, and the GAVI Alliance; new bilateral aid programs, one example of which is the U.S. President's Emergency Plan for AIDS Relief; and the involvement of private philanthropic foundations, most notably the Gates Foundation. All of these donors have sought to influence the policies of recipient countries, sometimes in conflicting ways and generally without reference to the host country's own priorities.

Although the global health funding revolution has dramatically changed the health landscape, this attention to global health needs has not been translated into greater realization of the right to health. One important reason is that much of this money has been designated for disease-specific programs, particularly for HIV/AIDS, malaria, and tuberculosis, rather than for strengthening health infrastructure and public health programs. Some programs directed toward tackling specific diseases have had beneficial results, for example the eradication of smallpox in the 1970s, and more recently, improvements in access to HIV/AIDS treatment services in some countries, but others have failed. Importantly, whatever their achievement of success, disease-based vertical programs have resulted in general problems of lack of integration of services and "disease-silo" approaches. Additionally, if this funding is channeled predominantly through nongovernmental actors and alternative providers rather than public funding providers – which often occurs – it can affect health personnel and practices (Koivusalo and Mackintosh 2009). Some critics claim that global health funding has drawn attention away from other health problems of the poor, weakened already fragile public health systems, attracted health professionals away from vital infrastructure positions, contributed to the brain drain, and failed to reach the populations in greatest need (Garrett, 2007; Taylor and Rowson 2009). Others have a more positive view of the benefits of this influx of money (Sachs, 2007; Bates and Boatend, 2007; de Waal, 2007), but even so, it is indisputable that this funding has further fragmented the health system and weakened the public health institutions on which the implementation of the right to health depends.

CONCLUSION

Globalization and the neoliberal structural macroeconomic reforms that have frequently accompanied it have significantly altered the health landscape from the one in which Article 12 of the ICESCR was drafted a half century ago, and raised issues that GC 14 does not directly address. Importantly, the changed global context makes the realization of many components of the right to health far more difficult. Like other economic and social rights, the realization of the right to health is predicated on the existence of a strong and activist government committed to fulfilling its human rights obligations, but neoliberal globalization has reduced the policy space of states and restricted the provision of health services by the state. The progressive realization of economic and social rights depends on the availability of resources that the state can invest. Neoliberal prescriptions have reduced the size of budgets for health expenditures and required the introduction of cost-recovery measures to the detriment of the provision of critical health inputs and the accessibility of health services. It is therefore relevant to consider to what degree health can be respected, protected, and progressively fulfilled as a universal right to which all human beings should have a claim if it is commodified to the extent that health care services, medicines, and essential social determinants such as clean water and adequate sanitation often come at a price that citizens cannot afford.

In a globalized world economy, states – particularly poor countries – have fewer incentives to bear the costs required to progressively fulfill the right to health, or many other economic rights that require significant expenditures on the part of the state. Involvement in the global market-place and the fulfillment of structural conditions imposed by World Bank policy makers or the WTO frequently overrule social policy expenditure. Hence, welfare states have contracted throughout the world, particularly in developing countries, as they have removed economic barriers and tried to integrate into a global economy (Rudra 2008). As states' resources for social spending have diminished and their autonomy has been increasingly constrained by IFIs and trade agreements, protection and fulfillment of the right to health have stagnated considerably in much of the developing world, and even industrialized countries have cut back on their entitlements.

Neoliberal globalization has affected the implementation of all three types of obligations of the right to health: to respect, protect, and fulfill the right. State parties are under the obligation to respect the right to health by refraining from imposing laws or policies that interfere directly or indirectly with the enjoyment of the right. Most of the examples of requirements to respect the right outlined in GC 14 (CESCR 2000: para. 34) are not directly affected by globalization. However, the paragraph that identifies potential violations of the obligation to respect (CESCR 2000: para. 50) indicates that "the failure of the State to take into account its legal obligation regarding the right to health when entering into bilateral or multilateral agreements with other States, international organizations and other entities, such as multinational corporations" would constitute a violation of the obligation to respect. That is, in fact, what many states have done in entering into many international and bilateral trade agreements and TRIPS, and by agreeing to the conditions imposed by the World Bank and the IMF.

Neoliberal globalization clearly constrains the obligation to protect the right to health. The General Comment specifically places an obligation upon states to ensure that privatization of the health sector does not constitute a threat to the availability, accessibility, acceptability, and quality of health facilities, goods, and services (CESCR 2000: para. 35), but it has. Privatization – not just of health services but of other social goods such as water and sanitation that are essential to realizing the right to health – has fragmented health provision and complicated the framing and implementation of coordinated health policies. Privatization also expands the scope of the obligations of the state to protect its residents from abuse by non-state actors, but doing so requires the government to assume different and more complex roles just as the state is being weakened by neoliberal policy prescriptions and the scarcity of resources and personnel. A 1999 UN Department of Economic and Social Affairs paper describes the role of government in the context of privatization as shifting from producing and delivering services to enabling and regulating them. The paper points out that these roles require governments to be able to analyze market conditions; set policy frameworks; draw up, negotiate, and enforce contracts; coordinate, finance, and support producers; and provide consumers with their options and remedies (De Feyter and Gómez Isa 2005). Many, perhaps most, governments – particularly in poor and middle-income countries – lack these capabilities.

The motivation and ability of governments to progressively fulfill the right have also been affected. The ontological view of health has been shifted by globalization and the economic reforms that have accompanied it over the past two decades. Health is viewed less as a right to be respected, protected, and fulfilled by the state and more as a commodity that can be bought by those with the requisite means. Progressive social policies with the aims of universal access, once the international norm, are becoming less frequent outside of a select band of states in Western Europe that have the infrastructure, provisions, and political will to identify and protect those who suffer below-average health standards.

In order to progressively fulfill the right to health, it is imperative that the state identifies and aids citizens without the economic means to ensure access to the full range of health services. The availability of services alone is not enough to fulfill the right to health. Integration into a global economy and neoliberal economic reforms have constrained state autonomy and capacity to cross-subsidize social and economic goods.

The CESCR has been aware of many of these developments and the issues they raise. Its 1998 statement on globalization mentions the increasing reliance upon the free market; deregulation of a range of activities; the growth in the influence of international financial markets and institutions in determining the viability of national policy priorities; the privatization of various functions previously considered to be the exclusive domain in the state; and a diminution in the role of the state and the size of its budget (CESCR 1998: para. 2). As it has also done on other occasions, the Committee reiterated that the realms of trade, finance, and investment are not exempt from human rights principles (CESCR 1998: para. 5), and called on the IMF and World Bank to pay enhanced attention to respect for economic, social, and cultural rights in their activities (CESCR 1998: para. 7). Although the Committee avers that none of these developments is necessarily incompatible with the principles of the Covenant or with the related obligations of governments, it acknowledges that "taken together, however, and if not complemented by appropriate additional policies globalization risks downgrading the central place accorded to human rights by the United Nations Charter in general and the International Bill of Rights in particular," especially in relation to economic and social rights (CESCR 1998: para. 3). The statement is upbeat, asserting that all of the risks can be guarded against, or compensated for, if appropriate policies are put in place, but the Committee acknowledges that most governments are not doing so (CESCR 1998: para. 4).

It is our sense that neither the Committee nor the human rights community has developed a truly effective strategy for dealing with globalization. The human rights community needs to address these issues with less rhetoric and more concrete and effective strategies.

REFERENCES

Abouharb, M. Rodwan and David Cingranelli, 2007. *Human Rights and Structural Adjustment*, New York: Cambridge University Press.

Acemoglu, Daron, 2003. "Patterns of Skill Premia," *Review of Economic Studies* 70(2): 199–230.

Aguilar Rivera, Ana Mylena, Ke Xu, and Guy Carrin, 2006. "The Bolivian health system and its impact on health care use and financial risk protection." Discussion paper no. 7:1–30. World Health Organization – Cluster 'Evidence and Information for Policy' (EIP). Retrieved from http://www.who.int/health_financing/documents/dp_e_06_7-bolivian_health_system.pdf.

Alexander, Nancy, 2005. "The Roles of the IMF, World Bank and WTO in Liberalization and Privatization of the Water Services Sector," *Citizen's Network on Essential Services*. Retrieved from http://www.servicesforall.org.

Barrientos, Armando, 2000. "Getting Better after Neoliberalism: Shifts and Challenges of Health Policy in Chile," in Peter Lloyd Sherlock (Ed.) *Healthcare Reform & Poverty in Latin America*, 94–111, London: Institute of Latin American Studies.

Bates, Roger and Katherine Boatend, 2007. "How to Promote Global Health," A Foreign Affairs Roundtable. Retrieved from http://www.foreignaffairs.com/discussions/roundtables/how-to-promote-global-health.

Birdsall, Nancy, 1999. "Globalization and the Developing Countries: The Inequality Risk." Remarks at Overseas Development Council Conference, International Trade Center, Washington, DC.

Birdsall, Nancy, 2005. "Debt and Development: How to Provide Efficient, Effective Assistance to the World's Poorest Countries." Working Paper, Washington, DC: Center for Global Development.

Braveman, Paula and Sofia Gruskin, 2003. "Defining Equity in Health," *Journal of Epidemiology and Community Health* 57: 254–258.

CEGAA (The Centre for Economic Governance and AIDS in Africa) and RESULTS Educational Fund (REF), 2009. "Evidence of the Impact of IMF Fiscal and Monetary Policies on the Capacity to Address HIV/AIDS and TB Crises in Kenya, Tanzania and Zambia."

CESCR (Committee on Economic, Social and Cultural Rights), 1998. Statement on Globalization, UN Doc. E/C.12/1999/11 and Corr.1, annex VII.

CESCR (Committee on Economic, Social and Cultural Rights), 2000. General Comment No. 14: *The right to the highest attainable standard of health* (article 12 of the International Covenant on Economic, Social and Cultural Rights), UN Doc. E/C.12/2000/4.

CESCR (Committee on Economic, Social and Cultural Rights), 2002. General Comment No. 15: *The Right to Water* (Arts. 11 & 12 of the International Covenant on Economic, Social and Cultural Rights), U.N. Doc. E/C.12/2000.

Chapman, Audrey, 2009. "Globalization, Human Rights, and the Social Determinants of Health," *Bioethics* 23(2): 97–111.

Connolly, Michelle, 2003. "The Dual nature of trade: measuring its impact on imitation and growth," *Journal of Development Economics* 72(1): 31–55.

Cornia, Giovanni Andrea, Stefano Rosignoli, and Luca Tiberti, 2009. "An Empirical Investigation of the Relation between Globalization and Health," in Ronald Labonté, Ted Screcker, Corinne Packer, and Vivien Runnels (Eds.) *Globalization and Health: Pathways, Evidence and Policy*, 34–62, New York and London: Routledge.

Correa, Carlos M., 2009. "Intellectual Property Rights and Inequalities in Health Outcomes," in Ronald Labonté, Ted Schrecker, Corinne Packer, and Vivien Runnels (Eds.) *Globalization and Health: Pathways, Evidence and Policy*, 263–288, New York and London: Routledge.

Daniels, Norman, Bruce P. Kennedy, and Ichiro Kawachi, 2007. "Why Justice Is Good for Our Health: The Social Determinants of Health Inequalities," in Ronald Bayer, Lawrence O. Gostin, Bruce Jennings, and Bonnie Steinbock (Eds.) *Public Health Ethics: Theory, Policy, and Practice*, 205–230, New York: Oxford University Press.

Davis, Donald, 2003. "Trade Liberalization and Income Distribution" NBER Working Paper No. 5693, National Bureau of Economic Research.

De Feyter, Koen and Felipe Gómez Isa, 2005. "Privatisation and Human Rights: An Overview," in Koen De Feyter and Felipe Gómez Isa (Eds.) *Privatisation and Human Rights in the Age of Globalisation*, 1–8, Antwerp and Oxford: Intersentia.

de Waal, Alex, 2007. "Major Challenges/Minor Response," A Foreign Affairs Roundtable. Retrieved from http://www.foreignaffairs.com/discussions/round-tables/how-to-promote-global-health.

DfID (Department for International Development, UK), 2004. "The case for abolition of user fees for primary health services," London: Health Systems Resource Centre, Department for International Development.

Dicklitch, Susan and Rhoda E. Howard-Hassmann, 2007. "Public Policy and Economic Rights in Ghana and Uganda," in Shareen Hertel and Alanson Minkler (Eds.) *Economic Rights: Conceptual, Measurement and Policy Issues* pp. 325–344, New York: Cambridge University Press.

Falk, Richard, 1999. *Predatory Globalization: A Critique.* Cambridge, UK: Polity.

Galiani, Sebastian and P. Sanguinetti, 2003. "The Impact of Trade Liberalization on Wage Inequality: Evidence from Argentina," *Journal of Development Economics* 72(2): 497–513.

Garrett, Laurie, 2007. "The Challenge of Global Health: Beware of What You Wish For," *Foreign Affairs* (January/February), accessed at www.foreignaffairs.com/articles/62268/laurie-garrett/...global-health.

Gates, Bill, 2010. "Rich Countries' Aid Generosity," *Annual Letter from Bill Gates.*

Gómez Isa, Felipe, 2005. "Globalisation, Privatisation and Human Rights," in Koen De Feyter and Felipe Gómez Isa (Eds.) *Privatisation and Human Rights in the Age of Globalisation*, 9–32, Antwerp and Oxford: Intersentia.

Gostin, Lawrence O. and James G. Hodge, Jr., 2007. "Global Health Law, Ethics, and Policy," *The Journal of Law, Medicine & Ethics* 35:519–525.

Grabel, Ilene, 1996. "Marketing the Third World: The Contradictions of Portfolio Investment in the Global Economy," *World Development* l 24(11): 1761–1776.

Hawkes, Corinna, Mickey Chopra, and Sharon Friel, 2009. "Globalization, Trade, and the Nutrition Transition," in Ronald Labonté, Ted Schrecker, Corinne Packer, and Vivien Runnels (Eds.) *Globalization and Health: Pathways, Evidence and Policy*, 2235–2262, New York and London: Routledge.

Homedes, Núria, Ana Carolina Paz-Narváez, Ernesto Selva-Sutter, Olga Solas, and Antonio Ugalde, 2000. "Health Reform: Theory and Practice in El Salvador," in Peter Lloyd Sherlock (Ed.) *Healthcare Reform & Poverty in Latin America*, 57–77, London: Institute of Latin American Studies.

Howard-Hassmann, Rhoda E. 2005. "The Second Great Transformation: Human Rights Leapfrogging in the Era of Globalization," *Human Rights Quarterly* 27(1): 1–40.

Howard-Hassmann, Rhoda E. 2010. *Can Globalization Promote Human Rights?* Philadelphia: University of Pennsylvania Press.

Hunt, Paul (2008). Draft Guidelines for Pharmaceutical Corporations. Retrieved from www2.ohchr.org/English/issues/health/right/docs/draftguid150508.doc.

Huong, Dang Boi, Nguyen Khanh Phuong, Sarah Bales, Chen Jiayang, Henry Lucas, and Malcolm Segall, 2007. "Rural Health Care in Vietnam and China: Conflict between market reforms and social need," *International Journal of Health Services* 37(3): 555–572.

International Covenant on Economic, Social and Cultural Rights (ICESCR), 1966. Retrieved from http://www2.ohchr.org/english/law/cescr.htm.

Jaumotte, Florence, Subir Lall, and Chris Papageorgiou, 2008. "Rising Income Inequality: Technology, or Trade and Financial Globalization?" IMF Working Paper 08185. Retrieved from http://www.imf.org/external/pubs/ft/wp/2008/wp08185.pdf.

Kamat, Sangeeta, 2004. "The Privatization of Public Interest: Theorizing NGO discourse in a public era," *Review of International Public Economy* 11(1): 155–176.

Katz, Alison, 2005. "The Sachs Report: Investing in Health for Economic Development – Or Increasing the Size of the Crumbs from the Rich Man's Table?" *International Journal of Health Services* 35(1): 171–188.

Koivusalo, Meri and Maureen Mackintosh, 2009. "Global public action in health and pharmaceutical policies: politics and policy priorities," Innovation Knowledge Development Working Paper No. 45, The Open University.

Kuehn, Bridget M., 2007. "Global Shortages of Health Workers, Brain Drain Stress on Developing Countries," *Journal of the American Medical Association* 298: 1853–1855.

Labonté, Ronald, Chantal Blouin, Mickey Chopra, Kelly Lee, Corinne Packer, Mike Rowson, Ted Schrecker, and David Woodward. 2007. *Towards Health Equitable Globalisation: Rights, Regulation, and Redistribution. Final Report to the Commission on Social Determinants of Health Globalization Knowledge Network.* Retrieved from http://www.who.int/social_determinants/resources/gkn_report_06_2007.pdf.

Leive, Adam and Ke Xu, 2008. "Coping with out of pocket health payments: Empirical evidence from 15 African countries," *Bulletin of the World Health Organization* 86: 849–856.

Levcovitz, Eduardo, 2007. "Processes of change and challenges for health systems based on the renewed PHC Strategy." VII Regional Forum: Strengthening PHC-Based Health Systems, PAHO.

Lister, John and Ronald Labonté, 2009. "Globalization and Health Systems Change," in Ronald Labonté, Ted Schrecker, Corinne Packer, and Vivien Runnels (Eds.) *Globalization and Health: Pathways, Evidence and Policy*, 181–212, New York and London: Routledge.

Maarse, Hans, 2006. "The Privatization of Health Care in Europe: An Eight-Country Analysis," *Journal of Health Politics, Policy and Law* 31(5): 981–1014.

Mazur, Jay, 2000. "Labor's New Internationalism," *Foreign Affairs*, 81(1): 79–93.

McGuire, James, 2010. *Wealth, Health and Democracy in East Asia and Latin America*, New York: Cambridge University Press.

O'Connell, Paul, 2007. "On Reconciling Irreconcilables: Neoliberal Globalisation and Human Rights," *Human Rights Law Review* 3: 483–509.

Ooms, Gorik and Rachel Hammonds, 2004. "World Bank Policies and the Obligations of Its Members to Respect, Protect and Fulfill the Right to Health," *Health and Human Rights* 8(1): 27–62.

Ooms, Gorik and Rachel Hammonds, 2008. "Correcting Globalisation in Health: Transnational Entitlements versus the Ethical Imperative of Reducing Aid-Dependency," *Public Health Ethics* 1(2): 154–170.

Oxfam International, 2009. "Blind Optimism: Challenging the myths about private health care in poor countries," Oxfam Briefing Paper No. 125.

Rodrik, Dani, 2006. "Goodbye Washington Consensus, Hello Washington Consensus," *Journal of Economic Literature* 44: 973–987.

Rousseau, Peter and Richard Sylla, 2003. "Financial Systems, Economic Growth and Globalization," in Michael Bordo, Alan M. Taylor, and Jeffrey G. Williamson (Eds.) *Globalization in Historical Perspective*, 373–413, Chicago: University of Chicago Press.

Rowden, Rick, 2009. *The Deadly Ideas of Neoliberalism: How the IMF Has Undermined Public Health and the Fight Against AIDS*, London and New York: Zed Books.

Rudra, Nita, 2008. *Globalization and the Race to the Bottom in Developing Countries: Who Really Gets Hurt?* Cambridge England and New York: Cambridge University Press.

Sachs, Jeffrey D., 2007. "Beware False Tradeoffs," A Foreign Affairs Roundtable. Retrieved from http://www.foreignaffairs.com/.../global-health.

SAPRIN (Structural Adjustment Participatory Review International Network), 2004. *Structural Adjustment: The SAPRIN REPORT: The Policy Roots of Economic Crisis, Poverty, and Inequality.* London: Zed Books.

Schrecker, Ted., 2009. "The power of money, global financial markets, national politics, and social determinants of health," in O.D. Williams & A. Kay (Eds.) *Global health governance: Crisis, institutions and political economy*, 150–181, New York: Palgrave Macmillan.

Schrecker, Ted, 2011. "The Health Case for Economic and Social Rights Against the Global Marketplace," *Journal of Human Rights* 10(2): 151–177.

Schrecker, Ted, Audrey R. Chapman, Ronald Labonte, and Roberto De Vogli, 2010. "Advancing health equity in the global marketplace: How human rights can help," *Social Science & Medicine* 71: 1520–1526.

Sen, Gita and Piroska Östlin, 2007. "Unequal, Unfair, Ineffective and Inefficient. Gender Inequity in Health: Why it exists and how we can change it." Final report to the WHO Commission on Social Determinants of Health, September 2007. Retrieved from http://www2.ids.ac.uk/ghen/resources/papers/wgekn_final_report.pdf.

Silva, Herland Tejerina, Pierre De Paepe, Werner Soors, Oscar V. Lanza, Marie-Christine Closon, Patrick Van Dessel, and Jean-Pierre Unger, 2011. "Revisiting Health Policy and the World Bank in Bolivia," *Global Social Policy* 11(22): 22–44.

Somers, Margaret R., 2008. *Genealogies of Citizenship: Market, Statelessness, and the Right to have Rights*, Cambridge: Cambridge University Press.

Srinivasan, T.N. and Jagdish Bhagwati, 1999. "Outward-Orientation and Development: Are Revisionists Right," Working Papers 806, Economic Growth Center, Yale University.

Stiglitz, Joseph, 2003. *Globalization and its Discontents*, New York: WW Norton & Co.

Taylor, Sebastian and Michael Rowson, 2009. "Global Financing for Health: Aid and Debt Relief," in Ronald Labonté, Ted Schrecker, Corinne Packer, and Vivien Runnels (Eds.) *Globalization and Health, Pathways, Evidence and Policy*, 152–180, New York: Routledge Press.

Toebes, Brigit, 2006. "The Right to Health and the Privatization of National Health Systems: A Case Study of the Netherlands," *Health and Human Rights* 9(1): 102–127.

UN (United Nations), 1948. *Universal Declaration of Human Rights*, adopted 10 Dec. 1948. United Nations General Assembly Res. 217 A (III). Retrieved from http://www.un.org/en/documents/udhr/.

UNICEF, 2008. "Nationwide Needs Assessment for Emergency Obstetric and Newborn Care Services in Sierra Leone," Reproductive and Child Health Programme, Ministry of Health and Sanitation.

Vreeland, James, 2003. *The IMF and Economic Development*, Cambridge: Cambridge University Press.

Waitzkin, Howard, Rebeca Jasso-Aguilar, and Celia Iriart, 2007. "Privatization of Health Services in Less Developed Countries: An Empirical Response to the Proposals of the World Bank and Wharton School," *International Journal of Health Services* 37(2): 205–227.

Wan, Guanghua, Ming Lu, and Zhao Chen, 2007. "Globalization and Regional Income Inequality: Empirical Evidence from within China," *Review of Income and Wealth* 53(1): 35–50.

Wilkinson, Richard, 2005. *The Impact of Inequality: How to Make Sick Societies Healthier*, New York and London: The New Press.

Wilkinson, Richard and Kate Pickett, 2009. *The Spirit Level: Why Equality Matters*, New York: Bloomsbury Press.

World Bank, 1993. *World Development Report 1993: Investing in Health*, New York: Oxford University Press.

World Bank, 2004. *World Development Report: Making Services Work for Poor People*, Washington, DC: World Bank.

WHO (World Health Organization), 1995. *The World Health Report 1995: Bridging the Gaps*, Geneva: WHO. Retrieved from http://www.who.int.who/1995/en/index.html

WHO, 2006. *The World Health Report 2006 – Working together for health*, Geneva: WHO. Retrieved from http://www.who.int/whr/2006/en/.

WHO, 2007. *The World Health Report 2007: Everybody's Business: Strengthening Health Systems to Improve Health Outcomes*, Geneva: WHO. Retrieved from http://who.int/healthsystems/strategy/everybodys_business.pdf.

WHO Commission on the Social Determinants of Health, 2008. *Closing the gap in a generation: Health equity through action on the social determinants of health*, Geneva: World Health Organization.

WHO, 2008. *The World Health Report: Primary Health Care – Now More Than Ever*, Geneva: WHO. Retrieved from http://www.who.int/whr/2008/en/index.html.

WHO CMH, 2001. "Macroeconomics and Health: Investing in Health for Economic Development," chaired by Jeffrey Sachs, Geneva: World Health Organization.

WTO (World Trade Organization), 2001. *Declaration on the TRIPS Agreement and Public Health*, Ministerial Conference, Fourth Session, Doha, WT/MIN(01)/DEC/W2.

Yamin, Alicia Ely, 2000. "Protecting and Promoting the Right to Health in Latin America: Selected Experiences from the Field," *Health and Human Rights* 5(1): 116–148.

4

Demolishing Housing Rights in the Name of Market Fundamentalism: The Dynamics of Displacement in the United States, India, and South Africa

Cathy Albisa, Brittany Scott, and Kate Tissington

I. INTRODUCTION

The right to housing is recognized as a fundamental human right within the international human rights system, initially adopted in 1948 by the United Nations General Assembly in Article 25 of the *Universal Declaration on Human Rights* as an essential aspect of an adequate standard of living, and reaffirmed in Article 11 of the *International Covenant on Economic, Social and Cultural Rights* in 1976. However, as is the case with most rights, housing rights violations occur throughout the world.[1] These violations include, inter alia, homelessness, forced eviction, demolition of shacks, lack of adequate low-income housing supply, and so forth (UN-HABITAT 2009).[2] An evolving jurisprudence intended to address these violations has developed in a number of countries (UN-HABITAT 2002). Although the right to housing is no different from a jurisprudential perspective than other human rights – insofar as, to fully realize a right to housing, there must be universal access that is adequate and afforded to all without discrimination – on a practical level, housing poses a particular set of challenges to which human rights law and policy work are currently limited in their ability to respond.

Housing situations may differ across regions, countries, provinces, states, cities and towns, but most places have at least two things in

---

[1] For example, according to the Executive Summary Report of the Advisory Group on Forced Evictions (AGFE) to the Executive Director of UN-HABITAT (AGFE 2007, 2), forced evictions will affect 38–70 million people worldwide between 2000 and 2020, as it has become "common practice in lieu of urban planning and inclusive social policies."

[2] In a 2011 report, UN-HABITAT noted that forced evictions are certainly on the rise across the globe, and that urban evictions, in particular, have seen a dramatic increase in recent years with the rising number of projects financed in cities.

common. First, the poor encounter both the greatest barriers to accessing adequate housing, as well as the greatest tenure insecurity and instability (i.e., the most forced displacement) (Advisory Group on Forced Evictions [AGFE] 2007). Second, unlike in education and health care, for example, there are few if any publicly designed or regulated comprehensive national systems for housing that ensure decent access and stability for all.[3] Formal, lawfully occupied housing is primarily market based, with some supplementary government housing for poor and eligible members of society.[4] As a result, housing is often an object of investment as much as a home or a part of a community.[5] Although informal settlements exist, there is generally little if any legal protection extended by the state to "unlawful" occupiers;[6] even within the formal market, security of tenure varies based on an occupant's status as an "owner" or "renter."

This poses a serious challenge to human rights activists advocating for laws, policies, and approaches that challenge the current housing paradigms. Within the human rights framework, needs, including basic and adequate housing, create obligations on the part of the government to not only fulfill human rights, but also to respect and protect them. That is, not only is the government required to refrain from forcibly evicting inhabitants itself, it must also prevent private actors – individuals, corporations, and any other institution – from doing the same. Despite this clear obligation to regulate the market, often very little is done.

Even where poor or economically distressed individuals have ownership rights – arguably the highest level of legal protection enforced by the state – displacement still occurs. The ongoing foreclosure crisis in the United States, as well as elsewhere, is a prime example. In this context,

---

[3] There are many government programs to create access to housing for the poor, from government housing to subsidies. However, these tend to be patchwork programs to address gaps left by the market, rather than a systemic approach. Considered another way, Kenna (2008) suggests that the development and maintenance of a housing market require legal instruments and state involvement in five essential categories: private property, housing finance, residential infrastructure, regulatory, and housing subsidy/public housing.

[4] For example, as of April 2, 2012, the U.S. Department of Housing and Urban Development (HUD) lists generally on its Web site: eligibility criteria, income limits, and waitlist process for its public and subsidized housing programs. HUD subsidizes roughly 3 million low-income housing units as of February 2012 (HUD 2012).

[5] Indeed, the global real estate investment trust (REIT) industry has more than doubled in the last ten years. There are 134 publicly traded U.S. REITs as of April 2, 2012. REITs are corporate entities that facilitate capital investment in real estate, designed to derive income from rents and mortgage interest.

[6] AGFE (2007) identifies as a central cause of evictions, limitations to acquiring property rights, and inter alia security of tenure, via the private market.

the role of private debt has led to tenuous living situations and massive displacement.[7] In particular, lower-income owners in the United States (as well as women and people of color) deemed "risky" by the market were forced to pay high, often fluctuating, interest rates and higher monthly payments than those with greater financial means (Fishbein and Bunce 2005). Moreover, in areas with rising land values, even debt-free owners may be subject to eviction as a result of rising property taxes and service costs, which can lead to unaffordable conditions and displacement.[8] Thus, ownership, as commonly conceived of today, is not a panacea. Where people living in poverty are renters instead of owners, or informal occupiers without any formal legal recognition, levels of protection against displacement are even lower. Irrespective of the status of inhabitants, current legal frameworks do not appear to protect against the massive levels of displacement witnessed globally (AGFE 2007).

This does not necessarily further an argument against private homeownership. In most places, people have a strong psychological and social investment in owning their homes.[9] The sense of autonomy and stability associated with homeownership is important and cannot be underestimated.[10] Yet, within that notion of property ownership is a "bundle of rights," and most of these rights (e.g., the right to use and enjoy the property in privacy) are not intrinsically tied to making a profit from the resale of property.[11] For many, the right to profit off the sale of their home is not a central concern; rather, the social, cultural, and economic values derived from its use are most important.[12]

As countries around the world struggle through a global economic crisis that many ascribe to the deregulation of the housing market under neoliberal economies (Kenna 2008),[13] this is an important moment to

---

[7] Goodman (2011) estimates that 8 million families have lost their homes to foreclosure since 2007, and that roughly 8–10 million more will join them before the mortgage crisis ends (out of 50 million outstanding mortgages). Growth of subprime mortgages soared from 1994 to 2006 from 5 in 100 mortgages to 1 in 5 (Schloemer 2006).

[8] For example, Zelinsky (2002) states that rising property values can absorb large percentages of retirees' incomes.

[9] See, for example, Kearns et al (2000).

[10] Ibid.

[11] IPS (1989) proposes, based on this premise, the expansion of *social ownership*, or housing operated solely for resident benefit, subject to resident control, with resale restrictions.

[12] Compare the analysis of Kearns et al. (2000) and Professor of Economics Michael Stone (2010), who points out the significant pressures – from thirty years of stagnant and falling wages at the same time housing, education, and health care costs rose – that basically forced homeowners to treat their homes as cash machines.

[13] See, for example, Önis and Güven (2010) and Kenna (2008). Kenna's article explores globalization's effects in housing systems across the world, including the growing role of

raise the question of what the relationship should be between housing and the market. The neoliberal worldview has become increasingly
influential since the 1980s and, in broad terms, posits that markets
have self-correcting mechanisms that function best without regulation,
and that governments are not as well situated as the private market
to address needs in a vast range of sectors, including housing (Peet and
Hartwick 2009). Therefore, a neoliberal restructuring of economies mandates deregulation and privatization (Peet and Hartwick 2009).

As human rights lawyers and practitioners, we recognize that these central assumptions of neoliberalism have significant relevance for the legal
concepts necessary to ensure government policies and practices meet obligations to both respect and protect the right to housing (Kenna 2008).[14]
How we resolve our understanding of the relationship between the state
and the market, as well as the relationship among rights such as the right
to property and profit and the right to housing as a component of the
right to life, is critical to ensuring stable communities and the protection
of security of tenure for vulnerable families and individuals. Thus, the
housing market and financial apparatuses that have been built up around
it should be examined extremely closely.

It appears that, rather than coexist in a careful balance, a right to
housing has been allowed to exist only within small spaces not already
claimed by market interests. Indeed, housing rights have been shaped by
(and have accommodated to) these forces, finding minimal recognition
when forced to come head to head with an increase in the profitability
of land and/or the economic benefits of development to wealthy elites in
society, both highly interrelated phenomena.

These concerns have been heightened by increasing wealth inequality in countries and across countries, which many ascribe to neoliberal economic policies (Mahmud 2010).[15] In countries where poverty
is low and there are also low levels of wealth inequality, there is far
greater access to housing even though a great deal of housing is market

global corporations and the globalization of housing finance and real estate investments,
as well as privatizations.

[14] Kenna (2008, 424), for example, quotes a European Federation of National Organizations Working with the Homeless (FEANTSA) report from 2005, which raised the
following issue: "Where states were once 'providers' they now increasingly adopt the
role of 'enablers', where they had little history of involvement, their new roles take on
a demonstrable 'support the market' function."

[15] According to Mahmud (2010, 23), "As interests of global finance capital took precedence over survival needs of the poor, the impact on the vulnerable was quick, and the
main single cause of increases in poverty and inequality during the 1980s and 1990s
was the retreat of the state."

based.[16] In democracies with adequate levels of wealth equitably distributed, the market may in fact function to meet housing needs overall. In countries where poverty is prevalent but wealth inequality is low, housing struggles remain serious; however, the nature of the threat to housing rights changes.[17] In countries where there is significant wealth inequality (always paired with significant poverty and representing the vast majority of countries in the world), market interests in the form of investment and development pose the most constant threat of displacement for poor communities, regardless of whether they own or rent formal housing or live in informal settlements.[18]

With a view to examine these dynamics more closely, this chapter will briefly focus on three case studies – Mumbai, Chicago, and Johannesburg – where the housing rights of poor communities have come into direct conflict with market interests. Two of these communities – Mumbai and Chicago – were displaced; one is fighting to remain – Johannesburg. Across the world, poor communities are routinely forcibly removed from their homes, without voice or vote over what happens to them or to the land and homes they are forced to leave.[19] The three case studies were chosen because they highlight specific occasions where communities attempted to use legal avenues to prevent their displacement, but the legal framework in place was inadequate to meet the obligation of government to protect residents from displacement of market forces. This chapter will discuss commonalities and differences between the case studies, and assess where existing legal concepts and avenues may be of use or fall short. Finally, this chapter will suggest some important concepts, currently absent in law and policy, which could assist in developing a systemic and coherent approach to protecting housing as a human right.

a. Mumbai, India: Whose World-Class City?

Mumbai is described as "the financial hub" of India, and seeks to be seen as a "world-class city," with companies from across the world submitting

---

[16] Sweden, Denmark, and Norway's combined average is slightly more than 20,000 homeless people (1 in 1,000 inhabitants) (Benjaminsen and Dyb 2008).

[17] For example, in Serbia there is a severe shortage of units, but most evictions and displacement stem from discrimination against minorities rather than economic incentives (Cirkovic and Terzic 2010).

[18] According to some, neoliberal policies advance particular understandings of development and poverty that "disregard the social context of provision, the lived experiences of the poor and dismiss and/or reinforce the way in which deprivations are constituted" (Higgott and Weber 2005, 435, 442).

[19] In the United States, this is currently also hitting the middle class hard in the form of foreclosure evictions. See Goodman (2011).

proposals and bids to the Maharashtra State in the hopes of redeveloping the city (Whiting 2008).[20] In 2003, a global management consulting firm issued an influential report – *Vision Mumbai* – detailing a comprehensive plan for turning Mumbai into a world-class city by 2013 (McKinsey & Company).[21] *Vision Mumbai* identifies housing and land availability as central obstacles to the city's achievement of world-class status, and recommends increased private-sector participation in slum redevelopment through the government's adoption of market principles. The report proposes such model policies as government auctions of public land as an incentive for private investment in the development of low-income housing (McKinsey & Company 2003).

Not surprisingly, with scarce land to develop in Mumbai, global investors have placed significant pressure on Maharashtra State to address informal settlements on government-owned property in the city center (McKinsey & Company 2003). At the same time, public attitudes and policies related to the city's slumdwellers have undergone a significant shift. Many of Mumbai's slums have been there for generations. Through the 1970s and 1980s, the housing rights of slumdwellers were met with some political and legal support.[22] Nonetheless, with the beginning of the 1980s – also coincidentally the beginning of the neoliberal period – the tide began to turn.

On July 13, 1981, the then-Chief Minister of Maharashtra Shri A.R. Antulay made an announcement that all slumdwellers in the city of Mumbai would be evicted forcibly and deported to their respective places of origin or removed to places outside the city.[23] In 1985, the legal groundwork for mass displacement was established, despite what was still sympathetic discourse. In *Olga Tellis & Others v Bombay Municipal Council*, the Supreme Court of India found that evicting slumdwellers – who created their livelihoods out of their makeshift homes – involved the right to life, stating that:

[20] The redevelopment of Dharavi – home to more than 1 million people – has drawn 26 bids involving 78 Indian developers (including DLF Ltd and Unitech) as well as 25 foreign firms (including Lehman Brothers, Dubai World, and China's Shimao Group) (Whiting 2008).

[21] Explained on McKinsey & Company's Web site, http://www.mckinsey.com/locations/india/communityservice/visionmumbai/, last accessed April 2, 2012.

[22] During this period, the World Bank began to fund slum upgrading, slum improvement, and sites and services programs in Indian cities. See also Ghertner (2008) for a discussion on the use of the nuisance law in Indian courts to force cities to provide services to slums.

[23] *Olga Tellis and Others v Bombay Municipal Council [1985] 2 Supp SCR 51.* Retrieved from http://www.escr-net.org/caselaw/caselaw_show.htm?doc_id=401006. The Supreme Court of India decision explains the original writ of 1981 at length.

An equally important facet of that right [to life] is the right to livelihood because, no person can live without the means of living, that is, the means of livelihood. If the right to livelihood is not treated as a part of the constitutional right to life, the easiest way of depriving a person of his right to life would be to deprive him of his means of livelihood to the point of abrogation. Such deprivation would not only denude the life of its effective content and meaningfulness but it would make life impossible to live.[24]

The Supreme Court also noted that this was a matter in "which the future of half of the city's population is at stake."[25] Still, the Court found that their presence was unauthorized and therefore illegal:

There is no doubt that the petitioners are using pavements and other public properties for an unauthorised purpose. But, their intention or object in doing so is not to commit an offence or intimidate insult or annoy any person, which is the gist of the offence of "Criminal trespass" under section 441 of the Penal Code. They manage to find a habitat in places which are mostly filthy or marshy, out of sheer helplessness. It is not as if they have a free choice to exercise as to whether to commit an encroachment and if so, where. The encroachment committed by these persons are involuntary acts in the sense that those acts are compelled by inevitable circumstances and are not guided by choice.[26]

Ultimately, the Court ruled that some slumdwellers – those who had been documented in a 1976 census and had identity cards – must be resettled and given alternative accommodation, and could not be evicted without process and notice. This falls far short of acknowledging a right to housing for the average resident (or, at least, the average resident in the lower half of the socioeconomic scale). Moreover, in practice, the slumdwellers were largely evicted without resettlement assistance (Centre for Development and Human Rights 2010). Thus, although the case contextualized the slumdwellers in a sympathetic manner, affording them some procedural rights, in reality this case became a "green light" for those looking to move the interests of outside investors and wealthier classes in the redevelopment of Mumbai.[27] By the end of the 1990s, slum redevelopment schemes were being tailored to attract private investors.[28]

[24] Ibid., 22.
[25] Ibid.
[26] Ibid., 31.
[27] See Ramanathan (2006).
[28] Mukhija (2001) notes that most redevelopment projects on public land in Mumbai resulted in the transfer of land to private actors.

The rhetoric of court cases going forward in time also reflects the loss of ground politically for the slumdwellers. In 2000, the Supreme Court shifted its paradigm dramatically and declared that, "Rewarding an encroacher on public land with an alternative free site is like giving a reward to a pickpocket for stealing."[29] Although previous cases supported the displacement as a "necessary evil," this change in rhetoric fueled an ever-present tactic against the poor: criminalization and exclusion as full rights holders. Five years later, the state began penalizing so-called illegal encroachers for occupation of public lands by denying slumdwellers voting rights, thus stripping them of recognition as legitimate members of society (D'Monte 2004).

In 2004, the state, with the assistance of the World Bank, began implementing *Vision Mumbai*.[30] To make land available for the myriad projects proposed to transform the city, the state began to rid government property of encroachers through demolition drives supervised by the state's police force (Katakam 2005). In the first year alone, more than 92,000 homes were demolished, displacing more than 400,000 people, with tens of thousands additional demolitions completed in each subsequent year (Kothari 2006). Under national regulation, "eligible" slumdwellers subject to demolition were still, in theory, entitled to resettlement in free government housing (COHRE 2002). The documentation required to establish eligibility, because of difficulty of proof and costs, has rendered as many as 70% of residents ineligible for resettlement and, ultimately, homeless (COHRE 2002). Living conditions have also become worse for those moved to resettlement sites far from work in the city center with few amenities, including water (COHRE 2002).

b. Chicago, Illinois: Left out of the Loop

Throughout the 1990s, Chicago increased in population, and the value of housing rose, as was the case in most cities in the United States (Levy, Comey, and Padilla 2006).[31] In part, the rising prices were driven by the "speculative fever" of private investors during the real estate boom

[29] *Almitra H. Patel v Union of India* WP 888/1996, February 15, 2000.
[30] For example, the World Bank's Web site establishes the Bank's contributions at approximately $542 million to the Mumbai Urban Transport Project. George Peterson (2006) explains the role of public-to-private land sales.
[31] Levy et al (2006) used data from the Urban Institute's Neighborhood Change Database, which is based on 1990 and 2000 U.S. Censuses.

(Silva 2011).[32] However, growth did not happen uniformly across the city (Silva 2011).[33] Neighborhoods bordering Lake Michigan north of the central business district (known as the Loop) and those immediately south and west of the downtown area were focal points of the city's housing market boom (Silva 2011). One of the Chicago Housing Authority's (CHA)[34] largest public housing complexes – Cabrini-Green – covered tens of acres in the middle of the heavily gentrified Near North Side.[35]

In 1992, Congress created the Urban Revitalization Demonstration program, commonly known as the Housing Opportunities for People Everywhere or HOPE VI program, to redevelop "severely distressed" public housing (Salama 1999).[36] In Chicago, before comprehensive demolition plans were even announced, real estate speculators began purchasing property adjacent to the Cabrini-Green projects with the explicit expectation that the complexes would be removed (Fleming 2008).[37] After sixteen years of public and legal battles against displacement, the last resident of Cabrini-Green's high- and mid-rise apartment buildings (most of whom were there as legal tenants renting government housing) was moved out in December 2010 (Terry 2010).[38] The *New York Times* reported:

> For pundits and politicians, the once-sprawling development on the Near North Side has long been a symbol – and a scapegoat – for all that is wrong with public housing. They saw Cabrini, and the city's other massive high-rise public housing developments, as hothouses for drugs, gangs and broken families, their dense poverty unsustainable. They will shed no tears

---

[32] See Silva (2011) reporting on Federal Reserve Bank of New York research.

[33] Silva (2011) cites Chicago Fact Book Consortium (1963), *Local Community Fact Book Chicago Metropolitan Area 1960* (U. of Ill. Chicago ed., 1963).

[34] The Chicago Housing Authority (CHA) is the local public agency authorized to engage and assist in the operation of low-income housing in Chicago. Public housing authorities (PHAs) administer federally funded programs, including 1.2 million publicly owned rental units.

[35] The Near North Side Neighborhood Change Chart created by Voorhees Center for Neighborhood and Community Improvement, http://www.uic.edu/cuppa/voorheesctr/Gentrification%20Index%20Site/NearNorthSide.htm, illustrates neighborhood change and patterns of gentrification between 1970 and 2000. See also Web site of Chicago Historical Society, http://encyclopedia.chicagohistory.org/pages/3712.html, for a map of CHA's public housing developments.

[36] The National Housing Law Project et al. (2002) in *False HOPE* published a critical assessment of the HOPE VI program, finding that it "worsened affordable housing needs."

[37] See also Peterson (1997).

[38] See also Black (2011).

when the 15-story building at 1230 North Burling Street comes down next year.

But for the last tenant, Annie Ricks, a 54-year-old teacher's aide and grand-mother of 10, it requires all of her strength and faith not to simply sit on the edge of her bed and weep. For her, Cabrini isn't a symbol. It is home. Now it is gone (Terry 2010, 1).

During the 1990s, public housing gained a widespread and gen-erally undeserved negative reputation.[39] With unsupported arguments that public housing caused crime and self-perpetuating concentrations of poverty,[40] political and business leaders set out to eliminate public housing – in particular public housing in high-value areas – in the United States.[41] In New Orleans, one of the primary arguments for eliminating the remaining public housing in the city despite the severe housing short-age after Hurricane Katrina was that it brought crime to the city.[42] As witnessed in many parts of the world, criminalization was a central tactic used to displace multigenerational communities living in public housing stock across the United States.

In Chicago, Cabrini-Green in particular became synonymous with this negative image, thanks to high-profile crimes that received national attention.[43] This targeting of Cabrini-Green occurred despite evidence that its residents did better on most indicators than residents in pub-lic housing that had been built far from high-opportunity areas (Terry 2010).[44] The mainstream media in Chicago generally promoted this

---

[39] See National Housing Law Project et al (2002); Venkatesh and Celimli (2004); and Steinberg (2010).

[40] Steinberg (2010, 217) argues that "dispossession and displacement are done in the name of deconcentrating poverty." In fact, it has been shown that concentrations of poverty are more likely when, for example, rental subsidies provided by the Section 8 program are paid to private landlords to house the poor. However, because this is a market-based program, and it is easier to displace families when rents rise, it has not engendered the same controversy (National Housing Law Project et al 2002).

[41] Greene (2008) provides a summary of a number of perspectives on the HOPE VI program.

[42] HUD's Web site hosts a factsheet on Katrina that cites "uninhabitable, crime-ridden, and unsafe" conditions as triggers for the projects' demolition. Those behind the destruction of multigenerational communities have never commented on the rising murder rate – despite no more public housing – that existed hand in hand with the displacement and inequitable redevelopment (Jervis 2011).

[43] See, for example, Stodghill (1998).

[44] Mr. Edwin Eisendrath, a former North Side alderman and HUD employee, quoted in Terry (2010): "Cabrini residents did better in school. . . . They were more likely to work. They took jobs eagerly when they were offered. They lived, after all, surrounded by some very healthy communities." See also Steinberg (2010).

narrative of Cabrini-Green as an untenable place to live, needing to be torn down, but residents tried to dispute this. The more independent (and often African-American) progressive media also took a different position:

> More to the point, HUD [the U.S. Department of Housing and Urban Development, the federal agency responsible for administering low-income housing programs] came to Chicago to bury an idea. One enshrined in a series of United Nations declarations and international covenants reaching back to the 1940s. One instituted by the practices of about seven decades of U.S. housing policy, beginning with the Depression-era's U.S. Housing Act of 1937, which declared it to be the "policy of the United States [Government] to remedy the unsafe and unsanitary housing conditions and the acute shortage of decent, safe and sanitary dwellings for families of lower income," and to produce a "decent home and suitable living environment for every American family" (Peterson 1997).

Moreover, although the government kept insisting the demolition was for the good of the residents, property owners and developers in the area were far more frank about the underlying motivation for tearing down Cabrini-Green, as opposed to other complexes that were far more troubled but far from the city center. As one independent media source reported in 1997:

> You can't miraculously invite market-rate people to buy on a nine-acre island in the shadow of Cabrini, developer Dan McLean noted last year. "There's just no point because it wouldn't fly." Mary McGinty, the president of the Near North Property Owners Association, was equally frank. "Middle-class and upper-class people won't move into Cabrini if it's surrounded by buildings that are a problem," she observed. "The majority of Cabrini-Green needs to be pulled down" (Peterson 1997).

Demolition of Chicago's large, centrally located public housing was accomplished both by de facto – or constructive – demolition and demolition by bulldozer. In 1996, HUD issued new eviction guidelines to local public housing authorities (PHAs). The "one-strike" policies encouraged PHAs to develop and enforce zero-tolerance rules, which gave PHAs the authority to evict residents based solely on allegations of criminal activity – even if charges were dropped or residents were affirmatively cleared – as well as a range of fairly ordinary human behavior, including such things as "poor housekeeping," using "abusive language" with a PHA employee, or missing two appointments with a PHA representative (Mahmud 2010).[45]

---

[45] Find HUD Lease Requirements in federal regulations, 24 C.F.R. § 966.4 (2004).

Furthermore, the U.S. Supreme Court upheld evictions under the one-strike policy that were based on a guest or family member's violation of the rules, even where the tenant had no knowledge.[46]

Between 1996 and 1998, occupancy rates in CHA properties declined by more than 20% (Rogal 2007). In 1997 alone, the CHA, wielding its new authority under the one-strike law, filed evictions against more than a quarter of the families living in the Cabrini-Green Homes Extension, a mix of mid- and high-rise buildings on the city's Near North Side (Rogal 2007). This compared with the less than 1% filed at Altgeld Gardens on the far South Side, an area removed from gentrification pressures (Rogal 2007). At its peak, Cabrini-Green housed as many as 18,000 people, but by the time the city announced a comprehensive redevelopment plan, only about 6,000 people remained.[47]

In 1998, the HOPE VI redevelopment tools were made permanently available to PHAs through HUD (Salama 1999). To date, HOPE VI provides grants to tear down severely distressed public housing units (a term that includes social connotations related to theories of crime and poverty concentration) and replace them with mixed-income developments (National Housing Law Project et al. 2002).[48] A central feature of the HOPE VI redevelopment model is its requirement of PHAs to retain private developers, leverage private investment, and enter the private real estate market.[49] In 2000, the CHA adopted the HOPE VI-funded *Plan for Transformation*, a ten-year redevelopment effort to replace all of Chicago's public housing with mixed-income housing. This has resulted in the demolition of roughly 20,000 public housing units across Chicago.[50]

Roughly 75% of all CHA families have expressed an interest in returning to their old neighborhood, yet fewer than 20% will be able to return

[46] See *Department of Housing and Urban Development v Rucker* 2002. 535 U.S. 125. This decision stated that the Anti-Drug Abuse Act of 1988 allows local PHAs to evict tenants for drug-related activity of non-tenant relatives or guests, regardless of whether tenants know, or should have known, about the activity.

[47] See the Coalition to Protect Public Housing et al. flier entitled "From Housing to Homelessness: The Truth Behind the CHA's Plan for Transformation." Retrieved from www.limits.com/cpph/Public%20Housing%20Flier.pdf.

[48] The National Housing Law Project et al. (2002) notes both the loose nature of the definition of "severely distressed" and HUD's shift away from the "'most' severely distressed" complexes.

[49] National Housing Law Project et al. (2002) cites the notes of auditors from the General Accounting Office and HUD's inspector general finding a shift in the HOPE VI program to sites with the greatest potential to attract private investment, not the most in need.

[50] For more on CHA's *Plan for Transformation*, visit the agency's Web site, http://www.thecha.org/pages/the_plan_for_transformation/22.php.

because of the higher rents of replacement units, in addition to prohibitive eligibility requirements for low-income families (Venkatesh and Celimli 2004). Although many families threatened with eviction walked away from their units without housing vouchers[51] (public subsidies that low-income families must use on the private market), those who did take a voucher faced new challenges on the private market, given the insufficient supply of available affordable units (Popkin et al. 2004).[52] More than 90% of CHA residents have been resegregated to high-poverty, high-crime neighborhoods under the *Plan for Transformation* (Fischer 2003).[53]

Although the residents engaged in a sixteen-year legal battle, the grounds upon which they brought their lawsuit did not include a right to housing or any argument involving the positive obligation of the government to respect residents' rights to remain. This is because there is no right to housing recognized in the U.S. Constitution or in most state constitutions. Instead, a great deal of the litigation stemmed from a 1969 consent decree that was still in effect in order to protect residents from racial discrimination.[54] Although most public housing constituted primarily poor African Americans, the location of Cabrini-Green appeared controversial from the start, and the government initially wanted to move mostly white families into the complexes, claiming it was necessary in order to avoid a hostile and perhaps violent reaction from the neighboring communities. This was rejected as unconstitutional by the courts, and a complex consent decree and receivership were set up to protect against discrimination.[55]

Thus, the focus of the litigation once the displacement plans were in place was whether the displacement would move residents into more segregated housing situations in violation of the 1969 consent decree

---

[51] For instance, in 1997, 86.3% of those who moved out of Cabrini did not leave with Section 8 vouchers (Rogal 2007).

[52] Popkin et al. (2004) found that former public housing residents face barriers to finding new stable homes in tight private rental markets. These include stigma related to public housing special needs (e.g., large families, a member with disabilities), as well as increased likelihood of housing instability.

[53] According to Fischer (2003), 78% of the involuntarily displaced families have been moved to census tracts in which the racial composition is more than 95% African American. More than 86% of the families have been moved to census tracts in which the racial composition is between 80% and 100% African American, and more than 93% have been moved to census tracts in which the racial composition is more than 50 percent African American.

[54] See *Gautreaux v Chicago Housing Authority Civ. A.* No. 66 C 1459 (1969).

[55] See *Hills v Gautreaux* 425 U.S. 284 (1976).

(Wilen 2006). Additionally, the local housing agency had entered into a contract regarding relocation, and the litigation was also focused on these contractual rights arising from the agreement between the local housing agency and the Local Advisory Council, which represented residents.[56] Another focus of the various lawsuits was whether the local government agency had meaningfully engaged residents in the relocation plans, in particular to avoid racially discriminatory relocation.[57] A review of the cases finds that most of the decisions hinged on procedural technicalities with no emphasis on the right of residents to live in a stable community or to, in fact, have access to basic and decent housing at all.

c. *Johannesburg, South Africa: Resisting Inner-City Evictions*

In the two case studies previously described, urban centers became more attractive to private investment over time. In Johannesburg, which bills itself as a "world-class African city," the local municipality embarked on a concerted process of inner-city regeneration in 2003 with the launch of its *Inner City Regeneration Strategy*.[58] The aim was to stimulate property values in the inner city by encouraging private-sector investment in the urban core, an area of around 12 square kilometers, which had experienced a period of decline during the 1990s.[59] When apartheid influx controls fell away in 1986, many African people, previously barred from living in the city center, began to move into the Johannesburg inner city. There was a rapid increase in demand for housing, and many property owners began to charge exorbitant rents to African tenants who moved into the inner city in the late 1980s and early 1990s (Wilson 2011). In response to the influx of black residents, white residents in neighboring apartments would often move out, rather than share their living space with black people. According to Stuart Wilson:

> While black tenants in the inner city were initially relatively affluent, profiteering by landlords meant that even salaried black tenants found it difficult to rent flats and/or houses without subletting their properties to other households and groups. In many residential blocks of flats, the consequent overcrowding put pressure on infrastructure and services in the inner city.

[56] See, for example, *Cabrini-Green Loc. Advisory Council v. Chicago Housing Authority*, No. 04 C 3792 (N.D. Ill., 2008).

[57] See, for example, *Cabrini-Green Loc. Advisory Council v. Chicago Housing Authority*. No. 96 C 6949 (N.D. Ill., 1997).

[58] See Ngwabi (2009).

[59] Ibid.

Demand for water and electricity skyrocketed, while lifts and sewerage systems struggled to cope. This led to a decline in the living environment in many residential areas of the Johannesburg inner city (Wilson 2011, 132).

A report published by the Centre on Housing Rights and Evictions (COHRE) in 2005 estimated about 67,000 people living in so-called bad buildings in the inner city of Johannesburg, many of whom were "paying no rentals or rentals (to slum lords) at rates far below market rates for residential accommodation in the inner city" (Wilson 2011, 134).

Between 2002 and 2006, mass evictions in the inner city of Johannesburg were a regular occurrence, and were presented as "a necessary corollary of development and rejuvenation" (Wilson 2011, 135). Property developers moved in to buy so-called bad buildings and convert them to middle- to upper-income accommodation, unaffordable to those families and individuals currently living there. The government evicted people on a regular basis from state-owned buildings on health and safety grounds, using a piece of national legislation called the National Building Standards and Building Regulations Act 103 of 1977 (NBRA). This process commenced with the issuing of a notice in terms of section 12(4)(b) of the NBRA, declaring a building unfit for occupation and ordering all its residents to vacate the building within one week of the date of the notice. It is estimated that between 2002 and 2006, about 10,000 residents of 122 properties in the inner city of Johannesburg were evicted in this way.[60] Evictions were not only state initiated; private-led evictions increased considerably over the years, as developers began buying properties in the inner city.[61]

This mechanism was an effectively speedy bypass to some of the obstacles posed by South Africa's more progressive national housing and eviction laws, which include a constitutional right to adequate housing and a clause that prescribes that "[n]o one may be evicted from their home, or have their home demolished, without an order of court made after considering all the relevant circumstances" (Constitution of the Republic of South Africa 1996, para. 26(3)). In terms of the latter, South Africa has national legislation that provides both procedural and substantive protections for unlawful occupiers facing eviction from privately or state-owned

---

[60] These figures are based on the outcome of an access to information request filed with the City of Johannesburg during 2006. See also Wilson (2006).

[61] These properties were, in effect, subsided by the state through the Urban Development Zone tax incentive, which is a tax allowance that covers an accelerated depreciation of investment made in either the refurbishment of an existing property or the creation of new developments within the inner city of Johannesburg.

land: the Prevention of Illegal Eviction from, and Unlawful Occupation of, Land Act 19 of 1998. In response to the rampant inner-city evictions and the recognized need for support to inner-city tenants, a community-based group called the Inner City Resource Centre (ICRC) emerged. In 2003, the ICRC began linking inner-city occupiers with public interest lawyers to challenge the mass evictions, and numerous challenges to eviction applications were launched. Two important precedent-setting cases in this regard are the *Olivia Road* and *Blue Moonlight* cases.

The *Olivia Road* case involved the city attempting to evict more than 300 people from two dilapidated buildings in the inner city.[62] The case was first heard in the Johannesburg High Court in February 2006, after which it was appealed twice and landed in the Constitutional Court in August 2007. The Court handed down an interim order requiring the parties to "engage with each other meaningfully" in an effort to resolve the differences and difficulties aired in the application in light of the values of the constitution. Negotiations were subsequently held between the parties and a settlement agreement was reached between the occupiers and the city, which provided inter alia that the city would install temporary interim basic services at the two buildings and provide the occupiers of the properties with accommodation in two refurbished inner-city buildings, on condition that they agreed to vacate the current buildings permanently and pending the formulation of permanent housing solutions for the occupiers.

The Constitutional Court endorsed the settlement agreement and handed down its judgment in February 2008, although much of the fate of the occupiers of the two buildings in question had already been negotiated as per the settlement agreement. The judgment discussed broader issues relating to inner-city evictions by local authorities, emphasizing that "the City must take into account the possibility of homelessness of any resident consequent upon a Section 12(4)(b) [in terms of the NBRA] eviction in the process of making the decision as to whether or not to proceed with the eviction" (*Olivia Road* 2008, para. 46).[63] Perhaps the most important aspect of the judgment was the stress it placed on the need for "meaningful engagement" between local authorities and occupiers in the event of a possible eviction.[64] The judgment criticized the

---

[62] *Occupiers of 51 Olivia Road, Berea Township and 197 Main Street, Johannesburg v City of Johannesburg and Others* 2008 (3) SA 208 (CC).

[63] Ibid.

[64] The court stated that some of the objectives of a two-way process of meaningful engagement would be to take into account: the potential consequences of an eviction on the

city's failure to facilitate "structured, consistent and careful engagement" during the implementation of its Inner City Regeneration Strategy, when it "must have been apparent that eviction of a large number of people was inevitable."[65]

The court chose not to pronounce on the question of permanent housing solutions for poor people living in the inner city, and accepted the city's willingness to engage with the residents as evidence of its good faith to further develop this plan in the future. Further, the court made no mention of the proximity issue in relation to the alternative accommodation, which could have acknowledged the importance of housing poor people near their places of work and livelihood opportunities, and the potential for gentrification of Johannesburg's inner city as a result of one-sided urban regeneration strategies.[66] The occupiers were eventually relocated by the city to the new buildings, where they currently reside on a temporary (albeit de facto permanent) basis, as no permanent housing solutions have been provided.

In the *Blue Moonlight* case, which concerns a community of eighty-six poor people living in a disused industrial building, a private developer attempted to evict the occupiers in 2006 after buying the property. The occupiers challenged the eviction application, arguing that they could not be evicted unless and until the City of Johannesburg discharged its constitutional obligation to provide them with temporary alternative accommodation. The occupiers joined the city to the proceedings and sought an order compelling the city to report on what steps it had taken, and would in future take, to provide accommodation to the occupiers (Tissington and Wilson 2011). The case was appealed to the Constitutional Court, which handed down a remarkable judgment on December 1, 2011, that solidified obligations on the part of the city to not render occupants homeless by eviction.[67] The court ordered the eviction of the occupiers in fourteen days, but only after the city provided those occupiers who were in need with temporary accommodation "in a location as near as possible to the areas where the property is situated."[68]

---

occupants; any measures the city could take to alleviate these "dire consequences"; whether it was possible to render the buildings concerned relatively safe and conducive to health for an interim period; whether the city had any obligations to the occupiers in the prevailing circumstances; and when and how the city could, or would, fulfill these obligations.

[65] See also Tissington (2008).

[66] Ibid., para. 6.

[67] *City of Johannesburg Metropolitan Municipality v Blue Moonlight Properties 39 (Pty) Ltd and Another* 2012 (2) SA 104 (CC).

[68] Ibid., para. 104 (e)(iv).

In essence, the court held that the city was both entitled and obliged to provide temporary accommodation to desperately poor people facing homelessness as a result of eviction. The court also criticized the city's failure to plan and budget for housing crises, and labeled its argument that it was not legally entitled to do so "unconvincing." The city's policy of providing shelter to people it removes from allegedly unsafe buildings, but refusing to provide shelter to equally desperate people evicted by private owners, was found to be unreasonable and unconstitutional. The court also held that, where a property owner purchases land knowing it to be occupied (as in this case), "an owner may have to be somewhat patient, and accept that the [owner's] right to occupation may be temporarily restricted" if an eviction would lead to homelessness. Further, "An owner's right to use and enjoy property at common law can be limited in the process of the justice and equity enquiry mandated by PIE."[69]

Therefore, the court established an implicit hierarchy of interests, in which the temporary shelter of the poor was placed at the top, and private investors' interests in developing property are temporarily frustrated until this has been achieved. This does not mean that private property is ignored or subverted, as some have claimed, but rather that the law responds to the emergency needs of the poor. *Blue Moonlight* will not end urban regeneration in inner-city Johannesburg. Instead, the obligations it imposes and the legal relationships it establishes will simply be factored into the cost analyses of the state and the private sector in their ordinary course of business. Nor will they impoverish municipalities, as the court made clear that national and provincial government must bear the cost of providing shelter when a municipality cannot (Dugard and Tissington 2011). Although shelter is not housing, and therefore the provision of which falls short of meeting more fundamental principles within the right to housing, at least this case established that no one can be dispossessed unless and until the state acts on its obligations to provide shelter and, thus, seeks to eliminate cases of homelessness by eviction.

Most importantly, the *Blue Moonlight* case challenges the view that municipalities must merely facilitate free enterprise, protect property rights, and minimally regulate the creation of nuisance in urban areas. Traditionally, South African cities have conceived of their role as being merely to ensure compliance with building regulations and the enforcement of health and safety by-laws. The cities argue that the primary responsibility for providing housing falls within the ambit of national government, and accordingly have dealt with housing quite

---

[69] Ibid., para. 40.

separately, merely by supporting ownership of houses in new township developments on the urban periphery. These have been funded by a capital subsidy provided by national government. The other view, embodied in *Blue Moonlight*, is that a municipality can and should have additional duties to protect its inhabitants and, notably, their interactions with powerful market interests.

Although a victory, it is also important to acknowledge that in practice, residents in the *Olivia Road* case report a lack of autonomy in the new buildings, which leads to a strong dissatisfaction with these temporary accommodations. They are not in homes where they can determine how to run their daily lives or are empowered to resolve their own problems. Instead, they are in settings where government sets the rules, which can create deep resentment. Thus, although the law has prevented abject street homelessness, its great shortfall is that it has regulated the residents via its balance of municipal obligations and power and not offered regulation of the market.[70]

2. CHANGING THE QUESTION

When land is at issue, the question most often asked is "What is the greatest market value that can be derived from a particular piece of land?" Too often, governments are asking this question in the same way a private corporation might, and, consequentially, attracting investors and maximizing financial returns become the overriding goals of housing provision schemes and redevelopment projects (Carty 2008).[71] Across the world, investors may be corporations seeking to set up businesses, developers seeking to make a profit through sales of high-value homes, or other governments seeking to exploit natural resources or simply invest abroad. Whatever the configuration, the underlying assumption remains the same: what the market values for a particular piece of land is deemed to be its optimal use for society, and any government intervention to stop community displacement – rare as it might be – is viewed as an interference with obtaining that highest value.[72] This is completely at

---

[70] Observations from a site visit to the new buildings, organized by the Socio-Economic Rights Institute of South Africa (SERI) in 2010.

[71] Carty (2008, 169–170) argues that the goal of neoliberalism is to turn the nation-state into the market-state.

[72] See, for example, HUD's Asset Management Overview Web page, which explains HUD's move to a "business model" on the basis of recommendations made in Harvard University Graduate School of Design's Public Housing Operating Cost Study in 2003.

odds with the human rights obligation of governments to both protect against displacement and to fulfill the right to housing by creating a system of land and housing that ensures stable communities for all. Moreover, the obligation to use maximum available resources must include resources within the private sector that require regulation by government.

Although poor communities may in fact highly value their right to remain in their homes and occupy certain land, they do not have the economic power to express that value in monetary terms. Therefore, land-use decisions based solely on market valuations do not take into account their interests. The employment of human rights values would perhaps lead to a different set of norms, as well as a different process for assessing the most valuable use of land. However, current legal concepts – even those grounded in human rights – often fail to address this fundamental challenge. One potential reason for this is because present legal human rights concepts are mostly shallow, particularly where conflicts with market interests and long-term security of tenure arise.

The reality is that the market's current presence in the realm of housing is so pervasive that it touches the life of every inhabitant. Even in informal settlements, there is generally a thriving informal economy in selling and renting shacks, and in accessing basic services, which also in turn feeds into the formal economy (Werbach 2011). Renters pay landlords for the use of their property. Yet, it is quite clear that these particular inhabitants – who are poorer and afforded lesser legal protections to varying degrees for their living arrangements – do not have an equal say in land-use decisions, nor do they equitably benefit from development, and, as a result, are subject to greater instability. The case studies discussed reflect how disparities in power in the market put poor communities at imminent risk of displacement. In all three cases, the market value of land rose due to gentrification processes.

Further, in all three cities, the criminalization of the communities became a primary tactic, along with arguments that the living conditions were not fit for anyone. Criminalization was both a political public-relations tool as well as a legal tool to justify displacement, stripping any perceived right of the occupants to have a voice in the redevelopment. In Chicago, the primary counterargument was that the displacement would lead to racially discriminatory effects, and in Mumbai that basic livelihoods would be threatened. Both arguments led to delay in the evictions, but neither appeared to ever have any possibility of preventing them.

In both the cases of Mumbai and Chicago, there were agreements to relocate and provide alternative accommodation that were not fully honored. Only 20% of Cabrini-Green residents were afforded new accommodation on-site (Fullerton 2011),[73] and only 30% of Mumbai's displaced residents were afforded alternative accommodation at all (Center for Development and Human Rights 2010). In inner-city Johannesburg, whole communities won rights to alternative accommodation in the nearby vicinity. The process of meaningful engagement required by the South African Constitutional Court was likely vital to this achievement, more vigorous than either Mumbai or Chicago's guidelines. This is likely attributable to South Africa's distinct legal framework, which acknowledges housing rights. Yet, even our most progressive examples fail to ensure that land and housing are used primarily toward meeting human needs in an equitable manner, and thus fail to ensure a human rights-based system of housing. Indeed, government is not only failing; it is in some very practical terms an accomplice to the abuses by implementing a legal system that regulates and subsidizes market interests. Thus, one can argue these cases demonstrate a failure to respect (by empowering the market to displace), protect (by failing to stop the market once displacement is a looming threat), and fulfill (by failing to develop a coherent housing policy framework that ensures stable communities) the right to housing.

3. CHALLENGING ASSUMPTIONS

Despite the three different legal frameworks (nondiscrimination, right to life and livelihood, and right to housing) utilized by communities in the case studies, there are assumptions in each of the cases the law did not in any way challenge, and in fact reinforced and affirmed.

a. Ownership Trumps All

The first concept is that an occupant's right to remain in a particular place is the exclusive determination of the owner of the property. In Mumbai and Chicago, the owner was the government; therefore, negotiating private property rights was not central. Yet, without even an articulation of housing rights, this is precisely the framework within which the government proceeded. In Chicago, where the residents had the most legal protection as subsidized renters, their security of tenure was – like private

---

[73] Despite being behind in building hundreds of public housing units promised, the CHA has made a deal with Target Company to build a four-story mega-store where William Green Homes used to stand (Fullerton 2011).

renters – subject to the changing interests of the property owner (in this case, political whim). Furthermore, the public housing residents' political clout to effectively respond to the shift was eroded by the process of criminalization. In Mumbai, the slumdwellers were never granted any formal legal recognition or protection, despite having occupied the land for generations. As a result, they were quickly deemed unlawful in relation to the government owner's interest. Similarly, in Johannesburg, the occupiers' unlawful status limited legal acknowledgment of their interests in relation to formal property owners.

b. State Provision of Alternative Accommodation

The second concept relevant in all three case studies is the obligation of unlawful occupiers to relocate and of the government to provide alternative accommodation. In Chicago, alternative accommodation simply could not lead to racial segregation, but nearly all other issues remained unaddressed. In the *Olivia Road* case in South Africa, the accommodation was agreed upon through a process of negotiation between the parties, although nothing specific was articulated by the court. Likewise in *Blue Moonlight*; however, the court did rule that the alternative accommodation should be "in a location as near as possible to the areas where the property is situated." Accommodations in both cases were temporary. Moreover, in both Chicago and Mumbai, stringent conditions were placed to determine eligibility of those being moved to the alternative accommodation. Finally, alternative accommodations were strangely perceived as a victory for tenants, when in fact once that concept became central they had clearly lost their right to stay in their homes.

c. Engagement

The third concept relevant in all these case studies was the obligation of the state to engage the occupants in a participatory process. Adequate engagement and participation failed to occur in any of these instances. In the *Olivia Road* case in South Africa, engagement was ordered as an antidote to the lack of engagement, and became the mechanism through which a settlement agreement was reached. In *Blue Moonlight*, the city refused to engage as it disputed the primary tenet of the case, that it had a responsibility to people under threat of homelessness because of private evictions. In Chicago, the obligation was to develop the relocation plans with the Local Advisory Council, which represented the public housing residents, and in Mumbai there was also supposed to be community notice and consultation. However, all three involved engagement after the fact – after a decision was made that the land had a higher value if the community was displaced. Although there have been cases where such engagement has been successful, as these case studies demonstrate, such success is far from universal.[74]

4. CONCLUSION

In terms of the relationship between housing rights and the market, the question should be asked whether available legal concepts properly align such a relationship in a way that gives housing rights at least as much weight as market interests. To begin with, why should communities accept alternative accommodation, even if well-defined, when without their participation it has been determined that their use of the land upon which they live is not of the highest value? That is, under current paradigms, the alternative accommodation doctrine is not being used by courts as a last resort, but rather a default whenever property rights are invoked. Furthermore, as the Supreme Court in India noted in the first slumdwellers lawsuit in 1985, an occupant's "lawfulness" is most often not a matter of choice.[75] It is apparent, from these case studies, that the South African Constitutional Court has come the closest to addressing the core conflicts of interest. Yet, the legal concepts wielded fall short of a comprehensive solution ensuring a human right to housing, giving weight only to factors that occurred after the highest value had been assigned and displacement was underway.

The authors of this chapter do not pretend to have a comprehensive solution to these issues or tensions, but we think it is important to rigorously examine the thinness and inadequacy of the legal concepts available to ensure communities' right to housing, giving particular attention to state obligations to respect and protect this right. These shortcomings are mostly based on the assumption that displacement is acceptable and simply attach conditions after the fact, such as notice, due

---

74 Wilen (2006) offers the Horner redevelopment as a "success," in part based on the creation of a representative resident body, with whom a judicial decree required the developers and property managers negotiate all aspects of the redevelopment effort. He compares the 63% of units promised at Horner with the lower numbers of promised units at other sites within Chicago (that did not benefit from judicial intervention, for one).

75 *Olga Tellis and Others v Bombay Municipal Council* (note 24).

process, some alternative accommodation obligations, and a limited form of ex post facto community engagement. Although these are undoubtedly important, the question yet to be answered – and rarely raised – is "What would a legal and policy framework look like based on the assumption that stable housing is a fundamental social value equal to, or greater than, increasing wealth (often at the expense of the quality of life for the poor)?"

It must be recognized that a state's obligation to protect the right to housing requires the government to regulate the market to this end. At minimum, a more serious right to participation and engagement should take effect prior to any decision to change land use; these decisions cannot be left exclusively to market valuations. Here, the government must step in to ensure these fundamental rights are protected. There are limited participation and engagement prior to these decisions in many areas, involving government hearings on zoning and redevelopment. However, it appears that the interests of occupants are rarely taken into account, arguably due to a lack of normative alternatives to market-based principles. Mechanisms to allow the needs of occupants to shape the outcome must be far better developed. One possible starting point may be legal concepts currently still under construction within the field of indigenous rights. Recognizing the rampant misuse of words such as "consultation" and "participation," advocates have begun to champion indigenous communities' right to "free, prior and informed consent" (Office of the President National Commission on Indigenous Peoples 1998).[76] In South Africa, the developing concept of meaningful engagement is also very useful in this regard.

Second, lawfulness should be reconceived. If housing is a human right, security of tenure cannot be left to the goodwill of property owners. Occupancy, particularly when it has existed for a significant period of time, should be protected. That is, it should be an important factor in determining not only prior lawfulness, but also the future lawfulness of continued occupancy.[77]

Finally, a serious balancing test should be developed that lends more weight to interests other than narrow profit margins in decisions

[76] The Office of the President National Commission on Indigenous Peoples (1998) recognizes the right of indigenous peoples to free, prior, and informed consent for all activities affecting their lands and territories, including development and use of natural resources.

[77] Oberlander (1985) argues that security in occupancy is an essential concern of the poor in securing land and a central component of an answer to poverty.

regarding land use and development. There are many values in addition to housing rights that might also be given weight (e.g., cultural, environmental, dignity, and equity). For the purposes of this chapter, however, we are primarily concerned with a test that would give value to the interests of occupiers. In addition to needing to make explicit the social value of land, the costs to the community of enduring displacement remain hidden and are rarely analyzed.[78] One suggestion is that courts conduct more rigorous evidence-based factual reviews of these social costs, as well, including the mortality and morbidity costs often associated with displacement (Fullilove 2004).[79] The resulting articulation of costs and benefits on both sides of the conflict may provide a platform for poor communities to at least begin articulating their interests.[80]

There is a need for the development and support of proactive, rather than merely defensive, legal and political concepts. Fundamental housing rights should be developed into a comprehensive framework. The notion that housing is a universal right, for example, needs to be further articulated to deal with prevailing assumptions that markets can serve all economic needs, and put an end to the retreat of the state from its human rights obligations. This could also serve to address the use of criminalization by market interests and similar tactics to exclude the poor from economic hubs and high-opportunity areas. Additionally, the notion of equity is underdeveloped and rarely, if ever, utilized. If housing is a human right, then governments must ensure processes are established that lead

[78] An important exception to this is a recent report from UN-HABITAT (2011), which maps out existing eviction impact assessment methodologies globally.

[79] One resident of Henry Street, the site of a mid-1970s urban renewal project in Pittsburgh, PA, told Fullilove that as the infrastructure of homes was destroyed, the community fell apart. The strain, particularly on the elderly, was enormous. "They were going to meetings and the next thing, we were going to funerals."

[80] In 2011, the South African Constitutional Court heard a case concerning a large property management company, which terminated residents' leases to allow for exorbitant rent increases in an inner-city building it had acquired. The case raised the issue of "social costs," and a central issue was that, although the occupiers put forward to the court the social costs in relation to their situation if their leases were terminated (they would either be rendered homeless on eviction or be forced to suffer a significant reduction in their standard of living), no information on the social costs borne by the company were provided, and that this lack of information could not be put at the feet of the tenant. The burden of proof in this regard lay with the landlord, and it simply did not and could not show the court that the social costs occurred by itself (e.g., costs of approaching a rental housing tribunal or insufficient profit from rentals) were disproportionately higher than those of the tenants. See *Maphango and Others v Aengus Lifestyle Properties (Pty) Ltd* [2012] ZACC 2.

to equitable use of housing and land resources.[81] There are three times as many empty homes as homeless people in the United States, and hundreds of thousands of these homes are actually owned, as of April 1, 2012, by the U.S. government (Olick 2012).[82] Equity may also be used to challenge the notion that redevelopment must be designed to attract higher-income residents – as was central to the gentrification in the Chicago and Mumbai case studies – when lower-income residents are struggling to access and keep housing. Looking more closely at the principle of equity would also importantly open the door to systemic assessments and responses to issues of housing finance and budgeting, which have also been subject to regression under neoliberalism (Dreier 2006).

As has already been introduced, traditional homeownership is not a panacea.[83] Therefore, there is a deep need to reexamine concepts of property rights in light of housing rights. Although there are not, again, any existing national systems that comprehensively address this question and provide a clear alternative to explore in this chapter, there are some fantastically creative alternative structures that have been created and experimented with at the local level. Through the use of contracts, community development practitioners have sought to establish different legal relationships and, as a result, have introduced the community land trust and other shared- and limited-equity arrangements that enhance certain rights within "the bundle," at the same time providing useful democratic checks on the "right" to profit and future development.[84] Also, alternative valuation processes for redevelopment have been explored through the use of public land banks in U.S. cities where the abandonment of the market has left large wastelands of old industry and empty homes (Alexander 2005). These, and certainly other, local efforts might have transferable concepts to more far-reaching policy development in determining how to structurally protect and promote housing rights given market realities.

In conclusion, although housing is deemed a human right under international law and in some domestic jurisdictions, market interests still regularly trump access to stable and secure housing for the poorest

[81] Although places like Mumbai and Johannesburg report housing shortages, the United States has a surplus. Christie (2011) uses U.S. Census data to show that 11.4% of all U.S. homes are vacant.

[82] Olick (2012) notes that there are currently 250,000 properties on federal agency books, with millions more to follow. The U.S. government is moving quickly to sell the properties in bulk to private investors who can afford "50, 100, 500 properties per deal."

[83] See Zelinsky (2002); Goodman (2011); and CRNHR (2011) for a U.S. grassroots response.

[84] See IPS (1989).

communities. Moreover, the current legal frameworks are at best defensive, and do not challenge the underlying neoliberal assumptions or the systemic conditions of chronic homelessness, ongoing displacement, and pervasive rent burdens. More vigorous concepts need to be developed to both defend housing rights and create a stronger set of obligations and vision for systemic solutions that ensure access to housing for all on an equitable basis.

REFERENCES

AGFE (Advisory Group on Forced Evictions), 2007. *Finding solutions to forced evictions worldwide: A priority to meet the MDGs and implement the Habitat Agenda*. Executive Summary Report of AGFE to the Executive Director of UN-HABITAT.

Alexander, Frank S., 2005. *Land Bank Authorities: A Guide to the Creation and Operation of Local Land Banks*. Local Initiatives Support Corporation.

Benjaminsen, Lars and Evelyn Dyb, 2008. "The Effectiveness of Homeless Policies – Variations among the Scandinavian Countries," *European Journal of Homelessness* 2: 45–68.

Black, Curtis, 2011. "Residents Fight Cabrini Rowhouse Evictions," *Newstips*. Retrieved from http://www.newstips.org/2011/09/residents-fight-cabrini-rowhouse-evictions/.

Carty, Anthony, 2008. "Marxism and International Law: Perspectives for the American (Twenty-First) Century?" in Susan R. Marks (Ed.) *International Law on the Left: Reexamining Marxist Legacies*, 169–198, Cambridge: Cambridge University Press.

Centre for Development and Human Rights, 2010. *Rights and Development Bulletin* 14.

Christie, Les, 2011. "11% of all U.S. Homes are Vacant," *CNN Money*. Retrieved from http://money.cnn.com/2011/03/28/real_estate/us_housing_vacancy_rates/index.htm.

Cirkovic, Ivana and Biserka Terzic, 2010. "Recognizing Homelessness in the Republic of Serbia." Paper for Peer Review on Building a Comprehensive and Participative Strategy on Homelessness, Portugal, November 4–5.

COHRE (Centre on Housing Rights and Evictions), 2000. *Legal Resources for Housing Rights: International Law and National Standards*. Geneva, Switzerland. Retrieved from http://sheltercentre.org/sites/default/files/COHRE_Sources4LegalResourcesForHousingRights.pdf.

COHRE, 2002. *Forced Evictions: Violations of Human Rights*. Global Survey 8.

CRNHR (Campaign to Restore National Housing Rights), 2011. "USA, 250,000 Empty Public Properties Should Be Used to Address the Housing Crisis." *Truthout*, September 29. Retrieved from http://truth-out.org/index.php?option=com_k2&view=item&id=3673:usa-250000-empty-public-properties-should-be-used-to-address-the-housing-crisis.

D'Monte, Darryl, 2004. "Banning the Majority from Voting," InfoChange. Retrieved from http://infochangeindia.org/governance/analysis/banning-the-majority-from-voting.html.

Dreier, Peter, 2006. "Federal Housing Subsidies: Who Benefits and Why?" in Rachel G. Bratt, Michael Stone, and Chester Hartman (Eds.) *A Right to Housing: Foundation for a New Social Agenda*, 105–133, Philadelphia: Temple University Press.

Dugard, Jackie and Kate Tissington, 2011. "In Defence of the Con-Court," *The Star*. Retrieved from http://www.iol.co.za/the-star/in-defence-of-the-concourt-1.1198152.

Fischer, Paul, 2003. *Where are the Public Housing Families Going? An Update.* Unpublished report, January 21.

Fishbein, Allen and Harold Bunce, 2005. *Subprime Market Growth and Predatory Lending: Housing Policy in the New Millennium*, U.S. Department of Housing and Urban Development Report from the Office of Policy Development and Resources. Retrieved from http://www.huduser.org/portal/publications/polleg/hpcproceedings.html.

Fleming, David, 2008. *City of Rhetoric: Revitalizing the Public Sphere in Metropolitan America*, New York: SUNY Press.

Fullerton, Ian, 2011. "Cabrini Target Reveals Design," *Skyline*. Retrieved from http://www.skylinenewspaper.com/News/07–27-2011/Cabrini_Target_reveals_design.

Fullilove, Mindy, 2004. *Root Shock: How Tearing Up City Neighborhoods Hurt America and What We Can Do About It*, New York: One World/Ballantine Books.

Ghertner, D. Asher, 2008. "Analysis of the New Legal Discourse Behind Delhi's Slum Demolitions," *Economic and Political Weekly* 43(20): 57–66.

Goodman, Laurie F., 2011. Amherst Securities. Testimony to the Subcommittee on Housing, Transportation and Community Development of the U.S. Senate Committee on Banking, Housing and Urban Affairs, September 20. Retrieved from http://banking.senate.gov/public/index.cfm?Fuseaction=Hearings.Hearing&Hearing_ID=16fe36f4-a0d1-4ef1-9a19-94a2a9f85e1a.

Greene, Matthew H., 2008. "The HOPE VI Paradox: Why Do HUD's Most Successful Housing Developments Fail to Benefit the Poorest of the Poor?" *Journal of Law and Policy* 17(1): 191–229.

Higgott, Richard and Heloise Weber, 2005. "GATS in Context: Development, An Evolving *Lex Mercatoria* and the Doha Agenda," *Review of International Political Economy*, 12(3): 434–455.

HUD (Housing and Urban Development), 2012. Resident Characteristics Reports. Select "all relevant characteristics," then "national." Retrieved from https://pic.hud.gov/pic/RCRPublic/rcrmain.asp.

IPS (Institute for Policy Studies Working Group on Housing with Dick Cluster), 1989. *The Right to Housing: A Blueprint for Housing the Nation*, Washington, DC: Community Economics Inc.

Jervis, Rick, 2011. "Crime Still Dogs New Orleans," *USA Today*. Retrieved from http://www.usatoday.com/news/nation/story/2011-12-29/new-orleans-murder-rate-violence/52275788/1.

Katakam, Anupama, 2005. "For a New Mumbai, At Great Cost," *Frontline* 22(2): 15–28. Retrieved from http://www.hindu.com/fline/fl2202/stories/20050128002004600.htm.

Kearns, Ade, Rosemary Hiscock, Anne Ellaway, and Sally Macintyre, 2000. "'Beyond Four Walls'–The Psycho-Social Benefits of Home: Evidence from West Central Scotland," *Housing Studies* 15(3): 387–410.

Kenna, Padraic, 2008. "Globalization and Housing Rights," *Indiana Journal of Global Legal Studies* 15(2): 397–469.

Kothari, Miloon, 2006. "Statement by the Special Rapporteur on adequate housing as a component of the right to an adequate standard of living to the World Urban Forum III (19–23 June 2006) in Vancouver," June 20. Retrieved from http://www.ohchr.org/EN/NewsEvents/Pages/DisplayNews.aspx?NewsID=4724&LangID=E.

Levy, Diane, Jennifer Comey, and Sandra Padilla, 2006. *In the Face of Gentrification: Case Studies of Local Efforts to Mitigate Displacement*, Washington, DC: Urban Institute.

Mahmud, Tayyab, 2010. "'Surplus Humanity' and the Margins of Legality: Slums, Slumdogs, and Accumulation by Dispossession," *Chapman Law Review* 14: 1–73.

McKinsey & Company, 2003. *Vision Mumbai – Transforming Mumbai into a World-Class City: A Summary of Recommendations*. Bombay First – McKinsey Report. Retrieved from http://www.letemps.ch/r/Users/lelievre/Textes/McKinseyReporton%20Mumbai%202003.pdf.

Mukhija, Vinit, 2001. "Enabling Slum Redevelopment in Mumbai: Policy Paradox in Practice," *Housing Studies* 18(4): 213–222.

National Housing Law Project, Poverty & Race Research Action Council, Sherwood Research Associates, and Everywhere and Now Public Housing Residents Organizing Nationally Together, 2002. *False Hope: A Critical Assessment of the Hope VI Public Housing Redevelopment Program*. Retrieved from http://www.nhlp.org/files/FalseHOPE_0.pdf.

Ngwabi, S.S.F., 2009. "Urban Regeneration and Private Sector Investment: Exploring Private Sector Perception of Urban Regeneration Initiatives in the Johannesburg Inner City," ch. 5 in unpublished PhD Thesis, Pretoria: Pretoria University.

Oberlander H. Peter, 1985. "Land: The Central Human Settlement Issue," *Human Settlement Issues* 7. Centre for Human Settlements, University of British Columbia.

Office of the President National Commission on Indigenous Peoples, 1998. "Rules and Regulations Implementing Republic Act No. 8371, Otherwise Known as 'The Indigenous Peoples' Rights Act of 1997.'" Administrative Order No. 1.

Olick, Diana, 2012. "Government Set to Sell Foreclosures in Bulk," CNBC, January 9.

Önis, Ziya and Ali Burak Güven, 2010. "The Global Economic Crisis and the Future of Neoliberal Globalization: Rupture versus Continuity," in Koç University GLODEM Working Paper. Retrieved from http://glodem.ku.edu.tr/10_001.pdf.

Peet, Richard and Elaine Hartwick, 2009. *Theories of Development: Arguments, Contentions, Alternatives*, 2nd edition, New York: Guilford Press.

Peterson, David, 1997. "A Great Chicago Land Grab," *Z Magazine*. Retrieved from http://www.zcommunications.org/a-great-chicago-land-grab-by-david-peterson.

Peterson, George E., 2006. *Land Leasing and Land Sale as an Infrastructure-Financing Option*. World Bank Policy Research Working Paper No. 4043. Retrieved from http://papers.ssrn.com/ sol3/papers.cfm?abstract_id= 940509.

Popkin, Susan J., Bruce Katz, Mary K. Cunningham, Karen D. Brown, Jeremy Gustafson, and Margery A. Turner, 2004. *A Decade of HOPE: Research Questions and Policy Challenges*, Washington, DC: The Urban Institute. Retrieved from http://www.urban.org/uploadedpdf/411002_HOPEVI.pdf.

Ramanathan, Usha, 2006. "Illegality and the Urban Poor," *Economic and Political Weekly*, July 22: 3193–3197.

Rogal, Brian J., 2007. "CHA Families Exit as Eviction Threat Grows," *The Chicago Reporter*. Retrieved from http://www.chicagoreporter.com/news/2007/09/cha-families-exit-eviction-threat-grows.

Salama, Jerry J., 1999. "The Redevelopment of Distressed Public Housing: Early Results from HOPE VI Projects in Atlanta, Chicago and San Antonio," *Housing and Policy Debate* 10(1): 95–136.

Schloemer, Ellen, Wei Li, Keith Ernst, and Kathleen Keest, 2006. Losing Ground: Foreclosures in the Subprime Market and Their Cost to Homeowners. Center for Responsible Lending, December, 7. Retrieved from http://www.responsiblelending.org/mortgage-lending/research-analysis/foreclosure-paper-report-2-17.pdf.

Silva, Cristina, 2011. "Speculative Investors Played Larger Role Than Thought in Driving Housing Bubble, Report Finds," *The Huffington Post*. Retrieved from http://www.huffingtonpost.com/2011/12/12/housing-bubble-real-estate-investors_n_1144437.html.

Steinberg, Stephen, 2010. "The Myth of Concentrated Poverty," in Chester Hartman and Gregory D. Squires (Eds.) *The Integration Debate: Competing Futures for American Cities*, 213–223, New York: Routledge.

Stodghill, Ron, 1998. "In the Line of Fire," *Time Magazine*. Retrieved from http://www.time.com/time/magazine/article/0,9171,988191,00.html.

Stone, Michael, 2010. "The Foundations of a Housing Crisis: How Did We Get Here?" in Christopher Niedt and Marc Silver (Eds.) *Forging a New Housing Policy: Opportunity in the Wake of Crisis*, 6–11, New York: Hofstra University.

Terry, Don, 2010. "The Final Farewell at Cabrini Green," *New York Times*. Retrieved from http://www.nytimes.com/2010/12/10/us/10cnccabrini.html?_r=1&pagewanted=all.

Tissington, Kate, 2008. "Challenging Inner City Evictions Before the Constitutional Court of South Africa: The Occupiers of *51 Olivia Road* Case," *Housing & ESC Rights Law Quarterly* 5(2): 5.

Tissington, Kate and Stuart Wilson, 2011. "SCA Upholds Rights of Urban Poor in *Blue Moonlight* Judgment," *ESR Review* 12(2): 3. Retrieved from http://www.communitylaw centre .org.za/clc-projects/socio-economic-rights/esr-review-1/previous-editions/ESR_Review12.2.pdf.

UN-HABITAT, 2002. *Housing Rights Legislation: Review of International and National Legal Instruments. United Nations Housing Rights Program. Report No. 1* (HS/638/01 E).

UN-HABITAT, 2009. *Right to Adequate Housing, Fact Sheet No. 21/Rev.*

UN-HABITAT, 2011. *Losing Your Home: Assessing the Impact of Eviction.* Retrieved from http://www.unhabitat.org/pmss/listItemDetails.aspx? publicationID=3188.

Venkatesh, Sudhir and Isil Celimli, 2004. "Tearing Down the Community," National Housing Institute. Issue No. 138, November/December. Retrieved from http://www.nhi.org/online/issues/138/chicago.html.

Werbach, Adam, 2011. "How a Classic Model of Social Commerce Can Teach the World How to Save," *The Guardian.* Retrieved from http://www.guardian .co.uk/sustainable-business/slumdwellers-savings-co-operative.

Whiting, Dominic, 2008. "India's Slum Dwellers Face Ruin in Development Blitz," *Reuters.* Retrieved from http://www.reuters.com/article/slideshow/ idUST29019920080608#a=1.

Wilen, William, 2006. "The Horner Model: Successfully Redeveloping Public Housing," *Northwestern Journal of Law and Social Policy* 1(1): 62–95.

Wilson, Stuart, 2006. "Human Rights and Market Values: Affirming South Africa's Commitment to Socio-economic Rights," in *Centre for Applied Legal Studies Newsletter 6.*

Wilson, Stuart, 2011. "Litigating Housing Rights in Johannesburg's Inner City: 2004–2008," *South African Journal on Human Rights* 27: 132–133.

Zelinsky, Edward A., 2002. "The Once and Future Property Tax: A Dialogue with My Younger Self," *Cardozo Law Review* 23: 2199–2221.

5

Implementation of the Human Right to Social Security around the World: A Preliminary Analysis of National Social Protections Laws

Lyle Scruggs, Christian Zimmermann, and Christopher Jeffords

I. INTRODUCTION

Article 22 of the 1948 Universal Declaration of Human Rights and Article 9 of the International Covenant on Economic, Social and Cultural Rights (ICESCR) require that parties recognize the right to social security, including social insurance. Realization of the right to social security is also a fundamental part of the mandate of the International Labor Organization (Cichon and Hagemejer 2007). General Comment 19 of the Committee on Economic, Social and Cultural Rights (CESCR) notes:

> [The right to social security] encompasses the right to access and maintain benefits, whether in cash or in kind, without discrimination in order to secure protection, inter alia, from (a) lack of work-related income caused by sickness, disability, maternity, employment injury, unemployment, old age, or death of a family member; (b) unaffordable access to health care; (c) insufficient family support, particularly for children and adult dependents (CESCR 2008, 2).

Despite the widespread international acceptance of the ICESCR, the implementation of its obligations is reportedly quite poor. According to the CESCR, approximately 80% of the world's population lacks access to meaningful social security protection (CESCR 2008; ILO 2010). The gap between policy and implementation highlights the need for monitoring and reporting on the status and progressive realization of the right to social security.

The views expressed in this chapter are those of the authors and do not necessarily reflect the views of the Federal Reserve System, the Board of Governors, or the regional Federal Reserve Banks.

Under the norms and obligations established by the ICESCR and broader international law, party states bear a primary duty to ensure the realization of the right to social security. As suggested in Article 2, national laws are considered an important means to fully realizing those rights (Sen 2004; CESCR 2008; Fukuda-Parr, Lawson-Remer, and Randolph 2009). Yet monitoring of progress has been limited. The ILO's recent *World Social Security Report* assesses social security laws, but looks only at a single point in time, the mid-2000s (ILO 2010). As useful as this snapshot is, it provides no insight into legislative and policy developments before or since the mid-2000s. Meanwhile, the ICESCR has been in force since 1976. What if any progress has been made in the realization of social security rights in the last three decades? Does the lack of meaningful protection suggested by the ILO report suggest insurmountable barriers to the realization of social security rights for the vast majority of the world's population? If not, to what extent can we credit the Covenant for what progress has been made to date?

In this chapter we provide a summary historical examination of the development of social protection rights laws since the 1960s. Using a mostly quantitative analysis of information about national legal commitments in several critical areas of social security protection, we trace the evolution of basic provisions for the human right to social security. We find evidence of growing state legal commitments to social security rights principles. By providing a longitudinal perspective on the scope of national social security laws, we hope to explain the limited progress that has been made to date in securing social security rights. We also hope to lay the groundwork for examining future progress.

Our project resembles other scholarly endeavors such as the Human Development Index pioneered by Amartya Sen (see Fukuda-Parr 2003), the Physical Integrity Rights Index (Cingranelli and Richards 2010), and the Social and Economic Right Fulfillment Index (Fukuda-Parr et al. 2009; Randolph, Fukuda-Parr, and Lawson-Remer 2010). Each of these projects aims to increase our understanding of human rights conditions over time. Each has produced cross-national indices of human rights outcomes. Our study is somewhat different, however, in that we gauge commitments by examining outputs (i.e., the existence of social security protection laws) rather than outcomes (e.g., number of substantive human rights abuses). The decision to look at outputs is due in part to the lack of adequate data on global outcomes over time.

Social protection did not begin with international institutions. Societies have often provided for individual protection from misfortune or vulnerability (Polanyi 1944). Throughout the course of the nineteenth and twentieth centuries, many states provided formal social protection to those in their territory, or, more exclusively, only to their citizens (Flora and Heidenheimer 1981). Because social protection may not necessarily derive from human rights norms, it is important to consider national social protection as potentially separate from formal human rights obligations.

In this chapter, we first lay out how we measure the scope of social security laws. We then describe the general international development of these legal provisions since the late 1960s. The next section examines some probable correlates of legal provision. The last section concludes with some caveats and further discussion of how to extend the study. To anticipate our results, we find that laws providing social protection have become quite widespread internationally, especially in the last two decades. Laws providing for old age and work injury security are, and have traditionally been, the most widespread. Provision for medical care, sick leave, and family benefits is somewhat less pervasive. Unemployment insurance protection has generally lagged, and remains absent in many countries, even many that are obligated under the Covenant. Our results also suggest that the legal scope of social security rights protection is correlated with the national standard of living (per capita income), a finding consistent with conventional explanations of the development of the welfare state in wealthier countries (Wilensky 1975). Being a party to the ICESCR is also associated with legal institutionalization. In addition, we find an association between a country's legal regime and scope of protection: civil law systems protect more than common law systems. We find very limited if any evidence that democracy increases the number of social security laws, or that ethnolinguistic division independently decreases them.

II. MEASURING THE SCOPE OF SOCIAL SECURITY LAWS

The right to social security and social insurance is stated very concisely in Article 9 of the Covenant: "The States Parties to the present Covenant recognize the right of everyone to social security, including social insurance." At eighteen words, it is by far the shortest article in the Covenant, and far and away the shortest substantive article.

The article is ambiguous with respect to which precise risks or misfortunes people should be protected from or to what degree; General Comment No. 19 declares that the article is intended to encompass protection from a loss of income due to: 1) sickness, 2) disability, 3) maternity, 4) work injury, 5) unemployment, 6) old age, 7) death of a family member, and 8) unaffordable access to health care (CESCR 2008). This list of conditions flows from the development of formal conventions adopted over the years by the International Labour Organization (ILO) (ILO 2010).

One interesting fact about the list of social insurance risks in General Comment 19 is that it corresponds quite closely to the framework created by the United States Social Security Administration (SSA) for collecting information on national social insurance provisions around the world, and published in regular reports entitled *Social Security Programs Throughout the World* (*SSPTW*) (SSA various years). Those reports provide detailed information about social insurance provision grouped into six basic categories: Old Age, Invalidity and Survivors; Sickness and Maternity; Health Care; Work Injury; Unemployment; and Family Allowances.

The *SSPTW* reports provide information at regular intervals back to 1937 (predating the United Nations Charter), including information about the existence and provision of legal protection, with the major groups covered by various social insurance schemes, the level and condition of benefits, and sources of funding. The level of detail in the report does vary from country to country, as does the correspondence between the published summary and the de facto coverage of social insurance laws (SSA 1969). Nonetheless, because the *SSPTW* reports do provide an international source of policy information over a very long period, they serve as a valuable source of information for comparing basic features concerning national achievement of the human right to social security.[1]

For this study, we coded whether or not countries have social protection laws providing cash (or in-kind) benefits for old age, illness, medical need, workplace injury, unemployment, and family allowances.[2] We looked for the presence of a major law in these six programs at five different points in time: 1969, 1977, 1989, 1999, and 2009–2010. The year 1977 represents a watershed year because it is the first *SSPTW* report subsequent to the entry into force (in 1976) of the Covenent.

In each year, a country is coded 1 if it has a law of the specified type in place. Each country thus has a score of 0 or 1 for each of the 6

---

[1] The 2010 *World Social Security Report* also relies extensively on information from the *SSPTW*, but it does not take advantage of the long history of those reports.

[2] We only coded the presence or absence of sickness insurance – that is, insurance against income loss in the event of non–work-related accident or illness – so we do not discuss the independent or joint existence of maternity benefits here.

different types of programs considered in each period. Ideally, we would have 5 (time points)*N (countries) observations for each of the 6 social protection categories. However, as is frequently the case with international administrative data, the actual number of observations is lower: 125, 156, 156, 173, and 173 in 1969, 1977, 1989, 1999, and 2009–2010, respectively.[3] The number of countries in the dataset at a given time changes primarily because the number of independent countries changes. The larger number of recognized states between 1969 and 1977 was driven mainly by decolonization (e.g., the independence of states like Angola or Papua New Guinea). The increase in states from 156 in 1989 to 173 in 1999 was driven primarily by the breakup of the Soviet Union. In order to keep a consistent unit of analysis – independent nation-states – political units are only coded when they come into existence. Larger units that are later divided are dropped after their division. For example, the Czech Republic and Slovakia do not appear in the data set until 1999 (their separation occurred in 1993), and Czechoslovakia is only in the dataset through 1989.

Missing information includes a few countries that are parties to the ICESCR and a few that are not.[4] Countries with a population greater than 1 million for which social security information is missing include (an asterisk indicates accession as of 2010): Angola*, Bhutan, Bosnia*, Cambodia*, Eritrea*, Guinea-Bissau*, North Korea*, Lesotho*, Macedonia, Mongolia*, Mozambique, Namibia*, Qatar, Tajikistan*, and United Arab Emirates.

III. SOCIAL PROTECTION RIGHTS AROUND THE WORLD 1969–2010

A. Expansion of Legal Protections

Table 5.1 provides the number of countries in each year (1969 1977, 1989, 1999, 2010) with a particular social protection law for each of the six types of social programs. As the table suggests, according to *SSPTW*,

---

[3] There were 193 UN member states in 2011.

[4] In three cases, – Iraq, Afghanistan, and Somalia – data for the most recent period are missing. Because legal retrenchment is empirically very rare in countries with information for all years, we coded them as experiencing no change in coverage between 1999 and 2010, although we recognize that de facto protections are likely poor. Because they are only 3 of more than 150 countries, how these countries are coded has no impact on our general conclusions.

TABLE 5.1. *National social insurance laws*

Program type	1969	1977	1989	1999	2009–10	By covenant party status in 2010 Party	By covenant party status in 2010 Non party
Old Age	99	132	145	166	169	141	29
Sick Pay	72	88	93	111	113	98	15
Medical Care	73	93	93	108	131	117	15
Work Injury	124	144	147	163	166	142	25
Unemployment	34	46	49	70	81	75	7
Family Allowance	63	73	70	86	99	93	7
At Least One Program	125	157	157	172	172	143	30

in 2010 almost all countries have some form of old-age pension. A large majority also have work-injury insurance laws. Countries without old-age pensions are Myanmar (Burma), Malawi, and Somalia. Antigua, Kuwait, Marshall Islands, Micronesia, Palau, and Vanuatu have no work-injury laws. Public medical care and sickness insurance are somewhat less widely protected legally, but those laws are nonetheless present in most countries. A majority of countries also have family allowance programs. Unemployment insurance is the least widespread type of legally provided social insurance: slightly less than half of the world's states had unemployment insurance programs in 2010. Table 5.1 does suggest considerable growth over time in the number of countries with all six types of social protection laws, which suggests states increasingly acknowledge legal social security protections.

B. ICESCR and Legal Protection

Table 5.2 provides the percentage of parties to the Covenant with each type of social insurance law starting in 1977. Signatories that have not ratified the Covenant – for example, Belize, Comoros, Cuba, Saõ Tomé, South Africa, and the United States – are counted as nonparties, as they are not legally bound by its provisions. The first thing of note is the evolution of ICESCR membership, indicated in the table row just below each year. Three years after the Covenant was opened for signature in December 1966, only six countries had signed and ratified it: Colombia, Costa Rica, Cyprus, Ecuador, Syria, and Tunisia. By 1977, the first year the Covenant was in force, only thirty-six countries were parties to the Covenant. By 2010, on the other hand, most countries (143) were parties.

TABLE 5.2. *National social insurance laws by covenant signatory status,*
1977–2010

	Covenant signatory status						
	1977		1989		1999		2010	
	Not party	Party (36)	Not party	Party (86)	Not party (41)	Party (123)	Not party (30)	Party (143)
Old Age	80%	100%	86%	99%	96%	96%	97%	98%
Sick Pay	51%	75%	46%	71%	47%	70%	50%	68%
Medical Care	55%	75%	44%	72%	45%	69%	50%	81%
Work Injury	89%	100%	89%	99%	87%	97%	83%	99%
Unemployment	23%	50%	23%	38%	21%	48%	23%	52%
Family Allowance	39%	72%	29%	58%	17%	62%	23%	65%

Note: In 1969, there was only one party to the Covenant.
SOURCE Table 5.2: National Social Insurance Laws by Covenant Signatory Status, 1977–
2010.

A year-by-year analysis shows the number of parties to the ICESCR by
year between 1968 (Figure 5.1) – when Costa Rica became the first party
to the Covenant – and 2008 – when the Bahamas acceded. The number
of states has grown steadily over the last forty years. There was a slight
surge in accession countries just after the treaty entered into force; but
the largest increase in accessions occurred between 1991 and 1993, due
primarily to the accession of newly independent countries of the former
Soviet Union, which has itself been a party.

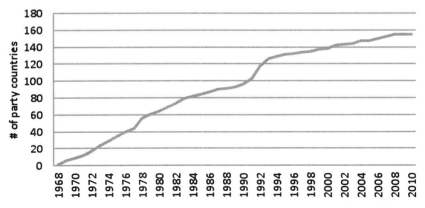

FIGURE 5.1. Parties to the Covenant on Economic, Social and Cultural Rights.

In terms of world population, the percentage of the world's people "covered" by the Covenant stands today at more than 90%. The expansion in population coverage is a relatively recent phenomenon. Nigeria and Brazil became parties to the treaty in the early 1990s; China became a party to the Covenant in 2001, Indonesia in 2006, and Pakistan in 2008. As of 2011, the United States is the only large country that is not a party.

What kind of evidence is there that becoming a party to the Covenant is associated with increasing the scope of legal social security rights? Table 5.2 shows that party states are more likely to have social protection laws in all six main categories. Whereas differences are apparent between parties and nonparties across the six categories, differences between party and nonparty countries are surprisingly stable over time. For example, in 2010, the 143 parties to the Covenant were not more likely to have old-age pensions than the 30 nonparties, and they were only slightly more likely to have work-injury protection. However, Covenant parties were much more likely than non-accession countries to have laws for sick pay (68% versus 50%), medical care (81% versus 50%), unemployment (52% versus 23%), and family allowance (65% versus 23%) laws.

B. An Index of the Breadth of Social Security Rights

As a summary measure of the scope of legal social security protection, we added up the presence of national laws in each of the six areas (old age, sickness, health care, work injury, family allowances, and unemployment) to produce a count of social security laws: SSCOUNT. A maximum (minimum) score of 6 (0) indicates that a country has social protection laws in all (none) of these areas, suggesting a full breadth of national commitment to the human right to social security. Figure 5.2 shows the distribution of SSCOUNT for each year: 1969, 1977, 1989, 1999, and 2010, normalized to the number of countries in that year. (Hence, each row sums to approximately 100%.) The figure clearly illustrates that there have been considerable increases in the degree of legal social protection over the years. In the late 1960s, only about 20% of countries had legislation covering all six areas of social security protection. However, in 2010, almost 40% had laws in all areas. Furthermore, the proportion of countries with two or fewer security laws (almost invariably pension and work injury) has fallen from a quarter of states to less than 10%. As of 2010, parties to the Covenant were much more likely to score high on the SSCOUNT. Almost half of the parties to the Covenant here have all

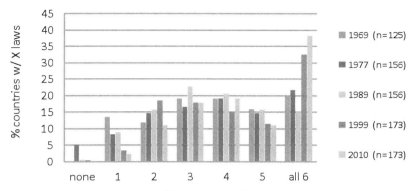

FIGURE 5.2. National laws on social security (SSCOUNT).

six types of social security laws; only one in five of the thirty nonparties to the Covenant achieved the maximum SSCOUNT score.

In terms of world population, in 2010 about half of the world's people lived in a country with a social security law in each of the six categories we examined. This stands in stark contrast to just a decade earlier, when less than 20% did. In some respects, recent increases in legal coverage are a basis for guarded optimism about future provision of de facto social security rights. After all, the experience of most Western countries during the twentieth century was first limited legal recognition in principle, followed in time by expanded de facto provision for the vast majority (Flora and Alber 1981).

IV. ACCOUNTING FOR LEGALIZATION OF SOCIAL PROTECTION

What factors are associated with a more comprehensive framework of social security laws? Before turning to any such analysis, it is important to recall that SSCOUNT measures only the presence of major social security laws in the areas of protection recommended by the international institutions. It does not measure the coverage or adequacy of such laws. Moving from 3 to 4 points or 5 to 6 points indicates the addition of a law in a distinct program that is a part of the framework for social security rights.

A. Treaty Accession

An obvious question for those interested in international human rights norms and conventions is whether or not the Covenant has affected state behavior (Hathaway 2001, Hafner Burton and Tsutsui 2005). The force of the Covenant (on parties and nonparties) presumably shifts the norm in the international community. Teasing out its actual influence on state behavior is not easy. One might infer that the Convention mattered simply because national laws have become more pervasive since the CSESCR entered into force. For example, the average SSCOUNT per country goes up between 1969 and 2009 from 3.7 to 4.4. However, it is hard to know whether the trend toward greater legal protection is due to the treaty and not other factors. For example, income has increased in many countries over time, and that is often linked to more social security protection. Moreover, the average SSCOUNT score per country changed little between 1969 and 1989, twelve years after the Covenant was in force. That the *World Social Security Report* paints a dim picture of the de facto population coverage in the mid-2000s might also argue against a strong positive effect of the Covenant on state behavior (ILO 2010).

B. Income

As just alluded, one criticism of analyses crediting international agreements or norms with fostering the national provision of economic rights is that differences in human rights achievement (especially for economic rights) reflect differences in national capabilities, not national commitments under international obligations. For example, poorer countries may face more difficulty in meeting some "positive" human rights obligations to protect their citizens compared to richer countries, because they cannot afford to protect them. Indeed, some measures of economic rights fulfillment attempt explicitly to "correct for" national resource constraints in evaluating country performance (Fukuda-Parr et al. 2009). Although such constraints are generally not viewed as permissible arguments for a state's failure to meet legal obligations, they are in fact recognized as practical constraints, explaining in part the idea of the progressive realization of these obligations. Whereas resource-based arguments might explain some variation in costly substantive protections, basic legal provisions to social security should not be heavily constrained by resource arguments. National capabilities may understandably limit the generosity of social protection, but providing a basic legal framework with modest substantive provisions should be within the capability of almost all states.

Table 5.3 compares SSCOUNT by level of national income. "Low income" is defined as national per capita income of less than $5,000, and "High income" is considered a per capita income of more than $15,000.

TABLE 5.3. *Count of social security laws and income (2010)*

(Cell entries are the percentage of countries in the World Bank income group with each count of SSLaws)		
Count of SSLaws	Low income (<$5K)	Middle income	High income (>$15K)
1	2%	6%	0%
2	23%	2%	6%
3	26%	15%	8%
4	31%	13%	12%
5	14%	13%	6%
6 (=maximum)	5%	50%	68%
Countries	65	52	50

Income data are from the Penn World Table and, to improve comparability, are converted to 2005 chained dollars at purchasing power parity (Heston, Summers, and Aten 2011). This comparison clearly shows that higher-income countries have more comprehensive legal frameworks for social security rights. More than two-thirds of high-income countries receive the maximum SSCOUNT score of 6; only about half of middle-income countries, and only three low-income countries, have the maximum score. Conversely, one-quarter of the low-income countries have laws in only one or two categories (almost exclusively old-age and work-injury laws); virtually no high-income countries have such low levels of framework legal protection of the human right to social security.

C. Other Influences: Democracy, Legal Traditions, Ethnic Fragmentation

Several other factors in addition to economic development and accession status to the Covenant might also be expected to affect the legal institutionalization of social security. We highlight political democracy, the presence of a civil law legal system, and national ethnolinguistic heterogeneity. First, we expect political democracies to enact more legal protections than nondemocracies. Social security rights are generally redistributive from the economically powerful to the economically marginalized. The literature on democracy and respect for civil and political human rights would also suggest a positive relationship (Davenport and Armstrong 2004). Furthermore, as Peter Lindert (2004) shows convincingly in his economic history of advanced democracies, democratic voice has done much to expand the remit of Western welfare states over the last two centuries. Information on the extent of democracy is the Freedom House measure of political freedom, which is converted here to a "Free" or "Not Free" designation (Freedom House 2011). Although there are other indicators of democratic regime type and much more complex methods of measuring regime, different indicators tend to be highly correlated over the period examined here.

Second, we think that social protection will be more comprehensive where there is a civil law or a socialist law tradition. The civil legal tradition is based more fundamentally on codified rights, so we expect this tradition to be more explicit in laying out social security protections in its legal framework. Civil law systems also tend to have more powerful legislatures and weaker judicial independence, higher taxes, and more redistribution (La Porta et al. 2004; Berkowitz and Clay 2011). Socialist legal traditions are based more fundamentally on economic rights than on liberal political rights. Information about the distinction between exclusively or dominantly civil law systems is from JuriGlobe (2011). La Porta, Lopez-de-Silanes, and Vishny (1999) distinguish socialist legal traditions from others.

A third important factor that should affect the legal provision of social security rights is the existence of significant social divisions. In particular, ethnic and linguistic differences have been suggested to be barriers to socially redistributive policies (Alesina, Glaeser, and Sacerdote 2001; Crepaz 2008; Dahlberg, Edmark, and Lundqvist 2011; Randolph et al. 2012). Such heterogeneity may similarly be associated with less comprehensive legal social security protection, as well. To measure social cleavages, we use an index of ethnolinguistic fractionalization that ranges between 0 and 1, with higher numbers implying more ethnolinguistic diversity (La Porta et al. 1999).[5] Obviously, the concept of ethnic or linguistic distinctions may be contentious (Laitin and Posner 2001), so some caution in interpreting these results may be warranted. However, as Easterly and Levine (1997) point out, different types of "national diversity"

---

[5] The index uses the average value of five different indices of national ethnolinguistic fractionalization: (1) index of ethnolinguistic fractionalization in 1960, which measures the probability that two randomly selected people from a given country will not belong to the same ethnolinguistic group; (2) probability of any two randomly selected individuals speaking the same language; (3) probability of two randomly selected individuals speaking different languages; (4) percent of the population not speaking the official language; and (5) percent of the population not speaking the most widely used language. Although there are only cross-sectional data for this measure, it is likely that the country scores will not change appreciably over time.

measures are correlated, so using an average of several measures as we do here helps to contain particular bias associated with a single indicator.

V. RESULTS

To explore these explanations of differences in legal rights to social security around the world, we employ a series of regression estimates. The dependent variable is SSCOUNT, which varies across countries and across time. We provide several sets of estimates. First, we provide estimates for a regression of SSCOUNT on each explanatory variable separately: 1) COVENANT = 1 when the country is a party to the Covenant; 2) INCOME, the natural log of national income per capita; 3) DEMOCRACY = 1 when the country has democratic institutions and is considered politically free; 4) CIVIL = 1 when the country has a predominantly civil law legal tradition; 5) SOCIALIST = 1 when the country has a socialist legal tradition; and 6) DIVISION, the ethnic fractionalization index.[6]

The general model estimated is:

SSCOUNT = constant + B1*COVENANT + B2*INCOME + B3*DEMOCRACY + B4*CIVIL + B5*SOCIALIST + B6*DIVISION

As we explain later, the results in Columns 1–6 of Table 5.4 are probably biased, but serve to illustrate some dangers of relying too much on bivariate relationships when dealing with international data. Columns 7 and 8 provide more reliable estimates of the average impact of these variables on SSCOUNT. They show multivariate regression results for each variable and hold the other five variables constant. Column 7 reports the results using a random effects estimator. Column 8 reports results with a fixed effect estimator.[7]

All results in Table 5.4 suggest at least some evidence in favor of all of the explanations we offered in the last section. Being a party to the Covenant, having a higher income per capita, being a liberal democracy,

---

[6] COVENANT, DEMOCRACY, CIVIL, and SOCIALIST take values of only 0 or 1, whereas DIVISION ranges more between 0 and 1.

[7] A fixed effects model estimates effects of all the independent variables simultaneously, at the same time essentially "controlling" for the average SSCOUNT in each country. This is a more reliable estimate of the impact of a change in one of the variables within a country. Because CIVIL, SOCIALIST, and DIVISION vary only from country to country, their effect on SSCOUNT cannot be estimated in this type of model. (It is not that we think that these factors cannot or have not changed at all in these countries; it is simply that we lack data on year-to-year change for these measures.)

TABLE 5.4. *Regression results for correlates of the number of social security laws (SSCOUNT)*

	1	2	3	4	5	6	7 Random effects	8 Fixed effects
COVENANT	1.16*** (0.13)						0.33*** (0.07)	0.29*** (0.07)
INCOME		0.68*** (0.04)					0.41*** (0.07)	0.29*** (0.10)
DEMOCRACY			1.23*** (0.13)				0.11 (0.09)	0.11 (0.10)
CIVIL				1.39*** (0.12)			1.23*** (0.18)	–
SOCIALIST					1.4*** (0.26)		0.83*** (0.3)	–
DIVISION						2.19*** (0.23)	–0.76* (0.43)	–
R-squared	0.13	0.29	0.14	0.18	0.04	0.13	0.505	0.38

N = 599, robust s.e. provided below estimates, *** = p-values < .01, ** = < .05, * = < .10.

having a civil law system, having a socialist legal tradition, and having low ethnolinguist diversity increase the number of social security laws.

Focusing on results in Columns 7 and 8, however, does suggest that once we control for the other variables and take into account fixed differences across countries, the effects of most of these factors are smaller. Controlling for other factors, being a party to the Covenant, on average, increases the number of social security laws by about .3. We cannot be certain that the correlation is due solely to the causal association we suggested. Some of the positive association may be due to causation running in the other direction; in other words, countries with more social protection laws becoming more likely to become parties to the Covenant. Separating the two directions of causality requires a more detailed empirical analysis.

Second, as countries get wealthier, they broaden the scope of their social security protection laws. Doubling a country's income per capita (i.e., a 1-unit change in the log of income per capita) raises the SSCOUNT by .3–.4, on average. This result is consistent with well-known findings about the effects of economic wealth on social protection spending more generally.

Third, the results in Column 7 suggest that a civil law system increases the number of social security laws. Compared with non-civil law systems – that is, common law, Islamic law, and countries with a mix of common or Islamic and civil law – civil laws systems have an SSCOUNT about 1.2 laws higher, on average. Countries with a socialist legal tradition also have more social security laws: about .8 more.[8]

Finally, two factors appear to have very uncertain impacts on the number of social security laws around the world. First, being a democracy does not have a very strong impact once we control for other factors such as income and a civil law tradition. That democracy does not necessarily result in more social protection laws, of course, should not be taken to mean that democracy is harmful to the protection of social security rights. It may be, for example, that democracies have more or better de facto social protection. Second, more ethnic heterogeneity (DIVISION) has an uncertain, but likely negative, effect on social protection laws. What is noteworthy here, however, is that the estimated negative effect of heterogeneity is much lower (and more uncertain) when we control for

---

[8] Most socialist law countries are now civil law countries. Analysis not reported here indicates that whether or not you consider the socialist law countries as a separate group makes little difference in the predicted effects of civil law.

the other factors in our analysis. Comparing the result of DIVISION in Columns 6 and 7 shows that failing to control for the other factors leads us to overstate the negative effect of ethnic heterogeneity by a factor of 3. Thus, although ethnic divisions may be seen as a barrier to the protection of social rights, they apparently have been overcome in many states.

VI. CONCLUSION

Social security protection is probably one of the most important accomplishments of the industrial countries during the twentieth century. Even in the industrial welfare states that provide limited social protection, illness, disability, and old age are much less likely to result in the loss of human dignity than they did a century ago. The degree to which progress has been motivated by a desire to provide social security as an economic human right – rather than national citizenship rights, for example – is more contentious (Esping-Andersen 1990). Perhaps this is why a human right to social security remains a relatively underexplored aspect of human rights.

In this chapter we have provided a very preliminary analysis of the evolution of a very basic degree of protection to the right to social security around the world. This includes the presence of national legislation in six areas of social security rights that states are obligated to protect under the International Covenant on Social Economic and Cultural Rights: old age, sickness, maternity, health care, work injury, and unemployment. Our examination of more than 170 countries spanning more than four decades suggests that, whereas substantive protections for most of the world's citizens remain inadequate, there has been progress in establishing a basic legal framework for protection in that period in more and more countries. Most people now live in a country that has most forms of social security protection in law.

Our results suggest that the national standard of living is likely the most important determinant of the presence of more social security laws, followed by the presence of a civil law legal system. Being a party to the CSECR matters somewhat for the scope of protection, but it is less strongly correlated with law count than one might have suspected. Democracy and ethnic heterogeneity both seem to have little independent effect on SSCOUNT, although what effects we can discern point in the direction we expected (positive and negative, respectively).

Much more work needs to be done in assessing and monitoring the right to social security. An important goal should be to move toward measuring and assessing changes in the coverage and adequacy of social protections, that is, de facto rather than de jure indicators. This study is a start of what we hope will be a larger examination of the evolution of national social insurance protection. More work should also be done to assess the impact of international institutions and norms on those developments. We would like to be able to both trace the evolution of social rights and evaluate what factors might promote their improvement. There is little doubt that an important part of that process is continuing projects such as the type of data collection and monitoring efforts embodied in the recent *World Social Security Report.*

REFERENCES

Alesina, Alberto, Edward Glaeser, and Bruce Sacerdote, 2001. "Why Doesn't the US Have a European-style Welfare State," NBER Working Paper 8524.

Berkowitz, Daniel and Karen Clay, 2011. *The Evolution of a Nation: How Geography and Law Shaped the American States*, Princeton, NJ: Princeton University Press.

CESCR (Committee on Economic, Social and Cultural Rights), 2008. *The Right to Social Security. General Comment Number 19*, E/C.12/GC/19. Retrieved from http://www.unhcr.org/refworld/publisher,CESCR,,,47b17b5b39c,0.html.

Cichon, Michael and Krzysztof Hagemejer, 2007. "Changing the development policy paradigm: Investing in a social security floor for all," *International Social Security Review* 60(2–3): 169–195.

Cingranelli, David L. and David L. Richards, 2010. *Cingranelli-Richards (CIRI) Human Rights Dataset*. Version 11–22-2010. Retrieved from http://ciri.binghamton.edu/.

Crepaz, Markus, 2008. *Trust beyond Borders: Immigration, the Welfare State, and Identity in Modern Societies*, Ann Arbor, MI: University of Michigan Press.

Dahlberg, Matz, Karin Edmark, and Heléne Lundqvist, 2011. "Ethnic Diversity and Preferences for Redistribution," Working Paper Series 860, Research Institute of Industrial Economics.

Davenport, Christian and David Armstrong, 2004. "Democracy and the Violation of Human Rights: A Statistical Analysis from 1976 to 1996," *American Journal of Political Science* 48(3): 538–554.

Easterly, William and Ross Levine, 1997. "Africa's Growth Tragedy: Policies and Ethnic Divisions," *The Quarterly Journal of Economics* 112: 1203–1250.

Esping-Anderesen, Gosta, 1990. *The Three Worlds of Welfare Capitalism*, Princeton, NJ: Princeton University Press.

Flora, Peter and Jens Alber, 1981. "Modernization, Democractization and the Development of Welfare States in Western Europe," in Flora and Heidenheimer (Eds.) *The Development of Welfare States in Europe and America*, New Brunswick, NJ: Transaction Books, 37–80.

Flora, Peter and Arnold Heidenheimer, (Eds.) 1981. *The Development of Welfare States in Europe and America*, New Brunswick, NJ: Transaction Books.

Freedom House, 2011. Freedom House Country Ratings. Retrieved from http://www.freedomhouse.org/ratings/index.htm.

Fukuda-Parr, Sakiko, 2003. "The Human Development Paradigm: Operationalizing Sen's Ideas on Capabilities," *Feminist Economics* 9(2–3): 301–317.

Fukuda-Parr, Sakiko, Terra Lawson-Remer, and Susan Randolph, 2009. "An Index of Economic and Social Rights Fulfillment: Concept and Methodology," *Journal of Human Rights* 8(3): 195–221.

Hafner Burton, Emilie and Kiyoteru Tsutsui, 2005. "Human Rights in a Globalizing World: The Paradox of Empty Promises," *American Journal of Sociology* 110(5): 1373–1411.

Hathaway, Oona, 2001. "Do Human Rights Treaties Make a Difference?" *Yale Law Journal* 111: 1935–2042.

Heston, Alan, Robert Summers, and Bettina Aten, 2011. *Penn World Table Version 7.0*, Center for International Comparisons of Production, Income and Prices at the University of Pennsylvania.

ILO, 2010. *World Social Security Report*, Geneva: ILO.

JuriGlobe, 2011. Les systèmes juridiques dans le monde/World Legal Systems, University of Ottawa. Retrieved from http://www.juriglobe.ca/.

La Porta, R., F. Lopez-de-Silanes, and R. Vishny, 1999. "The Quality of Government," *Journal of Law, Economics and Organization* 15(1): 222–279.

La Porta, Rafael, Florencio Lopez-de-Silanes, Cristian Pop-Eleches, and Andrei Shleifer, 2004. "Judicial Checks and Balances," *Journal of Political Economy* 112: 455–470.

Laitin, David and Daniel Posner, 2001. "The Implications of Constructivism for Constructing Ethnic Fractionalization Indices," *APSA-CP: The Comparative Politics Newsletter* 12: 13–17.

Lindert, Peter, 2004. *Growing Public: Social Spending and Economic Growth since the Eighteenth Century*, New York: Cambridge University Press.

Polanyi, Karl, 1944. *The Great Transformation*, Boston: Beacon Press.

Randolph, Susan, Sakiko Fukuda-Parr, and Terra Lawson-Remer, 2010. "Economic and Social Rights Fulfillment Index: Country Scores and Rankings," *Journal of Human Rights*. 9(3): 230–261.

Randolph, Susan, Michelle Prairie, and John Stewart, 2012. "Monitoring State Fulfillment of Economic and Social Rights Obligations in the United States," *Human Rights Review* 13: 139–165.

Sen, Amartya, 2004. "Elements of a Theory of Human Rights," *Philosophy and Public Affairs*, 34(4) 315–356.

SSA (Social Security Administration), various years. *Social Security Programs Throughout the World*, Washington, DC: US Government Printing Office.

Wilensky, Harold, 1975. *The Welfare State and Equality: Structural and Ideological Roots of Pubilc Expenditures*, Berkeley: University of California Press.

6

Why Is the Right to Work So Hard to Secure?

Philip Harvey

INTRODUCTION

Despite the crucial role it plays in facilitating the realization of other economic and social human rights (Harvey 2007), even the wealthiest countries in the world seem unable to secure the right to work. This chapter attempts to identify the source of this failure through a review of the policies American progressives have promoted to secure the right to work since the 1930s.

The first portion of this review focuses on Franklin D. Roosevelt's seminal twelve-year presidency. American progressives developed two distinct strategies for securing the right to work during this period. The first was a social welfare strategy involving the use of direct job creation to provide decent work for those job seekers whom the private sector could not employ at a particular moment in time. The second was a macroeconomic strategy that relied on the use of deficit spending by the federal government to raise aggregate demand enough to achieve full employment. In this chapter, the former strategy shall be referred to as the direct job-creation strategy and the latter as the aggregate demand management (ADM) strategy.

Direct job-creation programs such as the Civilian Conservation Corps (CCC) and the Works Progress Administration (WPA) occupied a central role in the mature New Deal of the second half of the 1930s. Moreover, the social welfare thinking that inspired these initiatives also inspired President Roosevelt's vigorous advocacy during World War II of a broadened conception of human rights. Nevertheless, American progressives lost interest in the direct job-creation strategy as war-related employment – both military and civilian – finally brought the nation's lingering unemployment crisis to an end in the early 1940s. Impressed by both the

ease with which war-related spending achieved this goal and the persuasiveness of John Maynard Keynes's teaching, progressives were easily
convinced that the Keynesian ADM strategy constituted both an easier
and a more effective means of securing the right to work that President
Roosevelt was talking about. It is hardly surprising, therefore, that it
was the ADM strategy rather than the direct job-creation strategy that
American progressives embraced as the cornerstone of their ongoing
efforts to secure the right to work following the end of World War II.

Unfortunately, because of its inflationary tendencies at the top of the
business cycle, the Keynesian ADM strategy proved incapable of achieving the full employment goal progressives had assigned it; and that failure, in turn, undermined the effectiveness of their efforts to secure other
aspects of the right to work such as the achievement of equal employment opportunity and adequate job quality. The conclusion drawn from
this analysis is that progressive efforts to secure the right to work will
continue to fail until an effective means is found to accomplish the task
the Keynesian ADM strategy proved incapable of accomplishing – the
elimination of the economy's job gap.

Fortunately, an alternative strategy is available – one that draws its
inspiration from the New Deal direct job-creation strategy abandoned by
American progressives when they embraced the Keynesian ADM strategy in the early 1940s. The advantages of this New Deal strategy are
only briefly identified in this chapter, but one worth special emphasis in
that unlike other strategies for combating unemployment, it is designed
to secure the right to work directly rather than indirectly through the
pursuit of other economic policy goals. It is a human rights policy that
produces desirable economic effects rather than an economic policy that,
hopefully, will produce desirable human rights effects. For this reason,
the direct job-creation strategy provides American progressives with more
than a remedy for the shortcomings of the Keynesian ADM strategy. It
furnishes them with the opportunity to reframe their efforts to combat unemployment – all types of unemployment – as a human rights
struggle.

THE UNITED STATES' FAILURE TO SECURE THE RIGHT
TO WORK

In other work, I have argued that the right to work has four aspects
or dimensions (Harvey 2007). The *quantitative* aspect of the right
requires that the number of jobs available in an economy be sufficient to

provide freely chosen employment for everyone who wants to work. The *qualitative* aspect requires that these jobs satisfy minimum standards of decency in terms of their pay, benefits, hours of work, working conditions, workplace governance, employment security, and opportunities for individual development. The *distributional* aspect of the right requires that equal employment opportunity be guaranteed to all members of society. Finally, the *scope* of the right requires that persons engaged in socially useful work that is not organized in the form of wage employment be guaranteed material support, conditions of work, and opportunities for personal development that are consistent with those to which wage workers are entitled, even if these guarantees are secured by other means than those that apply to wage employment.

The obligation of governments to respect, protect, and fulfill human rights applies to each of these aspects of the right to work, but the consequences of a failure to meet certain of these obligations can have a disproportionately negative effect on efforts to meet others among them. For reasons that will be explained later in this chapter, a failure to fulfill the quantitative aspect of the right to work tends to have a devastating effect on efforts to respect, protect, and fulfill other aspects of the right to work. This is not because ensuring that everyone has access to a job is inherently more important than ensuring that all job seekers have equal access to available jobs, that those jobs meet minimum standards of decency, and/or that nonwaged workers receive fair treatment and adequate support. Ensuring that everyone who wants paid employment has access to a job may even be less important than securing these other aspects of the right to work. What makes the obligation to respect, protect, and fulfill the quantitative aspect of the right to work so special is its functional role in efforts to adequately respect, protect and fulfill the other three aspects of the right to work – qualitative, distributional, and scope (Harvey 2007).

For this reason, rather than attempting to provide data that document the performance of the United States in meeting each of its obligations with respect to each aspect of the right to work, the following figures and table have been selected simply to highlight the overall failure of those efforts, with particular attention to the quantitative aspect of the right to work. Figure 6.1 illustrates the limitations of existing policies to secure the quantitative aspect of the right to work. The bottom line in the figure shows the number of vacant jobs employers in the United States have sought to fill from month to month over the past decade. The next line, labeled "Official Unemployment," shows the number of individuals who

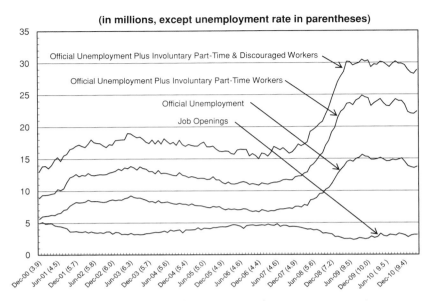

(in millions, except unemployment rate in parentheses)

Official Unemployment Plus Involuntary Part-Time & Discouraged Workers

Official Unemployment Plus Involuntary Part-Time Workers

Official Unemployment

Job Openings

FIGURE 6.1. Job Wanters and Job Openings in the U.S. Dec. 2000–Apr. 2011.

lacked jobs but were actively seeking work on a month-to-month basis over the same period of time. The next line adds "Involuntary Part-Time Workers" to official unemployment. These individuals are working part-time but want full-time jobs. Finally, the top line adds to these two groups jobless individuals who say they want a job but are not actively seeking work and hence are not counted as officially unemployed.

The distance between the bottom line in this figure and the three lines above it shows the size of the economy's job gap – the number of additional jobs needed to provide employment for everyone who wants to work. As one would expect, the figure shows that the Great Recession caused the economy's job gap to swell dramatically, to a peak of almost 28 million jobs in October 2009, based on the broadest measure of the job gap's size. The figure also shows, however, that even when the unemployment rate dipped below 4.0% in December 2000, there were 8 million fewer jobs than were needed to provide work for everyone who wanted it.

The reason this last statistic is so interesting is because at that level of unemployment, the Federal Reserve Bank is likely to be taking active steps to prevent the unemployment rate from falling further. Why? The simple answer is because of inflationary fears, and although progressive

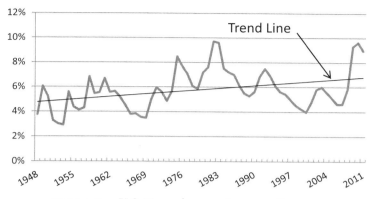

FIGURE 6.2. U.S. Unemployment Rate, 1948–2011.

economists might quarrel with whether it is necessary to put the brakes on the economy quite so soon to forestall unacceptable increases in the rate of inflation, there is no reason to believe the minimum level of unemployment they deem safe would ensure the availability of jobs for everyone who wants to work. Even if it did, Figure 6.1 makes it abundantly clear that the tool kit of macroeconomic policies on which economists rely is unable to maintain employment levels at whatever level they may deem acceptable. The economy's dips may be moderated, but they cannot be entirely thwarted.

Figure 6.2 shows that the performance of the United States in securing the quantitative aspect of the right to work has actually diminished rather than increased since the end of World War II. This trend is especially disheartening in light of the assumption, widely embraced in international human rights declarations and agreements, that although economic and social human rights may not be immediately enforceable, governments acting in good faith can and should be able to realize them progressively over time. Something has gone seriously wrong.

Figure 6.3 is suggestive of the failure of the United States government to secure the qualitative aspect of the right to work. The figure shows the failure of average hourly wages to keep pace with the growing wealth of the country as a whole since the early 1970s. Analogous data show that in contrast to the period portrayed in Figure 6.3, average wages grew as rapidly as per capita GDP from 1950 through 1965.

By itself this does not conclusively demonstrate that U.S. wage levels are either unjust or insufficient to support an adequate standard of living – two requirements for the realization of the qualitative aspect of the right

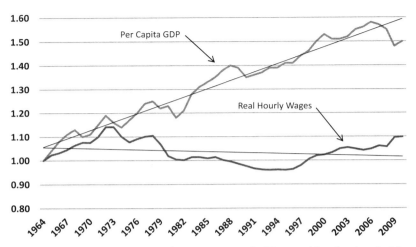

FIGURE 6.3. Per Capita GDP and Average Hourly Wages of Production & Non-supervisory Workers, 1964–2010.

to work. However, the fact that ordinary wage earners have shared none of the nation's growing wealth during the past four decades constitutes strong evidence that efforts to secure the qualitative aspect of the right to work have also stagnated in the United States.

Finally, Table 6.1 shows that disadvantaged workers bear a disproportionate share of the joblessness caused by the overall job gap in the United States, thus evidencing a failure to secure the distributive aspect of

TABLE 6.1. *Comparative unemployment rates, November 2010*

National Average Unemployment Rate	9.8%
Youths Aged 16–19	
Black Aged 16–19	46.5%
White Aged 16–19	20.9%
All Persons Aged 16 & over	
Black	16.0%
Hispanic	13.2%
White	8.9%
All Persons Aged 25 and Older	
Less Than High School Diploma	15.7%
High School Graduates, No College	10.0%
Some College or Associates Degree	8.7%
Bachelors Degree and Higher	5.1%

Source: BLS.

the right to work. Moreover, the fact that African Americans still suffer unemployment at approximately double the rate of whites is historically noteworthy, as that is the same differential cited in 1964 in justification of the need for federal legislation banning employment discrimination based on race.

Although extremely sketchy, this brief review of performance data should be sufficient to establish not only that the United States has a long way to go to secure the right to work, but that it is actually moving in the wrong direction. Whether the U.S. government has done as much as it reasonably could to counter these negative trends is another question, of course, one that depends on whether there are policy options available for achieving better results. That is the topic explored in the balance of this chapter.

THE NEW DEAL'S ANTICIPATION OF THE UNIVERSAL DECLARATION

When Franklin D. Roosevelt was sworn into office in March 1933, the U.S. economy had been contracting for more than three and a half years. Real per capita GDP had declined by almost 29%, and the nation's unemployment rate had increased from 3.2% to 25.2%. Almost 13 million workers were jobless in a labor force of just more than 50 million, and it was among those 13 million and their families (which at that time often included elderly parents as well as children) that the economy's loss of real income was concentrated. The Roosevelt Administration's response to the economic insecurity laid bare by this experience included a concerted effort both to provide aid to those who needed it and to create institutions that would reduce the economic insecurity to which people were exposed as a result of a variety of "hazards" in addition to unemployment.

The strategy devised by the New Dealers for addressing the needs of unemployed workers was conceived and developed not by economists, but by two social workers – Harry Hopkins and Aubrey Williams. Hopkins and Williams were the director and deputy director respectively of the New Deal agency created by Congress in the spring of 1933 to distribute federal dollars to shore up the nation's state-based public relief system. The philosophical underpinnings and legal structure of this system were based on the centuries old "poor law" regime the American colonies imported from Britain and retained following independence (Harvey 1999). Dissatisfied with the narrow range of reforms their agency was empowered to make in this antiquated system, Hopkins and Williams spent the summer and early fall of 1933 developing an alternative model for the delivery of public aid to the unemployed.

In a conceptual memo to Hopkins, Williams wrote that, "[R]elief as such should be abolished." Instead, the unemployed should be offered real jobs paying good daily wages, doing useful work suited to their individual skills. In other words, instead of offering public relief to the unemployed, they should be offered quality employment of the sort normally associated with contracted public works. However, to minimize both the cost of the undertaking and the amount of time needed to launch it, the government should serve as its own contractor, and the projects undertaken should be both less elaborate and more labor intensive than conventional public works (Schwartz 1984, 48–50).

In late October, as winter approached and the New Deal's conventional public works program, the Public Works Administration (PWA), had yet to stick a shovel in the ground, Hopkins pitched a job-creation proposal to President Roosevelt based on the model he and Williams had devised. Concerned about the PWA's slow start-up and rising levels of social unrest among the nation's jobless as the nation's fifth winter of depression approached, Roosevelt accepted Hopkins's proposal on the spot. A week later, the Civil Works Administration (CWA) was formally established by executive order, with Hopkins at its head and an initial budget allocation of $400 million diverted from the PWA.

The CWA was funded only through the winter of 1933–1934, but two months after the program was formally terminated, Hopkins was appointed to a presidential task force, the Committee on Economic Security (CES), which was charged with developing a series of legislative proposals to "promote greater economic security" for the American people (Roosevelt, 1934). Chaired by Secretary of Labor Frances Perkins,[1] the report submitted by the CES to the President in January 1935 described the goal of its proposals in the following terms:

> The one almost all-embracing measure of security is an assured income. A program of economic security, as we vision it, must have as its primary aim the assurance of an adequate income to each human being in childhood, youth, middle age, or old age–in sickness or in health. It must provide safeguards against all of the hazards leading to destitution and dependency (Committee on Economic Security, 1935).

---

[1] Hopkins was the only non-Cabinet Secretary appointed to the Committee. In addition to Perkins, the other members were Secretary of the Treasury Henry Morgenthau, Jr., Attorney General Homer Cummings, and Secretary of Agriculture Henry A. Wallace.

The CES proposed a two-legged social-welfare strategy to provide Americans this assured income. The first leg of the strategy adopted the plan Hopkins and Williams had developed and tested (via the CWA) for addressing the income security needs of unemployed workers. This part of the CES's social welfare strategy called for a commitment on the part of the federal government to provide unemployed workers with *employment assurance* by (a) doing what it could to stimulate private employment, and (b) providing employment itself for any workers the private sector was unable to employ at a particular time or in a particular place. Moreover, the CES made it clear that it was proposing its employment assurance strategy for use in "normal times" as well as during economic contractions:

> Since most people must live by work, the first objective in a program of economic security must be maximum employment. As the major contribution of the Federal Government in providing a safeguard against unemployment we suggest employment assurance – the stimulation of private employment and the provision of public employment for those able-bodied workers whom industry cannot employ at a given time. Public-work programs are most necessary in periods of severe depression, but may be needed in normal times, as well, to help meet the problems of stranded communities and overmanned or declining industries (Committee on Economic Security, 1935).

The second leg of the CES's assured income strategy was designed to meet the needs of people who were temporarily or permanently unable to support themselves and who lacked the support of someone who could. The best known of the programs proposed by the CES to perform this function is the nation's present Social Security system, but the CES's report included proposals addressing other income security needs as well.[2]

---

[2] To supplement Social Security until its pension entitlements matured, the CES proposed the establishment of a means-tested Old Age Assistance program. This latter program was larger and more important than Social Security for many years and still survives today as an important component of the Supplemental Security Income program. In addition to these programs targeting the elderly, the CES proposed a short-term Unemployment Insurance program to support unemployed workers until they were either recalled to their old jobs, found a new job, or went to work in the government's direct job-creation program. It also proposed the establishment of an income support program for needy children who had lost their father's support due to death or abandonment. This program, originally called Aid for Dependent Children, was later renamed Aid for Families with Dependent Children. For disabled persons, the CES proposed that the states should continue to bear responsibility for providing income support, but that those state-based programs should operate in accord with federal guidelines. Finally, the CES developed proposals for a range of public health initiatives, including the

The striking thing about the CES's recommendations is how closely they are mirrored by the economic and social rights recognized in the Universal Declaration. Except for the fact that the CES did not invoke the language of human rights to describe its proposals, its strategy for guaranteeing everyone an assured income is the same as that mandated by the Universal Declaration to secure everyone's right to an adequate standard of living. Both rely on an employment guarantee for those who can work and an income assistance guarantee for those who cannot.

All of the CES's published recommendations were implemented by Congress, to some degree or another, in the first half of 1935. The Social Security Act of 1935 was the vehicle used to implement the income security leg of the CES strategy, whereas the employment assurance leg was implemented by an Executive Order establishing the WPA accompanied by a legislated budget authorization to pay for the program.

Significantly, the president did not propose to fund the WPA at the level required to achieve the CES's goal of furnishing employment assurance to all workers. Instead, he requested only enough funding for the WPA to provide jobs for those unemployed workers who qualified as needy. This decision was consistent with the president's ingrained fiscal conservatism. He believed in balancing the federal government budget, with the caveat that deficits were justified when required to help people in need. What is puzzling, however, is why he allowed the CES to advocate a direct job-creation commitment that would have cost far more than he was willing to spend. His intervention to quash the CES's health insurance proposal shows that he was perfectly willing to limit the committee's proposals to those he thought he could get through Congress. Why, then, did he allow the CES to publish a proposal that would have cost three times as much as he was willing to spend?

One reason may be that the CES's employment assurance proposal so closely reflected his sense of the obligations of government in a market society – the moral grounding of his subsequent embrace of the language of human rights to describe the social welfare obligations of governments. In a widely reported campaign address delivered to the Commonwealth Club of California in the fall of 1932, presidential candidate

---

establishment of a national health insurance program that would have provided wage replacement benefits for sick workers as well as reimbursement for health care expenses that were beyond a family's means. However, due to the strength of opposition to the latter proposal by health care professionals, President Roosevelt directed the CES not to release that portion of its report.

Roosevelt opined that everyone has the "right to make a comfortable living...through his own work":

> Every man has a right to life; and this means that he has also a right to make a comfortable living. He may by sloth or crime decline to exercise that right; but it may not be denied him. We have no actual famine or death; our industrial and agricultural mechanism can produce enough and to spare. Our government formal and informal, political and economic, owes to every one an avenue to possess himself of a portion of that plenty sufficient for his needs, through his own work (Roosevelt, 1938, Vol. 1, 754).

Roosevelt made it clear in the same speech that he assigned primary responsibility for securing this right to the "princes of property" who "claim and hold control of the great industrial and financial combinations which dominate so large a part of our industrial life." Only if they failed to fulfill their responsibility, he continued, would it fall upon government to "assume the function of economic regulation...as a last resort." He also made it clear that he had not yet given up on the princes of property to fulfill their duty in this regard. "As yet there has been no final failure, because there has been no attempt, and I decline to assume that this nation is unable to meet the situation" (Roosevelt, 1938, Vol. 1, 754–755).

Four years later, in his acceptance speech to the Democratic National Convention after it nominated him to run for reelection, Roosevelt made it clear that the princes of property – whom he now referred to as "the royalists of the economic order" – had failed the test he set them four years earlier. In doing so, he once again referred to the right to work as the touchstone by which the legitimacy of their power should be judged:

> The royalists of the economic order have conceded that political freedom was the business of the government, but they have maintained that economic slavery was nobody's business. They granted that the government could protect the citizen in his right to vote, but they denied that the government could do anything to protect the citizen in his right to work and his right to live (Roosevelt, 1938, Vol. 5, 233–234).

In short, the CES's assertion that government should assume the duty of providing jobs for workers whom the private sector could not employ was an article of faith for Roosevelt, even if, as "Politician in Chief" he knew better than to ask Congress to authorize him to do it, and as "Fiscal Officer in Chief" he thought it was not something he could justify funding with additional deficit spending. Providing jobs for unemployed workers who were needy fell within his exception for justifying deficit spending.

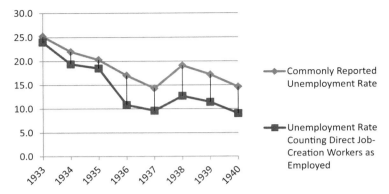

FIGURE 6.4. U.S. Unemployment Rate 1933–1940.

The rest of the unemployed would have to wait. Still, the broader commitment the CES advocated was close enough to his heart that he was willing to let the committee leave its employment assurance proposal in their report.

It is also important to note that even with the limited funding they were provided, the direct job-creation programs operated by the Roosevelt administration during this period made a far greater dent in the nation's unemployment problem than is generally recognized. Together, the WPA, CCC, and National Youth Administration (NYA) provided jobs for an average of about one-third of all unemployed individuals during the second half of the 1930s. This accomplishment is obscured by the unemployment statistics commonly reported for the New Deal period, which count workers employed in these programs as unemployed rather than employed. If workers employed in direct job-creation programs are counted as employed (as they are in unemployment statistics today), we see that the nation's unemployment rate dropped from 20.3% to 10.8% from 1935 to 1936 (the first full year of operations for the WPA) rather than to the 17.0% level commonly reported.

Figure 6.4 shows both the commonly reported and actual unemployment rate in the United States from 1933 through 1939 – with the difference between the two time series depending on nothing more than whether persons employed in the CCC, WPA, and NYA are counted as unemployed or employed. It should also be noted in this regard that the decline in private-sector unemployment portrayed by the top line in Figure 6.4 is at least partly attributable to the multiplier effect of the federal government's deficit spending on the CCC, WPA, and NYA

(Brown 1956). Evidence of this latter effect can be seen in the upward spike in unemployment that occurred in 1937 when President Roosevelt cut back on federal government spending – including spending on its direct job-creation programs – in an ill-conceived attempt to balance the federal budget. Thus, the overall job-creation effect of the New Deal's direct job-creation programs includes part of the decline shown in the top line of Figure 6.4 as well as the additional decline shown in the bottom line of the figure (Harvey, 2011).

Given what we now understand about the virtues of deficit spending during a recession, we can see the error not only in President Roosevelt's decision to reduce federal spending in 1937, but also in his broader decision to only partially implement the CES's employment assurance proposal. The federal government spent 2.2% of GDP on the WPA, NYA, and CCC combined in 1936. If it had increased that spending to 5.3% of GDP (the equivalent of about $750 billion in 2009), the nation's unemployment rate could have been reduced from more than 20% to less than 2% immediately; and due to the multiplier effect of that additional spending, the private sector's full recovery from the Great Depression probably would have been accelerated by several years. In short, we can see in retrospect that the CES's employment assurance plan was more than just a visionary social welfare proposal that anticipated the Universal Declaration. It also constituted a visionary economic policy that anticipated Keynes's advice for combating recessions. In fact, further on in this chapter, I shall argue that the CES's employment assurance proposal constitutes a better strategy for implementing Keynes's advice than the policies advocated by Keynesian economists over the past seventy-plus years.

THE NEW DEAL HUMAN RIGHTS VISION

Given Roosevelt's inclination to think of the right to live and the right to work as entitlements society has a duty to secure for its members, it required no great conceptual leap on his part to describe the New Deal's employment and social welfare goals in similar terms; and once the President started using that language, other New Dealers were quick to follow suit. The rhetorical turning point came in the President's "Four Freedoms Speech," which was delivered as a "fireside chat" with the American people, although it was formally his 1941 State of the Union Message to Congress (Roosevelt 1950). The four freedoms language Roosevelt used in this address resonated not only with the American public but with people around the world, and for that reason it was probably the most influential speech Roosevelt ever delivered.

The immediate goal of the speech (which followed Germany's conquest of France and its aerial bombardment of the United Kingdom – dubbed the Battle of Britain by Winston Churchill) was to encourage Congress to pass the Lend-Lease Act. However, despite its short-run political purpose and the fact that it was delivered eleven months before the United States formally entered the war, the speech came to serve as a kind of manifesto of the Allies's political objectives in their struggle with the Axis powers. It is also worth noting that the speech subsequently proved embarrassing to the allies when their colonial subjects sought to apply its principles in their own countries.

That an American president should talk about freedom and rights in a speech justifying a war is hardly surprising. What distinguished Roosevelt's speech was his insistence that the social welfare entitlements the New Deal had been seeking to secure were not only vital to maintain the morale of the defenders of democracy, but were constitutive of democracy itself – and therefore were among the rights the war was being fought to preserve at home and to extend to all the world's peoples (see Box 6.1).

Box 6.1. Excerpts from President Roosevelt's "Four Freedoms Speech" January 6, 1941

As men do not live by bread alone, they do not fight by armaments alone. Those who man our defenses, and those behind them who build our defenses, must have the stamina and the courage which come from unshakable belief in the manner of life which they are defending.

Certainly this is no time for any of us to stop thinking about the social and economic problems which are the root cause of the social revolution which is today a supreme factor in the world.

For there is nothing mysterious about the foundations of a healthy and strong democracy. The basic things expected by our people of their political and economic systems are simple. They are:

- Equality of opportunity for youth and for others.
- Jobs for those who can work.
- Security for those who need it.
- The ending of special privilege for the few.
- The preservation of civil liberties for all.

- The enjoyment of the fruits of scientific progress in a wider and constantly rising standard of living.

These are the simple, basic things that must never be lost sight of in the turmoil and unbelievable complexity of our modern world. The inner and abiding strength of our economic and political systems is dependent upon the degree to which they fulfill these expectations.

In the future days, which we seek to make secure, we look forward to a world founded upon four essential human freedoms.

- The first is freedom of speech and expression – everywhere in the world.
- The second is freedom of every person to worship God in his own way – everywhere in the world.
- The third is freedom from want – which, translated into world terms, means economic understandings that secure to every nation a healthy peacetime life for its inhabitants – everywhere in the world.
- The fourth is freedom from fear – which, translated into world terms, means a world-wide reduction of armaments to such a point and in such a thorough fashion that no nation will be in a position to commit an act of physical aggression against any neighbor – anywhere in the world.

That is no vision of a distant millennium. It is a definite basis for a kind of world attainable in our own time and generation.

Freedom means the supremacy of human rights everywhere. Our support goes to those who struggle to gain those rights or keep them. Our strength is our unity of purpose.

New Deal social welfare reformers were quick to embrace this rights talk. It fit perfectly with the policies they had been advocating to provide people with the economic security the New Deal was dedicated to providing the American people, and it provided a stronger argument for implementing those policies than appeals to either the charitable instincts or self-interest of voters.

The National Resources Planning Board (NRPB) was a research and advisory body housed in the Executive Office of the president and headed by a former railroad magnate (and "favorite uncle" of the president) Frederic Delano. Its Director of Research was a Columbia University economist, Eveline Burns, who had previously served as an advisor to the

Committee on Economic Security. At the time of the president's Four Freedoms Speech, the NRPB was engaged, among other tasks, in a detailed assessment of the social welfare initiatives undertaken by the Roosevelt administration since 1933, as a guide for planning the social welfare institutions it believed the country should be prepared to establish at the end of World War II. Recognizing the link between the freedom from want described in the president's speech and its social welfare planning initiative, the NRPB undertook the further task of developing, in consultation with the president, a nine-point "Declaration of Rights" that translated the freedom from want into a specific list of economic and social entitlements (see Box 6.2). The NRPB included this Declaration in its next annual report to the president, which he transmitted to Congress on January 14, 1942 (Roosevelt 1950).

Box 6.2. National Resources Planning Board Declaration of Rights 1942

FREEDOM OF SPEECH AND EXPRESSION, FREEDOM TO WORSHIP, FREEDOM FROM WANT, AND FREEDOM FROM FEAR, these are the universals of human life.

The translation of freedom into modern terms applicable to the people of the United States includes, as the National Resources Planning Board sees it, the following declaration of rights:

1 THE RIGHT TO WORK, usefully and creatively through the productive years;
2 THE RIGHT TO FAIR PAY, adequate to command the necessities and amenities of life in exchange for work, ideas, thrift, and other socially valuable service;
3 THE RIGHT TO ADEQUATE FOOD, CLOTHING, SHELTER, AND MEDICAL CARE;
4 THE RIGHT TO SECURITY with freedom from fear of old age, want, dependency, sickness, unemployment, and accident;
5 THE RIGHT TO LIVE IN A SYSTEM OF FREE ENTERPRISE, free from compulsory labor, irresponsible private power, arbitrary public authority, and unregulated monopolies;
6 THE RIGHT TO COME AND GO, TO SPEAK OR BE SILENT, from the spyings of secret political police;
7 THE RIGHT TO EQUALITY BEFORE THE LAW, with equal access to justice in fact;

8 THE RIGHT TO EDUCATION, for work, for citizenship, and for personal growth and happiness; and

9 THE RIGHT TO REST, recreation, and adventure; the opportunity to enjoy life and take part in an advancing civilization.

Source: National Resources Planning Board, 1942a.

The framing of the war effort as a human rights struggle also led the American Law Institute (ALI) to undertake the drafting of a *Statement of Essential Human Rights*. An influential private organization of judges, lawyers, and law professors dedicated to the improvement of the law, the ALI is best known for its authoritative "Restatements" of the common law and its "Model Codes"; but it also undertakes studies for the purpose of expressing its views as to what it believes the law, or the principles underpinning the law, should be in particular areas. The director of the ALI from its founding in 1923 until 1949 was William Louis Draper, a former dean of the University of Pennsylvania Law School. Under Draper's leadership, and with funding from the Carnegie Endowment for International Peace and the American Philosophical Society of Philadelphia, the ALI convened an international drafting committee to enumerate the human rights, acceptable to all the peoples of the world, on which a lasting peace could be based following the end of World War II. The effort took three years of study and discussion.

The ALI Council, the organization's governing body, decided not to put the *Statement of Essential Human Rights* to a vote of the organization's members – in significant part because of disagreement over the inclusion of social rights in the document (see Box 6.3) – but it did direct that the *Statement* be distributed to all members and condoned its private publication so the public could benefit from the work. What distinguishes this document from other similar lists, other than its international provenance, is its inclusion of detailed explanations and commentary concerning each of the rights enumerated in it (American Law Institute 1945).

In 1944, with the end of the war in sight, Roosevelt chose to use his State of the Union Message to summarize his argument that the employment and social welfare entitlements his administration had sought to secure were in fact human rights that the federal government had a duty to secure (Roosevelt 1950). Invoking the natural rights language of the U.S. Declaration of Independence, Roosevelt criticized the nation's original Bill of Rights as "inadequate" in an industrial age "to assure

Box 6.3. American Law Institute Statement of Essential Human Rights (Social Rights Provisions) 1945

Article 12. WORK
Every one has the right to work.

  The state has a duty to take such measures as may be necessary to insure that all its residents have an opportunity for useful work.

Article 13. CONDITIONS OF WORK
Every one has the right to reasonable conditions of work.

  The state has a duty to take such measures as may be necessary to insure all [workers] reasonable wages, hours, and other conditions of work.

Article 14. FOOD AND HOUSING
Every one has the right to adequate food and housing.

  The state has a duty to take such measures as may be necessary to insure that all its residents have an opportunity to obtain these essentials.

Article 15. SOCIAL SECURITY
Every one has the right to social security.

  The state has a duty to maintain or insure that there are maintained comprehensive arrangements for the promotion of health, for the prevention of sickness and accident, and for the provision of medical care and of compensation for loss of livelihood.

us equality in the pursuit of happiness." He then proceeded to list eight economic and social entitlements (a refinement of the NRPB's earlier nine-item list) which he claimed the American people had already "accepted, so to speak" as "a second Bill of Rights under which a new basis of security and prosperity can be established for all – regardless of station, race, or creed" (see Box 6.4).

Box 6.4. FDR's Second Bill of Rights January 11, 1944

It is our duty now to begin to lay the plans and determine the strategy for the winning of a lasting peace and the establishment of an American standard of living higher than ever before known. We cannot be content, no matter how high that general standard of living may be, if some fraction of our people – whether it be one third or one fifth or one tenth – is ill fed, ill clothed, ill housed, and insecure.

This Republic had its beginning, and grew to its present strength, under the protection of certain inalienable political rights – among them the right of free speech, free press, free worship, trial by jury, freedom from unreasonable searches and seizures. They were our rights to life and liberty.

As our nation has grown in size and stature, however – as our industrial economy expanded – these political rights proved inadequate to assure us equality in the pursuit of happiness.

We have come to a clear realization of the fact that true individual freedom cannot exist without economic security and independence. "Necessitous men are not free men." People who are hungry and out of a job are the stuff of which dictatorships are made.

In our day these economic truths have become accepted as self evident. We have accepted, so to speak, a second Bill of Rights under which a new basis of security and prosperity can be established for all – regardless of station, race, or creed.

Among these are:

- The right to a useful and remunerative job in the industries or shops or farms or mines of the nation;
- The right to earn enough to provide adequate food and clothing and recreation;
- The right of every farmer to raise and sell his products at a return which will give him and his family a decent living;
- The right of every businessman, large and small, to trade in an atmosphere of freedom from unfair competition and domination by monopolies at home or abroad;
- The right of every family to a decent home;
- The right to adequate medical care and the opportunity to achieve and enjoy good health;
- The right to adequate protection from the economic fears of old age, sickness, accident, and unemployment;
- The right to a good education.

All of these rights spell security. And after this war is won we must be prepared to move forward, in the implementation of these rights, to new goals of human happiness and well being.

America's own rightful place in the world depends in large part upon how fully these and similar rights have been carried into practice for our citizens.

It is clear that this proposed "Second Bill of Rights" was (and still is) an aspirational document, but it was aspirational in the strong sense that New Deal progressives believed that policies existed that would secure the rights in question immediately. It was not just a set of goals they were determined to work toward; it was a set of goals they thought they could achieve – if only they had the votes in Congress to enact the necessary reforms. After all, it was their policy vision that came first. The idea that their policy goals were human rights goals came later.

This expanded human rights vision – developed by American progressives and promoted by them both at home and abroad during World War II – was strongly embraced by progressives at the international level, as well. Just four months after President Roosevelt delivered his Second Bill of Rights speech, the International Labour Organization (ILO) met in Philadelphia to prepare for the organization's reactivation following the end of World War II. The "Declaration of Philadelphia" adopted on May 10, 1944, by the ILO's General Conference provided the first clear indication of the central role the economic and social human rights promoted by American progressives during World War II would occupy in the subsequent development of international human rights law (see Box 6.5).

Box 6.5. ILO Declaration of Philadelphia May 10, 1944

I

(a) labour is not a commodity;

(c) poverty anywhere constitutes a danger to prosperity everywhere;

* * *

II

(a) all human beings, irrespective of race, creed or sex, have the right to pursue both their material well-being and their spiritual development in conditions of freedom and dignity, of economic security and equal opportunity;

(b) the attainment of the conditions in which this shall be possible must constitute the central aim of national and international policy;

III
* * *

The Conference recognizes the solemn obligation of the International Labour Organization to further among the nations of the world programmes which will achieve:

(a) full employment and the raising of standards of living;

(b) the employment of workers in the occupations in which they can have the satisfaction of giving the fullest measure of their skill and attainments and make their greatest contribution to the common well-being;

(c) the provision, as a means to the attainment of this end and under adequate guarantees for all concerned, of facilities for training and the transfer of labour, including migration for employment and settlement;

(d) policies in regard to wages and earnings, hours and other conditions of work calculated to ensure a just share of the fruits of progress to all, and a minimum living wage to all employed and in need of such protection;

(e) the effective recognition of the right of collective bargaining, the cooperation of management and labour in the continuous improvement of productive efficiency, and the collaboration of workers and employers in the preparation and application of social and economic measures;

(f) the extension of social security measures to provide a basic income to all in need of such protection and comprehensive medical care;

(g) adequate protection for the life and health of workers in all occupations;

(h) provision for child welfare and maternity protection;

(i) the provision of adequate nutrition, housing and facilities for recreation and culture;

(j) the assurance of equality of educational and vocational opportunity.

This trend was confirmed when the United Nations (UN) undertook the drafting of an "International Bill of Rights," the first fruit of this undertaking being the adoption of the Universal Declaration of Human Rights. The fact that the drafting committee that performed this task was chaired by Eleanor Roosevelt (an official U.S. Delegate to the UN from 1946 through 1952, and the first elected chair of the organization's Human Rights Commission) underscores the role played by the New Dealers's human rights vision in this undertaking. The influence of the ALI's *Statement of Essential Human Rights* in shaping the structure and content of the Universal Declaration (Humphrey 1984) provides more concrete evidence of the linkage.

The strategy for securing economic and social human rights mandated by the Universal Declaration is essentially the same strategy the CES endorsed in 1935 and the NRPB after it in 1942 (National Resources Planning Board, 1942b). Everyone has a right to a standard of living allowing them to live in dignity. For those members of society who are able to support themselves (and their dependents), this right can be realized by securing their right to work. For those members of society who are unable to support themselves, income security must be provided by other means.

The consonance between the New Dealers's human rights vision and the human rights vision embodied in the Universal Declaration could not be clearer. Suggestions that the economic and social provisions of the Universal Declaration are somehow alien to American values could not be further from the truth. The values embodied in the Universal Declaration are American values in a very literal sense.

THE SUBSTITUTION OF KEYNESIAN FISCAL POLICY FOR DIRECT JOB CREATION IN THE PROGRESSIVE EMPLOYMENT STRATEGY

The combination of policy experimentation and ideological innovation described in the preceding two sections of this chapter provided American progressives with a coherent social welfare strategy for guaranteeing a decent standard of living to all Americans (as outlined in the CES's report), a tested means of implementing that strategy (as demonstrated by the establishment of the WPA along with income transfer programs such as Social Security), and a powerful rights-based justification for pursuing the strategy (as articulated in Roosevelt's Second Bill of Rights and the Universal Declaration).

The success of that overall strategy, however, depended on the success of its employment-assurance/right-to-work leg. This is true partly because, as the CES noted, most people must live by work, but more importantly because of the linkage between the success of the employment leg of the strategy and its income-support leg. As unemployment rates rise, the number of people who need income support to achieve an adequate standard of living increases, while the tax revenue available to meet their needs decreases. Furthermore, given the centuries-old and deeply imbued tendency in market societies to view the able-bodied but jobless poor as morally suspect and likely responsible for their own deprivation, it is harder to sustain political support for income-transfer programs that provide income support for population groups that include persons who are able to work but remain jobless. For all of these reasons, any significant failure in the employment-assurance/right-to-work leg of the New Deal/Universal Declaration strategy for guaranteeing everyone an adequate standard of living is likely to affect the success of the income-support leg of the strategy, as well.

This is why the shift in progressive thinking about employment policy that occurred during World War II is so momentous. As noted earlier, it was social welfare planners rather than economists who designed and implemented the New Deal's direct job-creation strategy for providing workers with employment assurance. The primary purpose of that strategy in the minds of those who devised and implemented it was to help people survive the Depression, not to hasten the end of the Depression. The beneficial effects of jobs-program spending on the economy were well recognized – especially after the disastrous consequences of Roosevelt's premature attempt to balance the federal budget in 1937. However, it is safe to say that no one recognized the unique macroeconomic advantages of using the direct job-creation strategy to combat the Depression. Briefly, those advantages are that it (1) creates more jobs per dollar of stimulus spending, (2) creates those jobs much faster than other types of stimulus spending, (3) targets the job-creation effect of stimulus spending in a fairer way, and (4) provides superior protection against downward recessionary spirals (Harvey 2011a; 2011b).

If the New Dealers had understood these advantages, and if Keynes's insight concerning the desirability of running budget deficits during economic downturns had been absorbed more quickly, the WPA could have been used to provide all American workers with employment assurance rather than just the neediest third. Involuntary unemployment could have been eliminated as early as 1937, and the economy's full recovery from the Depression would have been substantially accelerated.

Because direct job-creation programs such as the CCC and WPA were viewed as social welfare measures during the 1930s rather than economic policy initiatives, progressive economists entered the 1940s with no particular interest in or commitment to the strategy proposed by the CES for providing workers with employment assurance. Instead, their attention was focused, as it had been throughout the 1930s, on how to promote recovery in the private sector. For progressive economists, Keynes's *General Theory* provided what they had been looking for – a persuasively reasoned theory that supported a relatively simple and clear-cut policy intervention to right the economy. When the nation's unemployment problem evaporated in response to war-time spending, the Keynesians had practical confirmation of Keynes's teaching. As John Kenneth Galbraith noted, "One could not have had a better demonstration of the Keynesian ideas, and I think it's fair to say that as a young Keynesian in Washington, in touch with the other Keynesians there, we all saw that very clearly at the time" (Galbraith 2000, 6). The conclusion progressive economists drew from this experience was that providing jobs for everyone who wanted to work was not nearly as hard as people thought. All that was required was an adequately high level of aggregate demand – something the federal government could easily achieve by engaging in deficit spending.

There was no reason, of course, why Keynes's ideas could not have been used to buttress the arguments advanced by the CES in support of the direct job-creation strategy. This was, in fact, the stance adopted by the NRPB. Most progressives, however, saw no reason to take on the political and administrative challenges of creating programs like the WPA – which were always controversial – when it seemed that the needed jobs could be created much more easily simply by having the government spend more money. As Galbraith commented, "We saw the war, which we regretted, and I still regret it. I don't easily tell other people they should get killed, but we saw the war as a justification of the Keynesian theory, the Keynesian doctrine, and the Keynesian recommendation" (Galbraith 2000, 6).

Keynes himself supported this notion with his famous quip in the *General Theory* that burying bank notes at the bottom of abandoned mines and inviting capitalists to dig them up would create jobs just as well as any other type of spending. So if it was politically easier to enact wasteful spending than useful spending, it would be better to let the wastrels have their way than to tolerate unemployment by not spending enough to achieve full employment (Keynes 1936, 129).

What progressives missed, and Keynes never emphasized, is that how stimulus money is spent does make a difference for reasons that are not adequately captured by the widely-recognized fact that different types of deficit spending can have different multiplier coefficients. This is clearly true at the top of the business cycle. When writing about the use of the ADM strategy to achieve full employment a few years after the publication of the *General Theory*, Keynes noted that adding demand to industries that are already operating at close to full capacity can cause inflation rather than a further expansion of employment. For this reason, he advocated the use of public works spending at that point in the business cycle to ensure further increases in aggregate demand were targeted on the unemployed (Tcherneva 2011). In Keynes's example of the buried bank notes, he simply assumed that there were unemployed miners in the neighborhood.

How stimulus dollars are spent also matters at the bottom of the business cycle if you want to provide employment assurance for unemployed workers. Only if stimulus spending is delivered to the economy via a direct job-creation program can unemployed workers be guaranteed immediate temporary employment while they wait for the multiplier effect of the stimulus spending to create jobs for them in the private sector (Harvey, 2011a; 2011b).

In any event, the lesson progressive economists took away from the economy's performance during World War II was that fiscal policy alone could achieve full employment. This was a subtly different objective than providing workers with employment assurance or securing their right to work. Still, the achievement of full employment can be defined in a way that is functionally equivalent to the employment-assurance/right-to-work goal, and that is how it was understood in the 1940s when Keynesian economists won the hearts and minds of progressives in general. William Beveridge's widely cited definition of full employment captures this intent very well, provided the gendered language of his description is ignored:

> [Full employment] means having always more vacant jobs than unemployed men, not slightly fewer jobs. It means that the jobs are at fair wages, of such a kind, and so located that the unemployed men can reasonably be expected to take them; it means, by consequence, that the normal lag between losing one job and finding another will be very short (Beveridge 1944, 18).

It is also important to understand that the substitution of Keynesian ADM policies for direct job creation in the progressive strategy for ensuring everyone an adequate standard of living did not involve any change in the income-support leg of that strategy. The only thing that changed was the method adopted for ensuring the availability of decent jobs for everyone who wanted to work.

This substitution was complete before the war was over. The NRPB's 1942 report was the last clear call for the retention of the CES strategy. By the time progressive New Dealers in Congress drafted a bill in 1944 to secure the right to work proclaimed in the president's Second Bill of Rights speech, the strategy they adopted was wholly Keynesian – an automatic authorization for the government to spend enough to achieve full employment, with no role at all assigned to the New Deal's signature direct job-creation strategy. In fact, the use of direct job creation for the construction of public works (the signature activity of both the CCC and WPA) was expressly prohibited by the bill unless it was deemed "necessary by reason of special circumstances," or was "authorized by other provisions of law" (Bailey 1950, 245).

There was no real push-back to this shift in progressive thinking. As John Kenneth Galbraith has noted, "[t]he Keynesian view of economic policy collected the whole liberal left movement in the United States. That became part of the accepted policy, the accepted doctrine. And you ask was [Keynes] influential? Nobody could have been more influential. He changed the nature of what we call liberal economics" (Galbraith 2000, 6).

PROGRESSIVE EMPLOYMENT POLICY FROM THE END OF WORLD WAR II TO THE END OF THE "60s"

The full-employment strategy American progressives have pursued since the end of World War II has combined three distinct types of policy interventions. The first has consisted of macroeconomic interventions to ensure the availability of adequate numbers of jobs to provide work for all job seekers. The second has consisted of the promotion of unionization and labor market regulation to ensure that all of these jobs meet minimum quality standards. The third has consisted of policy initiatives designed to ensure equal employment opportunity. These latter initiatives (which I shall refer to as structuralist, for reasons described later) can be further subdivided under four headings: (1) education and training measures, (2) antidiscrimination measures, (3) community development initiatives, and (4) the provision of employment-enabling services such as child care and public transportation.

During the 1940s and 1950s, economists of all persuasions in the United States tended to view the unemployment problem in market economies as wholly cyclical in nature. In keeping with this view, progressive employment policy was limited, as a general rule, to the advocacy of Keynesian ADM policies to counter cyclical downturns and the support of unionization and regulatory measures such as minimum wage legislation to enhance job quality.

This combination of policies worked well enough in the immediate postwar period to keep average unemployment rates at the 4.5% level from 1947 through the end of the 1950s. Meanwhile, a still-vibrant union movement succeeded in keeping average wage growth in line with per capita GDP growth (see commentary accompanying Figure 6.2), thereby lifting millions of blue-collar workers into the middle class.

It was not sufficient, however, to achieve full employment as that term was understood by American progressives during World War II. To achieve full employment in that sense, there must be enough jobs available to provide work for everyone who wants it. Both Figure 6.1 and the achievement of unemployment rates less than 2% from 1943 through 1945 demonstrate that 4.5% unemployment does not come close to doing that. Moreover, as Table 6.1 illustrates, the harmful effects of a failure to achieve genuine full employment are not borne equally by all population groups. Disadvantaged workers bear a disproportionate share of the unemployment and poverty caused by an aggregate job shortage, and those problems continued to fester in the United States during this period, even if they attracted little public notice.

The "rediscovery" of poverty in the United States following the publication of Michael Harrington's book, *The Other America*, in 1952 and the attention the civil rights movement drew to the labor market effects of racial discrimination led progressives to add a third leg to their overall employment strategy in the 1960s. Although continuing to rely on the adequacy of the Keynesian ADM strategy to secure the quantitative aspect of the right to work, and the combined effects of unionization and labor market regulation to secure the qualitative aspect of the right, 1960s-era progressives saw that additional measures were needed to secure the distributive aspect of the right.

The recognition thus accorded the problem of unequal access to employment opportunities was long overdue in the United States. The unwillingness of New Deal progressives to challenge racism – a compromise they viewed as necessary to achieve social reforms that would benefit African Americans along with all other disadvantaged Americans – was their greatest failure (Hamilton and Hamilton, 1998). Still, commitment does not necessarily translate into effectiveness, and the failure of

1960s-era progressives to recognize and respond to shortcomings in their strategy for securing the quantitative aspect of the right to work undermined their otherwise well-conceived strategy for securing the distributive aspect of the right.

In assessing the causes of the unemployment and poverty problems that beset African Americans and other disadvantaged population groups, 1960s-era progressives focused their attention on the many barriers to equal employment opportunity that existed in American society. Employment discrimination denied the members of certain population groups access to available jobs; unequal access to educational and training opportunities prevented them from qualifying for available jobs; the tendency for businesses to shun minority communities left the residents of those communities with too little access to available jobs; and inadequacies in the provision of public services made it harder for them to find transportation, child care, and other services that would enable them to seek and remain in available jobs.

Based on this understanding of the labor market problems faced by disadvantaged population groups, progressives began to promote a wide range of policy initiatives in the 1960s that were designed to remove barriers to equal-employment opportunity. For ease of exposition, I shall refer to these barriers as "structural," and the policy initiatives adopted to remove them as "structuralist." In so doing, I am using the term in the way labor economists do when they distinguish structural from cyclical and frictional unemployment. *Structural unemployment* is unemployment caused not by a lack of jobs in the aggregate, but because workers are not being hired due to a mismatch between their skills and those required to fill available jobs (a *skills mismatch*) or a mismatch between the location of available jobs and qualified job seekers (a *geographic mismatch*). A mismatch between the personal characteristics of qualified job seekers – such as their race or gender – and the characteristics that employers prefer or require their employees to possess (*employment discrimination*) can be viewed similarly as a structural barrier to equal employment opportunity, as can the absence of employment-enabling support services such as child care (Harvey 2000).

Virtually all of the employment-related reform measures initiated by progressives in the 1960s were structuralist in this sense of the term; and these measures did succeed in helping large numbers of individuals achieve a better life. On the other hand, when success is measured in aggregate rather than individual terms, it is harder to judge the structuralist strategy pursued by 1960s-era progressives a success. The strategy failed to improve the relative position of African Americans (and most other disadvantaged population groups) as measured by high-profile statistics such as their comparative employment, unemployment, and poverty rates. This is the result that permitted Ronald Reagan to claim that liberals fought "poverty, and poverty won" (Wooldridge and Micklethwait 2004, 11).

Progressives have blamed the limited success of the structuralist measures they pioneered in the 1960s (and have promoted ever since) on the complexity of the problems they address and the resistance of groups whose privileges are threatened by the equalization of economic opportunities. There undoubtedly is truth in this charge, but it overlooks an inherent weakness in the structuralist strategy when it is pursued in a job-short economy. This weakness can be called the "musical chairs effect." Imagine a group of concerned teachers who noticed that some children regularly lose when they play the game of musical chairs. In response to this problem, the teachers might offer these children special help. They could teach them how to move faster when the music stops (job training), coach them to linger near vacant chairs when the music is playing (overcoming geographic mismatch between jobs and job seekers), or counsel them concerning the best ways to overcome efforts by cliques of players to prevent disfavored children from claiming seats (combating discrimination). Moreover, these strategies might work in helping those children do better when they play the game. What the strategy will not do, however, is reduce the number of children left standing at the end of each game. Moreover, those "newly deprived" children are likely to be the ones who are most similar to those who got the extra help – rather than the players who consistently do well in the game.

If jobs were plentiful in the aggregate, structural barriers to equal-employment opportunity could still prevent disadvantaged job seekers from finding work as readily as other job seekers, but in that instance, efforts to help people surmount these barriers would not result in other individuals being left unemployed. It would simply mean jobs would be filled that otherwise would remain vacant or that there would be some shuffling among the occupants of particular jobs. No one would lose their livelihood.

In contrast, if an aggregate shortage of jobs exists in the labor market, successful efforts to help jobless individuals overcome structural barriers to employment necessarily result in someone else remaining jobless who would otherwise be employed. Moreover, those individuals who end up jobless are likely to be those who suffer from the same kind of problems as the assisted workers. More privileged workers are unlikely to lose out, because they have more resources to devote to the competition, so the result will be job churning among disadvantaged workers accompanied by a high level of resentment on the part of those who do not get special help directed at those who either do get special help or are perceived as getting it.

In short, the overall level of job availability in an economy is likely to have a profound effect on the success of the structuralist strategy. In a job-short economy, even a "successful" intervention as measured by the post-intervention employment experience of the assisted population is unlikely to make much difference in the overall incidence of the social problems the intervention addresses. It will simply shift the burden of those problems onto the shoulders of the next most disadvantaged group of job seekers in the community who, because of their increased joblessness, are likely to experience more of the problems that originally inspired the effort to help the assisted group. In the meantime, individuals and population groups who rightly or wrongly feel threatened in their job security by the special assistance offered disadvantaged job seekers will grow more resentful, doing what they can – by fair means or foul – to hang on to their own jobs.

It is important to emphasize that I am not suggesting the opportunity-equalizing measures progressives deployed beginning in the 1960s were or are useless. My point is simply that the success of these measures in eradicating the problems they target depends to a large extent on whether or not an aggregate job shortage exists in the economy. If jobs are plentiful, opportunity-equalizing measures have an excellent chance of succeeding on both an individual and aggregate level – with the result being a reduction in inequality. However, if there are not enough jobs to go around, the chances that measures of this type will succeed are greatly reduced. That is the point that 1960s-era progressives failed to appreciate.

PROGRESSIVE EMPLOYMENT POLICY SINCE THE END OF THE "60S"

Notwithstanding the less than stellar results produced by the structuralist strategy during the 1960s, progressives have continued to rely on it ever since. This is partly attributable to the strong commitment progressives feel to the equal opportunity goals of these policies; but it also reflects the fact that the achievement of full employment has virtually disappeared from the progressive reform agenda. I am not suggesting that the full employment goal itself has lost its appeal. The problem is that progressives have lost faith in their ability to achieve it.

The turning point came during the recession of 1973–1975. The challenge posed by that particular economic downturn was that declining GDP and rising unemployment were accompanied by continued high rates of inflation. Called "stagflation" at the time, this confluence of normally opposing tendencies shattered the confidence of both the general public and most policy makers in the Keynesian ADM strategy.

The problem was that the standard Keynesian prescription for combating unemployment is the opposite of its prescription for combating inflation. Stymied by this conundrum, even progressives lost faith in the ability of the Keynesian ADM strategy to raise employment levels without aggravating inflationary tendencies in the economy, and that meant giving up on the achievement of full employment. In 1972, the Democratic Party Platform defined "full employment" as "a guaranteed job for all," and described the achievement of that goal as "the primary economic objective of the Democratic Party." In the Party's 1980 platform, the goal of achieving full employment received only a single oblique affirmation in a laundry list of other goals, and by 2002 the goal had disappeared entirely, never to return (Harvey 2008, 173 n. 49).

In other words, rather than confronting the challenge of developing a new strategy for achieving full employment following their loss of faith in the ability of the Keynesian ADM strategy to do the job, progressives simply abandoned their efforts to secure the quantitative aspect of the right to work and doubled down on the two remaining elements of their post-World War II employment strategy – the promotion of unionization and increased labor market regulation to secure the qualitative aspect of the right to work, and the pursuit of structuralist policy initiatives to secure the distributive aspect of the right.

In light of our earlier analysis of the shortcomings of progressive efforts to achieve equal employment opportunity during the 1960s, it is hardly surprising that the truncated employment strategy progressives have pursued since then has produced similarly disappointing results. During the 1960s, unemployment averaged 4.8%, and during the crucial half-decade from 1965 through 1969 it averaged 3.8%. Over the four decades that have passed since then, unemployment rates have averaged 6.3%.

The fortuitous confluence of circumstances that caused unemployment to fall to the 4% level in the late 1990s did succeed in reminding progressives of the benefits of full employment. Unfortunately, support for the goal as it was originally conceived and promoted in the 1940s had so atrophied by then that even progressives confused the economy's performance in the late 1990s with full employment (see, e.g., Bernstein and Baker 2003). The resurgence in support among progressives for a vigorous Keynesian response to the so-called Great Recession also failed to reverse this trend. Paul Krugman, the most visible spokesperson for progressive Keynesianism in recent years, has made it clear that he conceives of a return to full employment as a return to the 5% unemployment he thinks is consistent with reasonable price stability (Krugman, 2009). The definition of full employment that served as the foundation of the progressive reform agenda for three decades still commands support among progressives (Goldberg, Harvey, and Ginsburg 2007), but in the absence of a coherent strategy for achieving it, the goal has become aspirational in the weak sense of a wish rather than in the strong sense of an immediate policy goal.

Conservative promises over the past several decades to create jobs with tax and spending cuts have not worked either, of course, but progressives have not been able to take consistent advantage of this failure because they can neither point to a proven track record of managed job creation of their own, nor articulate a coherent alternative strategy to the one conservatives promote. Criticism of conservative policies, by itself, does not win public support for the existing progressive reform agenda. What is needed is an alternative strategy that promises actually to work – and that means finding a substitute for the failed Keynesian ADM strategy, one that is capable of achieving full employment as the goal was originally conceived by progressives in the early 1940s.

THE FUTURE OF PROGRESSIVE EMPLOYMENT POLICY

It has been four decades since the last period of concentrated progressive reform ended in the United States, arguably the longest gap without such a period in the nation's history. It is certainly longer than the periods of conservative retrenchment that divided the Progressive Era from the New Deal and the New Deal from the 1960s. The explanations American progressives usually offer for their forty-year exile in the political wilderness focus on the relative strength of the conservative interests arrayed against them. This chapter suggests a different reason – the substantive failure of the Keynesian ADM policy prescription on which progressives have relied since the end of World War II to achieve full employment.

The reason this failure has been so consequential, this chapter suggests, is because securing the quantitative dimension of the right to work is essential for the success of the progressive reform project as a whole. The achievement of sustained full employment is necessary to ensure the effectiveness of policies designed to ensure that all jobs satisfy minimum standards of decency, thereby securing the qualitative aspect of the right to work. It also is essential for the success, on the aggregate level, of policies designed to achieve equal employment opportunity, thereby securing the distributive aspect of the right to work. Further, by making it possible for society to secure all aspects of the right to work, the achievement of sustained full employment would also make it easier for society to secure the right to income support of persons who cannot or are not expected to work. It would do this by adding to the resource base from which transfer benefits are funded while simultaneously reducing the number of persons needing such benefits. Incidentally, it would also make it politically easier to decide who is and who is not entitled to income assistance (Harvey, 2008, 2005). Finally, by making it possible to secure both the right to work and to income security, the achievement of sustained full employment is essential for securing the right of all persons to an adequate standard of living (i.e., the eradication of poverty, once and for all, from the human condition). In other words, the failure of the full-employment/employment-assurance/right-to-work leg of the progressive employment strategy really does matter a great deal.

There is, however, a silver lining to this cloud. An alternative employment strategy does exist that would correct the deficiencies in the existing progressive strategy without undermining its strong points. This alternative is the New Deal strategy of providing all workers with employment assurance by using direct job-creation programs to close the economy's job gap. In other work, I have explored the use of this strategy as a means of securing the right to work that President Roosevelt advocated and that has been recognized in numerous international agreements (Harvey 2005; 2002; 1995a; 1993; 1989), reforming public assistance programs (Harvey 2008; 1995a; 1989), achieving sustained full employment (Harvey 2006; 2000; 1995b; 1989), combating recessions (Harvey 2011a), and promoting local economic development (Harvey 2011b). There is also a growing post–Keynesian literature advocating the use of direct job creation to achieve full employment with price stability (Mitchell and Wray 2005; Wray 1999; Mosler 1997–1998; Mitchell and Watts 1997).

This is not the place to review this literature, but the account provided in this chapter of the policy options available to American progressives during World War II shows that the Keynesian ADM strategy is not the only means available for closing the economy's job gap. Indeed, the inability of the Keynesian ADM strategy to achieve genuine full employment suggests that American progressives made a fateful if understandable mistake when they chose to ground their overall employment policy on it rather than the New Deal's direct job-creation strategy. They were right that it would have been far more difficult to gain the political support needed to implement the New Deal strategy in the post–World War II period. Still, opportunities to do so would have presented themselves, especially in light of the fact that, unlike the Keynesian ADM strategy, the New Deal strategy can be implemented on the local as well as national level (Harvey 2011b). Successful experiments implementing the New Deal strategy at the state or local level would have led to further such opportunities, and the strategy's success in securing the quantitative aspect of the right to work would have provided the necessary foundation for the success of progressive efforts to secure the qualitative and distributive aspect of the right, as well.

My most enduring recollection of my paternal grandmother is her telling me that if I did not learn from my mistakes, what was the use of making them. It is important for progressives to acknowledge the weaknesses in their employment strategy. It is not that Keynes was wrong in his analysis of macroeconomic dynamics. Nothing in this chapter supports such a contention. The problem is that it does not follow that the conventional Keynesian ADM strategy has ever been capable of performing the role assigned to it in securing the right to work. The effort by progressives to soldier on without a full employment strategy once the flaws in the Keynesian ADM strategy became apparent in the 1970s has been disastrous. A new strategy for securing the quantitative aspect of the right to work is desperately needed.

This also presents an opportunity for progressives to re-embrace the human rights vision and language of their New Deal predecessors. Full employment is a muddy policy goal whose substantive content varies dramatically depending on whether it is defined in terms of job availability or price stability. Moreover, because of the rhetorical appeal of the job-availability definition, even economists whose analytic work is based entirely on the opposing, price-stability definition of the term have little interest in making a point of the distinction. Why call attention to the fact that the "full" employment you are discussing is really just "half-full" employment? In other words, the term is not only muddy; it is perversely muddy because so many economists have a positive interest in maintaining its ambiguity.

The meaning of the right to work can also be confusing, of course. The use of the term by antiunion groups in the United States demonstrates this. Still, the relative clarity with which the right has been defined in international human rights agreements makes it a far less ambiguous goal than the achievement of full employment. This clarity is further enhanced by the fact that whether or not the right has been secured is amenable to easy demonstration, whereas the achievement of full employment is notoriously difficult to measure.

Nor is it just the elimination of ambiguity that should cause progressives to replace the full-employment goal with that of securing the right to work. The more important reason is provided by the enhanced moral force of human rights claims. Absent its association with the right to work, the achievement of full employment would be just one of many discretionary goals a majoritarian government could pursue – or not pursue – based on voter preferences. If voters prefer lower taxes or less inflation to the achievement of full employment, who are we to question their preferences? Rights-based claims are different. Philosophers describe them as moral trumps precisely because we accept their priority over claims based on mere preferences – even when those preferences are expressed in fully democratic elections.

Progressives have readily embraced the language of human rights in their efforts to secure the qualitative and distributive aspects of the right to work. Why, then, have they not embraced similar language in their efforts to secure the quantitative aspect of the right? Lack of confidence in the ability of the Keynesian ADM strategy to achieve sustained full employment provides part of the answer. Another reason may be that the achievement of full employment is not readily translatable into an enforceable right on either an individual or collective level. Finally, progressive economists may be hesitant to embrace human rights goals in their work because of the methodological difficulties involved in reconciling the moral mandates of human rights claims with the preference-satisfaction norms of modern economic theory.

Substituting the direct job-creation strategy for the Keynesian ADM strategy would resolve most of these difficulties. It would provide a credible means of achieving and measuring the achievement of genuine full employment. It would also allow the quantitative as well as the qualitative and distributive aspects of the right to work to be enforced on an individually justiciable basis. Finally, the ease with which the strategy's results can be measured, combined with the fact that it can be implemented on a local as well as national level, would facilitate empirical economic research, even if the problem of reconciling the preference-based norms of contemporary theoretical economics with the moral obligations of modern human rights doctrine remained.

In short, embracing the direct job-creation strategy would make it easier for progressives to renew their commitment to the New Dealers's expanded human rights vision; and the strong historical and conceptual association between the strategy and that vision would provide a further impetus for them to do so. The failure of American progressives over the past two-thirds of a century to fully exploit the human rights vision of their New Deal predecessors constitutes a missed opportunity of monumental proportions. It is time to correct that mistake along with the weaknesses in progressive employment policy that have crippled its effectiveness.

REFERENCES

American Law Institute Drafting Committee, 1945. *Statement of Essential Human Rights*, New York: Americans United for World Organization, Inc.

Bailey, S.K., 1950. *Congress Makes a Law: The Story Behind the Employment Act of 1946*, New York: Columbia University Press.

Bernstein, J. and D. Baker, 2003. *The Benefits of Full Employment*, Washington, DC: Economic Policy Institute.

Beveridge, W.H., 1944. *Full Employment in a Free Society*, London: Allen and Unwin.

Brown, E.C., 1956. "Fiscal Policy in the Thirties: A Reappraisal," *The American Economic Review* 46: 857–879.

Committee on Economic Security, 1935. Report of the Committee on Economic Security. Retrieved from http://www.ssa.gov/history/reports/ces.html.

Galbraith, J.K., 2000. Interview Broadcast on *Commanding Heights: The Battle for the World Economy* [Television series]. Boston, MA: WGBH. PDF transcript of interview retrieved from http://www.pbs.org/wgbh/commandingheights/hi/resources/pdf_index.html#int_johnkennethgalbraith.

Goldberg, G.S., P.L. Harvey and H.L. Ginsberg, 2007. "A Survey of Full Employment Advocates," *Journal of Economic Issues* 41: 1161–1168.

Hamilton, D.C. and C.V. Hamilton, 1998. *The Dual Agenda: The African American Struggle for Civil and Economic Equality*, New York: Columbia University Press.

Harvey, P.L., 1989. *Securing the Right to Employment: Social Welfare Policy and the Unemployed in the United States*, Princeton, NJ: Princeton University Press.

Harvey, P.L., 1993. "Employment as a Human Right," in William J. Wilson (Ed.) *Sociology and the Public Agenda*, 351–374, Newbury Park, CA: Sage Publications.

Harvey, P.L., 1995a. "Fashioning a Work-Based Strategy for Welfare Reform Based on International Human Rights Doctrine," *Journal of Public Health Policy* 16: 269–285.

Harvey, P.L., 1995b. "Paying for Full Employment: A Hard-Nosed Look at Finances," *Social Policy* Spring 1995: 21.

Harvey, P.L., 1999. "Joblessness and the Law Before the New Deal," *Georgetown Journal on Poverty Law and Policy* 6: 1–41.

Harvey, P.L., 2000. "Combating Joblessness: An Analysis of the Principal Strategies that Have Influenced the Development of American Employment and Social Welfare Law During the 20th Century," *Berkeley Journal of Employment and Labor Law*, 21: 677–758.

Harvey, P.L., 2002. "Human Rights and Economic Policy Discourse: Taking Economic and Social Rights Seriously," *Columbia Human Rights Law Review* 33: 363–471.

Harvey, P.L., 2004. "Aspirational Law," *Buffalo Law Review* 52: 701–726.

Harvey, P.L., 2005. "The Right to Work and Basic Income Guarantees: Competing or Complementary Goals?" *Rutgers Journal of Law and Public Policy* 2: 8–59.

Harvey, P.L., 2006. "Funding a Job Guarantee," *International Journal of Environment, Workplace and Employment* 2: 114–132.

Harvey, P.L., 2007. "Benchmarking the Right to Work," in Shareen Hertel and Lanse Minkler (Eds.) *Economic Rights: Conceptual, Measurement and Policy Issues*, 115–141, New York: Cambridge University Press.

Harvey, P.L., 2008. "Is There A Progressive Alternative to Conservative Welfare Reform," *Georgetown Journal on Poverty Law and Policy* 15: 157–208.

Harvey, P.L., 2011a. *Back To Work: A Public Jobs Proposal for Economic Recovery*, New York: Demos. Retrieved from http://www.demos.org/sites/default/files/publications/Back_To_Work_Demos.pdf.

Harvey, P.L., 2011b. *Securing the Right to Work at the State or Local Level with a Direct Job Creation Program*, Berkeley, CA: Institute for Research on Labor and Employment. Retrieved from http://www.bigideasforjobs.org/job-briefs/employment/.

Humphrey, J.P., 1984. *Human Rights and the United Nations: A Great Adventure*, Dobbs Ferry, New York: Transnational Publishers.

Keynes, J.M., 1936. *General theory of employment, interest and money*, London: Macmillan.

Krugman, P.R., 2009. "Stimulus Arithmetic," *New York Times* blog. January 6, 2009. Retrieved from http://krugman.blogs.nytimes.com/2009/01/06/stimulus-arithmetic-wonkish-but-important/.

Mitchell, W.F. and M.J. Watts, 1997. "The Path to Full Employment," *The Australian Economic Review* 30: 436–443.

Mitchell, W.F. and L.R. Wray, 2005. "In Defense of Employer of Last Resort: A Response to Malcolm Sawyer," *Journal of Economic Issues* 39: 235–244.

Mosler, W., 1997–1998. "Full Employment and Price Stability," *Journal of Post Keynesian Economics* 20: 167–182.

National Resources Planning Board, 1942a. "Our Freedoms and Rights," quoted in Marion Clauson, *New Deal Planning: The National Resources Planning Board*, Baltimore: Johns Hopkins Press, 1981, 183–184.

National Resources Planning Board, 1942b. *Security, Work and Relief Policies*, Washington, DC: U.S. Government Printing House.

Roosevelt, F.D., 1934. *Executive Order No. 6757*, June 29, 1934.

Roosevelt, F.D., 1938. *The Public Papers and Addresses of Franklin D. Roosevelt*, Vols. 1–5 (1928–1936). Samuel I. Rosenman, compiler, New York: Random House.

Roosevelt, F.D., 1941. *The Public Papers and Addresses of Franklin D. Roosevelt*, Vols. 6–9 (1937–1940). Samuel I. Rosenman, compiler, New York: MacMillan.

Roosevelt, F.D., 1950. *The Public Papers and Addresses of Franklin D. Roosevelt*, Vols. 10–13 (1941–1945). Samuel I. Rosenman, compiler, New York: Harper and Brothers.

Schwartz, B.F., 1984. *The Civil Works Administration, 1933–1934*, Princeton NJ: Princeton University Press.

Tcherneva, P., 2012. "Permanent On-The-Spot Job Creation – The Missing Keynes Plan for Full Employment and Economic Transformation," *Review of Social Economy* 70: 57–80.

United Nations, 1948. Universal Declaration of Human Rights, G.A. Res. 217A (III), U.N. GAOR, 3d Sess., *Resolutions, Part I, U.N. Doc. A/810* (1948).

Wooldridge, J. and J. Micklethwait, 2004. *The Right Nation: Conservative Power in America*, New York: Penguin Press.

Wray, L.R., 1999. *Understanding Modern Money: The Key to Full Employment and Price Stability*, Aldershot, England: Edward Elgar.

II

Nondiscrimination

7

The Rights of the Child to an Adequate Standard of Living: Applying International Standards to the U.S. Case

Kathryn Libal and Ken Neubeck

A society that possesses sufficient resources for all children and allows some of its children to go without necessary health care, food, and education is failing in its moral duty *(Woodhouse, 2008, p. 40)*.

INTRODUCTION

The idea that children have economic and social rights has been articulated in international law since the 1920s, when the Geneva Declaration of the Rights of the Child was drafted by the League of Nations (1924) and the International Labour Organization created standards for child labor. The landmark children's human rights treaty, the UN Convention on the Rights of the Child (UN CRC 1990) underscores that children are rights bearers, despite not having reached the age of majority for full citizenship. Thus, the full range of human rights, including social, economic, cultural, civil, and political rights that states are obligated to respect, protect, and fulfill for adult citizens, are also to be accorded to children.

State ratification of the CRC is nearly universal, and efforts to implement the treaty at the country level have been considerable in the past twenty years (Todres 2011). Yet, neither the Committee on the Rights of the Child nor state parties to the CRC have adequately addressed the question of children's economic and social rights and eliminating child

The authors wish to thank Lanse Minkler, Cathy Albisa, and Phil Harvey, as well as members of the Economic and Social Rights Group and its affiliates at the University of Connecticut, Human Rights Institute, for their critical feedback on an earlier draft of this chapter.

poverty as a core obligation of states.[1] In the past few years, however, interest has grown among children's rights advocates and the Committee on the Rights of the Child to address children's rights to an adequate standard of living.

Key concerns have been to examine child poverty elimination in developing countries, including the question of extraterritorial obligation to fulfill children's economic and social rights (Vandenhole 2009) and measuring the realization of children's rights (Carvalho 2008). Growing interest in the measurement of fulfillment of children's rights generally, and children's economic and social rights specifically, is evidenced in the work fostered by the United Nations Children's Fund (UNICEF) for developing general measures of children's rights attainment (UNICEF Innocenti Research Centre 2006) and efforts to develop indices capturing child poverty at the local and national levels, including a proposed Child Poverty Index and Child Development Index.[2]

Yet, despite such efforts, attention on how to effectively use the CRC and other human rights treaty processes to reduce and eventually eliminate child poverty in both wealthy and developing countries has been inadequate (Aber, Hammond, and Thompson 2010). This chapter serves a two-fold purpose: to bring together analysis of existing international standards on addressing child poverty – particularly in the growing body of general comments by the Committee on the Rights of the Child – and to underscore the importance of addressing persistent structural inequalities shaped by racism, sexism, and anti-immigrant sentiment in wealthy states such as the United States when addressing the child's right to an adequate standard of living.

In this chapter, we first outline the growing interest at the United Nations to better monitor and foster the implementation of children's right to an adequate standard of living, primarily through the committee charged with monitoring the CRC. Although the right to an adequate standard of living is a pervasive question in developing countries, the

---

[1] The Committee on the Rights of the Child, which is charged with monitoring state progress to implement the treaty, underscores that four principles are fundamental to the convention: the principle of nondiscrimination (Art. 2); the best interests of the child (Art. 3); due consideration of the child's evolving capacities (Art. 5); and the right of the child to life, survival, and development (Art. 6) (CRC 1990).

[2] The UNICEF Innocenti Research Centre is currently funding several projects to examine inequalities in rich and poor countries, including UK-based research on developing multidimensional child poverty estimates in rich countries that are possible to compare. See the Institute of Development Studies at http://www.ids.ac.uk/go/idsproject/multidimensional-child-poverty-in-rich-countries.

focus of this chapter is on the conceptualization of a child's right to an adequate standard of living in wealthy states. Recent deliberations by the Committee on the Rights of the Child have emphasized the importance of obligations of states' parties to take immediate action to implement policies providing a minimum level of social protection, or the "minimum core obligations" of states. These include: "essential foodstuffs, equal access to primary health care, basic shelter and housing, social security or social assistance coverage, family protection, and basic education" (UN Committee on the Rights of the Child 2007, 13).[3] As we show in this chapter, many wealthy countries have implemented policies that effectively tackle child poverty, although the Committee on the Rights of the Child also notes significant gaps for even the wealthiest states in collecting data on child poverty and developing a robust understanding of how marginalized groups of children, including racial and ethnic minority and immigrant children, disproportionately experience poverty.

A second aim of this chapter is to address the economic and social rights implications of social welfare policy in the United States, in large part because of its failings to comprehensively address the right of all children to an adequate standard of living. The United States, which is party to neither the CRC nor the International Covenant on Economic, Social and Cultural Rights (ICESCR), has signed both human rights treaties and arguably has obligations to address the economic and social rights of children within its borders in light of these signatures. Such obligations are reinforced by the United States's long-standing recognition of the Universal Declaration of Human Rights and participation as a state party to the Convention on the Elimination of All Forms of Racial Discrimination (CERD), as well. Using tools for human rights analysis offered by the Committee on the Rights of the Child and obligations of the United States under CERD, we draw attention to the necessity of examining child poverty in wealthy states (as well as those with more limited means). Our analysis underscores the importance of addressing how racism and

---

[3] This emphasis has been borrowed from the UN Committee on Economic, Social, and Cultural Rights (CESCR) standards of "minimum core obligations" of states parties to the ICESCR. Although considerable attention has focused on the question of progressive realization of economic rights in developing countries, it is our aim to shed light on the demands this places on wealthy states, as well, including the United States, which still officially denies the existence of economic human rights. Despite the fact that the United States is party to neither the ICESCR nor CRC, it is our contention that scholars and human rights advocates can scrutinize U.S. governmental effort and progress to combat child poverty within its borders in light of international human rights standards.

structural inequality affect the realization of children's economic and social rights by focusing attention on the wealthiest country in the world, where child poverty – especially among children of color and newcomer immigrant children – is a pervasive and growing problem. U.S. children's right to an adequate standard of living has not been fulfilled, despite the country's capacity to eliminate child poverty. Framing this matter as one not only of economic rights but also of civil rights to protection from discrimination on the basis of race, and obligations to respect children's rights to equality may provide added leverage to catalyze government effort in addressing child poverty.

INTERNATIONAL LAW ON THE PROVISION OF AN ADEQUATE STANDARD OF LIVING FOR CHILDREN

The international human rights system has long recognized the obligations of governments to support families in protection and provision of children's economic and social rights (Taylor 2006). Majka and Ensalaco (2005) point to the considerable harm caused to children by poverty and social inequality, whether or not children are from poor or wealthy countries. Echoing the principle of indivisibility of (children's) human rights, Majka and Ensalaco assert: "It is impossible to give a better life to all children without promoting their economic, social, and cultural rights, as well as protecting their civil and political rights" (2005, 3). As early as the adoption of the Geneva Declaration of the Rights of the Child by the League of Nations (1924), international standards have recognized children's economic and social rights, or their rights to "the means requisite for normal material and spiritual development." According to the Geneva Declaration, "The child that is hungry . . . must be fed, the child that is sick must be helped . . . the orphan and the waif must be sheltered and succored."

The 1959 UN Declaration on the Rights of the Child, which preceded the adoption of the International Covenant on Civil and Political Rights (1966) and ICESCR (1966), expanded the framework for economic and social rights accorded to children. These included provision of adequate nutrition, medical care, education, addressing the needs of children with disabilities, state or social assistance to children without a family, and adequate housing (Ensalaco 2005). Measures to protect children from exploitation and dangerous work and establish a minimum wage for employment in the 1959 declaration signaled principles that would become enshrined in the International CRC some three decades later. Children's rights as workers were also addressed in treaties regarding minimum wage and exploitative labor by the International Labour Organization (Ensalaco 2005).

The CRC was adopted as a treaty by the UN General Assembly in late 1989 and entered into force in 1990. It became the most quickly and widely ratified of all human rights treaties (Rutkow and Lozman 2006), including all UN member states except the United States and Somalia. The treaty encompasses the full range of human rights, foregrounding state obligations for child protection, to assure provision of basic needs, and to foster child participation in communities and society attendant to the "evolving capacities" of the child. Article 4 underscores that states parties "shall undertake all appropriate legislative, administrative, and other measures for the implementation of the rights recognized in the present Convention. With regard to economic, social, and cultural rights, States Parties shall undertake such measures *to the maximum extent of their available resources*, and, where needed, within the framework of international co-operation (emphasis added)."

Article 6 reinforces that children have an "inherent right to life" and that states parties "shall ensure *to the maximum extent possible* the survival and development of the child" (emphasis added). Whereas the treaty recognizes that parents have responsibilities for the upbringing and development of the child, states parties are obligated to "render appropriate assistance to parents and legal guardians in the performance of their child-rearing responsibilities and shall ensure the development of institutions, facilities and services for the care of children" (Article 18). Moreover, the treaty elaborates standards for the child's "enjoyment of the highest attainable standard of health" (Article 24).

The CRC articulates a state's obligation to fulfill children's economic and social rights directly in Article 27, underscoring, "States Parties recognize the right of every child to a standard of living adequate for the child's physical, mental, spiritual, moral and social development." According to Article 27, parents or other guardians of the child "have the primary responsibility to secure, within their abilities and financial capacities, the conditions of living necessary for the child's development." Yet, in circumstances where parents or guardians cannot meet the child's basic needs, states parties are charged with securing supports for parents who are unable to work or earn sufficient resources. Thus, "States Parties, in accordance with national conditions and within their means, shall take appropriate measures to assist parents and others responsible for the child to implement this right and shall in case of need provide material assistance and support programmes, *particularly with regard to nutrition, clothing and housing*" (emphasis added). The treaty does not distinguish whether or not a child is deserving of support based on parental or guardian life choices and conditions; the obligation for support is framed as an economic and social rights entitlement universally available to children, regardless of family size, parental "behavior," social group membership, or household income.

Human rights committee work often entails publishing general comments on thematic issues that more fully interpret the meaning of specific rights contained within a treaty. The Committee on the Rights of the Child has issued thirteen general comments addressing concerns, including elaborating the meaning of a specific right and guidance for implementation. General comment topics have included the right to education (*General Comment No. 1*), HIV/AIDS and the rights of the child (*General Comment No. 3*), the rights of children with disabilities (*General Comment No. 9*), and most recently, the right of the child to be free of all forms of violence (*General Comment No. 13*, 2011). Although many of the general comments address children's economic and social rights in some way, children's right to an adequate standard of living is underdeveloped as a theme throughout the corpus of general comments. In *General Comment No. 7* on "Implementing the Rights of the Child in Early Childhood" (2005), the Committee has attended to Article 27 specifically with the following interpretation:

> Young children are entitled to a standard of living adequate for their physical, mental, spiritual, moral and social development (art. 27). The Committee notes with concern that even the most basic standard of living is not assured for millions of young children, despite widespread recognition of the adverse consequences of deprivation. Growing up in relative poverty undermines children's well-being, social inclusion and self-esteem and reduces opportunities for learning and development. Growing up in conditions of absolute poverty has even more serious consequences, threatening children's survival and their health, as well as undermining the basic quality of life. States parties are urged to implement systematic strategies to reduce poverty in early childhood as well as combat its negative effects on children's well-being. All possible means should be employed, including "material assistance and support programmes" for children and families (art. 27.3), in order to assure to young children a basic standard of living consistent with rights. Implementing children's right to benefit from social security, including social insurance, is an important element of any strategy (art. 26) (*General Comment No. 7* 2005, para. 26).

This short paragraph underscores the necessity of states parties to create systematic strategies to address childhood poverty (in this instance in early childhood), underscoring that "[a]ll possible means should be employed, including 'material assistance and support programmes' for children and families," to assure young children "a basic standard of living" consistent with their rights.

Discrimination

The Committee notes in its general comment on "General Measures of Implementation for the Convention on the Rights of the Child" that children from disadvantaged groups, including racial and ethnic minorities, require a heightened level of policy attention: "Whatever their economic circumstances, States are required to undertake all possible measures towards the realization of the rights of the child, paying special attention to the most disadvantaged groups" (*General Comment No. 5* 2003, para. 8). In monitoring implementation of the CRC with respect to Article 27, the committee has not spared wealthy countries from criticism.

In its 2004 "Concluding Observations," the Committee on the Rights of the Child charged Germany to:

> Take all necessary measures to the "maximum extent of... available resources" to accelerate the elimination of child poverty, notably to eliminate the disparities between the eastern and western parts of the country... [and continue to] provide material assistance and support to economically disadvantaged families, notably single-parent families and families of foreign origin, to guarantee the right of children to an adequate standard of living (UN Committee on the Rights of the Child 2004, para. 51).

Committee "Concluding Observations" for Sweden in 2009 cite concern with "large disparities" that remain "between municipalities, counties and regions concerning the implementation of the Convention, including with regard to levels of child poverty, resources available to the social services for children at risk, and academic results between different schools and region" (UN Committee on the Rights of the Child 2009, para. 11). Again attending to the principle of nondiscrimination in redressing child poverty concerns:

> While noting an overall decrease in the number of children living in poverty in recent years, the Committee expresses its concern at the large disparities in the level of child poverty within and between municipalities, and urban

boroughs. It also notes with concern the very high proportion of immigrant children living in households with a persistently low income and the continuing deterioration in the economic situation of children from non-Swedish backgrounds and children living in single-parent households (UN Committee on the Rights of the Child 2009, para. 52).

The Committee focused its recommendations on state party obligations to "ensure that all children are not living below the poverty line," noting that "special support measures" must be taken to address the right of children from "social disadvantaged families" to have an adequate standard of living and to be free from poverty (UN Committee on the Rights of the Child 2009, para. 53). Although the Committee does not define what those special support measures should be, in other documentation it notes the importance of social assistance and cash transfers in assuring children do not live in poverty.

Devolution and Privatization of Social Welfare

Prompted by widespread practices of privatization and devolution of social welfare assistance within many wealthy countries since the 1980s, the Committee on the Rights of the Child has also taken a general stance on the potential human rights consequences of these processes on children. In *General Comment No. 7* on "Implementing the Rights of the Child in Early Childhood," the Committee notes that, "Decentralization of power, through devolution and delegation of government, does not in any way reduce the direct responsibility of the State party's Government to fulfil its obligations to all children within its jurisdiction, regardless of the State structure" (2005, para. 40). Importantly, "There must be safeguards to ensure that decentralization or devolution does not lead to discrimination in the enjoyment of rights by children in different regions" (2005, para. 41). Regarding widespread practices of privatization of social services for children (particularly within the United States), the Committee observes, "Enabling the private sector to provide services, run institutions and so on does not in any way lessen the State's obligations to ensure for all children within its jurisdiction the full recognition and realization of all rights in the Convention" (2005, para. 44).

The Committee's position on devolution and the privatization of social welfare supports in wealthy countries represents an attempt to grapple with the erosion of rights accorded low-income and marginalized children and families in the past twenty to thirty years (Kamerman and Kahn

2003). Such work requires fuller coordination and incorporation of standards being set by other bodies, such as that of Independent Expert on the Question of Human Rights and Extreme Poverty Magdalena Sepúlveda Carmona, who operates under the auspices of the UN Human Rights Council. In a recent report on cash-transfer programs, Sepúlveda Carmona outlines the obligations of states to implement and ensure that cash-transfer programs reach the most vulnerable and excluded members of a society (UN Human Rights Council 2009). Among those considered most vulnerable are children, although because children are often not treated as subjects of rights, evaluations of cash-transfer programs are "very often not adequately child-focused" (2009, para. 77).[4]

THE CRISIS OF CHILD POVERTY IN THE UNITED STATES

Child Poverty Rates and Characteristics

Although many children thrive in the United States, persistent inequalities related to race, social class, gender, and regional location undermine the human security and well-being of a large proportion of children. Child and family poverty are intimately entwined. In 2009, a family of four was considered poor by the federal government if its income for that year was less than $22,050; for a family of three, the poverty threshold was $18,310. It is important to emphasize that the poverty rate for U.S. children is greater than the overall poverty rate for the nation as a whole. Whereas in 2009 the overall rate was 14.3% (43.6 million people), for children less than eighteen years of age the rate was 20.7% (15.5 million children) (U.S. Census Bureau 2010, 16). Children accounted for 35.5% of those in poverty in 2009, whereas they were only 24.5% of the U.S. population (U.S. Census Bureau 2010, 16).

Conditions look even worse for U.S. children when one examines their rate of extreme poverty, defined as living below 50% of the poverty income threshold. In 2009, almost 7 million of the nation's 15.5 million

---

4   Based on available research, Sepúlveda Carmona underscores that the impact of cash-transfer programs on children living in poor households is influenced by: the volume of transfers; the extent to which the program is child-oriented; who controls transfers within the household; and the availability of complementary social services (2009, para. 82). The Committee on the Rights of the Child, and other committees such as those monitoring CERD, CEDAW, the Convention on the Rights of Persons with Disabilities, and ICESCR, would be well served to require fuller responses from states' parties as to their efforts to use cash-transfer programs to address vulnerable and marginalized children's right to an adequate standard of living.

impoverished children were extremely poor. Children's extreme poverty rate was 9.3%. That year, children comprised 36.3% of those living on less than 50% of the poverty line (U.S. Census Bureau 2010, table 6, 18). Such numbers are particularly striking when considering the fact that families are estimated to need an annual income that is twice the poverty threshold in order to meet their basic needs (Wight, Chou, and Aratani 2011). That would be $44,100 for a family of four, an impossible income to achieve for millions of families given structural conditions such as declining wages, high unemployment rates, and the rising cost of housing and health care.

Poverty conditions for children have been deteriorating in recent years in the United States, particularly since the "Great Recession" began in December 2007 (Neubeck 2011). For example, the numbers of poor children increased by 33% between 2000 and 2009, such that by 2009 there were almost 4 million more poor children in the United States, and extreme poverty rates among children rose from 7% in 2000 to more than 9% in 2009 (Wight et al. 2011).

As has often been pointed out, lone-mother-headed families are far more likely to be poor than families two-parent households. In 2009, the poverty rate for children in married-couple households was 11%, whereas in female-headed households it was more than 44% (U.S. Census Bureau 2010, 16). In large part, this is due to the economic challenges facing lone mothers in the labor market, where women are less likely to be employed than men and more likely to earn less when they are employed (Casey, Fata, Orloff, and Ragu 2009). Most members of lone-mother-headed families are children. Moreover, poverty rates are highest among young children. In 2009, more than half of U.S. children who were under age six and lived with only their mother were poor (Kaufmann, 2011).

Children of color are far more likely to be poor than white children, pointing to the effects of structural and institutional racism and uneven access to opportunities and resources, in some cases over generations. In 2009, 12% of white children lived below the poverty line, whereas 36% of black children, 33% of Latino children, and 34% of Native American children lived in poor households (Wight et al. 2011). Immigrant children, many of whom are children of color, had a poverty rate of 27% in 2009 and were a third more likely than those with native-born parents to be poor (Wight et al. 2011).

Given the disproportionate representation of children of color living under the poverty threshold, ignoring economic and social human rights obligations is an especially notable expression of U.S. human rights indifference. Although the United States is party to CERD, in its most recent review by the committee (Committee on the Elimination of Racial Discrimination 2008), no mention was made of the disproportionate experience of poverty and hunger faced by children of ethnic and racial minority groups. The committee's critical remarks focused on structural inequalities in access to quality education, efforts to promote desegregation, and a range of civil rights issues, including high incarceration rates of children of color. It also tackled the question of access to decent and affordable housing and health care, yet the committee was silent on issues of the intersection of race, poverty, and social exclusion, not only for children but also for adults.

Comparing Child Poverty Rates Cross-Nationally

The crisis of poverty for children in the United States is underscored by comparisons with other wealthy developed nations (Neubeck 2006b). For example, data from the Luxembourg Income Study (LIS) of fifteen Western nations found that U.S. children in lone-mother-headed families, when compared to similar families in other nations, had the highest rate of poverty based on the percentage of children living in households with incomes below 50% of the national median. Moreover, the United States had the highest percentage of extremely or severely poor children among the fifteen nations (Rainwater and Smeeding 2003a; see also Rainwater and Smeeding 2003b). LIS researchers using larger numbers of nations for their comparisons of child poverty rates have come up with similar findings (Gornick and Jantti 2009).

In 2007, UNICEF published a "report card" on overall child well-being in "rich countries," focusing on twenty-five nations in the Organisation for Economic Co-operation and Development (OECD) (UNICEF 2007). One of the items measured for each nation was material well-being. The latter measure was based on the percentage of children in homes with incomes below 50% of the national median; the percentage of children in homes where no adult was employed; and the percentage of children reporting low family affluence, few educational resources, and fewer than ten books in the home. The United States ranked seventeenth out of the twenty-five OECD nations on overall material well-being. However, it ranked at the bottom of the list of nations when it came to the percentage of children in households with incomes below 50% of the national median (UNICEF 2007).

U.S. Child Poverty Is Not Adequately Addressed by Government

Although poverty levels experienced by children in the United States have generally been found to be among the highest, if not the highest, of those in affluent industrialized nations, U.S. government policies that would greatly reduce or eliminate child poverty are weak. Let us look briefly at two key government programs bearing on the poverty circumstances and economic and social human rights of U.S. children.

Temporary Assistance for Needy Families

Recall that in 2009 the poverty rate for children in the United States was 20.7%, meaning that 15.5 million children were living under the official poverty threshold that year. However, the principal government income assistance program for impoverished families, Temporary Assistance for Needy Families (TANF), came nowhere near addressing these children's needs, not to mention the millions of children who were considered "near poor" (having family incomes less than 25% above the poverty line). Although 15.5 million children lived in poverty in 2009 and 7 million of those lived in extreme poverty, TANF provided income assistance to a monthly average of only 3.1 million children that year (U.S. Department of Health and Human Services, 2011). Not only does the program fail to serve almost half of the children eligible for support, it is also insufficient for meeting the basic needs of those who do receive cash assistance. In all but five states, TANF cash-assistance transfers fail to lift children (and their families) out of extreme poverty (Urban Institute, n.d.).[5]

Disaggregating data related to TANF-funded social transfers (cash assistance) by state reveals considerable discrimination toward children on the basis of state residence, a clear violation of the principle of nondiscrimination considered fundamental to the CRC. Whitaker (2001) points to the extreme inequalities of support for children in the United States depending upon the state in which the child resides. He notes that state discretion in "implementing the TANF program has resulted in a program that treats poor families with children quite differently across state lines," emphasizing that "children are especially vulnerable in many Southern states, which have significantly poorer outcomes for children than their counterparts in the Northeast and the West" (2001, 147). Whitaker's study provides important insight into the consequences of extreme

---

[5]   Alaska, California, Delaware, Minnesota, Tennessee, and Virginia all provide levels of assistance to lift children and families out of extreme poverty.

federalism and devolution of key social welfare policies, but he does not disaggregate data further by race, gender, and immigration status. If these factors are taken into account, then the disparities compound not only along regional lines but also on the basis of social group membership.

"Welfare" for the very poor was created under the Social Security Act of 1935 as a means-tested, federal-state funded entitlement program. The "entitlement" to cash assistance and other forms of support, including transportation and child care subsidies and educational training programs, was ended by welfare reform legislation adopted by Congress in 1996 (Neubeck 2006b). The Personal Responsibility and Work Opportunity Reconciliation Act of 1996 (PRWORA) subjected recipients to new eligibility standards, including stringent work requirements for adults and strict time limits for families who received aid. PRWORA eliminated the requirement that states assist all families who are income-eligible for welfare by giving the individual states a great deal of autonomy and discretion in this regard. States quickly began cutting the welfare rolls. They discouraged new TANF applications, routinely "sanctioned" recipients for TANF rule violations and dropped them off the rolls, and established eligibility time limits for income assistance that ranged from five to as little as two years (Neubeck 2006b).

Enrollment of families in TANF dropped precipitously with the implementation of PRWORA. Between 1995 and 2008, the number of children supported by TANF fell from 9 million to 3 million. By 2008, fewer than a quarter of the children who economically qualified for TANF assistance actually received it, down from 62% in 1995 (Legal Momentum 2009b) Nor is there any national standard for the income assistance provided under TANF. Under PRWORA, states are allowed to determine not only whether and to whom to extend assistance, but also the amount that families are eligible to receive. In all but one state, a family of three (most often a mother and two children) receives assistance of less than $8 per day, and the assistance is less than $5 per day in thirty states (Legal Momentum 2009c). There is great variation in income benefits by state, and the average benefit for a family nationally is only 29% of the official poverty threshold (Legal Momentum 2009a).

Finally, it is important to note that TANF is a one-size-fits-all program. PRWORA does not require states to adapt TANF eligibility requirements or time limits to the characteristics of those in need of assistance. The diversity of the poverty population essentially goes unrecognized and ignored. This diversity includes impoverished adults and children who are able-bodied versus challenged by disabilities; urban versus rural dwellers; immigrants versus native born; documented immigrants versus undocumented; housed versus homeless; tribal members living on Indian reservations versus those living off Indian reservations; and those whose sexuality or identity is straight versus those who are lesbian, gay, bisexual, transgender, or queer (Neubeck 2006b).

Adding to this diversity, one of the fastest-growing segments of the TANF rolls is *child-only* cases, parental and nonparental caregiving households in which only the child is eligible for TANF (Anthony, Vu, and Austin 2008). The growth in cases where only children are eligible for cash assistance under TANF is due to adult caregivers no longer receiving cash assistance due to eligibility time limits, having been sanctioned and removed from the TANF rolls for program rule violations, [6] because their immigration status renders them ineligible for TANF assistance, or because they are receiving assistance from another source (such as Federal Supplemental Security Income for people with disabilities). In many cases, children are being reared by kin other than their parents, often by grandparents. Children in such households often have even fewer resources to support and ensure their well-being than households in which adults are also on the TANF rolls (Anthony et al. 2008). Grandparents are typically on a limited low income that barely supports them, and the TANF child-only payments do not add enough to adequately provide for the added expenses of supporting a child. Child-only cases have markedly increased as a proportion of the TANF rolls even as the overall rolls have been dramatically decreasing.

Supplemental Nutrition Assistance Program

Family impoverishment is often accompanied by food insecurity and hunger. This can be particularly serious for children, as they are vulnerable to problems stemming from nutrition that is inadequate for their physical and mental development. The principal government program created to address food insecurity is the Supplemental Nutrition Assistance Program (SNAP), more popularly known as Food Stamps. Access to SNAP benefits by low-income families is far greater than is the case

---

[6] One example of such an effect is the lifetime ban on accessing TANF for recipients who are convicted of drug offenses. The American Civil Liberties Union has attempted to challenge laws enacted at the state level that require random drug testing of those receiving cash assistance. See ACLU, "Welfare Drug Testing," accessed at http://www. aclu.org/drugpolicy/testing/10757res20030415.html, April 10, 2009.

for TANF. SNAP is a federal means-tested entitlement program that theoretically is available to anyone who meets income criteria.[7]

In general, people with incomes below 130% of the official poverty threshold are entitled to SNAP benefits, although most recipients are living below that threshold. In 2009, 33.5 million people received assistance purchasing food through SNAP (U.S. Department of Agriculture 2010). Eighty-six percent of SNAP households lived in poverty that year, and 42% lived in extreme poverty. Of the 33.5 million people served by SNAP in 2009, 47% or 15.7 million were children (U.S. Department of Agriculture 2010). Although these statistics would suggest that the SNAP program is providing comprehensive coverage and meeting the food needs of low-income and poverty-stricken children, in reality about a third of those who are eligible are still not being served (Food Research and Action Center 2011). Whereas some poor families may reject reliance on SNAP as "taking welfare," far more are unaware that they are income-eligible for this program. In part, this is due to states' insufficient outreach to and education of low-income families, although this is changing (Biggerstaff, McGrath Morris, and Nichols-Casebolt 2002).

Moreover, the actual benefits provided under SNAP are meager. SNAP provides monthly benefits that average out to little more than $1 per meal per person, making it very difficult for impoverished families to purchase the fruit, vegetables, and protein necessary for a child's healthy diet. Many such families find that they must turn to food pantries or soup kitchens because they have run out of food before the end of the month (Food Research and Action Center 2011; U.S. Conference of Mayors 2010).

Despite the benefits provided to millions of impoverished households and their children by SNAP, food insecurity remains a major problem in the United States. In 2009, the federal government found that almost 15% of U.S. households, or 17.4 million people, were *food insecure*, meaning that they had trouble at some point during the year providing enough food for household members. This is the highest number of people suffering food insecurity since the federal government began systematically gathering data in 1995. In 2009, children were food insecure in 4.2 million households or 10.6% of all U.S. households with children. Higher than average food-insecurity rates were found to exist for households

---

[7] Government-subsidized food stamps have been around on and off since 1939 and the Great Depression, but were only permanently made available as an entitlement program under the Food Stamp Act of 1964. The Food and Nutrition Act of 2008 changed the food stamp program's name to SNAP.

near or below the poverty threshold, in single-parent households, and in households whose members were African American or Latino. Low-income households with children were more likely to be food insecure than those without children (Nord et al. 2010, tables 5 and 6).

In 2011, conservative members of the U.S. House of Representatives introduced a bill called the Welfare Reform Act of 2011 (H.R. 1167). Its provisions include a requirement that single-parent households with dependent children work or receive training for a minimum of 120 hours per month in order to be eligible for SNAP benefits. Noncompliance would lead to loss of SNAP benefits for the entire family unit (U.S. House of Representatives 2011). The bill's work requirements resemble those of the PRWORA, and if the bill is ever passed by Congress, it is likely to exacerbate rather than help solve the conditions of food insecurity that are endemic and that afflict millions of children in the United States.

HOW OTHER NATIONS ADDRESS CHILD POVERTY

What are some of the key policies implemented by affluent nations whose child poverty rate is lower – in some cases significantly lower – than that of the United States? Three types of policies appear to be of central importance (this section relies heavily on Neubeck, 2006b). First, many affluent nations have robust income-transfer policies (direct income assistance or tax benefits) that help families economically, regardless of their structure or composition. Second, many such nations provide free or subsidized services to low-income families (e.g., health care, child care) from which children as well as adults benefit. Third, many affluent nations have "family friendly" policies in place (regulating pay, working hours, leave) that are supportive of women who are balancing employment with parenting responsibilities.[8]

As we have seen, the United States does not consider impoverished children and their families to have any entitlement to welfare. The road out of poverty is largely framed by the U.S. government and political elites as an individual's personal responsibility. In contrast, most affluent

---

[8]   The United Kingdom stands out as recently having taken particularly proactive steps to reduce its child poverty levels. Reacting to the United Kingdom's failure to reach child poverty-reduction goals set by Parliament in the late 1990s, Parliament passed the Child Poverty Act of 2010. The Act, which passed with multiparty support, calls for establishment of a Child Poverty Commission and sets forth strategies for the elimination of child poverty by the year 2020 (Parliament of United Kingdom 2010). The United States has no similar plans on the horizon.

European nations, to use an example, consider income assistance that reduces exposure to poverty a right of citizenship if not a basic human right. Data from the LIS have shown that children in affluent European nations, particularly children of lone mothers, benefit greatly from income-transfer policies and the help they provide in mitigating poverty (Rainwater and Smeeding 2003a).

Income-transfer policies take a variety of forms, including annual cash child allowances to help families provide for their children; child support assistance for lone mothers when their children's fathers are unable or unwilling to pay; and generous unemployment insurance benefits with few eligibility or time-limit restrictions (Neubeck 2006b). Most income-transfer assistance is available to all families. Lone-mother-headed families are neither unnecessarily singled out nor are they highly stigmatized and demonized for "dependency on the dole," as has historically been the case for so-called welfare mothers in the United States (Neubeck 2001; Neubeck 2006a).

Just as in the United States, many European mothers, particularly lone mothers, find that they must be employed in order to help support their families. Unlike many affluent European nations, the U.S. government has failed to devote resources sufficient to meet the need for subsidized child care, which can be a major expense for mothers who are employed. Given that impoverished recipients of TANF must meet work requirements or lose eligibility for cash assistance, the shortage of child care is a major impediment to staying on the TANF rolls.

Nor does the United States have a national health care system that provides free or low-cost preventive care and medical treatment for all, as is the case in virtually every other affluent industrialized nation. Low-income families and children are eligible for Medicaid, created in 1965 through an amendment to the Social Security Act. This joint federal-state–funded means-tested program is administered by individual states. The states set the eligibility threshold for participation, and have been finding ways to exclude low-income participants due to rising health care costs and the lingering negative impact of the Great Recession on state budgets. Many impoverished children are able to get assistance through Medicaid under a program known as the Children's Health Insurance Program (CHIP). In 2009, CHIP covered more than two-thirds of children living in poverty, but less than half of all low-income children (Kaiser Family Foundation 2010). Clearly, the lack of universal health-insurance coverage poses heavy economic and other burdens on many impoverished families and their children. Poor children and adults are more likely to be ill, lack health care, and die prematurely than their more affluent counterparts in the United States. In 2008, the United States ranked in the bottom quartile in life expectancy among thirty OECD nations (Anderson and Squires 2010).

Finally, affluent European nations often provide family friendly policies that support women who must be in the labor force. These policies, when supplemented by income-transfer policies and free or low-cost services, comprise a "package" that contributes to the reduction of child poverty rates and supports children in a variety of different ways. Working mothers, for example, are often eligible for extended, and usually paid, maternal and post-maternal parental leave without penalty from their employers. In a number of affluent European nations, no discrimination between part-time and full-time work is permitted when it comes to rates of pay and benefits, a boon to mothers who must or prefer to work part-time. There is also a tradition of extended vacation time in European nations, which provides working mothers with generous opportunities to be with their children. The United States offers limited opportunities for (unpaid) parental or family leave, allows employers to discriminate in pay rates and benefits between full- and part-time workers, and leaves vacation decisions up to employers (who typically allow workers very little time off).

U.S. OPPOSITION TO THE CRC AND ARTICLE 27

The United States is often characterized by human rights advocates as an "outlier" or as "exceptionalist," due to its failure to join other nations in ratifying such major human rights treaties as the ICESCR, CEDAW, and the CRC (Libal and Hertel 2011; Schulz 2009). Although President William J. Clinton ordered the secretary of state to sign the CRC in 1995, thus signaling U.S. government interest in joining other nations in addressing children's rights, ratification of the CRC was blocked by conservative members of the U.S. Senate Foreign Relations Committee (Blanchfield 2009; Cook 2009). As one of only two UN member states that have failed to join the CRC, the term "outlier" certainly seems appropriate to apply to the United States.

The near-universal endorsement of the CRC's principles and standards arguably renders the United States subject to its norms as a matter of "customary international law." Interestingly, the United States played a major role in crafting many of the CRC's provisions (Todres 2006). Much of what is included in the CRC is already a matter of law, policy, and practice at U.S. federal and state levels of government. In at least some policy areas, the United States could easily serve as a model for ratifying nations whose actual implementation of the CRC's provisions is lagging (Todres 2011). Thus, it is significant that U.S. ratification of the CRC remains highly and successfully contested. Some observers argue that, of all the human rights treaties that the United States has yet to ratify, the CRC is the one least likely to receive U.S. Senate support at any time in the foreseeable future (Weissbrodt 2006).

There are a number of reasons that ratification of the CRC continues to be strongly resisted (Todres 2006, 2011; Rutkow and Lozman 2006). Oddly enough, none of them directly address Article 27, the right of all children to an adequate standard of living. Here we briefly review issues commonly raised by CRC opponents, who are primarily political and religious conservatives (Smolin 2006; Cook 2009).

Threats to U.S. Sovereignty

Some of the fundamental objections to ratification of the CRC are basically the same as conservative objections to U.S. ratification of other major human rights treaties and international treaties in general. CRC opponents argue that with ratification the United States, a sovereign nation, would lose control over its own affairs and become subject to the decision-making power of international bodies, such as treaty-monitoring committees of the United Nations (Blanchfield 2009). UN member nations hold membership on such committees, meaning that foreign nationals, who may not share the political and moral values that prevail in the United States, would be in a position to influence if not dictate internal U.S. policies regarding the treatment of children.

Undermining U.S. System of Federalism

Opponents of the CRC, similar to opponents of other treaties, point to the important role that the federalist system plays within the United States (Blanchfield 2009). Under the U.S. Constitution and rulings by the U.S. Supreme Court, the power of the federal government has been limited in ways that leave a good deal of legislative, judicial, and executive power in the hands of the individual states. This is certainly the case with many current policies and practices regarding the protection and treatment of children. CRC's opponents fear the loss of states' rights were the CRC to be ratified, as under the U.S. Constitution international treaties, once ratified, are the "law of the land." All branches of state and local government as well as the federal government must conform to provisions of ratified international treaties, which trump existing domestic laws, including existing laws affecting children.

Ironically, some liberal proponents of the CRC could be accused of playing into the hands of conservatives by suggesting that states' rights could simply be protected by Senate ratification of the CRC with "reservations, understandings, and declarations" (an option suggested by Todres 2006, 31). Reservations, understandings, and declarations (RUDS) have been attached to the three core human rights treaties that the United States has thus far ratified.[9] In essence, those RUDS state that the United States is ratifying the given treaty with the understanding that individual states will continue to retain their existing legal powers and authority over those matters the treaty provisions affect. Without the protection of RUDs, states, for example, would not be allowed to continue to house child and adult prisoners together or imprison children for life without chance of parole or allow corporal punishment to be administered in schools.

U.S. ratification of these human rights treaties has also been based on the requirement that they not be *self-executing*, meaning that federal and state legislation is necessary for any of the treaty's provisions to be enforceable by the courts. Together with various RUDs, a statement disallowing treaty self-execution has been attached to each of the human rights treaties the United States has ratified to date. In this way, whereas the nation appears to be a champion of human rights, in practice it is avoiding being held fully subject to these treaties' provisions under international law (Schulz 2009; Venetis 2011).

Encroachment on the Rights of Parents

One of the most emotionally driven and successful arguments of CRC opponents relates to what they see as the treaty's erosion of parents' rights when it comes to rearing their children (Fagan 2001; www.parentalrights. org). CRC's focus on the rights of children raises conservatives' fears that the child's rights will be elevated above those of his or her parents, a

---

[9] These are the International Covenant on Civil and Political Rights, Convention against Torture and Other Cruel, Inhuman, or Degrading Treatment or Punishment, and the International Convention on the Elimination of All Forms of Racial Discrimination. The United States has also ratified the Convention on the Prevention and Punishment of the Crime of Genocide and the 1967 Protocol Relating to the Status of Refugees.

fear reinforced by the fact that parents' own rights vis-à-vis their children are not directly addressed by the CRC. Opponents suggest the CRC empowers children, which in a zero-sum game way of thinking means disempowering parents.

Conservatives are also concerned that the CRC fails to adequately acknowledge children's immaturity, their limited understanding of the meaning of human rights, and the likelihood they will not know how and when to appropriately exercise such rights. Opponents portray parents being rendered powerless as their children proceed to demand their rights as if they are as capable as adults, but then make impulsive and poor decisions with harmful and irreversible results for their own and others' lives (Fagan 2001).

Finally, there is concern that the CRC will essentially mean the transformation and breakdown of the traditional family, by which conservatives mean a legally married heterosexual couple – mother and father – who are rearing children born within wedlock. If children are accorded rights that mean they are no longer required to abide by the behavioral rules and moral norms of their parents, the fear is that traditional lines of authority within the family will break down, parental socialization of their children will suffer disruption, and children will grow out of control and prone to ever more serious forms of deviant behavior (Fagan 2001). Opponents of the CRC typically suggest that the decay and breakdown of the traditional family structure will inevitably undermine the functioning of society as a whole. The need to hold on to the traditional family structure at all costs is a common conservative mantra.

Reproductive and Family Planning Concerns

Perhaps the most visceral conservative opposition comes from those who regard the CRC as a threat on matters of abortion and contraception (Fagan 2001; www.parentalrights.org). The CRC appears neutral on these topics, leaving policies up to individual nations to handle as they see fit. Nonetheless, conservatives believe that CRC advocates have a hidden agenda of promoting "the right to abortion" (a phrase CRC's opponents systematically privilege over "a woman's right to choose").

By now, the reader may be wondering where economic and social human rights fit in to the broad litany of concerns expressed by CRC's U.S. opponents. The manifest objections to the CRC seem to ignore Article 27 and children's right to an adequate standard of living (Taylor 2006), for reasons unknown. This does not mean that conservative hostility to the notion of economic and social human rights in the case of children is nonexistent. When it comes to economic and social human rights in general, the United States has either refused to ratify relevant treaties or largely ignored economic and social rights provisions in those it has ratified (e.g., CERD) (Thornberry 2005). Thus, it is likely that critiques of the economic and social human rights provisions in the CRC would be made into an issue by conservative opponents were the CRC to become subject to Senate debate over ratification. For now, with their other message strategies working, that is not a weapon that CRC opponents have felt a need to engage yet.

CONCLUSION

Some children's rights advocates in the United States have begun to reinvigorate a movement for CRC ratification in the past five years (Todres 2011; Libal, Mapp, Ihrig, and Ron 2011). Although discussions of children's economic and social rights have not been central to this movement (Imig 2006), working to build a broader coalition of support for ratification may present an opportunity to shape a new public discourse on children's economic and social rights (Cook 2009).

Adoption and implementation of the CRC require a marked shift in the idea of childhood. The treaty enjoins states to recognize children as rights holders themselves, rather than as mere objects of philanthropic concern or parental or state guardianship. The idea of children as both beneficiaries of state provision and as individuals with at least a limited capacity to make claims on the state for the realization of their rights is a challenging innovation. Ambivalence about what kind of citizen a child is and establishing mechanisms to recognize the claims of children as legitimate is evident in both social policy and juridical practices in the United States. Legal scholar Jacqueline Bhabha (2006) argues that children (minors under the age of eighteen) are treated within U.S. law as inchoate citizens, and often are not able to make recognized claims for protection and provision. They are at once idealized and sentimentalized as the bearers of special entitlements to protection, even as the actual guarantees for children who are particularly disadvantaged or poor remain quite weak.

As agents or claim makers in their own rights, children face substantial barriers to individually or collectively advocating for adequate and nondiscriminatory access to schooling, for policy change concerning health care, and basic income supports and in-kind services (such as Food

Stamps, WIC, and so forth). Is it reasonable to expect children to be able to make effective claims for more robust entitlements, when few avenues for mobilizing the collective voices of their caregivers have gained the attention of key political leaders and policy makers in recent years?[10]

These barriers point to the need for a revitalized children's human rights movement that necessarily involves a range of actors, including practitioners who work regularly with children and their families (social workers, doctors, nurses, day care providers and preschool teachers, elementary and secondary teachers, academics, etc.), human rights and social justice activists, lawyers, and political leaders, as well as to the extent possible, a mobilization of allies within faith communities, community organizations, and low-income and middle-class Americans. A revitalized movement could challenge not only the stereotypical portrayals of individuals on public assistance (welfare), but also the real barriers to lifting a family from poverty in the U.S. economic system. It would entail grappling with racism, classism, and sexism in a more meaningful way than focusing primarily on prejudice that is exhibited between individuals.

Enlisting the support of prominent nongovernmental organizations to examine economic and social rights violations experienced by children in the United States more carefully is an important step. In general, prominent human rights, civil rights, and feminist organizations in the United States have not prioritized the economic and social rights of children. A notable exception to this can be seen in the work of the National Economic and Social Rights Initiative, but this group is relatively new and the effects of its advocacy have yet to be felt widely in the United States.

Leading professional associations, such as the American Medical Association, the American Bar Association, the National Association of Social Workers, and teachers' unions have historically been committed to the U.S. ratification of the CRC. These organizations, which have very large membership bases, have not engaged advancing the economic and social rights of children in a way that builds visibility (with the possible exception of children's rights to access adequate health care). Issues of hunger, homelessness, and adequate schooling for all children remain largely "invisible" to the broader public, and these associations could be doing much more to amplify their advocacy on behalf of children's economic and social rights.

---

[10] See the work of the Kensington Welfare Rights Union, the Poor People's Economic Human Rights Campaign, as well as grassroots efforts to mobilize homeless and displaced persons in the aftermath of Hurricane Katrina.

Yet even without or prior to U.S. ratification of the CRC, much can be done to implement policies at a state and federal level that adhere to human rights principles vis-à-vis economic and social rights for children. Advocates shaping policy, public interest lawyers, and professionals involved in the apparatuses of child protection and providing (limited) supports to low-income families and children can and should engage the corpus of human rights law and standards set at the international level to address the social and economic rights of children in the United States. Such work is already taking place at the municipal level in Chicago, Illinois, and at the state level in Hawaii (Kaufman 2011).

Moreover, fuller engagement of children's rights advocates with the CERD review process, as well as ongoing engagement with the Human Rights Council through the Universal Periodic Review process and other special investigative efforts, stands to further embed the idea that children in the United States have economic and social rights that the government is failing to meet. Indeed, Aber et al. (2010) argue that U.S. ratification and implementation of the CRC would provide a tool for reducing child poverty in the United States "if and only if they can be used to promote change in the political economy of children's issues in the United States" (2010, 160). Central to transforming that political economy regarding the rights of children must be a recognition of the enduring effects of structural racism and inequality that continue to shape the face of child poverty in the United States.[11] In the United States, this may mean working through treaty-monitoring processes before the Committee on the Elimination of Racial Discrimination or the Human Rights Committee to tackle linked issues of poverty and racial discrimination experienced by children of color.

More generally, this chapter has sought to call attention to the importance of examining child poverty as a core human rights concern, not only in developing countries, but also in countries with ostensibly the greatest capacity to respect, protect, and fulfill the human rights of children. The CRC, which has been in force for more than twenty years,

---

[11]   Aber et al. (2010) give an intriguing analysis that draws upon comparisons with other Anglophone countries that have implemented the CRC. They argue that joining the CRC has not provided sufficient impetus to address child poverty in the United Kingdom, Canada, or Australia to date. Unfortunately, their analysis does not take up the question of racial disparities and the experience of child poverty in the United States or other Anglophone countries. Addressing structural racism and the disproportionate experience of poverty by children of color in the United States is a crucial element in changing "the political economy of children's issues" (Aber et al. 2010, 160).

has played a foundational role in "fostering positive changes in law, policy, and attitudes toward children in numerous countries" (Todres 2011, 132). Although the Committee on the Rights of the Child has been active in investigating and setting standards on many children's rights issues, it has not focused extensively on the implementation of Article 27. Better coordination with the committees charged with monitoring ICESCR, CEDAW, and ICERD would be an important step in addressing child poverty and children's rights to an adequate standard of living. Another step would be to develop a general comment on Article 27 that articulates children's rights to an adequate standard of living. This general comment would present an opportunity to underscore insights of other committees on how to best implement social assistance programs that assure the economic and social rights of children, and highlight some of the disparate (and too often brief) discussions on fulfilling the most basic standard of living for young children and children belonging to marginalized and disadvantaged groups as core obligations of states (see, e.g., *General Comment 7* [2005] and *General Comment 13* [2011]). In light of ongoing restructuring and reduction of social welfare supports for low-income families and evidence of declining economic fortunes of children in the United States (Lim, Yoo, and Page 2010) and other countries that arguably have the capacity to effectively eliminate child poverty within their borders, such renewed attention in the coming decade is warranted.

REFERENCES

Aber, J.L., A.S. Hammond, and S.M. Thompson, 2010. "U.S. ratification of the CRC and reducing child poverty: Can we get there from here?" *Child Welfare* 89(5): 159–175.

Anderson, G.F. and D.A. Squires, 2010. "Measuring the U.S. health care system: A cross-national comparison. Commonwealth Fund," *Issues in International Health Policy*, June.

Anthony, E.K., C.M. Vu, and M.J. Austin, 2008. "TANF child-only cases: Identifying the characteristics and needs of children living in low-income families," *Journal of Children and Poverty* 14(1): 1–20.

Bhabha, J., 2006. "The child – What sort of human?" *PMLA* 121(5): 1526–1535.

Biggerstaff, M.A., P. McGrath Morris, and A. Nichols-Casebolt, 2002. "Living on the edge: Examination of people attending food pantries and soup kitchens," *Social Work*, 47(3): 267–277.

Blanchfield, L., 2009. *The United Nations Convention on the Rights of the Child: Background and policy issues*, Washington, DC: Congressional Research Service.

Carvalho, E., 2008. "Measuring children's rights: An alternative approach," *International Journal of Children's Rights* 16: 545–563.

Casey, T., S. Fata, L. Orloff, and M. Raghu, 2009. *TANF reauthorization round II: An opportunity to improve the safety net for women and children*, New York: Legal Momentum.

Cook, D.T., 2009. "Ratifying the Convention amidst the messy cultural politics of American childhood (editorial)," *Childhood* 16(4): 435–439.

Ensalaco, M., 2005. "The right of the child to development," in M. Ensalaco and L.C. Majka (Eds.) *Children's human rights: Progress and challenges for children worldwide*, 9–29, Lanham, MA: Rowman & Littlefield Publishers, Inc.

Ensalaco, M. and L.C. Majka (Eds.), 2005. *Children's human rights: Progress and challenges for children worldwide*, Lanham, MA: Rowman & Littlefield Publishers, Inc.

Fagan, P.F., 2001. "How U.N. conventions on women's and children's rights undermine family, religion, and sovereignty," Heritage Foundation *Backgrounder*, No. 1407, February 5, 1–21.

Federal Interagency Forum on Child and Family Statistics, 2009. "America's children: Key national indicators of well-being." Retrieved from http://www.childstats.gov/americaschildren/eco.asp.

Food Research and Action Center, 2011. Retrieved from http://frac.org/.

Gornick, J.C. and M. Jantti, 2009. "Child poverty in upper-income countries: Lessons from the Luxembourgh Income Study" in S.B. Kamerman, S. Phipps, and A. Ben-Arieh (Eds.) *From child welfare to child well-being: An international perspective on knowledge in the service of policy making*, 339–370, New York: Springer.

Imig, D., 2006. "Building a social movement for America's children," *Journal of Children and Poverty* 12(1): 21–37.

Kaiser Family Foundation, 2010. *The uninsured, a primer: Key facts about Americans without health insurance*, Menlo Park, CA: Kaiser Family Foundation.

Kamerman, S.B. and A.J. Kahn, 2003. "Child and family policies in an era of social policy retrenchment and restructuring," in K. Vleminckx and K.L. Smeeding (Eds.) *Child well-being, child poverty, and child policy in modern nations: What do we know?* Revised edition, 501–526, Bristol, UK: The Policy Press.

Kaufman, R., 2011. "State and local commissions as sites for domestic human rights implementation," in S. Hertel and K. Libal (Eds.) *Human rights in the United States: Beyond exceptionalism*, 89–110, New York: Cambridge University Press.

Kaufmann, G., 2011. "U.S. poverty: Past, present and future," *The Nation*, March 22.

League of Nations, 1924. *Geneva Declaration of the Rights of the Child*. Geneva: League of Nations.

Legal Momentum, 2009a. *Advocate for an improved safety net for women and children: An agenda for TANF reform*, New York: Women's Legal Defense and Education Fund.

Legal Momentum, 2009b. *The bitter fruit of welfare reform: A sharp drop in the percentage of eligible women and children receiving welfare*, New York: Women's Legal Defense and education Fund.

Legal Momentum, 2009c. *Meager and diminishing welfare benefits perpetu-ate widespread material hardship for poor women and children*, New York: Women's Legal Defense and Education Fund.

Libal, K. and S. Hertel, 2011. "Paradoxes and possibilities: Domestic human rights policy in context," in S. Hertel and K. Libal (Eds.) *Human rights in the United States: Beyond exceptionalism*, 1–22, New York/London: Cambridge University Press.

Libal, K., S.C. Mapp, E. Ihrig, and A.L. Ron, 2011. "The United Nations Conven-tion on the Rights of the Child: Children can wait no longer for their rights," *Social Work* 56(4): 367–370.

Lim, Y., J. Yoo, and T. Page, 2010. "Losing ground: The persistent declining economic fortunes of children," *Journal of Children and Poverty* 16(2): 145–160.

Majka, L. C. and M. Ensalaco, 2005. Introduction: "A human rights based approach to the needs of children," in M. Ensalaco and L.C. Majka (Eds.) *Children's human rights: Progress and challenges for children worldwide*, 1–7, Lanham, MA: Rowman & Littlefield Publishers, Inc.

Neubeck, K., 2011. "Human rights violations as obstacles to escaping poverty: The case of lone mother-headed families," in S. Hertel and K. Libal (Eds.) *Human rights in the United States: Beyond exceptionalism*, 234–254, New York: Cambridge University Press.

Neubeck, K.J., 2006a. "Welfare racism and human rights," in R.E. Howard-Hassmann and C.E. Welch, Jr. (Eds.) *Economic rights in Canada and the United States*, 87–102, Philadelphia: University of Pennsylvania Press.

Neubeck, K.J., 2006b. *When welfare disappears: The case for economic human rights*, New York: Routledge.

Neubeck, K.J., 2001. *Welfare racism: Playing the race card against America's poor*, New York: Routledge.

Nord, M., A. Coleman-Jensen, M. Andrews, and S. Carlson, 2010. *Household food security in the United States, 2009*, Washington, DC: U.S. Department of Agriculture, Economic Research Service.

Parliament of United Kingdom, 2010. *Child Poverty Act 2010*. Retrieved from http://www.legislation.gov.uk/ukpga/2010/9/contents.

Rainwater, L. and T.M. Smeeding, 2003a. *Poor kids in a rich country: America's children in a comparative perspective*, New York: Russell Sage Foundation.

Rainwater, L. and T.M. Smeeding, 2003b. "Doing poorly: U.S. child poverty in cross-national context," *Children, Youth and Environments* 13(2): 48–76.

Rutkow, L. and J.T. Lozman, 2006. "Suffer the children?: A call for United States ratification of the United Nations Convention on the Rights of the Child," *Harvard Human Rights Journal* 19(Spring): 161–190.

Schulz, W.F., 2009. *The power of justice: Applying international human rights norms to the United States*, Washington, DC: Center for American Progress.

Smolin, D.M., 2006. "Overcoming religious objections to the Convention on the Rights of the Child," *Emory International Law Review* 20(1): 81–110.

Taylor, C.T., 2006. "Children's right to an adequate standard of living," in J. Todres, M.E. Wojcik, and C.R. Revaz (Eds.) *The U.N. Convention on the*

Rights of the Child: An analysis of treaty provisions and implications for U.S. ratification, 237–250, Ardsley, NY: Transnational Publishers.

Thornberry, P., 2005. "Confronting racial discrimination: A CERD perspective," *Human Rights Law Review* 5(2): 239–269.

Todres, J., 2011. "At the cross-roads: Children's rights and the U.S. government," in S. Hertel and K. Libal (Eds.) *Human rights in the United States: Beyond exceptionalism*, 132–152, New York: Cambridge University Press.

Todres, J., 2006. "Analyzing the opposition to U.S. ratification of the U.N. Convention on the Rights of the Child," in J. Todres, M.E. Wojcik, and C.R. Revaz (Eds.) *The U.S. Convention on the Rights of the Child: An analysis of treaty provisions and implications of U.S. ratification*, 19–31, Ardsley, NY: Transnational Publishers.

Twill, S. and S. Fisher, 2010. "Economic human rights violations experienced by women with children in the United States," *Families in Society* 91(4): 356–362.

UN (United Nations), 1990. *United Nations Convention on the Rights of the Child*, Geneva: UN.

UN CERD (United Nations Committee on the Elimination of Racial Discrimination), 2008. Concluding observations of the Committee on the Elimination of Racial Discrimination: United States of America, CERD/C/USA/CO/6, UN: Geneva.

UN CRC (United Nations Committee on the Rights of the Child), 2011. *General Comment No. 13: The right of the child to freedom from all forms of violence*, CRC/C/GC/13, UN: Geneva.

UN CRC, 2009. *Concluding observations: Sweden*, 51st Session, CRC/C/SWE/CO/4.

UN CRC, 2007. Day of general discussion on resources for the rights of the child – responsibility of states, UN: Geneva. Retrieved from http://www2.ohchr.org/english/bodies/crc/discussion.htm.

UN CRC, 2006. *General Comment No. 9: The rights of children with disabilities*, CRC/C/GC/9, UN: Geneva.

UN CRC, 2005. *General Comment No. 7: Implementing child rights in early childhood*, CRC/C/GC/7/Rev.1, UN: Geneva.

UN CRC, 2004. *Concluding observations: Germany*, 35th Session, CRC/C/15/Add.226, UN: Geneva.

UN CRC, 2003a. *General Comment No. 5: General measures of implementation of the Convention on the Rights of the Child (arts. 4, 42 and 44, para. 6)*, CRC/GC/2003/5, UN: Geneva.

UN CRC, 2003b. *General Comment No. 3: HIV/AIDS and the rights of the child*, CRC/GC/2003/3, UN: Geneva.

UN CRC, 2001. *General Comment No. 1: Article 29(1): The aims of education*, CRC/GC/2001/1, UN: Geneva.

UN HRC (United Nations Human Rights Council), 2009. *Promotion and protection of all human rights, civil, political, economic, social and cultural rights, including the right to development. Report of the independent expert on the question of human rights and extreme poverty, Magdalena Sepúlveda Carmona*, A/HRC/AA/9, UN: Geneva.

UNICEF (United Nations Children's Fund), 2007. *Child poverty in perspective: An overview of child well-being in rich countries*, UNICEF Innocenti Research Centre: Florence, Italy.

UNICEF Innocenti Research Centre, 2006. *The general measures of the Convention on the Rights of the Child: The process in Europe and Central Asia*, UNICEF: Florence, Italy.

Urban Institute, n.d. Welfare Rules Database. Retrieved from http://anfdata.urban.org/wrd/WRDWelcome.cfm.

U.S. Census Bureau, 2010. *Income, poverty, and health insurance coverage in the United States: 2009*, Washington, DC: U.S. Government Printing Office.

U.S. Conference of Mayors, 2010. *Hunger and homelessness survey: A status report on hunger and homelessness in American cities*, Washington, DC: U.S. Conference of Mayors.

U.S. Department of Agriculture, 2010. *Characteristics of Supplemental Nutrition Assistance Program Households: Fiscal Year 2009*, Alexandria, VA: USDA Food and Nutrition Service, Office of Research and Analysis.

U.S. Department of Health and Human Services, 2011. TANF Caseload Data 2009, Administration for Children and Families. Retrieved from www.acf.hhs.gov/programs/ofa/data-reports/caseload/monthly/caseload2009.htm.

U.S. House of Representatives, 2011. *Welfare act of 2011, H.R. 1167*, 112th Congress. Retrieved from http://thomas.loc.gov.

Vandenhole, W., 2009. "Economic, social, and cultural rights in the CRC: Is there a legal obligation to cooperate internationally for development?" *International Journal of Children's Rights* 17: 23–63.

Venetis, P.M., 2011. "Making human rights treaty law actionable in the United States: The case for universal implementing legislation," *Alabama Law Review* 63(1): 97–160.

Weissbrodt, D., 2006. "Prospects for ratification of the Convention on the Rights of the Child," *Emory International Law Review* 20(1): 209–216.

Whitaker, I.P., 2001. "Unequal opportunities among unequal states: The importance of examining state characteristics in making social welfare policies regarding children," *Journal of Children and Poverty* 7(2): 145–162.

Wight, V.R., M. Chou, and Y. Aratani, 2011. *Who are America's poor children?: The official story*, New York: Columbia University, National Center for Children in Poverty.

Woodhouse, B.B., 2008. *Hidden in plain sight: The tragedy of children's rights from Ben Franklin to Lionel Tate*, Princeton, NJ: Princeton University Press.

8

Achieving Women's Economic Rights, in Policy and in Practice

Catherine Buerger

I. INTRODUCTION

In March 2010, representatives to the Commission on the Status of Women gathered in New York to assess the progress that has been made in the achievement of global women's rights. This meeting marked the 15th anniversary of the Fourth World Conference on Women, held in Beijing in 1995. Although the regional reports compiled for this fifteen-year review showed notable progress in some areas, including the development of domestic legislation, there remained a considerable gap in many countries between the de jure and de facto status of women. This was particularly evident in the categories of poverty alleviation and women's economic empowerment.[1] A lack of disaggregated data, combined with context-specific barriers as well as the historical prioritization of civil and political rights, has hindered the process of translating legal respect for women's economic rights into their fulfillment. Through considering the case study of women's employment protections and property rights in Ghana, this chapter illustrates that it is not simply a lack of legal protections that results in rights being left unfulfilled. Local information about the ways that individuals engage with these laws on an everyday basis is essential in implementing human rights-related policies. Legal reforms must be coupled with programs that account for the social, political, and cultural conditions that lead to barriers in rights attainment.

---

[1] Based on a review of the Beijing +15 Regional Synthesis Reports: Economic Commission for Africa (2009); Economic Commission for Europe (2009); Economic Commission for Latin America and the Caribbean (2009); Economic and Social Commission for Asia and the Pacific (2009); Economic and Social Commission for Western Asia (2009).

A. Women's Human Rights: A Brief History

The current state of women's economic rights has its roots in the history of the women's rights movement. Many cite The First World Conference on Women, held in Mexico in 1975, as a starting point for the entrance of women's issues into the international intergovernmental agenda (Friedman 1995). Notably, this conference also marked the start of the United Nations (UN) Decade for Women. Although women had been involved in the UN since its inception, human rights documents had mainly dealt with rights through gender-neutral language. Critics soon acknowledged that this philosophy could, however, be seen as a "double-edged instrument if it is used to punish women for failing to conform to the conventional norms expected of men" (Kaufman and Lindquist 1995, 121). If gender were to remain missing from the discussion of rights, topics such as maternity leave, pregnancy-related health care, and discrimination in employment and education would also continue to be absent in human rights documents. Although the Universal Declaration of Human Rights (UDHR) states that all individuals "are entitled without any discrimination to equal protection of the law" (UDHR, Article 7), and "everyone, without any discrimination, has the right to equal pay for equal work" (UDHR Article 23[2]), The Convention of the Elimination on All Forms of Discrimination against Women (CEDAW), which entered into force in 1981, became the first official convention to shed light on specific gender-based forms of discrimination.

Following the adoption of CEDAW, the focus on women's rights continued to grow. Advocates for women's rights at the World Conference on Human Rights, held in Vienna in 1993, turned the focus to discussing violence against women as a human rights violation. Sullivan (1994, 160) argues that this "unprecedented emphasis" on violence was "not matched by comparable attention to the denial of women's economic, social and cultural rights." Two years later, at the Fourth World Conference on Women in Beijing, the discourse surrounding women's rights was altered yet again to reflect the new push to discuss human rights as they pertain to women as opposed to just discussing women's rights (Bunch and Fried 1996). The fact that all rights were now being considered would seem to imply that greater attention was paid to social and economic issues. In reality, however, the focus still remained primarily on the topics of violence and civil and political rights (Hemment 2004).

Despite the increased attention placed on the importance of women's human rights, Apodaca's 1998 study on discrimination and achievement of social and economic rights revealed that there were still many barriers in place to the attainment of human rights for women. Although life expectancy, literacy, primary school enrollments, and rates of economic activity had increased for both men and women since 1975, the achievement gap between gender groups had only marginally closed. Rights were being slowly, progressively realized, but "the degree of discrimination against women in the enjoyment of their rights has not significantly improved" (Apodaca 1998, 151). Unfortunately, it seems little changed after Apodaca's study. When representatives from the Commission on the Status of Women met in New York in 2010 to report on the progress of women's rights, this pattern of discrimination was still evident. Synthesis reports from the regions of Africa, Europe, Latin America, Asia, and the Middle East suggested continued gender gaps in the achievement of rights for women.

B. The State of Women's Economic Rights Today

A recent development in the fight for women's human rights has come in the shape of institutional reform within the UN. In an effort to increase the cohesive promotion of gender equality throughout the UN, four previously distinct parts of the UN were combined into one overarching office, UN Women. The office became operational in January of 2011. The four agencies – the Office of the Special Adviser on Gender Issues and Advancement of Women, the Division for the Advancement of Women, the United Nations Development Fund for Women (UNIFEM), and the International Research and Training Institute for the Advancement of Women – were combined with the intention of increasing the coordination, resources, and impact of all agencies working on women's issues within the UN (UN Secretary General 2010). The centralized nature of the organization is intended to allow for a quicker flow of information between national-, regional-, and international-level offices as well as enable more efficient monitoring of the various UN entities working to advance women's issues (UN Secretary General 2010). At a press conference held following the opening of the office in January 2011, the executive director of the new organization, Ms. Michelle Bachelet, again noted the continued struggles in the comprehensive achievement of rights for women: "Ninety-six percent of the gap between women and men in the field of health and 93 percent of the gap in education have been closed; 41 percent of the disparity in economic participation and 82 percent of that in political empowerment remain to be narrowed"(UN Women 2011).

The regional synthesis reports released in 2009, describing regional progress made concerning women's rights since the Beijing Conference, shed light on another complex challenge facing women's rights advocates. Nearly all of the regions acknowledge the progress that has been made legislatively toward the achievement of women's rights through either the development of new laws or legal reform. For example, the African Synthesis Report (Economic Commission for Africa 2009, 19) states that "notable progress has been made in legal reforms and policies for gender equality and women's empowerment." At the same time, all five regional reports state that there has been difficulty in the enforcement and translation of these laws into actual equality. The difference between legislative ideals and actual experience seems particularly strong for women's economic rights; that is, the rights to an adequate standard of living, employment without discrimination, and a basic income guarantee (Hertel and Minkler 2007). Additionally, economic rights may include supporting rights such as the rights to education, fair wages, and safe working conditions. Although many countries "systematically refer to the principle of equality" within the laws and constitutions, women still earn less, are more concentrated in informal and vulnerable employment (UNIFEM 2009, 54), and lack power in economic decision making (Economic Commission for Europe 2009). The continuing gap between policy and reality suggests that although progress has been made in the respecting and protecting of women's economic rights, these rights are still not being adequately fulfilled.

There are many contributing factors to why this may be the case. One challenge facing advocates for women's economic rights is a continued lack of adequate data and measurement tools to allow for the monitoring of rights. As Chapman (2007, 151) states, without adequate measurement tools, "countries that ratify or accede to specific human rights instruments cannot assess their own performance" or be held accountable for the enforcement of rights. Although several measurement tools have been developed, researchers still struggle with a dearth of accurate data. Specifically, a lack of gender disaggregated data (Hertel and Minkler 2007) and a lack of accurate statistics about the informal economy (Sweeney 2007) have both proven to be significant barriers in precisely monitoring the achievement of women's economic rights.

Not all of the data-collection challenges stem from a lack of methodology, however. Chapman (1996, 26) notes that "currently, neither the political will nor the methodological capabilities required for effective monitoring is present." At present, there are 186 state parties to the

CEDAW. Many of these countries, however, do not have, or do not enforce, domestic legislation concerning gender discrimination (Okin 1998). This pattern was also revealed in Sweeney's (2007) study that showed no correlation between the level of national commitment to the CEDAW and women's economic rights. An additional challenge related to political will stems from the process of reporting to the Committee on the Elimination of Discrimination Against Women. Although CEDAW requires state parties to file reports noting the progress made on enforcing the Convention "(a) Within one year after the entry into force for the State concerned; (b) Thereafter at least every four years and further whenever the Committee so requests," late reporting by member countries has inhibited the process of tracking global progress (CEDAW, Article 18). In fact, by 2000, there were 242 overdue reports to CEDAW from 165 state parties (Merry 2006). Additionally, Article 20 of the Convention mandates that the Committee will meet "for a period of not more than two weeks annually" to review the reports submitted by member states (CEDAW, Article 20). The short amount of time allotted for meetings adds further obstacles to the process of considering the diverse barriers facing women around the world in their quest to claim rights.

As noted by Merry (2006) in her study of gender violence and the practices of CEDAW, context-specific social and cultural barriers are particularly difficult to fully consider within the short amount of time allowed for review by the committee, and thus present a significant challenge to the translation of large-scale policy and legislation into the fulfillment of rights. In her research concerning the development of economic and social rights indicators, Apodaca notes that although her findings reveal geographic region to be a significant predictor of women's economic and social human rights achievement, the data cannot explain why this is so. The problem of explanation is common in the literature, and "most cross-cultural human rights researchers simply accept region as an obvious category in no need of explanation" (Apodaca 1998, 164). This acceptance of a lack of explanation by researchers, however, likely limits the potential of research and policy to be translated into the fulfillment of human rights. A further integration of country- and region-specific data into the study of women's rights can help identify how exactly the context-dependent barriers operate in women's engagement with human rights laws at the local level (Apodaca 2007).

II. CASE STUDY: WOMEN'S ECONOMIC RIGHTS IN GHANA

A closer look into the case study of women's economic rights in Ghana provides an illustrative example of the importance of country-level contextualization of rights implementation. Ghana's postcolonial history, experience with legal and political corruption, as well as the continued cultural importance of customary systems of law, politics, and kinship all combine to influence the ways in which women engage with the law. The 1992 Ghanaian Constitution pays extensive attention to the rights and freedoms of the people. It makes many of the human rights listed in documents such as the Universal Declaration of Human Rights (UDHR) and the International Covenant of Economic, Social, and Cultural Rights (ICESCR) legally binding in Ghana. Despite this legal effort, however, individuals (women especially) continue to struggle to achieve the rights guaranteed to them by their constitution. As a whole, Ghana ranks 130th on the Human Development Index (HDI), with a score of 0.467 in 2010. This data points to the fact that although Ghana is outperforming many African nations in education, standard of living, and the ability to live a long and healthy life, globally, it still ranks in the category of "low human development" (Human Development Reports Office 2010). Additionally, based on data from 2008, Ghana scores a 0.729 on the Gender Inequality Index, meaning that women suffer a 72.9% loss of achievement in the areas of reproductive health, empowerment, and labor market because of their gender (Human Development Reports Office 2010) This data illustrates that although laws are in place to protect the rights of Ghanaians, social and cultural challenges still exist. On the topic of economic rights, the ability of women to use laws guaranteeing rights to own and inherit property and be protected during employment becomes especially important. In Ghana, the parallel legal system, cultural understanding of group identity, and established traditional authority create context-specific challenges for the use of these laws to claim economic and human rights.

Ghana's legal system has its roots in British common law and the system of indirect rule instituted under the British colonial administration. Indirect rule incorporated local institutions such as customary law and traditional leaders into "a single Government in which Native Chiefs have well-defined duties" along with colonial officials (Lugard 1918, 298, quoted in Roberts and Mann 1991, 20). The plural legal system instilled during colonialism has continued since Ghana gained independence in

1957. The power given to customary law and the political structure of chieftaincy has remained constant, although the levels of official incorporation into the governmental structure of the country have varied. Since independence, the system of chieftaincy has often been favored because of the negative impression of the statutory system. Over the last fifty years, the people of Ghana have witnessed multiple coups and constitutions, as well as a ten-year period of oppressive military rule. Especially during the period of military control, the judiciary was often used by those in power to "legally" imprison and repress opponents (Oquaye 2000). Udogu (2003) argues that this history of repressive government may affect average citizens' belief in the power of law to protect their rights. Although the 1992 constitution attempts to break with the past by emphasizing civil rights and liberties, there has not been a serious attempt at "legitimation and redefinition of the ideology" of the police and courts in Ghana, resulting in a continued skepticism of the populace toward the criminal justice system (Tankebe 2009, 256).

A. Property and Inheritance

Many scholars agree that a woman's ability to own property plays a central role in her standard of living and also in her quest for equality in gender relations (Agarwal 1994; Rao 2007; Razavi 2007). This is especially true in Ghana, where agriculture accounts for 37.3% of the GDP and employs about 55% of the workforce (CIA World Fact Book 2010). Outside of agriculture, much of the industrial sector in Ghana (accounting for 25.3% of the GDP) also revolves around land, including the timber and mining industries. Because of this, an individual's ability to secure use of land is essential to the maintenance of living standards.

Marriage and kinship patterns strongly affect the distribution of property in Ghanaian society. Although marriages may occur under either statutory or customary law, most Ghanaians still prefer to enter into customary unions (Bond 2008). Under customary law, marriages do not result in spouses becoming part of each other's lineage systems (Kuenyehia and Ofei-Aboagye 1998). As most land (nearly 80%) is officially held by lineages (i.e., kinship groups) and not by individuals, when one spouse dies, property is passed back to the lineage (Alden Wily and Hammond 2001). Although this would seem to affect women and men equally, because of societal norms, women tend to find it much more difficult than men to later acquire land independently (Kludze 1988). Because of this, widows face particular difficulties in maintaining living standards after the death of their spouses. These challenges will be discussed in more detail in the following section.

Cultural heritage also plays a role in a woman's ability to become the primary owner of a parcel of land. Ghana's largest ethnic group, the Akan, are matrilineal and are therefore more likely to have female-owned property. In fact, one-fifth (21.1%) of Akan land parcels are held by women, compared to only 11.7% of non–Akan land parcels (Quisumbing and Otsuka 2002). Additionally, Quisumbing and Otsuka's (2002) study of evolving land tenure in Ghana revealed that female-held land in Ghana was primarily acquired as a gift as opposed to being inherited or privately purchased. Although men were also likely to acquire land as a gift, the distribution of acquisition was far more balanced between the modes of inheritance, private acquisition, and gift.

In 1985, with the passing of the Intestate Succession Law, Ghana made its first legislative effort to mitigate the discriminatory effects of traditional land holdings. Before this time, all inheritance was controlled through the customary system (Fenrich and Higgins 2001). The Intestate Succession Law, which guarantees widows a portion of the couple's property in the case that a will was not previously made, was a first attempt to codify the process of widows seeking property inheritance. There are, however, several procedural barriers to the use of this law by women. For example, the law only applies to property that was self-acquired by the couple (not to property acquired with the assistance of extended family). Especially in rural areas, records of land ownership are scarce (Kasanga and Kotey 2001). In addition, women are often not involved in the process of land ownership, and therefore may not be privy to the specific details of how the property was acquired (Fenrich and Higgins 2001). Extended families may wish to keep the land of the deceased and therefore assert that they assisted the couple in originally acquiring the land (Kuenyehia and Ofei-Aboagye 1998). If the family contests the claim in this way, and records are not available, the case becomes the group's word against that of the individual. These challenges reduce the emancipatory potential of the Intestate Succession Law when it comes to women's land rights issues.

Another law created to help assert individual rights to land is Ghana's Land Title Registration Law, passed in 1986. This law theoretically allows for individual titling of land, even if it is lineage land. Having an official title would greatly increase the chances that a widow would be able to maintain ownership of the land after her husband's death. This practice, however, is uncommon. In rural areas, only 10% of families attempt to register land. Meanwhile, only 5% of urban families have titled land

(Kasanga and Kotey 2001). This suggests that the barrier to registration is something more than simple proximity to the government offices. For those who did make the effort to attempt registration, only one-half were able to complete the process within one year; others spent as many as ten years in the process (Center for Democracy and Development 2000). Time and financial resources are clear barriers to successful formal land registration.

Gender also plays a roll in the potential success of land registration as a path to economic rights. Dicklitch and Howard-Hassmann (2007) argue that when the government of Ghana chose to pursue a policy of structural adjustment in 1983, the eventual changes made to increase privatized property (among other structural adjustment polices) resulted in positive economic growth. When individuals have the ability to register their land, they are better able to use it to increase capital through rent, sale, or use of the land as collateral. Dicklitch and Howard-Hassmann rightly note, however, that although this may be the case for men, women's access to land often decreases during privatization because of their inability to participate in the registration process.

A third legal instrument dealing with inheritance rights is Article 22 of the 1992 Ghanaian Constitution. This article makes allowances for a widow's inheritance rights, requiring widowed spouses to be provided "a reasonable provision out of the estate" regardless of whether or not a will was written. Part two of the article also mandates the legislature to create legal protections for the property rights of spouses "as soon as practicable." In theory, this constitutional provision extends beyond the powers of the Intestate Succession Law by requiring the courts to override an individual's will if the document does not adequately provide for the widowed spouse (Fenrich and Higgins 2001). Unfortunately, however, the Ghanaian legislature has yet to take action to create the mandated legislation. Although individuals could still use the constitutional provision to challenge a will (or lack of one) through the courts, research in 2001 revealed that no one had, at that point, attempted to do so (Fenrich and Higgins 2001).

As these examples illustrate, many of the laws put in place to grant economic rights for women in Ghana are underutilized. This situation reflects data trends at the regional level that show progress in the creation of laws, but a lack of translation into results. In Ghana, part of the reason for this divergence is the highly embedded nature of customary law coupled with a weak state judiciary. A study conducted on court usage in land disputes in Ghana revealed that, although state courts are used in dispute resolution, they are not the first method chosen in most areas. The study primarily focused on one rural district and one urban center.[2] Only in the urban center was the state court the dominant choice for settling land disputes. In the rural areas, it was much more likely that a traditional court, chief, or elder was consulted first (53.2% of the cases in the rural district and 100% of the time in the village). Even though they were not chosen the majority of the time, traditional sources of conflict resolution were still sought first 29.6% of the time in the urban center (Crook 2004). This study illustrates the prevalence of customary law and traditional authority in regard to property in Ghana, and also suggests the extralegal nature of the challenges to establishing economic rights for women in Ghana.

Even when women choose to claim their rights within the statutory system, other practical barriers exist in the fulfillment of that right. One of these barriers is a judiciary that, to date, has been ineffectual on the topic of property rights, often deferring to traditional custom (Fenrich and Higgins 2001). In addition to this barrier, Blocher (2006) notes that even when the court finds in favor of individual landholders, it is difficult and expensive to enforce its decisions. In a country such as Ghana that has a parallel legal system, statutory decisions are not always seen as legitimate and therefore decisions about land ownership made through the formal courts may also be seen as illegitimate. As Platteau (1996, 76) writes, "If property has no social legitimacy, it is not property because it lacks the basic ingredient of property, recognition by others." The right may be respected and even protected, but in this case, it still remains unfulfilled.

The weak judiciary has often made widows hesitant to bring legal cases in the state courts for fear of the potential social ostracization that often accompanies challenging traditional rulings (Mikell 1992). Social ostracization is an especially dim prospect because, although customary law does not require a lineage to provide land or property to a widow, the lineage is often expected to care for her, at least minimally, despite the death of her husband (Higgins 2005). To bring a court case through the statutory system is to risk a double loss: one in the court system and one in the traditional lineage system. A loss of both land and family support is very difficult for widowed rural women to overcome. Because

---

[2] Data from a rural village court was also included, although due to the low number of cases brought in this court (ten), the study's conclusions were primarily based on the data from the two other sites.

of this, some women have chosen to pursue property disputes within the customary system, such as the Asante[3] Queen Mother's court. This court is a component of the Queen Mother's efforts to maintain the welfare of Asante women (Stoeltje 2000). Although customary courts may help the women meet immediate economic needs, they do not address overarching problems of gender inequality and discrimination. Stoeltje (2000, 78) describes how the act of a woman bringing a dispute against a man to the Asante Queen Mother's customary court "challenges the dominant ideology of gender," but does not serve to redefine the overarching gender ideologies.

The dilemma that exists between choosing to settle a dispute in either a customary court or the statutory system is exacerbated by migration within modern African states. As people move to more urban areas, family structures are changed and individuals receive less social support from the family and become more reliant on the state apparatus. Yet the state does not always have adequate resources to enforce statutory decisions. As Ibhawoh (2000, 854) writes, "The community and extended family are no longer able to play their social welfare roles, while the state is not yet able to replace them in doing this. Put differently, cultures are no longer able and constitutions are not yet able."

B. Labor Protections

Research has shown that, similarly to many countries, Ghanaian women experience greater amounts of poverty than men (Wrigley-Asante 2008). As previously discussed, the Ghanaian Constitution generally mirrors international standards regarding human rights. There are, however, notable exceptions. First, Ghana's constitution does not guarantee the right to work, although Article 24 is consistent with international law in mandating that:

(1) Every person has the right to work under satisfactory, safe and healthy conditions, and shall receive equal pay for equal work without distinction of any kind.
(2) Every worker shall be assured of rest, leisure and reasonable limitation of working hours and periods of holidays with pay, as well as remuneration for public holidays.

---

[3] The Asante (also referred to as Ashanti or Akan), are the largest ethnic group in Ghana.

(3) Every worker has a right to form or join a trade union of his choice for the promotion and protection of his economic and social interests.
(4) Restrictions shall not be placed on the exercise of the right conferred by clause of this article except restrictions prescribed by law and reasonably necessary in the interest of national security or public order or for the protection of the rights and freedoms of others.

In addition to these constitutional provisions, Article 27(1) mandates that women be accorded paid maternity leave for a reasonable period before and after the birth of a child. There are also legal provisions protecting employees from sexual harassment in the workplace.

As was the case with property law, however, there are many sociocultural conditions present in Ghana that limit the potential of these laws. One of the primary barriers confronting women in Ghana is their overrepresentation in the informal employment sector. As a region, sub-Saharan Africa has the highest global rates of women working in the informal sector (84%) (Fawole 2008). In Ghana, most women work as either food crop farmers or market women (Fallon 2003). In both of these lines of work, women do not have access to certain rights, such as maternity leave (Wrigley-Asante 2008). It is also much more difficult for women to hold employers accountable by seeking formal recourse through the court system if they are employed in the informal sector. This is largely because, in this form of employment, it is less likely that there would be the kind of formal documentation that is generally required as evidence in a statutory case. Formal sector employment brings its own set of challenges for women seeking recourse. If a court case becomes necessary to claim rights, an extensive commitment of resources, of both finances and time, is often required. Additionally, a study concerning workplace conditions in Ghana revealed that most women are concerned that filing a formal complaint will result in backlash. As Aryeetey (2004, 58) writes, the assumed "backlash from seeking redress invariably affected the victims more than the offender, considering that victims risked being transferred, fired, demoted, or marginalized."

Outside of procedural difficulties, there are also historical influences that affect the way Ghanaian women engage with labor laws. As discussed earlier, Ghana's history of corruption within the judiciary has left many residents skeptical of the court's ability to protect their rights. This is specifically poignant for women working in the markets throughout the country. In 1979, under the military regime of Jerry Rawlings, when market women attempted to organize into cooperatives, they were met with hostility from the government. The regime accused the women of hurting the nation by hoarding commodities and artificially inflating prices. In retaliation, the government burned down the central market place in Accra, Ghana's capital city (Mikell 1992). Although the period of military control in Ghana ended in 1992, the memory of retaliation remains. Oquaye (1995) argues that human rights abuses during the period of military control in Ghana have left a lasting legacy of fear and continue to inspire distrust of government-controlled legal processes. In this way, the history and culture of Ghana continue to affect the barriers that women face in using local laws intended to protect their rights.

III. CONCLUSION

Although a case study such as this is clearly not enough to fix the problem of attainment gaps between policy and practice, taken along with a growing collection of data sets and indicators, one is able to see a more complete picture of the challenges that lie ahead in fulfilling women's economic rights. The case study used in this chapter illustrates how a country's history, social makeup, and political practices all work in complex ways to influence how individuals are able to use legislation for the claiming of rights. Policies designed without taking a country's sociopolitical context into account are likely to face challenges in implementation that may only reinscribe the current gaps between legislation and experience. UN Women appears to be attempting to change this pattern. By prioritizing the country-level presence of UN Women (UN Secretary General 2010) and attempting to serve as a "a hub of knowledge on the situation of women and girls in a given country and the practices that have proved successful ("what works") in advancing gender equality" (UN Secretary General 2010, 7), the organization appears to be attempting to implement a more context-responsive policy plan. In addition to the increased local presence of UN Women, the engagement of local NGOs in both the creation of programs, as well as in the monitoring and review process, will likely add more breadth of understanding at the country level (Edwards and Sen 2000; Chapman 1996). In Ghana, both women's employment protections and property rights are protected through law, and yet the rights remain unfulfilled in practice. If the laws in a country are not succeeding in fulfilling the rights of individuals, they must be accompanied by programs targeting the specific challenges faced by those individuals. Only through the understanding of local barriers will we see human right move beyond policy into practice.

REFERENCES

Agarwal, Bina, 1994. *A Field of One's Own: Gender and Land Rights in South Asia*, Cambridge: Cambridge University Press.

Alden Wily, L. and D. Hammond, 2001. "Land Security and the Poor in Ghana: is there a way forward?" Study for Department for International Development, Commissioned by the Ghana Rural Livelihoods Programme, August.

Apodaca, Clair, 1998. "Measuring Women's Economic and Social Rights Achievement," *Human Rights Quarterly* 20(1): 139–172.

Apodaca, Clair, 2007. "Measuring the Progressive Realization of Economic and Social Rights," in Shareen Hertel and Lanse Minkler (Eds.) *Economic Rights: Conceptual, Measurement, and Policy Issues*, 165–181, New York: Cambridge University Press.

Aryeetey, Ernest, 2004. *Coming to Terms with Sexual Harassment in Ghana*, Legon, Ghana: University of Ghana, Institute of Statistical, Social, and Economic Research (ISSER).

Blocher, Joseph, 2006. "Building on Custom: Land Tenure Policy and Economic Development in Ghana," *Yale Human Rights and Development Law Review* 9(1): 166–202.

Bond, Johanna, 2008. "Pluralism in Ghana: The Perils and Promise of Plural Law," *Oregon Review of International Law* 10: 391–418.

Bunch, Charlotte and Susana Fried, 1996. "Beijing '95: Moving Women's Human Rights from Margin to Center," *Signs: Journal of Women in Culture and Society* 22(1): 200–204.

Center for Democracy and Development, 2000. "Corruption and Other Constraints on the Land Market and Land Administration in Ghana: A Preliminary Investigation," Ghana.

Chapman, Audrey, 1995. "Monitoring Women's Right to Health Under the International Covenant on Economic, Social and Cultural Rights," *The American University Law Review* 44: 1157–1175.

Chapman, Audrey, 1996. "A 'Violations Approach' for Monitoring the International Covenant on Economic, Social and Cultural Rights," *Human Rights Quarterly* 18(1): 23–66.

Chapman, Audrey, 2007. "The Status of Efforts to Monitor Economic, Social, and Cultural Rights," in Shareen Hertel and Lanse Minkler (Eds.) *Economic Rights: Conceptual, Measurement, and Policy Issues*, 143–164, New York: Cambridge University Press.

CIA World Fact Book, 2010. "Ghana." Retrieved from https://www.cia.gov/library/publications/the-world-factbook/geos/gh.html.

Convention on the Elimination of All Forms of Discrimination Against Women (CEDAW). 1979. 1249 U.N.T.S. 13; 19 I.L.M. 33(1980)

Crook, Richard, 2004. "Access to Justice and Land Disputes in Ghana's State Courts: The Litigants' Perspective," *Journal of Legal Pluralism and Unofficial Law* 1–28.

Dicklitch, Susan and Rhoda E. Howard-Hassmann, 2007. "Public Policy and Economic Rights in Ghana and Uganda," in Shareen Hertel and Lanse Minkler

(Eds.) *Economic Rights: Conceptual, Measurement, and Policy Issues*, 325–344, New York: Cambridge University Press.

Economic Commission for Africa, 2009. "A Fifteen-Year Review of the Implementation of the Beijing Platform for Action in Africa (BPfA) +15, from 1995–2009," Banjul, the Gambia, 1–28.

Economic Commission for Europe, 2009. "Regional Review of Progress," Geneva, Switzerland, 1–20.

Economic Commission for Latin America and the Caribbean, 2009. "Review of the Implementation of the Beijing Declaration and Platform for Action and the Outcome of the Twenty-Third Special Session of the General Assembly in Latin America and Caribbean Countries," Santiago, Chile, 1–38.

Economic and Social Commission for Asia and the Pacific, 2009. "Review of the Implementation of the Beijing Platform for Action in the ESCAP Region," Bangkok, Thailand, 1–16.

Economic and Social Commission for Western Asia, 2009. "Consolidated Arab Report on the Implementation of the Beijing Platform for Action +15," Beirut, Lebanon, 1–25.

Edwards, Michael and Gita Sen, 2000. "NGOs, Social Change, and the Transformation of Human Relationships: A 21st Century Civic Agenda," *Third World Quarterly* 21(4): 605–616.

Fallon, Kathleen, 2003. "Transforming Women's Citizenship Rights Within an Emerging Democratic State: The Case of Ghana," *Gender and Society* 17(4): 525–543.

Fawole, Olufunmilayo, 2008. "Economic Violence to Women and Girls: Is It Receiving the Necessary Attention?" *Trauma, Violence, and Abuse* 9(3): 167–177.

Fenrich, Jeanmarie and Tracy Higgins, 2001. "Promise Unfulfilled: Law, Culture, and Women's Inheritance Rights in Ghana," *Fordham International Law Journal* 25: 259–341.

Friedman, Elisabeth, 1995. "Women's Human Rights: The Emergence of a Movement," in Julie Peters and Andrea Wolper (Eds.) *Women's Rights, Human Rights: International Feminist Perspective*, 18–35, New York: Routledge.

Hemment, Julie, 2004. "Global Civil Society and the Local Cost of Belonging: Defining Violence Against Women in Russia," *Signs: Journal of Women in Culture and Society* 29(3): 815–840.

Hertel, Shareen and Lanse Minkler, 2007. "Economic Rights: The Terrain," in Shareen Hertel and Lanse Minkler (Eds.) *Economic Rights: Conceptual, Measurement, and Policy Issues*, 1–36, New York: Cambridge University Press.

Higgins, Tracy, 2005. "A Reflection on the Uses and Limits of Western Feminism in a Global Context," *Thomas Jefferson Law Review* 28: 423–448.

Human Development Reports Office, 2010. "Human Development Report 2010, The Real Wealth of Nations: Pathways to Human Development," New York: United Nations Development Programme (UNDP).

Ibhawoh, Bonny, 2000. "Between Culture and Constitution: Evaluating the Cultural Legitimacy of Human Rights in the African State," *Human Rights Quarterly* 22: 838–860.

Kasanga, Kasim and Nii Ashie Kotey, 2001. *Land Management in Ghana: Building on Tradition and Modernity*, London: International Institute for Environment and Development.

Kaufman, Natalie Hevener and Stefanie Lindquist, 1995. "Critiquing Gender-Neutral Treaty Language: The Convention on the Elimination of All Forms of Discrimination Against Women," in Julie Peters and Andrea Wolper (Eds.) *Women's Rights, Human Rights: International Feminist Perspective*, 18–35, New York: Routledge.

Kludze, A. Kodzo Paaku, 1988. *Modern Law of Succession in Ghana*. New Jersey: Foris Pubns USA.

Kuenyehia, Akua and Esther Ofei-Aboagye, 1998. "Family Law in Ghana and its Implications for Women," in Akua Kyenyehia (Ed.) *Women and Law in West Africa Situational Analysis of Some Key Issues Affecting Women*, 23–61, Ghana: Sedco Publishing.

Lugard, Frederick, 1918. "Revisions of Instructions to Political Officers on Subjects Chiefly Political and Administrative," in A.H.M. Kirk-Greene (Ed.) *The Principles of Native Administration in Nigeria: Selected Documents, 1900–1947*, 68–148, London: Oxford University Press.

Merry, Sally Engle, 2006. *Human Rights and Gender Violence: Translating International Law into Local Justice*, Chicago: University of Chicago Press.

Mikell, Gwendolyn, 1992. "Culture, Law, and Social Policy: Changing the Economic Status of Ghanaian Women," *Yale Journal of International Law* 17(1): 225–240.

Okin, Susan, 1998. "Feminism, Women's Human Rights and Cultural Difference," *Hypatia* 13(2): 32–52.

Oquaye, Mike, 1995. "Human Rights and the Transition to Democracy Under PNDC in Ghana," *Human Rights Quarterly* 17(3): 556–573.

Oquaye, Mike, 2000. "The Process of Democratisation in Contemporary Ghana." *Commonwealth and Comparative Politics*. 38(3): 53–78.

Platteau, Jean-Phillippe, 1996. "The Evolutionary Theory of Land Rights as Applied to Sub-Saharan Africa: A Critical Assessment," *Development and Change*. 27: 29–86.

Quisumbing, Agnes and Keijiro Otsuka, 2002. *Land, Trees, and Women: Evolution of Land Tenure Institutions in Western Ghana and Sumatra (Research Report 121)*, Washington, DC: International Food Policy Research.

Rao, Nitya, 2007. "Custom and the Courts: Ensuring Women's Rights to Land, Jharkhand, India," *Development & Change* 38(2): 299–319.

Razavi, Shahra, 2007. "Liberalisation and the Debates on Women's Access to Land," *Third World Quarterly* 28(8): 1479–1500.

Roberts, Richard and Kristin Mann, 1991. "An Introduction: Law in Colonial Africa," in Kristin Mann and Richard Roberts (Eds.) *Law in Colonial Africa*, 3–60, Portsmouth, NH: Heinemann Educational Books, Inc.

Stoeltje, Beverly, 2000. "Gender Ideologies and Discursive Practices in Asante," *PoLAR: Political and Legal Anthropology Review* 23(2): 77–88.

Sullivan, Donna, 1994. "Women's Human Rights and the 1993 World Conference on Human Rights," *American Journal of International Law* 88: 152–167.

Sweeney, Shauna, 2007. "Government Respect for Women's Economics Rights: Across-National analysis, 1981–2003," in Shareen Hertel and Lanse Minkler (Eds.) *Economic Rights: Conceptual, Measurement, and Policy Issues*, 233–266, New York: Cambridge University Press.

Tankebe, Justice, 2009. "Self-Help, Policing, and Procedural Justice: Ghanaian Vigilantism and the Rule of Law," *Law and Society Review* 43(2): 245–270.

Udogu, E.Ike, 2003. "National Constitutions and Human Rights Issues in Africa," *African and Asian Studies* 2(2): 101–135.

UN (United Nations) Secretary-General, 2010. "Comprehensive Proposal for the Composite Entity for Gender Equality and the Empowerment of Women, Report of the Secretary-General (A/64/588)," New York: UN.

UN Women, 2011. "New UN Women's Body Plans to Reinforce Presence at Country Level." Retrieved from http://www.unwomen.org/2011/01/new-un-women-body-plans-to-reinforce-presence-at-country-level/

(UNIFEM) United Nations Development Fund for Women, 2009. "Who Answers to Women?: Gender and Accountability: Progress of the World's Women 2008/2009," New York: UN, 1–152.

Wrigley-Asante, Charlotte, 2008. "Men are Poor, but Women are Poorer: Gendered Poverty and Survival Strategies in the Dangme West District of Ghana," *Norwegian Journal of Geography* 62: 161–170.

9

Statelessness and Economic and Social Rights

Kristy A. Belton

INTRODUCTION

We live in a world where millions of people acquire citizenship[1] automatically each year through *jus soli* (birth on the territory), *jus sanguinis* (citizenship via descent), and other state-approved channels of citizenship acquisition. We also live in a world where an estimated 12 to 15 million people lack citizenship altogether (Southwick and Lynch 2009; Manly 2007; see Figure 9.1). These stateless people are "not considered . . . national[s] by any State under the operation of its law" (UN 1954, Article 1). Statelessness is often described as a condition of invisibility and heightened vulnerability.[2] Without citizenship from anywhere, the stateless are susceptible to myriad human rights violations from: indefinite or unnecessary detention, torture, and enslavement to family separation, the refusal of identity documents, and inadequate housing and health care, among others.[3]

---

[1] Citizenship and nationality are used interchangeably in this chapter, as is common in the literature on statelessness (see, for instance, Batchelor 2006; Forced Migration Review 2009; Perks and de Chickera 2009; Sokoloff 2005; United Nations High Commissioner for Refugees and Inter-Parliamentary Union 2005). "Citizenship" refers to the legal bond between a person and a state at the domestic level; "nationality" refers to this bond at the international level.

[2] See, for instance, Adam (2009); Bosniak (2007); Lynch (2005); Lynch and Teff (2009); McDougall (2008); and the United Nations High Commissioner for Refugees (2009).

[3] On indefinite or unnecessary detention, see Equal Rights Trust (2010); and Weissbrodt and Collins (2006). Refer to Lynch and Ali (2006) on torture; Lewa (2009, 14) and Aird, Harnett, and Shah (2002, 7) on enslavement; and Bhabha (2009) and Belton (2010a) on family separation. With regard to the refusal of identity documents, see Korir Sing'oei (2009, 43); and van Selm (2009). As concerns inadequate housing and health care, refer to Lynch (2005); Heffernan (2002); and Kingston, Cohen, and Morley (2010).

-Stateless --> Stateless, Stateless Persons,
Sum over all periods, From 2004 to 2009
Source: UNHCR

0-999
1000-1999
2000-4999
5000-9999
10000-14999
15000-24999
>25000

FIGURE 9.1. Statelessness around the Globe: Official Figures Source: UNHCR Statistical Online Population Database (2011).[4]

[4] Bear in mind that this map is based on "official" figures and consequently does not illustrate the presence of all known, but "uncounted," stateless populations.

Unlike the highly developed international protection regime that exists for refugees, and the protection extended in international law by states to their own citizens, stateless people are without recourse to such protection. They are outcasts in an international system of states that requires each person to be a citizen of somewhere (League of Nations 1930). In contrast to refugees or internally displaced persons (IDPs), stateless persons "lack the assistance, benefits or attention of government or humanitarian communities" (Cordell 2011). They are thus "perhaps even more vulnerable than refugees due to their near-total lack of ability to exercise their human rights" (Glickman 2010). Their lack of formal membership in any state translates into violations of their economic, social, cultural, civil, and political rights, as well. Despite the multitude of human rights violations that often attach to the condition of being stateless, statelessness has yet to garner the attention given by practitioners and the international community to other groups of concern, such as migrants, refugees, and IDPs.[5] Statelessness continues to be a "blind spot" on the international community's agenda (Lynch 2009) and, until recently, the United Nations High Commissioner for Refugees (UNHCR) – the body mandated with the identification and protection of the stateless[6] – admitted that it was not doing enough to address this issue (UNHCR 2007). Additionally, stateless groups rarely figure into academic research on human rights, especially economic and social (ES) rights work, although their lack of citizenship typically translates into an inability to enjoy many basic rights and protections.

The existing literature on statelessness consists of two primary strains. The first is legal and/or technical, which consists of analyses on the causes of statelessness, examinations of extant treaties on nationality and statelessness, and differences between types of statelessness (Batchelor 1995 and 1998; Bosniak 2000; Donner 1994; Massey 2010; van Waas 2008). The second is more advocacy oriented, and comprised of works that

---

[5] Stateless people are recognized in international law as a distinct category to refugees and IDPs. Refugees cross international borders in order to evade persecution, whereas IDPs are forced to leave their homes because of armed conflicts, natural and man-made disasters, and other similar circumstances (see the Guiding Principles on Internal Displacement [OCHA 2004] for further information). Stateless people, on the other hand, do not necessarily cross state borders (see the de jure versus de facto distinction provided in this chapter), nor do they necessarily face outright persecution or undergo forced migration within their states of residence. Unlike refugees and IDPs, the stateless are not recognized as citizens of or by any state.

[6] The UN General Assembly established this mandate for UNHCR via resolution 3274 (XXIX) in 1974.

describe the situation of stateless people and what should be done to improve their plight (Lynch 2005; Lynch and Southwick 2009; Perks and de Chickera 2009).[7] Although few comparative analyses of statelessness exist, Blitz and Lynch's 2009 volume examines the benefits of citizenship for formerly stateless populations from a comparative perspective. Even though this volume does not explicitly address statelessness from an ES rights framework, it arguably provides several examples of how the acquisition of nationality can fail to improve the lot of formerly stateless populations without a concomitant improvement in their socioeconomic situation.[8]

As a complement, but in distinction to the aforementioned bodies of literature, this chapter specifically provides an overview of the relationship between statelessness and economic and social rights enjoyment. Through an examination of the Articles of the International Covenant on Economic, Social and Cultural Rights (ICESCR) and the experiences of stateless groups, this chapter demonstrates that the international community is generally failing to respect, protect, and fulfill the ES rights of the stateless. The chapter offers suggestions as to how the stateless' ES rights might be better fulfilled and concludes with avenues for future research on this largely understudied area of scholarship.

THE RIGHT TO A NATIONALITY AND STATELESSNESS

The UN Charter (1945) gives the Economic and Social Council (ECOSOC) the authority to make recommendations and set up commissions concerning the promotion of "respect for, and observance of, human rights and fundamental freedoms for all" (Articles 62 and 68). One of the first acts of ECOSOC was the creation of a Human Rights Commission (HRC), tasked with the formulation of an international bill of human rights. Among the rights included in the Universal Declaration of Human Rights (UDHR) was the assertion that everyone has the right to a nationality (Article 15). The inclusion of such a right was hotly contested during the meetings of the HRC. Some of the eighteen-member team thought that such a right would provide leeway for UN incursions upon state sovereignty and insisted that it be removed from the draft bill of rights. Other delegates believed that the right to a nationality was

---

[7] See the introductory chapter of Blitz and Lynch (2009) for a more comprehensive examination of the literatures that touch upon noncitizens generally.

[8] Refer to the Korir Sing'oei and Sivapragasam chapters of Blitz and Lynch (2009) especially (more said on this later in the chapter).

"essential to a declaration on human rights" (Morsink 1999, 82). Eleanor Roosevelt, Chairperson of the HRC at the time, argued that the right to a citizenship was of "vital importance,"[9] and this opinion gained acceptance among the majority of the delegates. Although the majority finally agreed that the right to citizenship was fundamental to maintain in the bill, all references to the role of the UN in implementing this right were omitted from the final declaration. From that time, other international human rights instruments have included the right to a nationality,[10] and the UN has crafted two conventions dealing specifically with statelessness.

The 1954 Convention relating to the Status of Stateless Persons defines a stateless person and enumerates the rights and freedoms that he or she possesses in the absence of state membership. As noted earlier, a stateless person is "not considered as a national by any State under the operation of its law" (Article 1). This is the de jure definition of statelessness, and among those who are de jure stateless one finds: Palestinians, Bidun, and Kurds in Syria (Shiblak 2009, 39), Banywarwanda in the Democratic Republic of Congo, and Hill Tribes in Thailand, among others (Open Society Justice Initiative 2011). De facto statelessness refers to those "outside the country of their nationality who are unable or, for valid reasons, are unwilling to avail themselves of the protection of that country" (Massey 2010, 60). De facto stateless groups include the children of undocumented Haitian migrants in the Bahamas (Belton 2010a), the descendants of Indochinese refugees in Thailand and Japan (Komai and Azukizawa 2009), Roma in Europe (Hammarberg 2009 and 2010), and others. Regardless of type of statelessness, however, the de jure and de facto stateless face similar obstacles in rights enjoyment and both suffer a lack of state protection in practice. It is this realization that led the UNHCR to declare that the de facto stateless should be treated as much as possible as if they were de jure stateless (Massey 2010).

---

[9] Mrs. Roosevelt considered the rights to a nationality, freedom of thought and conscience, and participation in the government of one's country to be the three key rights in any declaration on human rights (Roosevelt 1948). Events surrounding the establishment of the UN – World War II and the Holocaust – likely influenced Mrs. Roosevelt's opinion about these three articles. Many people were denationalized during this time and most of them lost their lives as a consequence of being deprived of these three rights.

[10] Article 5 of the International Convention on the Elimination of All Forms of Racial Discrimination states that citizenship is a civil right (UN 1965). Articles 24 and 7 of the International Covenant on Civil and Political Rights (UN 1966) and the Convention on the Rights of the Child (UN 1989), respectively, assert the right of every child to acquire a citizenship, and Article 9 of the Convention on the Elimination of All Forms of Discrimination Against Women (UN 1979) states that a woman has the right to acquire, change, and retain citizenship.

The 1954 Convention lays out several rights and freedoms for stateless people, but permits states party to the convention to limit many of these rights and freedoms only to the stateless who are "lawfully staying" on their territory. For example, the ES rights to employment (Articles 17–19 and 24), unionization (Article 15), housing (Article 21), public relief (Article 23), and social security (Article 24) can be limited to those who are lawfully staying on a state party's territory.[11] Unlike the 1951 Convention relating to the Status of Refugees, neither statelessness convention contains an Article directing states to refrain from imposing penalties on those stateless who are "unlawfully" on the state's territory provided they can "show good cause for their illegal entry or presence" (United Nations 1951, Article 31). Additionally, and in contradistinction to the 1951 refugee Convention, the 1954 Convention on statelessness provides "a *minimalist commitment at the lowest common denominator*" when it comes to the treatment of stateless people and their right to work (van Waas 2008, 310). That is, whereas refugees must be treated like nationals when it comes to employment, the stateless only need be treated "on a par with non-nationals generally" (ibid.). As van Waas points out, "[A]ll three articles on the right to work [in the 1954 Convention] provide the same low level of protection" (ibid., 311).

Beside these "qualified" ES rights, the 1954 Convention asks that contracting state parties provide administrative assistance to the stateless and facilitate their naturalization. It also states that state parties allow the stateless to transfer assets and own property, access primary education and the courts, have their artistic and scientific works protected, and be provided identity documents. Furthermore, the convention is clear that the stateless should not be expelled (provided they are lawfully present in the territory) and that they have the right to practice religion freely.

The 1961 Convention on the Reduction of Statelessness, on the other hand, provides a series of guidelines aimed to decrease the occurrence of statelessness globally. It directs contracting state parties to prevent statelessness at birth and asserts that changes in personal status (such as marriage, divorce, or adoption) must not generate statelessness. The 1961 Convention also asks that states refrain from denationalizing a person until said person has acquired the nationality of another state first. Just as the 1954 Convention contains statements that qualify the applicability of its Articles to the stateless, so does the 1961 Convention. It allows states

---

[11] Civil rights can also be limited by this clause; for instance, the right to freedom of movement (Article 26).

party to the convention to limit the grant of their nationality in some instances to a person who "has always been stateless" (Articles 1 and 4). This is in marked distinction to the 1951 Convention on Refugees. That is, one does not always have to have been a refugee in order to acquire formal refugee status and recognition in the present. This particular limitation on the grant of nationality to stateless persons is particularly troubling when one considers that statelessness is a condition that may be acquired at any time in a person's life. Statelessness may result from inadequate and/or sexist nationality laws (Donner 1994), bureaucratic inefficiencies (Aird, Harnett, and Shah 2002; Belton 2010a), outright discrimination (Wooding 2008), state dissolution (Council of Europe 2006a and 2006b; van Waas 2008), and revocation based on residence abroad, among other means.

Additionally, unlike many other human rights, which can be provided by non-state actors, the human right to a nationality, as currently conceived, can only be provided by the state. International law is clear that the state alone has the authority to decide who constitutes its citizenry (League of Nations 1930, Article 1; Weis 1956). Thus, an international norm on the prohibition of statelessness exists (Donner 1994; Adjami and Harrington 2008), and international law posits that a "genuine and effective" link should cement the citizen-state bond,[12] but international law does not delineate how states should grant nationality.[13] This is a matter of municipal law (Weis 1956).

As the Westphalian order is allegedly weakened by the various flows of globalization (Castles and Davidson 2000; Hettne 2000), states have begun to redefine their conception of sovereignty "in terms of control over people rather than control over territory or policy generally" (Dauvergne 2007; see also Hindess 2005). This emphasis on control over people and the state's right to determine its citizenry has consequences for the stateless. No state can be made to give these people citizenship. Consequently, some groups languish in camps for decades, unable to pass on a citizenship they do not possess to their children who, in turn, inherit their stateless status. Even when court sentences are handed down prohibiting a state's engagement in the arbitrary denial of nationality, states

---

[12] The genuineness and the effectiveness of the citizen-state bond can be demonstrated via residency, work, and marriage and family ties, among other means. This principle was elaborated in the Nottebohm case (International Court of Justice 1955).

[13] No law exists at the international level dictating which state should give citizenship on what basis to whom.

do not always comply with judicial decisions.[14] Moreover, ratification of the 1954 and 1961 statelessness Conventions has been notoriously weak. Of the 192 Member States of the UN, only 66 are party to the 1954 Convention relating to the Status of Stateless Persons (United Nations 2011b) and even fewer (38) are party to the 1961 Convention on the Reduction of Statelessness (United Nations 2011a). In total, less than 20% of the member states of the UN have ratified both statelessness Conventions.

Despite lack of accession to the statelessness Conventions, even if states do not formally provide for the ES rights of the stateless in their laws and policies, they are still obliged to do so if they are party to ICESCR (UN 1966b). That is, unless states made specific reservations to the Articles in these Conventions regarding stateless (or noncitizen) populations in their territory, the ES rights of ICESCR apply to stateless persons. These ES rights are the "resources necessary for a minimally decent life" (Hertel and Minkler 2007, 2) and consist of "adequate food, adequate clothing, adequate shelter, and minimal preventive public health care" (Shue 1996, 23), among others. The following section examines how well the stateless' ES rights are being respected, protected, and fulfilled in practice.

INFRINGEMENTS OF ICESCR

The ICESCR is clear that the rights within it apply to all people regardless of nationality (Article 2.2). The Committee on Economic, Social and Cultural Rights (CESCR) reiterates this claim in General Comment No. 20 on Non-Discrimination in Economic, Social and Cultural Rights when it states: "[I]nternational treaties on racial discrimination, discrimination against women and the rights of refugees, stateless persons, children, migrant workers and members of their families, and persons with disabilities include the exercise of economic, social and cultural rights" (United Nations 2009, paragraph 5). Additionally, a recent UN publication, "The Rights of Non-citizens," declares: "Governments shall take progressive measures to the extent of their available resources to protect the rights of everyone – regardless of citizenship – to: social security; an adequate standard of living including adequate food, clothing, housing,

---

[14] Consider *The Case of Yean and Bosico v. Dominican Republic* (Inter-American Court of Human Rights 2005), wherein the Inter-American Court of Human Rights judged that the Dominican Republic (DR) was arbitrarily depriving children born of Haitian descent in the DR of their right to Dominican nationality. The DR has yet to change its approach to Dominican-born children of Haitian descent and continues to hold that they are "in transit" and therefore ineligible for Dominican citizenship.

and the continuous improvement of living conditions; the enjoyment of the highest attainable standard of physical and mental health; and education" (Office of the High Commissioner for Human Rights 2006, 25).

The inclusiveness of ICESCR's Article 2.2 and the positive stances of the CESCR and Office of the High Commissioner for Human Rights (OHCHR) regarding ES rights and statelessness are marred, however, by the fact that Article 2 continues with the following caveat: "Developing countries, with due regard to human rights and their national economy, may determine to what extent they would guarantee the economic rights recognized in the present Covenant to non-nationals" (Article 2.3).

Because ICESCR does not distinguish which of the articulated rights are economic from those that are social, this qualification leaves developing states with broad leeway to deny ES rights to the stateless. This is a concern when one considers that many stateless people are found within "developing" states.[15] The statement by the UN Independent Expert on minority issues regarding Article 2.3 of ICESCR does not clarify the situation either. She asserts that "[r]eference to 'due regard to human rights' must be interpreted to secure that this discretion is not applied discriminatorily and therefore may not disproportionately affect certain non-national minorities" (McDougall 2008, 13). This assertion raises several questions. Does this mean that the stateless, or formerly stateless populations, count as non-national minorities in this situation? If so, what does it mean that certain non-national minorities, but not all, may not be disproportionately affected by this clause? Additionally, if the stateless do not fall within this category of non-national minorities, how does Article 2.3 affect them specifically?

Assuming for the time being that Article 2.3 must be "interpreted narrowly" (International Commission of Jurists 1987, 127), how are the stateless faring when it comes to the enjoyment of the ES rights delineated in ICESCR? Article 1 of ICESCR asserts that everyone has the right to self-determination when it comes to economic and social development. Although this Article does not specify what is meant by self-determination or economic development, the following survey of the status of the stateless' ES rights enjoyment illustrates that the lack of ES rights fulfillment likely limits the stateless' ability to be fully self-determining agents. Articles 6 and 7, which are the first Articles enumerated in Part III of ICESCR that deal with specific ES rights, concern the rights to work and "just

---

[15] Van Waas additionally observes that neither the Committee nor the Covenant explain what is meant by the term "developing countries" (2008).

and favourable conditions of work." These rights are frequently violated when one is stateless. Although a few countries offer a legal status to the stateless and provide identity documents so they may lawfully work in their country of residence, many countries do not offer the stateless this opportunity. Consequently, the stateless are often confined to the informal labor market, where discrimination and exploitation are pervasive.

Although no work has yet systematically documented the treatment of the stateless in the labor market (whether formal or informal), several studies provide glimpses into the precarious situation of stateless groups when it comes to the right to work and decent conditions of work (Lynch 2005). These studies show that stateless people are regularly channeled into "3D jobs" – those that are dirty, dangerous, or degrading. Sokoloff, for example, notes that the Rohingya of Burma are forcefully employed by the Burmese army, without pay, "for construction and maintenance of [the army's] facilities, as well as for a variety of other tasks required by the authorities" (2005, 21). For those Rohingyas who are not forcefully employed, food is often their "only source of income" (Medecins Sans Frontieres 2002, 14). Estate Tamils in Sri Lanka, although de jure citizens since the passage of the Grant of Citizenship to Persons of Indian Origin Act (Government of Sri Lanka 2003), continue to work for low wages in dangerous conditions (Immigration and Refugee Board of Canada 2006; Helle 2011). Additionally, stateless women and children are especially vulnerable to trafficking[16] and sexual violence (Aird et al. 2002; Hussain 2011; Lynch 2008 and 2009; Lynch and Southwick 2009; Sokoloff 2005).

Stateless people are also routinely denied the opportunity to own land and property or to access credit and business licenses, which affects their ability to earn a livelihood (Human Rights Watch 2010 and 2011; Lynch and Ali 2006; Sokoloff 2005). As van Waas notes in the case of Syria, "[S]tateless Kurds cannot obtain property deeds, register cars or businesses, open a bank account or obtain a commercial driver's license and in Bahrain, Bidoon have been prohibited from buying land, starting a business or obtaining a government loan" (2010, 25). These practices further inhibit the enjoyment of the stateless' right to work. Furthermore, stateless people are sometimes denied "childcare supplements, protections against unfair discrimination, promotions, job security, and end-of service bonuses" because of their precarious employment status (Human Rights Watch 2011, 7).

---

[16] This, in turn, leads to a violation of ICESCR's Article 10.3 right of a child not to be exploited.

While more research needs to be done on statelessness and the fulfillment of Articles 8 and 9 of ICESCR – the right to form trade unions and to strike, and to enjoy access to social security, respectively – it is likely that these rights are not respected, protected, or fulfilled when it comes to the stateless. In some states, such as Kazakhstan, Kyrgyzstan, and Tajikistan, the stateless are explicitly prohibited from "joining groups with political aims... mak[ing] it hard for them to improve their conditions" (Farquharson 2011, 69), and in Syria, stateless Kurds are prohibited from joining professional labor unions (Lynch and Ali 2006). Even if expressed prohibitions against association do not exist, as individuals who lack secure status in the state within which they reside, the stateless are likely to want to avoid detection by state authorities so as to evade possible deportation or detention (Belton 2010b). Thus, the stateless probably do not formally organize, protest, and/or engage in strike activities to the degree that those with a secure or lawful status do.[17] As regards access to social security, although further research is needed in this area as well, we know that stateless people have been denied pensions (Adam 2009; Lynch 2005) and that it is difficult, if not impossible, to access government social security services if one does not possess a recognized legal status from the state. Farquharson notes, for example, that in Kazakhstan, Kyrgyzstan, Tajikistan, and Turkmenistan, pensions are not accessible to those employees who work outside the formal sector, "such as undocumented stateless persons" (2011, 67).

Article 10 of ICESCR, which articulates the right to family assistance and protection – as well as special protection of the mother who has recently given birth – is typically violated when children and parents are separated from each other during detention and deportation activities. Additionally, when poverty compels stateless parents to send their children to work (Lynch and Ali 2006) as opposed to school, the parents are consequently unable to fully protect their children. Reports exist of Sri Lankan Estate Tamils who are unable to breastfeed their children in a clean and safe environment (Helle 2011) or who receive little to no prenatal care (Gajanayake, Caldwell, and Caldwell 1991). Women in some

---

[17] This is a subject in need of empirical investigation, however, as *sans papiers* and undocumented migrant workers in several developed countries have been known to engage in protest activity of various types regardless of their insecure status in their country of residence. See, for example, McNevin (2006); and Monforte and Dufour (2011), among others. Additionally, in 2011 the stateless bidun protested against the Kuwaiti government for "years of disenfranchisement and discrimination" (Human Rights Watch 2011, 3 and 11). The Kuwaiti government responded with "tear gas, smoke bombs... water cannons... [and] batons" and arrested many of them (ibid., 11).

states face the added barrier of sexist nationality laws – wherein they cannot pass on their nationality to their children if married to a noncitizen – which leads some to divorce their stateless husbands.[18] Moreover, when stateless parents are denied marriage or birth certificates, as often occurs, families have few state-recognized means of proving they are a unit and are consequently susceptible to separation (Lynch 2008). Protection of the family unit is therefore quite tenuous for the stateless.

One of the most common ICESCR rights violated when one is stateless is the Article 11 right to an adequate standard of living. Whether it is in the camps of northern Kenya (Opala 2011), the confines of northeastern India (Singh 2010) or western Burma (Garcia and Olson 2008), or the shanty-towns of the Bahamas, the stateless often do not enjoy "adequate food, clothing and housing, and the continuous improvement of living conditions" (Article 11.1). During the 1990s, for example, the stateless Chakmas of Arunachal Pradesh in India were denied ration cards and forbidden to sell their produce as part of an "economic blockade" against them (Singh 2010). This dramatically threatened their right to an adequate standard of living and, in a few cases, it threatened their right to life. The Meskhetian Turks of Russia were "brought...to the brink of famine" when their land leases were revoked and they could no longer cultivate food (Sokoloff 2005, 21). Stateless Rohingya in camps in Malaysia are known to lack adequate food, and those living in Bangladesh are "completely dependent on UN and aid agencies for food" (Lynch 2005, 37 and 32; see also Hussain 2011). Physicians for Human Rights noted that in the Cox's Bazaar area, Rohingya families often go for days without food, a situation exacerbated by the fact that the government of Bangladesh "strictly forbids any delivery of food aid to them" (2010, 11). In the unofficial camps in Bangladesh, stateless people have been found eating twigs and several were dying of starvation (ibid.). Stateless children often feel the brunt of this malnutrition (Heffernan 2002), which can lead to corporal disfigurement (Physicians for Human Rights 2010).

The abysmal conditions in which many stateless people live either generate or exacerbate health-related problems. Camps and stateless people's settlements typically lack adequate sanitation facilities and running water. Kelley notes that the Biharis of Bangladesh, who were stateless until quite recently, lived in dismal conditions:

---

[18] These women often feel forced to make this decision so that their children will no longer be stigmatized by the father's stateless status and be able to go to school and engage in other activities (Barbieri 2007).

They lack adequate water supplies. Sanitation services are practically non-existent, with few toilets, washing facilities, garbage disposal or proper drainage. In Geneva camp, one of the largest, for example, there are only 250 public latrines for 25,000 inhabitants. Ten to twelve family members typically live in spaces averaging 8 feet × 8 feet. There is no privacy and poor health is endemic (2010, 10).

Sokoloff (2005) makes a similar observation, and other reports on stateless settlements elsewhere likewise remark on the generally dismal living environments of the stateless. Physicians for Human Rights, for example, notes that the Kutupalong camp for stateless Rohingya in Bangladesh contains "stagnant raw sewage next to refugees' makeshift dwellings. Human excrement and open sewers were visible throughout the camp" (2010, 6; see also Hussain 2011).[19] Consequently, water-borne infectious diseases result in high levels of diarrhea among camp residents, especially children. The stateless are also susceptible to other health problems that run the gamut of chronic illness, sexually transmitted diseases, and drug abuse to psychological issues such as depression, which sometimes results in alcoholism, domestic violence, and suicide (Sokoloff 2005). These poor living conditions, in addition to the types of employment and poor working conditions of many stateless persons, clearly negatively affects the stateless' Article 12 right of enjoying the highest attainable standard of physical and mental health.

Additionally, in those states where the stateless lack legal standing, they are routinely denied access to public health services (Lynch and Ali 2006; Kingston, Cohen, and Morley 2010; Lynch 2009), which further exacerbates their ability to enjoy their Article 12 right to health. Stateless children, for example, are often routinely denied vaccinations: "[I]n at least 20 countries, stateless children cannot be legally vaccinated... In many other countries, children without citizenship documents cannot receive treatment in health centers or participate in food programs" (Aird et al. 2002, 6). Human Rights Watch notes that even when governments, such as Kuwait, allegedly offer health care insurance, the stateless have problems accessing what limited coverage exists. They state that "Bidun interviewed for this report said they could not afford their health care costs, and that the government policy failed to cover testing, medication, or surgical care that medical professionals had recommended to them"

---

[19] Depending on whether they remain in the confines of Burma or have crossed an international border, the Rohingya may be stateless or stateless and refugees. Although many stateless people are not refugees, refugees often end up becoming de facto stateless.

(2011, 7). Stateless Kurds in Syria are routinely denied access to health care and hospitals, and "are instead forced to seek the services of private doctors and health clinics, where costs can be prohibitive and the numbers of which are limited" (Lynch and Ali 2006, 5). Because many of the stateless are confined to work in the low-paying informal sector, they lack sufficient funds to afford these nonpublic health services. They therefore have to rely on nongovernmental organizations and charities to assist them with their physical and mental health issues (Human Rights Watch 2011).

Similarly, the stateless often cannot rely on governments to fulfill their ICESCR right to an education (Articles 13 and 14). In many countries, such as Egypt (Lynch 2005), Kuwait (Barbieri 2007; Human Rights Watch 2011), Libya, and Saudi Arabia (van Waas 2010), stateless children are unable to attend public school, but are instead relegated to private schools that often "have inferior resources and standards to those found in government schools" (Human Rights Watch 2011, 6). In some countries, stateless children with disabilities are refused special needs education (Lynch and Ali 2006; Barbieri 2007), and it is not unheard of for governments to take specific retaliatory action against stateless children's school facilities. In Arunachal Pradesh, for example, the local government "began a campaign of school closings, burnings, and relocations which has effectively denied the Chakmas and Hajongs their right to education under international law" (South Asia Human Rights Documentation Centre, no date, 9). In more liberal states, discrimination often prevents stateless children from fully enjoying their right to an education (Belton 2010a). In those instances where a stateless child is able to attend school, she or he may be prohibited from participating in school activities or receiving scholarships (Lynch and Ali 2006), all of which affect the child's ability to be a self-determining person.

This survey demonstrates that stateless people often face myriad obstacles in the realization of their ES rights. The limits on their educational and employment opportunities, in addition to the stateless' susceptibility to poverty, malnutrition, and various diseases, make it difficult for them to be fully self-determining people in the areas of economic and social development. The fact that these people lack a nationality altogether – unlike migrants, IDPs, and other types of noncitizens – makes their condition particularly harsh. Without citizenship, they are in limbo, without a recognized identity, and fall through a gap in the international community's protection system (UN News Centre 2010). Unlike refugees and IDPs whose precarious situation elicits humanitarian responses, the international community is hesitant to label the situation of stateless groups a humanitarian issue for fear of infringing upon state sovereignty (Bloom 2009). These and other factors consequently place the stateless in a particularly vulnerable position when it comes to enjoying their human rights. The next section offers some suggestions as to how the lives of the stateless might be improved so that their ES rights are better respected, protected, and fulfilled.

RESPECTING, PROTECTING, AND FULFILLING THE RIGHTS OF THE STATELESS

An obvious first step in respecting the ES rights of the stateless is to grant them nationality. As noted earlier, the UHDR is clear that each person has the right to a nationality (Article 15), and several other human rights instruments reiterate this claim. Although the possession of a nationality in no way guarantees substantive equality or generates respect from co-citizens, it at least provides people legal standing and some measure of protection against the threat of arbitrary deportation and detention. Assuming that the right to a nationality becomes fully enshrined in international practice,[20] and more stateless persons acquire citizenship, the grant of citizenship must be accompanied by policy changes. Such changes must allow for the equal treatment and societal inclusion of the formerly stateless in practice. As Special Rapporteur on Nationality, Including Statelessness Manley Hudson observed during the fourth session of the International Law Commission:

> Any attempt to eliminate statelessness can only be considered as fruitful if it results not only in the attribution of a nationality to individuals, but also in *an improvement of their status*. As a rule, such an improvement will be achieved only if the nationality of the individual is the nationality of that State with which he is, in fact, most closely connected, his "effective nationality," if it ensures for the national the enjoyment of those rights which are attributed to nationality under international law, and the enjoyment of that status which results from nationality under municipal law. Purely formal solutions which do not take account of this desideratum might reduce the number of stateless persons but not the number of unprotected persons. They might lead to a shifting from statelessness *de jure* to statelessness *de facto* which, in the view of the Rapporteur, would not be desirable (Hudson 1952, 20).[21]

[20] That is, more states ratify the statelessness conventions and adhere to these conventions' precepts to the best of their abilities.

[21] The italicized phrase in the first sentence is not in the original.

An improvement of their status must consequently consist of the fulfillment of ES rights, especially the stateless' integration into the formal labor market. In a recent work analyzing the benefits of citizenship for formerly stateless populations (Blitz and Lynch 2009), several authors note that the acquisition of citizenship has not always improved the living conditions of formerly stateless groups, or their enjoyment of ES rights. Korir Sing'oei, for example, explains how the granting of citizenship to stateless Nubians in Kenya "is not sufficient without a corresponding integration into the labour market," as "structural barriers still consign the Nubians to the same state of poverty and destitution from which they were seeking escape through their struggle for citizenship" (2009, 45 and 46). Korir Sing'oei thus concludes that in the case of the Nubians, the acquisition of citizenship "has not brought complete relief" (ibid., 46).

Similarly, Sivapragasam notes that those Estate Tamils who have managed to acquire citizenship in Sri Lanka have not witnessed an improvement in their economic situation as their wages have not increased, they remain heavily in debt, and they lack land upon which to grow their own foodstuffs (2009). Additionally, "[T]here also appears to be little improvement with regard to [the] educational development of the population" (ibid., 73). Ablyatifov, discussing the situation of the stateless Crimean Tatars of Ukraine, observes that citizenship acquisition has not led to an overall improvement in ES rights for those who managed to acquire citizenship.[22] He states that citizenship acquisition has been unable to "address some of the systemic problems of unemployment, the lack of decent housing and public infrastructure, high levels of morbidity, the lack of access to sufficient medical care, limited social integration, the restoration of property rights and the multiple challenges involved in the allocation of land" (2009, 83). If citizenship acquisition alone is not enough to improve the situation of the stateless, and if millions continue to live in conditions that are not conducive to self-determination, what can be done to ensure that the ES rights of the stateless are respected, protected, and fulfilled?

Firstly, the CESCR needs to issue a General Comment on the Economic and Social Rights of the Stateless, with a special emphasis on the stateless in developing countries. Although The Limburg Principles on the Implementation of the International Covenant on Economic, Social and Cultural Rights state that "[a]s a general rule the Covenant applies

---

[22] There are still several thousand Crimean Tatars who have yet to obtain Ukrainian citizenship (Butkevych 2011).

equally to nationals and non-nationals," and that the exception provided in Article 2.3 "should be interpreted narrowly" (International Commission of Jurists 1987, 127), it does not provide guidance on how the clause should be interpreted regarding the ES rights of the stateless in developing countries. This is particularly important when one considers that millions of stateless peoples are found in the developing world and that their ES rights can be limited by their unlawful presence in a state. It would thus behoove the CESCR to issue a General Comment on the ES rights of stateless people in order to elucidate the scope and application of their ES rights.

Additionally, the UN should consider establishing a formal complaints mechanism for the stateless akin to the individual petitions and communications that are permitted regarding violations of the International Covenant on Civil and Political Rights (ICCPR) (UN 1966a), the International Convention on the Elimination of all forms of Racial Discrimination (UN 1965), the Convention Against Torture (UN 1984), and the Convention on the Elimination of All Forms of Discrimination Against Women (UN 1979). This petition's mechanism allows any person who believes that his or her rights under these conventions have been violated to bring a complaint against a state as long as the state is party to the convention of concern. According to OHCHR:

> [Petitions can be brought for] violations of your right to life; arbitrary arrest and detention; torture; prison conditions; unfair trial; arbitrary interference with your family, privacy or home; failure to protect the family or children; violations of your freedom of thought, religion or expression; violations of your right to peaceful assembly and freedom of association; violations of the right of minorities to enjoy their culture; discrimination based on race, sex and other grounds (Office of the High Commissioner for Human Rights, no date, 3).

The relevant Convention committee to which the person has petitioned may then request compensation for the affronted individual or recommend other remedies to states such as a retrial, commutation of a death sentence, an investigation, and so forth. Although all such recommendations are simply suggestions, as "States parties have a moral obligation to implement the decisions, but these are not legally binding" (Office of the High Commissioner for Human Rights, no date, 5), this mechanism at least allows individuals to present their human rights claims within an international body when their state of residence is ignoring or, at worst, violating their human rights. As the stateless suffer many of the violations noted by the OHCHR earlier, in addition to the aforementioned infringe-ments of their ES rights, they too should be provided with a Committee that a) monitors the implementation and violations of their human rights as elucidated in the statelessness conventions, ICESCR, and other human rights instruments and b) hears individuals' petitions regarding potential violations of their human rights.

If such a Committee is not presently feasible, the UN should consider the creation of a Special Rapporteur on Statelessness. Special Rappor-teurs, or special procedures mandate holders, exist for the express pur-poses of:

> examin[ing], monitor[ing], advis[ing] and publicly report[ing] on human rights situations in specific countries or territories, known as country man-dates, or on major phenomena of human rights violations worldwide, known as thematic mandates. Various activities are undertaken by spe-cial procedures, including responding to individual complaints, conducting studies, providing advice on technical cooperation at the country level, and engaging in general promotional activities (OHCHR 2011).

Special Rapporteurs exist for indigenous peoples (James Anaya), migrants (Jorge A. Bustamante), and internally displaced peoples (Chakola Beyani). It is not, therefore, a stretch to ask that such an individual be assigned to stateless persons. In fact, the need for such a position was estab-lished nearly fifty years ago when the International Law Commission – part of the UN's Committee on the Progressive Development of International Law and its Codification – created the position of Special Rapporteur on Nationality, Including Statelessness (International Law Commission 2007). This position was held by Manley O. Hudson and Roberto Córdova, respectively (International Law Commission 2008), and consisted of addressing the nationality of married women, elimina-tion of present and future statelessness, situations of multiple nationality, and drafting of the statelessness conventions, among other nationality-related topics (International Law Commission 2007). Because the ILC "decided to defer any further consideration of . . . questions relating to nationality" in 1954 (United Nations 1960, 149), and the need to address and resolve statelessness persists, the UN should create a position for a Special Rapporteur on Statelessness, which could complement the work of UNHCR in this area.

A more radical step could be the establishment of a UN body autho-rized to provide a special status to the stateless when the state of residence refuses to grant them citizenship. This special UN-issued status would go beyond the previously used Nansen passports. Nansen passports, which are no longer in use, were UN-issued documents provided to refugees who lacked the protection of their state of citizenship. Nansen passports "gave refugees a recognizable status and allowed them to travel freely" (Barnett 2002, 242). The special UN-issued status for the stateless, however, would provide the stateless with the additional rights to work, health care, and an adequate standard of living. Although this status could not be imposed upon a state – that is, the UN status-issuing body could not make a state accept a person with the special status – incentives could be provided so that it becomes beneficial for states to accept the special status of these persons and to protect their ES rights. For example, the yearly dues owed by a state to the UN could be reduced by a given amount for each person who resides in a state that recognizes the special UN-issued status and respects, protects, and fulfills the stateless' ES rights to the best of its abilities.

Although some may find the issuance of such a special status outside of the UN's purview, it is important to bear in mind that the inclusion of a right to a nationality in the UDHR "points to an implicit acknowledgement on the part of the drafters that the United Nations has duties in this area" (Morsink 1999, 82). This claim was supported by Eleanor Roosevelt, one of the drafters of the UDHR, who remarked that Article 15 of the UDHR was of vital importance, and that those persons "who are without [the protection of some government] shall be protected by the United Nations" (Roosevelt 1948, 474). The International Law Commission, in its 1953 session, echoed Mrs. Roosevelt's position when it declared that "[s]tateless persons, or persons threatened with statelessness . . . should be protected, in conformity with international conventions, by the United Nations" (United Nations 1959, 228). Arguably, this protection should at least include a committee or Special Rapporteur devoted to monitoring the rights and hearing the claims of the stateless, even if it does not go as far as providing a special UN-issued status to them.

CONCLUSION

This survey of statelessness and economic and social rights demonstrates that more work needs to be done in this area of human rights research. The CESCR needs to elaborate how Article 2.3 of ICESCR applies to the stateless in developing countries, and scholars need to engage with the subject of statelessness in a wide variety of research contexts and in a comprehensive way, as well. Although we are aware that state-lessness often limits work and educational opportunities and hinders the stateless' ability to access public services of various kinds, we know very little about how each specific ES right is respected, protected, or ful-filled when it comes to the stateless. Comparative analyses specifically and systematically addressing ES rights and statelessness do not exist. What we currently have is a series of NGO reports, supplemented by a few academic case studies, of the general situation of the stateless with-out a comprehensive investigation into the specific relationship between statelessness and the enjoyment of particular ES rights.

Not only do we know very little about the relationship between state-lessness and the enjoyment of specific ES rights– such as the rights to form trade unions and strike – we do not know whether certain ES rights – such as the rights to social security and an adequate standard of living – are more often violated than other ES rights – such as the rights to an educa-tion or basic health care. That is, are all ES rights as likely to be violated when it comes to the stateless? Which ES rights are the stateless most likely to enjoy, which are they most likely to be denied, and what accounts for the difference? Additionally, we have not yet adequately analyzed the relationship between poverty and statelessness. Is it a general feature of statelessness that those without citizenship from anywhere are poorer on average than the typical citizen in the state within which they reside? If so, is statelessness a cause or a consequence of poverty? Is poverty – or the denial of an adequate standard of living – the primary barrier to the stateless' enjoyment of other ES rights? In other words, is statelessness as limiting a status if a person is not impoverished?

In terms of fulfilling the ES rights of the stateless, little has been writ-ten on the practical means by which these rights can be enjoyed by the stateless when they do not hold any legal status in the state within which they reside, or are discriminated against by society. Although it is gener-ally recognized that all human rights are interdependent and indivisible (International Commission of Jurists 1987), is it possible that by focusing on the fulfillment of a particular ES right – such as the right to work – that the enjoyment of other ES rights may follow for the stateless? That is, if they could be provided some recognized work status that allows them to work freely in the formal sector at the same level of pay as a citizen with similar qualifications and with equal treatment to said citizen, could this improve their situation in the ES rights arena? Similarly, although Blitz and Lynch's edited volume (2009) on the benefits of citizenship for for-merly stateless populations is a welcome contribution to the literature on statelessness, further research needs to be conducted on the improvement in a person's ability to be self-determining in the economic and social spheres once citizenship has been acquired. Many of the authors of the volume, and the editors themselves, note that citizenship acquisition alone is not enough to improve the lot of the formerly stateless, yet we do not know what the best practices are in terms of respecting, protecting, and fulfilling the ES rights of the stateless.

Finally, our knowledge is limited regarding how the stateless go about trying to achieve their ES (or any other human) rights when violated. To whom do they turn, what do they do, and how do they react when their ES rights are ignored? What sort of collective actions do they engage in and what are some of the common mechanisms used by the stateless in order to ameliorate violations of their ES rights? Which forms of collective action have been successful for them and which coping mechanisms are most commonly used? Additionally, do the stateless think in terms of ES rights and, if so, do they feel that particular ES rights would better assist them to become fully self-determining agents? Survey research, although difficult with these populations due to their invisible and often unlawful status, will be important in addressing these questions.

In conclusion, statelessness is a continuing problem that affects millions of people globally. Although stateless people arguably have all the rights enumerated in the UDHR, ICCPR, and ICESCR,[23] this study shows that the stateless' lack of citizenship status often severely limits their ability to enjoy these rights. The possession of a citizenship from somewhere is still closely tied to the ability to have one's human rights respected, protected, and fulfilled in practice. Although statelessness is making a slow comeback on the international agenda,[24] the international community – especially the UN and its member states – should be doing more to address this issue. Scholars, in turn, need to consider seriously the relationship between statelessness and the denial of ES rights.

[23] With the exception of those rights expressly reserved for nationals or those that are contingent upon a country's development status for fulfillment.

[24] Notably, the UNHCR has accomplished several important objectives over the past few years, including: assistance to states regarding citizenship laws, paving the way for thousands of people to acquire citizenship in Sri Lanka, Bangladesh, and Nepal; a proposed new budget structure that focuses upon statelessness as one of its four core areas (United Nations High Commissioner for Refugees 2007); the promotion of the eradication of statelessness by the High Commissioner, along with the High Commissioner of the Office for Human Rights, in an editorial (Guterres and Arbour 2007); and an educational campaign on its Web site to inform people about statelessness.

REFERENCES

Ablyatifov, Rustem, 2009. "Citizenship Reform and Challenges for the Crimean Tatars in Ukraine," in Brad K. Blitz and Maureen Lynch (Eds.) *Statelessness and the Benefits of Citizenship: A Comparative Study*, 75–84. Oxford Brooks University, UK. Retrieved from http://www.udhr60.ch/report/statelessness_paper0609.pdf.

Adam, Adam Hussein, 2009. "Kenyan Nubians: Standing Up to Statelessness," *Forced Migration Review* 32: 19–20. Retrieved from http://www.fmreview.org/statelessness.htm.

Adjami, Mirna and Julia Harrington, 2008. "The Scope and Content of Article 15 of the Universal Declaration of Human Rights," *Refugee Survey Quarterly* 27(3): 93–109.

Aird, Sarah, Helen Harnett, and Punam Shah, 2002. *Stateless Children: Youth Who are without Citizenship*, Washington, DC: Youth Advocate Program International.

Barbieri, Patrick, 2007. *About Being Without: Stories of Stateless in Kuwait*, Washington, DC: Refugees International. Retrieved from http://www.refugeesinternational.org/sites/default/files/Kuwait_statelessrpt.pdf.

Barnett, Laura, 2002. "Global Governance and the Evolution of the International Refugee Regime," *International Journal of Refugee Law* 14(2/3): 238–262.

Batchelor, Carol, 1995. "Stateless Persons: Some Gaps in International Protection," *International Journal of Refugee Law* 7(2): 232–259.

Batchelor, Carol, 1998. "Statelessness and the Problem of Resolving Nationality Status," *International Journal of Refugee Law* 10(1): 156–183.

Batchelor, Carol, 2006. "Transforming International Legal Principles into National Law: The Right to a Nationality and the Avoidance of Statelessness," *Refugee Survey Quarterly* 25(3): 8–25.

Belton, Kristy A., 2010a. "Arendt's Children in the Bahamian Context: The Children of Migrants without Status," *International Journal of Bahamian Studies* 16: 35–50.

Belton, Kristy A., 2010b. "Dry Land Drowning or Rip Current Survival? Haitians Without Status in the Bahamas," *Ethnic and Racial Studies* 34(6): 948–966.

Bhabha, Jacqueline, 2009. "Arendt's Children: Do Today's Migrant Children have a Right to have Rights?" *Human Rights Quarterly* 31(2): 410–451.

Blitz, Brad K. and Maureen Lynch (Eds.), 2009. *Statelessness and the Benefits of Citizenship: A Comparative Study*. Oxford Brooks University, UK. Retrieved from http://www.udhr60.ch/report/statelessness_paper0609.pdf.

Bloom, Jane E., 2009. "Challenges to Finding Solutions to Statelessness," International Catholic Migrations Commission. Retrieved from http://www.crsprogramquality.org/storage/events/Statelessness_Challenges-to-Solutions.pdf.

Bosniak, Linda, 2000. "Citizenship Denationalized," *Indiana Journal of Legal Studies* 7(2): 447–509.

Bosniak, Linda. 2007. "Roundtable on Citizenship: An Emerging International Law of Citizenship?" *Proceedings of the Annual Meeting (American Society of International Law)* 101: 91–94.

Butkevych, Maksym, 2011. "Mr Oldrich Andrysek assumes responsibilities as the Regional Representative of the United Nations High Commissioner for Refugees," United Nations High Commissioner for Refugees. Retrieved from http://www.unhcr.org.ua/news.php?in=1&news_id=205.

Castles, Stephen and Alastair Davidson. 2000. *Citizenship and Migration: Globalization and the Politics of Belonging.* New York: Routledge.

Cordell, Kristen, 2011. "Expert Perspective: Kristen Cordell, advocate at Refugees International, talks about long term solutions for refugees." Retrieved from http://zunia.org/post/expert-perspective-kristen-cordell-advocate-at-refugees-international-talks-about-long-term-soluti/.

Council of Europe, 2006a. *Convention on the Avoidance of Statelessness in Relation to State Succession.* Retrieved from http://conventions.coe.int/Treaty/EN/Treaties/Html/200.htm.

Council of Europe, 2006b. Explanatory Report on the *Convention on the Avoidance of Statelessness in Relation to State Succession.* Retrieved from http://conventions.coe.int/Treaty/EN/Reports/Html/200.htm.

Dauvergne, Catherine, 2007. "Citizenship with a Vengeance," *Theoretical Inquiries in Law* 8(2): 489–508.

Donner, Ruth, 1994. *The Regulation of Nationality in International Law*, 2nd edition, Irvington-on-Hudson, NY: Transnational Publishers, Inc.

Equal Rights Trust, 2010. *Unravelling Anomaly: Detention, Discrimination and the Protection Needs of Stateless Persons,* London.

Farquharson, Marjorie, 2011. *Statelessness in Central Asia,* United Nations High Commissioner for Refugees. Retrieved from http://www.unhcr.org/4dfb592e9.html.

Forced Migration Review. 2009. "Stateless." *Refugees Studies Center.* Issue 32. Retrieved from http://www.fmreview.org/sites/fmr/files/FMRdownloads/en/FMRpdfs/FMR32/FMR32.pdf.

Gajanayake, Indra, John C. Caldwell, and Pat Caldwell, 1991. "Why is Health Relatively Poor on Sri Lanka's Tea Estates?" *Social Science & Medicine* 32(7): 793–804.

Garcia, Sean and Camilla Olson, 2008. "Rohingya: Burma's Forgotten Minority," Refugees International. Retrieved from http://www.refugeesinternational.org/sites/default/files/RohingyaDec19.pdf.

Glickman, Dan, 2010. "Testimony of The Honorable Dan Glickman," United States Senate Committee on the Judiciary. Retrieved from http://www.judiciary.senate.gov/hearings/testimony.cfm?id=e655f9e2809e5476862f735da15dabae&wit_id=e655f9e2809e5476862f735da15dabae-1-1.

Government of Sri Lanka, 2003. Grant of Citizenship to Persons of Indian Origin Act, No. 35. Supplement to Part II of the *Gazette of the Democratic Socialist Republic of Sri Lanka.*

Guterres, António and Louise Arbour. 2007. "The Hidden World of Stateless People." Retrieved from http://www.unhchr.ch/huricane/huricane.nsf/view01/950096EC42521C75C12573A1004FF9E9?opendocument.

Hammarberg, Thomas, 2009. "Many Roma in Europe are stateless and live outside social protection," Council of Europe: Commissioner for Human

Rights. Retrieved from http://www.unhcr.org/refworld/country,,COECHR,, CZE,,4a7023c72,0.html.

Hammarberg, Thomas, 2010. "The Rights of Stateless Persons must be Protected," Council of Europe. Retrieved from https://wcd.coe.int/wcd/ViewDoc .jsp?id=1722017&Site=COE.

Heffernan, John W., 2002. "Being Recognized as Citizens: A Human Security Dilemma in South and Southeast Asia," Commission on Human Security, 1–34. Retrieved from http://www.humansecurity-chs.org/activities/research/ citizenship_asia.pdf.

Helle, Knut-Erik, 2011. "The Dirty Secret of Ceylon Tea." Retrieved from http: //keh.nu/Articles/the-dirty-secret-of-ceylon-tea.html.

Hertel, Shareen and Lanse Minkler, 2007. "Economic Rights: The Terrain," in Shareen Hertel and Lanse Minkler (Eds.) *Economic Rights: Conceptual, Measurement, and Policy Issues*, 1–35, Cambridge: Cambridge University Press.

Hettne, Bjorn, 2000. "The Fate of Citizenship in Post-Westphalia," *Citizenship Studies* 4(1): 35–46.

Hindess, Barry, 2005. "Citizenship and Empire," in Thomas Blom Hansen and Finn Stepputat (Eds.) *Sovereign Bodies: Citizens, Migrants, and States in the Postcolonial World*, 241–256, Princeton, NJ: Princeton University Press.

Hudson, Manley O., 1952. *Nationality, Including Statelessness*, UN, A/CN.4.50. Retrieved from http://untreaty.un.org/ilc/documentation/english/a_cn4_50.pdf.

Human Rights Watch, 2010. "Stateless again: Palestinian-Origin Jordanians Deprived of their Nationality," New York. Retrieved from http://www.hrw. org/reports/2010/02/01/stateless-again.

Human Rights Watch, 2011. "Prisoners of the Past: Kuwaiti Bidun and the Burden of Statelessness," New York. Retrieved from http://www.hrw.org/reports/ 2011/06/13/prisoners-past.

Hussain, Misha, 2011. "Stateless Mothers Fall Through the Cracks in Bangladesh," Association for Women's Rights in Development. Retrieved from http://www.awid.org/News-Analysis/Issues-and-Analysis/Stateless-refugee-mothers-fall-through-the-cracks-in-Bangladesh.

Immigration and Refugee Board of Canada, 2006. "Sri Lanka: Plantation Tamils; their Number, Location, Relations with Sri Lankan Tamils, Legal Status and Treatment by Members of the Government Security Forces and Police (2004–2006)." Retrieved from http://www.unhcr.org/refworld/docid/ 45f1476b20.html.

Inter-American Court of Human Rights, 2005. *The Case of Yean and Bosico v. the Dominican Republic*. Retrieved from http://www.unhcr.org/refworld/ country,,IACRTHR,,DOM,,44e497d94,0.html.

International Commission of Jurists, 1987. "The Limburg Principles on the Implementation of the International Covenant on Economic, Social and Cultural Rights," *Human Rights Quarterly* 9(2): 122–135.

International Court of Justice, 1955. *Nottebohm Case (Second Phase), Judgment of April 6th*, 4–27. Retrieved from http://www.icj-cij.org/docket/files/18/2674. pdf.

International Law Commission, 2007. "Introduction: Origin and background of the development and codification of international law," in *The Work of the*

International Law Commission, 7th edition. Retrieved from http://untreaty.un.org/ilc/ilcintro.htm.

International Law Commission, 2008. "Nationality Including Statelessness." Retrieved from http://untreaty.un.org/ilc/guide/6_1.htm.

Kelley, Ninette, 2010. "Ideas, Interests, and Institutions: Conceding Citizenship in Bangladesh," *University of Toronto Law Journal* 60(2): 349–371.

Kingston, Lindsey N., Elizabeth F. Cohen, and Christopher P. Morley, 2010. "Limitation on Universality: The 'Right to Health' and the Necessity of Legal Nationality," *International Health and Human Rights* 10(11): 1–12.

Komai, Chie and Fumie Azukizawa, 2009. "Stateless persons from Thailand in Japan," *Forced Migration Review* 32.

Korir Sing'oei, Abraham, 2009. "Promoting Citizenship in Kenya: The Nubian Case," in Brad K. Blitz and Maureen Lynch (Eds.) *Statelessness and the Benefits of Citizenship: A Comparative Study*, 37–49. Oxford Brooks University, UK.

League of Nations. 1930. "Convention on Certain Questions Relating to the Conflict of Nationality Laws," *American Journal of International Law* 24(3): 192–200.

Lewa, Chris, 2009. "North Arakan: An Open Prison for the Rohingya in Burma," *Forced Migration Review* 32: 11–13.

Lynch, Maureen, 2005. "Lives on Hold: The Human Cost of Statelessness," Washington, DC: Refugees International. Retrieved from http://www.refintl.org/policy/in-depth-report/lives-hold-human-cost-statelessness.

Lynch, Maureen, 2008. "Futures Denied: Statelessness among Infants, Children and Youth," Washington, DC: Refugees International. Retrieved from http://www.refugeesinternational.org/sites/default/files/Stateless_Children_FINAL.pdf.

Lynch, Maureen, 2009. "Statelessness: International Blind Spot Linked to Global Concerns," Washington, DC: Refugees International. Retrieved from www.refugeesinternational.org/node/3758.

Lynch, Maureen and Perveen Ali, 2006. "Buried Alive: Stateless Kurds in Syria," Washington, DC: Refugees International. Retrieved from http://www.refugeesinternational.org/policy/in-depth-report/buried-alive-stateless-kurds-syria.

Lynch, Maureen and Katherine Southwick, 2009. "Nationality Rights for all: A Progress Report and Global Survey on Statelessness," Washington, DC: Refugees International. Retrieved from http://www.refugeesinternational.org/policy/in-depth-report/nationality-rights-all.

Lynch, Maureen and Melanie Teff, 2009. "Childhood Statelessness," *Forced Migration Review* 32: 31–33.

Manly, Mark, 2007. "The Spirit of Geneva – Traditional and New Actors in the Field of Statelessness," *Refugee Survey Quarterly* 26(4): 255–261.

Massey, Hugh, 2010. *UNHCR and De Facto Statelessness*, LPPR/2010/01. Geneva: UN. Retrieved from http://www.unhcr.org/refworld/pdfid/4bbf387d2.pdf.

McDougall, Gay, 2008. *Promotion and Protection of all Human Rights, Civil, Political, Economic, Social and Cultural Rights, Including the Right to Development*, A/HRC/7/23. Geneva: UN.

McNevin, Anne. 2006, "Political Belonging in a Neoliberal Era: The Struggle of the Sans-Papiers," *Citizenship Studies* 10(2): 135–151.

Medecins Sans Frontieres, 2002. "10 Years for the Rohingya Refugees in Bangladesh: Past, Present and Future," 1–45. Retrieved from http://www.msf. org/source/downloads/2002/rohingya.doc.

Monforte, Pierre and Pascale Dufour, 2011. "Mobilizing in Borderline Citizenship Regimes: A Comparative Analysis of Undocumented Migrants' Collection Actions," *Politics & Society* 39(2): 203–232.

Morsink, Johannes, 1999. *The Universal Declaration of Human Rights: Origins, Drafting, and Intent*, Philadelphia, PA: University of Pennsylvania Press.

Office for the Coordination of Humanitarian Affairs, 2004. "Guiding Principles on Internal Displacement." Retrieved from http://www.unhcr.org/43ce1cff2. html.

Office of the High Commissioner for Human Rights, No Date. "23 Frequently Asked Questions about Treaty Body Complaints Procedures." Retrieved from http://www2.ohchr.org/english/bodies/petitions/docs/23faq.pdf.

Office of the High Commissioner for Human Rights, 2006. "The Rights of Non-Citizens," HR/PUB/06/11. New York and Geneva.

Opala, Ken, 2011. "Refugee Camps Teeming with a New Generation of Youth Who are Stateless," *Daily Nation*. April 1. Nairobi, Kenya. Retrieved fromhttp://www.nation.co.ke/News/-/1056/1137308/-/view/printVersion/-/1fi8obz/-/index.html.

Open Society Justice Initiative, 2011. "*De Jure* Statelessness in the Real World: Applying the Prato Summary Conclusions." Retrieved from http://www.soros.org/initiatives/justice/focus/equality_citizenship/articles_publications/publications/prato-20110302/prato-statelessness-20110303.pdf.

Perks, Katherine and Amal de Chickera, 2009. "The Silent Stateless and the Unhearing World. Can Equality Compel Us to Listen?" *Equal Rights Review* 3: 42–55.

Physicians for Human Rights, 2010. *Stateless and Starving: Persecuted Rohingya Flee Burma and Starve in Bangladesh*, Cambridge, MA: Physicians for Human Rights. Retrieved from http://physiciansforhumanrights.org/library/documents/reports/stateless-and-starving.pdf. Accessed Apr. 2, 2011.

Refugees Studies Center, 2009. "Stateless," *Forced Migration Review* 32: 1–76.

Roosevelt, Eleanor, 1948. "The Promise of Human Rights," *Foreign Affairs* 26: 470–477.

Shiblak, Abbas, 2009. "The lost tribes of Arabia," *Forced Migration Review* 32: 37–38.

Shue, Henry, 1996. *Basic Rights: Subsistence, Affluence, and U.S. Foreign Policy*, 2nd edition, Princeton, NJ: Princeton University Press.

Singh, Deepak K., 2010. *Stateless in South Asia: The Chakmas between Bangladesh and India*, Thousand Oaks, CA: Sage.

Sivapragasam, P.P., 2009. "From Statelessness to Citizenship: Up-Country Tamils in Sri Lanka," in Brad K. Blitz and Maureen Lynch (Eds.) *Statelessness and the Benefits of Citizenship: A Comparative Study*, 65–74. Oxford Brooks University, UK.

Sokoloff, Constantin, 2005. *Denial of Citizenship: A Challenge to Human Security*, New York: Advisory Board on Human Security, Office for the Coordination of Humanitarian Affairs, UN. Retrieved from http://ochaonline.un.org/ochalinkclick.aspx?link=ocha&docid=1003253.

South Asia Human Rights Documentation Centre, no date. "The Stateless Chakmas and Hajongs of the Indian State of Arunachal Pradesh: A Study of Systematic Repression." New Delhi.

UN (United Nations), 1945. *Charter of the United Nations*. Retrieved from http://www.un.org/en/documents/charter/index.shtml.

UN, 1984. *Convention Against Torture and Other Cruel, Inhuman or Degrading Treatment or Punishment*. Retrieved from http://www2.ohchr.org/english/law/cat.htm.

UN, 1979. *Convention on the Elimination of all Forms of Discrimination Against Women*. Retrieved from http://www2.ohchr.org/english/law/cedaw.htm.

UN, 1961. *Convention on the Reduction of Statelessness*. Retrieved from http://www2.ohchr.org/english/law/statelessness.htm.

UN, 1989. *Convention on the Rights of the Child*. Retrieved from http://www2.ohchr.org/english/law/crc.htm.

UN, 1951. *Convention Relating to the Status of Refugees*. Retrieved from http://www.unhcr.org/3b66c2aa10.html.

UN, 1954. *Convention Relating to the Status of Stateless Persons*. Retrieved from http://www2.ohchr.org/english/law/stateless.htm.

UN, 2009. *General Comment no. 20: Non-Discrimination in Economic, Social and Cultural Rights*, Economic and Social Council, E/C.12/GC/20. Retrieved from http://www2.ohchr.org/english/bodies/cescr/comments.htm.

UN, 1965. *International Convention on the Elimination of all Forms of Racial Discrimination*. Retrieved from http://www2.ohchr.org/english/law/cerd.htm.

UN, 1966a. *International Covenant on Civil and Political Rights*. Retrieved from http://www2.ohchr.org/english/law/ccpr.htm.

UN, 1966b. *International Covenant on Economic, Social and Cultural Rights*. Retrieved from http://www2.ohchr.org/english/law/cescr.htm.

UN, 2011a. "Status of Ratifications – Convention on the Reduction of Statelessness," *Treaty Series* 989: 175. Retrieved from http://treaties.un.org/pages/ViewDetails.aspx?src=UNTSONLINE&tabid=2&mtdsg_no=V-4&chapter=5&lang=en#Participants.

UN, 2011b. "Status of Ratifications – Convention Relating to the Status of Stateless Persons," *Treaty Series* 360: 117. Retrieved from http://treaties.un.org/pages/ViewDetailsII.aspx?&src=UNTSONLINE&mtdsg_no=V~3&chapter=5&Temp=mtdsg2&lang=en.

UN, 1948. *Universal Declaration of Human Rights*. Retrieved from http://www.un.org/en/documents/udhr/index.shtml.

UN, 1959. *Yearbook of the International Law Commission 1953, vol. II*. Retrieved from http://untreaty.un.org/ilc/publications/yearbooks/Ybkvolumes(e)/ILC_1953_v2_e.pdf.

UN, 1960. *Yearbook of the International Law Commission 1954, vol. II*. Retrieved from http://untreaty.un.org/ilc/publications/yearbooks/Ybkvolumes(e)/ILC_1954_v2_e.pdf.

United Nations High Commissioner for Refugees, 2007. *Biennial Programme Budget 2008–2009 of the Office of the United Nations High Commissioner for Refugees*, A/AC.96/1040, General Assembly. Retrieved from http://www.unhcr.org/excom/EXCOM/46ea53192.pdf.

United Nations High Commissioner for Refugees, 2009. *Global Appeal 2009 Update.* Retrieved from http://www.unhcr.org/publ/PUBL/4922d4370.pdf.

United Nations High Commissioner for Refugees, 2011. *Global Appeal 2011 Update.* Retrieved from http://www.unhcr.org/4cd917c99.html.

United Nations High Commissioner for Refugees, 2007. "Q&A: The World's 15 Million Stateless People Need Help." Retrieved from http://www.unhcr.org/cgi-bin/texis/vtx/news/opendoc.htm?tbl=NEWS&id=464dca3c4.

United Nations High Commissioner for Refugees. 2012. "Statistical Online Population Database." Retrieved from http://apps.who.int/globalatlas/default.asp.

United Nations High Commissioner for Refugees and Inter-Parliamentary Union, 2005. *Nationality and Statelessness: A Handbook for Parliamentarians.* Retrieved from http://www.unhcr.org/436774c62.html.

UN News Centre, 2010. "UN agency appeals for better protection for world's stateless people." Retrieved from http://www.un.org/apps/news/story.asp?NewsID=36355&Cr=unhcr&Cr1=.

van Selm, Joanne, 2009. "Stateless Roma in Macedonia," *Forced Migration Review* 32: 46–47. Retrieved from http://www.fmreview.org/statelessness.htm.

van Waas, Laura, 2008. *Nationality Matters: Statelessness Under International Law*, Antwerp, Belgium: Intersentia.

van Waas, Laura, 2010. *The Situation of Stateless Persons in the Middle East and North Africa*, United Nations High Commissioner for Refugees. Retrieved from http://www.unhcr.org/4ce63e079.html.

Weis, Paul, 1956. *Nationality and Statelessness in International Law*, London: Stevens & Sons Limited.

Weissbrodt, David S. and Clay Collins, 2006. "The Human Rights of Stateless Persons," *Human Rights Quarterly* 28(1): 245–276.

Wooding, Bridget, 2008. "Contesting Dominican Discrimination and Statelessness," *Peace Review* 20(3): 366–375.

III

Meta

10

Establishing a Social and International Order for the Realization of Human Rights

Mark Gibney

UDHR Article 28. Everyone is entitled to a social and international order in which the rights and freedoms set forth in this Declaration can be fully realized.

INTRODUCTION

In his definitive study of the drafting history of the Universal Declaration of Human Rights (UDHR), Johannes Morsink (1999) has little to say about the purpose and meaning behind Article 28, giving only slightly more attention to accompanying Article 22,[1] which serves as an introduction to the "new" economic, social, and cultural rights (ESCR) set forth in Articles 23–27. According to Morsink, some of the drafters of the UDHR took the view that the two articles essentially covered the same ground, and thus there was no need to include both of them together. However, this position was ultimately rejected. The only substantive discussion of Article 28 that Morsink (1999, 231–232) provides involves the use of the word "good" in the original draft: "Everyone has the right to a good social and international order in which the rights and freedoms set forth in this Declaration can be fully realized." This vague adjective was later removed.

Based on this thin history, it is apparent that Article 28 was not one of the more hotly contested provisions during the drafting of the UDHR, and with the notable exception of the work of Thomas Pogge, which is

---

[1] Article 22 provides: "Everyone, as a member of society, has the right to social security and is entitled to realization, through international effort and international co-operation and in accordance with the organization and resources of each State, of the economic, social and cultural rights indispensable for his dignity and the free development of his personality."

referenced later, there has not been a great deal of scholarly attention given to this article since that time, either. Thus, it would be easy to dismiss Article 28 (as well as Article 22) on the basis that it offers no new substantive right, but only the appropriate and proper conditions to achieve certain rights.

Yet, Article 28 is important for at least two reasons. The first is the use of the term "everyone," which is one of many affirmations in the UDHR that all human beings have human rights by the mere fact of their existence. Related to this, what Article 28 underscores is that human rights are not primarily for states and the maintenance of peace and security between countries, as has been suggested from time to time. Instead, human rights are for people.

The second reason Article 28 is important is that it places human rights protection within the broadest possible framework: the entire international order. To a modern audience this might not strike a responsive chord because in the decades that have followed, the concept of human rights has remained decidedly state-based and state-centered. That is, individual states decide whether to become parties to international and regional human rights treaties; whether they are complying with international human rights standards as they report on their own practices to the United Nations (UN) treaty bodies; whether they have afforded victims the necessary means of procuring an effective remedy; and as a final example and one that relates to the focus of this chapter, decide the geographic scope of their own human rights obligations.

A telling example of this last point occurred a few years ago involving Paul Hunt, who at the time was the UN Special Rapporteur on the right to health. During the course of a country study of Sweden, Hunt asked government officials whether Sweden was legally obligated to provide foreign aid. To be fair, Sweden is arguably the single most generous country in the world in terms of the amount of aid it provides per GDP, and there is absolutely no indication that this state of affairs will change anytime soon. However, to Hunt's surprise and consternation, the Swedish government took the position that it was under no legal obligation to provide any aid. Hunt rejects this view of human rights:

> Sweden does not accept that it has a legal obligation of international assistance and cooperation. While other high-income states share Sweden's view, middle-income and low-income countries disagree.

> However, if there is no legal obligation underpinning the human rights responsibility of international assistance and cooperation, inescapably all

international assistance and cooperation fundamentally rests upon charity. While such a position might have been tenable in years gone by, it is unacceptable in the twenty-first century (Hunt 2007, para. 113).

Who is correct – Paul Hunt or the Swedish government? I would argue that the answer to this question is vastly more important than it might otherwise seem. Sweden's position is one that is based on a traditional notion of state sovereignty. The international human rights revolution changed this, but only to some degree. According to the dominant position, whereas international human rights standards changed state practices, this was only true within a country's domestic realm and it only applied to a state's relationship to those who were within its own territorial borders. What international human rights law did not address – or so it is commonly thought – is the "diagonal" relationship between one state and citizens of another country. In that way, the reason why the response of the Swedish government will seem uncontroversial to many is that we have conceptualized human rights in such a way that each state is to take care of its "own" – but there is no obligation to go beyond this (literally). Thus, although a country such as Sweden might provide aid and assistance to another state where human rights standards are not being met, it is under no legal obligation to do so. Or so it is readily assumed.

Perhaps if every state were to meet its human rights obligations, this approach would not pose a problem in the sense that "everyone" would still enjoy the protections that international human rights law mandates. This, however, is anything but the case, especially in terms of ESCR, as Pogge has pointed out:

> It is estimated that 850 million human beings are chronically undernourished, over 1,000 million lack access to safe water and 2,600 million lack access to basic sanitation. About 2,000 million lack access to essential medicines. Some 1,000 million have no adequate shelter and 2,000 million lack electricity. Some 781 million adults are illiterate and 250 million children between 5 and 14 do wage work outside their household – often under harsh or cruel conditions: as soldiers, prostitutes, or domestic servants, or in agriculture, construction, textile, or carpet production. Roughly one-third of all human deaths, 18 million annually or 50,000 each day, are due to poverty-related causes, easily preventable through better nutrition, safe drinking water and sewage systems, cheap rehydration packs, vaccines, antibiotics, and other medicines. People of color, females, and the very young are heavily overrepresented among the global poor, and hence also among those suffering the staggering effects of severe poverty (Pogge 2007: 12–13, citations omitted).

It should be clear that the countries where these horrors are taking place are not meeting their obligations under international human rights law, or to state this more succinctly, these states are committing human rights violations, just as they would be doing if they tortured or killed these people instead. Unfortunately, this is as far as our thinking has gone, or at least as far as we have allowed it to take us. The argument I will develop here is that this state of affairs is also an indictment of the international community in that these "outside" states see themselves as having no legal obligations to eliminate these atrocities themselves – or to establish an international order that would be designed to do so.

I begin by briefly examining some of the work of philosopher Thomas Pogge. Although I find myself in agreement with Pogge's argument that the present international order is immoral, my view is that his analysis is mainly based on ethical considerations. What is missing is a more serious discussion of international human rights law, although I will readily concede that this realm has not performed any better. I spend some time examining why this has been the case and why even countries such as Sweden refuse to acknowledge the human rights obligations they have outside their own borders. However, there has been some recent indication of change, and I analyze three examples of this: 1) the Responsibility to Protect (R2P) initiative; 2) the "duty to prevent" (genocide); and 3) the creation of the Extraterritorial Obligations (ETO) Consortium. Finally, I end by positing certain steps that could be taken immediately that would bring the world much closer to the international order that has been called for, but which has yet to materialize.

THOMAS POGGE AND ARTICLE 28

Thomas Pogge is outraged at the state of the world – and justifiably so. The simple truth is that we live in a world where hundreds of millions of people are still denied at least some form of human rights protection. Pogge's work is aimed at addressing this, and in doing so he has taken at least two different tacks. In his book *World Poverty and Human Rights* (2002) Pogge's focus is more on severe world poverty as a moral issue, but more precisely, how and why we generally do not view this nightmarish state of affairs as constituting a moral issue in the first place. Pogge has a simple answer: "Extensive severe poverty can continue, because we do not find its eradication morally compelling. And we cannot find its eradication morally compelling until we find its persistence and the relentless rise in global inequality troubling enough to warrant serious moral reflection" (Pogge 2002, 3). However, in a later work, Pogge (2007) deals more with the establishment of an institutional order to help achieve this moral imperative. He takes the position that the moral quality, or justice, of any institutional order depends primarily on its success in affording all its participants secure access to the objects of their human rights. In addressing Article 28 in particular, he sets forth what this particular provision of the UDHR is asking of the citizens and governments of the developed states:

> [I]t is not that we assume the role of a global police force ready to intervene to aid and protect all those whose human rights are imperiled by brutal governments or (civil) wars. It requires instead that we support institutional reforms toward a global order that would strongly support the emergence and stability of democratic, rights-respecting, peaceful regimes and would also tend to reduce radical economic deprivations and inequalities, which now engender great vulnerabilities to civil rights violations as well as massive premature mortality from malnutrition and easily preventable diseases (Pogge 2007, 18).

Pogge goes on to say that the point of human rights is to ensure that all human beings have secure access to certain vital goods, but that many persons lack such security. He agrees that it makes "good sense" to assign responsibility for such insecurity to the governments and citizens where this insecurity occurs. However, he also points out the severe limitations inherent in this approach: "For the hope that these countries will, from the inside, democratize themselves and abolish the worst poverty and oppression is entirely naïve so long as the institutional context of these countries continues to favor so strongly the emergence and endurance of brutal and corrupt elites" (Pogge 2007, 23).However, the real thrust of Pogge's argument is to point the finger of moral blame squarely at Western states and the citizens of those countries: "[T]he primary responsibility for this institutional context, for the prevailing global order, lies with the governments and citizens of the wealthy countries because we maintain this order, with at least latent coercion, and because we, and only we, could relatively easily form it in the directions indicated" (Pogge 2007, 23).

GOING BEYOND MORALITY: THE ROLE OF INTERNATIONAL HUMAN RIGHTS LAW

Like many, I find Pogge's condemnation of the present world order compelling. However, although he invokes human rights standards and Article 28 in particular, his argument is often lacking in terms of drawing upon international human rights law more specifically. In that way, it sits at a juncture somewhere between law and morality, but he is mainly presenting a moral argument. My own approach is to rely more on law, and thus, what follows is the argument that there is a legal obligation to establish an international order that would be conducive to the promotion and protection of human rights. One of the most important first steps in achieving this is by recognizing that states have human rights obligations that extend outside their own territorial borders.

The place to begin is with the UDHR itself, which in the view of many international lawyers has long passed into the realm of customary international law. Because of this, the UDHR can now be considered to be legally binding on all states. Yet, it is important to note that Article 28 is not the only human rights provision that deals with issues of an international order. Under Articles 55 and 56 of the United Nations Charter, member states obligate themselves to take "joint and several action in cooperation with the Organization" in order to achieve "conditions of economic and social progress and development."

Given the fact that the overwhelming majority of human rights abuses in the world are violations of ESCR, one of the key human rights instruments is the International Covenant on Economic, Social and Cultural Rights (ICESCR). Unlike many other human rights treaties, there is no mention in the treaty of either territory or jurisdiction. Furthermore, Article 2 requires that the state parties undertake to take steps "individually and through international assistance and co-operation, especially economic and technical, to the maximum of its available resources, with a view to achieving progressively the full realization of the rights recognized in the present Covenant."

What is also noteworthy is that the CESCR, the UN body that is assigned the task of overseeing and implementing the Covenant, has repeatedly pressed the issue that the obligations of the state parties transcend their own territorial borders. Thus, in one of its earliest General Comments (No. 3, 1990), the Committee explained that the term "maximum available resources" referred to "both the resources existing within a State and those available from the international community through international cooperation and assistance" (para. 13). The General Comment continues:

> It is particularly incumbent upon those states that are in a position to assist others in this regard . . . . It [the Committee] emphasizes that, in the absence of an active programme of international assistance and cooperation on the

part of all those States that are in a position to undertake one, the full realization of economic, social and cultural rights will remain an unfulfilled aspiration in many countries (par. 14).

Similarly, in *General Comment No. 12* on the Right to Food (1999), the Committee asserted that member states have a legal obligation to "take steps to respect the enjoyment of the right to food in other countries, to protect that right, to facilitate access to food and to provide the necessary aid when required" (para. 12). Further developing this theme, in its *General Comment No. 14* on the Right to Health (2000), it stated that "depending on the availability of resources, States should facilitate access to essential health facilities, goods and services in other countries, wherever possible and provide the necessary aid when required" (para. 39). In its *General Comment No. 15* on the Right to Water, the Committee stated that "International assistance should be provided in a manner that is consistent with the Covenant and other human rights standards and sustainable and culturally appropriate. The economically developed States parties have a special responsibility and interest to assist the poorer developing States in this regard" (para. 34). Finally, in its *Concluding Observations* of state reports, the Committee has repeatedly encouraged developed states to provide 0.7% of their GDP in foreign assistance, providing yet another indication that the Committee believes that richer states have an obligation to assist poorer ones.

Taking a cue from the ICESCR, some of the more recent international human rights treaties, most notably the Convention on the Rights of the Child and the Disabilities Convention, mandate "international cooperation" between and among the contracting parties. Among soft law instruments, certainly the strongest commitment to the principle that human rights are an international concern comes from the 2000 Millennium Declaration, where world leaders reaffirmed the following proposition:

> We recognize that, in addition to our separate responsibilities to our individual societies, we have a collective responsibility to uphold the principles of human dignity, equality and equity at the global level. As leaders we have a duty therefore to all the world's people, especially the most vulnerable and, in particular, the children of the world, to whom the future belongs.

Yet, despite these various provisions mandating international cooperation and assistance between states, there is still no international order as such, and states continue to act under the belief that their own human rights obligations extend no further than their territorial boundaries. I believe there are several reasons for this.

Misunderstanding the Meaning and Scope of Human Rights. The first problem is that there is an unfortunate tendency to make the concept of human rights more difficult and more complicated than it should be. Furthermore, and often because of this, human rights are often dismissed as unrealistic and even utopian in nature. The truth is that human rights represent the bare minimum that is required for each person to live a human existence. Thus, human rights are more properly thought of as serving as a floor below which no individual is to be allowed to fall. Yet, human rights should not be viewed as taking care of people so much as creating conditions – within states, but through the international order as well – where individuals are able to care for themselves.

What also has to be said about human rights in general, and international human rights law in particular, is that it is nonreciprocal in nature. States become parties to international human rights treaties not because they hope to gain some kind of advantage or because other states have done so. Rather, they do so in recognition that all human beings have human rights. Thus, in becoming a party to an international human rights treaty, each state obligates itself to ensuring the human rights of all.

Citizens' Rights and Human Rights. Ironically enough, one of the reasons for the ascendancy of the state-centric approach to human rights is the growing trend toward democratization and the natural connection between human rights, on the one hand, and the rights that citizens of these states enjoy. Given the enormous overlap between these two sets of rights, it is easy to see how the two are often conflated. However, human rights and citizens' rights might not always dovetail with one another (the right to vote, for example). More importantly, individuals have human rights not because they are citizens of a particular state, but because they are human beings.

The converse of this is also true. The obligations that states have to protect human rights have (or should have) nothing to do with a person's citizenship. Rather, states are assigned the (primary) role of protecting human rights within their own territory for two reasons. The first involves international law. It is always lawful for a state to act within its own territorial boundaries, whereas under most circumstances outside states have to get the consent of the territorial state in order to do this. The second reason involves efficiency. All else being equal, it is more efficient for a territorial state to serve as the main actor in protecting human rights within its own borders than to assign this role to outside countries.

The essential point is that this distribution of human rights obligations is only appropriate so long as human rights are protected. However, when there is a gap in human rights protection – and we know for a fact that there is a yawning gap – it is incumbent on the international community to respond and to provide this protection.

State Responsibility and the Crossing of National Borders. Under international law, a state is responsible for the unlawful acts that it carries out (Crawford 2002). Within the domestic realm, there is seldom any question of when a state has acted, and therefore little question of when a state is responsible for violating international legal standards. Or to state this more bluntly, a state that tortures its citizens has committed an internationally wrongful act; likewise, a state that does not make every effort at its disposal to feed its starving population has committed an internationally wrongful act, as well.

However, what international law has generally struggled with is assigning responsibility when a state acts outside its own borders, or else when it acts domestically but the human rights consequences are felt by individuals living in some other country. When either of these two situations arises, state responsibility becomes contested in ways that it would not be if the practices in question had occurred exclusively within the state's domestic sphere. One of the clearest examples of the primacy of territory in determining state responsibility is *Sale v. Haitians Centers Council* (1993), where the U.S. Supreme Court upheld the legality of the Coast Guard's Haitian interdiction policy on the grounds that the *nonrefoulement* provisions under domestic (U.S.) and international law, which prohibit a state from sending an individual to a country where his/her life or freedom might be threatened, did not apply unless and until an individual was actually on American soil – but not before then.

Unfortunately, *Sale* is no anomaly. Similarly, in *Bosnia v. Serbia* (2007), a case we will come back to later in this chapter, the International Court of Justice held that the Serbian government was not responsible for genocide carried out by its Bosnian Serb allies. In arriving at its decision, the ICJ ruled that notwithstanding the extraordinarily close ties between these two, the Bosnian Serbs were not acting as state agents of Serbia, nor were they operating under the "effective control" of Serbia. Because of this, Serbia was deemed not to have any legal responsibility for the genocidal horrors carried out by a dangerous paramilitary group that was in large part a creation of the Serbian government.

There are at least two problems with the standards employed by the ICJ. The first involves the standards themselves. Not only are many of these impossible (or virtually impossible) to meet, but the ICJ has provided no indication of where these standards come from and why they are the appropriate standards to employ.

The second problem is that responsibility is treated in an either-or fashion, where states have either met these standards – in which case they would be fully responsible – or else (and more likely) they would not meet this level of effective control, in which case the state would bear absolutely no responsibility. In that way, at least according to the Court's analysis, Serbia was no more responsible for committing genocide or for aiding and assisting in genocide in Bosnia than Canada or Tanzania would be. It is difficult to see how this kind of analysis helps to advance the law of state responsibility. Or as my colleagues and I (Gibney, Tomasevski, and Vedsted-Hansen 1999) have termed this in a slightly different context, rather than constituting the law on state responsibility this is more akin to the law on state (non)responsibility.

The point is that if Serbia's actions were a completely internal or domestic matter, there would be little question of Serbian responsibility. However, what apparently changes things is that the Bosnian Serb allies that were receiving massive amounts of aid and assistance from Serbia were located in another country (Bosnia). Seemingly because of this, the Serbian government was deemed not to bear any responsibility for the genocidal atrocities carried out by its allies.

Sovereign Immunity and Human Rights. There is another way in which states are able to avoid responsibility for violating human rights standards, and it is through the principle of sovereign immunity. One of the ways this issue often comes up is when one state is sued in the courts of another country for violating human rights standards. In this regard, perhaps the single most fascinating (but frustrating) legal decision in the entire realm of human rights is the European Court of Human Rights ruling in *Al-Adsani v. United Kingdom* (2002). The case involved a Kuwaiti-UK dual national who was tortured in Kuwait during the first Persian Gulf War. After being released from the hospital and returning to his home in the UK, Al-Adsani brought suit against the Kuwaiti government. The case went all the way up to the House of Lords, the highest judicial body in the UK, but his claim was repeatedly dismissed on the basis of the sovereign immunity provisions under British law.

Thus far there are no great surprises, but after these unsuccessful proceedings Al-Adsani brought another suit. Rather than suing Kuwait, he sued the UK, and he did so on the grounds that by providing sovereign immunity to a state (Kuwait) that carried out torture against him, the

UK itself has violated his rights under the European Convention. This case made it all the way to the Grand Chamber of the European Court of Human Rights, but in a torturous (no pun intended) 9–8 ruling, the Court held that the UK had not violated Al-Adsani's rights.

In mentioning this case it is perhaps obvious that I strongly disagree with this holding. I am also of the mind that an opposite ruling – 9–8 in favor of Al-Adsani – would have helped establish a much different conceptualization of human rights. The larger point is that there are many instances where the principle of sovereign immunity stands directly in the path of human rights. This might seem to be the clash of two competing rights under international law – sovereign immunity versus human rights – however, many human rights (such as torture) are considered to be *jus cogens* norms, which is to say that they are (supposed) to have a preferred position in the hierarchy of international law standards. Instead, just the opposite has been true, and the principle of sovereign immunity has repeatedly served to trump human rights claims.

EVIDENCE OF A NEW INTERNATIONAL ORDER

Human rights are declared to be universal, yet as these and other examples show, human rights remain territorially bound, resulting in a world where hundreds of millions are denied at least some form of human rights protection, particularly in terms of violations of ESCR. Yet, there is evidence of a decided change, and I now turn to three examples where states' extraterritorial human rights obligations have been recognized. Although the focus of this chapter is on ESCR, note that two of these examples relate specifically to civil and political rights and only one has a direct bearing on economic rights as such. The more important consideration is that these are manifestations of a much different way of conceptualizing human rights than we have seen in the past. No doubt, these initiatives or measures, by themselves, do not come anywhere close to establishing the kind of international order that is called for under international human rights law. On the other hand, I would maintain that these things are strong evidence that we are much closer to achieving this end than we had been before.

The Responsibility to Protect

At the time this is being written, an international effort (of sorts) has been created in order to protect civilians (and aid insurgents) in Libya. This intervention is based on the principles set forth in the Responsibility to Protect (R2P) initiative (International Commission on Intervention and State Sovereignty 2001), which posits that whereas each state has an obligation to protect human rights within its own territorial borders (and outside states have an obligation to assist the territorial state), a failure by that country to do so that results in gross and systematic human rights violations will give rise to interventionist measures by the international community – including military intervention.

Despite this expansion of state responsibility, there are at least two potential weaknesses in the initiative itself. The first is that it remains unclear whether states have a legal obligation to act, or whether, such as Sweden's approach to foreign assistance, states may respond to human suffering in other lands if they so choose – but they are under no legal obligation to do so. A second problem relates to the limitations of R2P in the sense that the initiative only speaks of a small category of violations of Civil and Political Rights (CPR). As the Secretary General's 2009 Report on implementation notes:

> The responsibility to protect applies, until Member States decide otherwise, only to the four specified crimes and violations: genocide, war crimes, ethnic cleansing and crimes against humanity. To try to extend it to cover other calamities, such as HIV/AIDS, climate change or the response to natural disasters would undermine . . . consensus and stretch the concept beyond recognition or operational utility (UN General Assembly 2009, para. 9[b]).

However, this same report goes to some length to acknowledge some of the reasons why conflict arises in the first place, particularly the problem of underdevelopment and the social, economic, and political dislocations this invariably brings about: "Chronic underdevelopment does not, in and of itself, cause strains among different ethnic, religious or cultural communities. But it can exacerbate the competition for scarce resources and severely limit the capacity of the State, civil society, and regional and subregional organizations to resolve domestic tensions peacefully and fully" (UN General Assembly 2009, para. 43).

The implementation report continues: "On balance, substantial increments in levels of general development assistance could well reduce the aggregate incidence of crimes and violations relating to the responsibility to protect, because some of the worst cases of mass domestic violence have occurred in very poor countries, where the poorest of the poor lack the capacity to resist" (UN General Assembly 2009, para. 43).

The R2P initiative represents the single most visible recognition that states have an interest – and perhaps even a legal obligation – in attending to human rights conditions in other states. We now return to the ICJ decision in *Bosnia v. Serbia*, which, ironically enough, constitutes the strongest judicial endorsement of this same principle.

Bosnia V. Serbia: *The Obligation to Prevent (Genocide)*

Article 1 of the Genocide Convention provides: "The Contracting Parties confirm that genocide, whether committed in time of peace or in time of war, is a crime under international law which they undertake to prevent and to punish." According to one reading of the Convention, the only obligation that states parties have is one of prevention and punishment. However, as we saw in our earlier discussion of this case, before attending to these particular issues, the ICJ first addressed whether Serbia was responsible for committing genocide itself by means of its Bosnian Serb allies, or else, whether it had aided and assisted those who carried out genocide. Applying an extraordinarily rigorous standard, the Court ruled that Serbia had not done either of these two things.

Although this part of the ICJ's opinion garnered most of the world's attention, what is equally important is the second part of the Court's ruling, where it held that Serbia had failed to meet its obligations to prevent and punish genocide, which it treated as constituting two separate and distinct obligations. The Court ruled that Serbia had violated both of these obligations – the first and only time that an international adjudicatory body has ruled that a state has violated the Genocide Convention – but our focus will only be on the obligation to prevent genocide.[2]

In terms of providing some more background, Serbia had taken the position that the Genocide Convention only applies to individuals but not to states, and it also made the argument that if states did have a legal responsibility to prevent genocide, those obligations were completely internal or domestic in nature. The Court rejected both of these positions. Thus, states (and not just individuals) can violate the Genocide Convention, and the responsibility to prevent genocide also extends to other lands. In its analysis, the Court ruled that the duty to prevent genocide is an obligation of conduct and not of result. In that way, a state is not responsible for achieving the desired result, but only for failing to

---

[2] In terms of the duty to punish, the Court ruled that Serbia had failed to fully cooperate with the International Criminal Tribunal for the Former Yugoslavia.

"take all measures to prevent genocide which were within its power, and which might have contributed to preventing genocide" (para. 430). What this demands is a standard of due diligence, which is to be determined on a case-by-case basis, according to the following factors:

> The first, which varies from one State to another, is clearly the capacity to influence effectively the action of persons likely to commit, or already committing genocide. The capacity itself depends, among other things, on the geographical distances of the States concerned from the scene of the events, and on the strength of the political links, as well as links of all other kinds, between authorities of that State and the main actors in the events. The State's capacity to influence must also be addressed by legal criteria, since it is clear that every State may only act within the limits permitted by international law; seen thus, a State's capacity to influence may vary depending on its particular legal position vis-à-vis the situations and persons facing the danger, or the reality, of genocide (para. 430).

Applying this standard, the ICJ ruled that because of the close relationship between Serbia and its Bosnian Serb allies, the former's failure to act to prevent genocide constituted a violation of the Genocide Convention. This part of the ICJ's ruling truly is revolutionary in positing that each state party to the Genocide Convention has a legal obligation to take all conceivable measures within its own powers (which will vary from state to state) to prevent genocide – in other lands. What does not matter is whether these efforts would ultimately prove to be successful or not, and what also does not matter is whether other countries are meeting (or even attempting to meet) their own obligations under the Convention. In that way, this part of the Court's ruling in *Bosnia v. Serbia* represents the strongest judicial endorsement of the principle that human rights obligations are both territorial and extraterritorial in scope. In addition, although the Court only addressed the issue of genocide, it also recognized that such a duty to prevent might exist in other human rights instruments as well. Whereas a general duty to prevent, by itself, will not necessarily lead to the creation of a social and international order conducive to the promotion and protection of human rights, what it does is mandate that states can no longer turn a blind eye to human rights atrocities occurring elsewhere. Instead, international human rights treaties (and not only the Genocide Convention) create an interlocking web where state parties (and perhaps even those that are not) share one another's fate.

The Extraterritorial Obligations

The last initiative I will reference is the newly established Extraterritorial Obligations (ETO) Human Rights Consortium, which is made up of a unique blend of international law experts and nongovernmental organizations such as Amnesty International, Human Rights Watch, FIAN, the International Commission of Jurists (ICJ), ESCR-Net, and so on.[3] The goal of the ETO Consortium is to promote the principle that states have both territorial and extraterritorial human rights obligations, and in September 2011 a group of distinguished international lawyers signed the Maastricht Principles on Extraterritorial Obligations of States in the area of Economic, Social and Cultural Rights.[4] The ETO Consortium, which focuses on ESCR, works under a few core principles. One is the affirmation that each state has the primary responsibility for protecting human rights within its own territorial borders. If these obligations are met, there is no need to proceed any further. However, and similar to R2P and the duty to prevent standard set forth in *Bosnia v. Serbia*, if a state is either unable or unwilling to protect the ESCR of its inhabitants, then this task is to be assumed by the international community.

Related to this, another core principle relates to states' tripartite duties – respect, protect, and fulfill. According to the tenets of the ETO Consortium, each state has a legal obligation to respect ESCR – within its own domestic borders, but outside its territory as well; each state has an obligation to protect against ESCR violations by private actors – within its own domestic borders, but outside its territory as well; and finally, each state has a legal obligation to fulfill ESCR – within its own domestic borders, but outside its territory as well. In that vein, what should also be noted about Hunt's country report of Sweden referred to earlier is that as part of this same study, he also traveled to Uganda, which is the largest recipient of Swedish foreign assistance, and to Washington DC, to meet with IMF and World Bank officials. As Hunt explains in his report, in addition to its domestic responsibilities, Sweden's obligation to protect the right to health extends outside its own territorial borders (and not merely to Swedish citizens living overseas), and the purpose of these trips was to ensure that Sweden was meeting its extraterritorial obligations to protect the right to health.

---

[3] By way of full disclosure, I was one of the founding members of the ETO Consortium and am presently a member of the Steering Committee.

[4] See http://www.icj.org/dwn/database/Maastricht%20ETO%20Principles%20-%20FINAL.pdf.

STEPS TOWARD THE ESTABLISHMENT OF AN
INTERNATIONAL ORDER

I am not naïve enough to believe that many readers will be convinced by the argument I am presenting here, and one reason for this is that it presents such a different way of conceptualizing human rights than we have been exposed to before. So I will end this chapter by presenting three small steps that could easily and immediately be undertaken that would help lead toward the creation of the kind of international order envisioned by Article 28 of the UDHR. In each instance, the proposal serves as a reminder that states must not ignore the consequences of their own actions in the world, nor can they continue to ignore the plight of those living in other lands.

Human Rights Reporting. One thing that reinforces the dominant state-centric approach is the nature of human rights reporting. The annual U.S. State Department and the Amnesty International reports on human rights practices focus solely (or almost solely) on the manner in which a state protects human rights within its own territory. Thus, there is virtually no attention given to how state A's actions or inactions might have affected human rights practices and protections in state B, and there is certainly no mention of how and what state A has done to help establish the social and international order envisioned by Article 28. As far as I know, the same is true for all other reports that relate to human rights, such as the UN Development Index. So as a first step, annual human rights reports should not only look at domestic practices, but also how states operate in the world.

Human Rights Impact Statements. Related to this, another thing that states could do is to issue something on the order of a human rights impact statement regarding the manner in which its own policies affect human rights practices in other lands. I will make no pretense of providing an exhaustive list, but consider the following situations: arms sales, economic sanctions, trade barriers, and foreign assistance. In each of these scenarios, the policies and practices of one state can have (and certainly have had) a profound effect on human rights protections in another country, and yet there is simply no indication that the first state has ever stopped to consider what that impact might be. One thing that could be done is that when states file their reports with the various UN human rights treaty bodies, they would also be required to analyze the effect that their policies and practices have had on human rights protections in other countries.

Complaint Mechanisms. Related to this, one of the things that should be attended to is the creation of a complaint mechanism by which foreign nationals whose human rights have been violated might pursue a claim and issue a complaint when appropriate. Let's say that some Ugandan sugar farmers are harmed by the nature and distribution of Swedish foreign aid, or else, they are no longer able to farm because they are not able to compete with sugar that is produced by the European Union (EU).[5] What recourse do they have? As far as I can tell, at the present time they have none. According to the case law of the European Court of Human Rights, it is quite clear that such farmers would not be able to press a claim before the Strasbourg court because they would be found to be outside the jurisdiction of Sweden as well as all of the other EU states.[6] Could such farmers make use of the new ICESCR Optional Protocol for these purposes?[7] Once again, this is not likely, unless the Committee takes an expansive view of what constitutes jurisdiction. Thus, what is needed is some means by which individuals whose human rights are negatively affected by the actions or inactions of another state are able to press their claims.[8]

CONCLUSION

I will close by reiterating two things. The first is to underscore the truly revolutionary aspect of human rights. Not only do all people in all countries have human rights, but all states have an obligation to ensure these

---

[5]   The reference here is to Wouter Vandenhole's study (2007) of the EU sugar industry. Vandenhole found that it was EU policy to overproduce (beyond domestic demand) by approximately 25% and to then place this excess sugar on the world market. What his study also found was that this was having a deleterious effect on sugar farmers in a number of Third World countries, who were not able to compete with the cheaper (heavily subsidized) EU sugar.

[6]   Article 1 of the European Convention provides: "The High Contracting Parties shall secure to everyone within their jurisdiction the rights and freedoms defined in ... this Convention." In *Bankovic et al. v. Belgium et al.* (2001), the Court dismissed a case as inadmissible claims brought by thirty-six Serb citizens (Serbia is not a party to the Convention) who were either harmed or killed during a NATO bombing mission over Belgrade on the basis that these individuals were not within the jurisdiction of any of the contracting states.

[7]   Article 2 provides:

> Communications may be submitted by or on behalf of individuals or groups of individuals, under the jurisdiction of a State Party, claiming to be victims of a violation of any of the economic, social and cultural rights set forth in the Covenant by that State Party. Where a communication is submitted on behalf of individuals or groups of individuals, this shall be with their consent unless the author can justify acting on their behalf without such consent.

[8]   It should be noted that there has been some increasing attention given to the idea of an international human rights tribunal. See generally, Gibney (2002), Nowak (2007), and Scheinin (2009).

rights. Article 28 of the UDHR calls for the establishment of a social and international order where human rights can flourish. However, there has been little apparent progress toward that end, and one of the primary reasons for this is that states continue to operate under the (mistaken) belief that their human rights obligations end at their own national borders.

One of the strongest objections against the position that I am taking is that it would be too expensive to undertake. Others, most notably Pogge (2002), Sachs (2005), and Collier (2007), have computed that these costs would be nowhere near as expensive as we allow ourselves to think they are. Rather than talking about money, however, I think a better way of thinking about our shared human rights obligations is Henry Shue's notion of full coverage, and although he is speaking about the obligations of individuals, the same holds true for the human rights responsibilities of states as well:

> Universal rights . . . entail not universal duties but full coverage. Full coverage can be provided by a division of labor among duty bearers. All negative duties fall upon everyone, but the positive duties need to be divided and assigned among bearers in some reasonable way. Further, a reasonable assignment of duties of any one individual must be limited, ultimately because her total resources are limited and, before the limit is reached, because she has her own rights, which involve perfectly proper expenditures on some resources on herself rather than fulfilling duties toward others. . . . One cannot have substantial positive duties toward everyone, even if everyone has basic rights. The positive duties of any one individual must be limited (Shue 1988, 690).

The last point is to suggest how we might (and should) conceptualize human rights differently than we have to date. When we see civilians being killed in Libya or people starving in Somalia, we (naturally) think of this as a human rights violation by Libya and Somalia, respectively. This, of course, is correct, but only partially. It is this other part – the part that all states are assigned the responsibility of preventing these (and other) horrors from taking place – that has for too long been ignored.

REFERENCES

Books and Articles

Collier, Paul, 2007. *The Bottom Billion: Why the Poorest Countries Are Failing and What Can Be Done About It*, Oxford: Oxford University.

Crawford, James, 2002. *The International Law Commission's Articles on State Responsibility: Introduction, Text and Commentaries*, Cambridge: Cambridge University Press.

Gibney, Mark, 2002. "On the Need for an International Civil Court," *The Fletcher Forum of World Affairs* 26: 47–58.

Gibney, Mark, Katarina Tomasevski, and Jens Vedsted-Hansen, 1999. "Transnational State Responsibility for Violations of Human Rights," *Harvard Human Rights Journal* 12: 267–209.

Hunt, Paul, 2006. Implementation of General Assembly Resolution 60/251 of 15 March 2006 Entitled "Human Rights Council." Report of the Special Rapporteur on the right of everyone to the enjoyment of the highest attainable standard of physical and mental health, Addendum

International Commission on Intervention and State Sovereignty, 2001. *The Responsibility to Protect*. Retrieved from http://responsibilitytoprotect.org/ICISS%20Report.pdf

Morsink, James, 1999. *The Universal Declaration of Human Rights: Origins, Drafting, and Intent*, Philadelphia: University of Pennsylvania Press.

Nowak, Manfred, 2007. "The Need for a World Court of Human Rights," *Human Rights Law Review* 7: 251–259.

Pogge, Thomas, 2002. *World Poverty and Human Rights*, Cambridge: Polity.

Pogge, Thomas, 2007. "Severe Poverty as a Human Rights Violation," in Thomas Pogge (Ed.) *Freedom from Poverty as a Human Right: Who owes what to the very poor?*, 11–54. Oxford: Oxford University Press.

Sachs, Jeffrey, 2005. *The End of Poverty: Economic Possibilities for Our Time*, New York: Penguin Press.

Scheinin, Martin, 2009. *Towards a World Court of Human Rights*. Research report to the Swiss Initiative to Commemorate the 60th Anniversary of the Universal Declaration of Human Rights. Retrieved from http://www.udhr60.ch/report/hrCourt_scheinin0609.pdf.

Shue, Henry, 1988. "Mediating Duties," *Ethics* 98: 687–704.

UN General Assembly, 2009. *Implementing the Responsibility to Protect*, report of the Secretary-General, A/63/677.

UN General Assembly, 2008. *Optional Protocol of the International Covenant on Economic, Social and Cultural Rights*, General Assembly Res. A/RES/63/117.

(UN) CESCR (UN Committee on Economic, Social and Cultural Rights), 1990. *General Comment 3: The Nature of States Parties' Obligations*, Fifth Session, UN Doc. E/1991/23, annex III at 86 (1991), reprinted in Compilation of General Comments and General Recommendations Adopted by Human Rights Treaty Bodies, UN Doc. HRI/GEN/1/Rev.6 at 14 (2003).

CESCR, 1999. *General Comment 12: Right to Adequate Food*, Twentieth Session, UN Doc. E/C.12/1999/5 (1999), reprinted in Compilation of General Comments and General Recommendations Adopted by Human Rights Treaty Bodies, UN Doc. HRI/GEN/1/Rev.6 at 62 (2003).

CESCR, 2000. *General Comment 14: The Right to the Highest Attainable Standard of Health*, Twenty-second Session, UN Doc. E/C.12/2000/4 (2000), reprinted in Compilation of General Comments and General Recommendations Adopted by Human Rights Treaty Bodies, UN Doc. HRI/GEN/1/Rev.6 at 85 (2003).

CESCR, 2002. *General Comment 15: The Right to Water*, Twenty-ninth Session, UN Doc. E/C.12/2002/11 (2002), reprinted in Compilation of General

Comments and General Recommendations Adopted by Human Rights Treaty Bodies, UN Doc. HRI/GEN/1/Rev.6 at 105 (2003).

CESCR, 2007. *On the right of everyone to the enjoyment of the highest attainable standard of physical and mental health*, report of the Special Rapporteur (Paul Hunt), A/HRC/4/28/Add.2 28 February 2007.

Vandenhole, Wouter, 2007. "Third State Obligations Under the ICESCR: A Case Study of EU Sugar Policy," *Nordic Journal of International Law* 76: 71–98.

Cases

Al-Adsani v. United Kingdom, 2002. Judgment of November 21, 2001, 34 ECHR 11.

Bankovic et al. v. Belgium et al., 2001. App. No. 52207/99 ECHR.

Case Concerning the Application of the Convention on the Prevention and Punishment of the Crime of Genocide (Bosnia and Herzegovina v. Serbia and Montenegro), 2007. Judgment of February 27, 2007.

Sale v. Haitians Centers Council, 1993. 509 U.S. 155.

11

Beyond a Minimum Threshold: The Right to Social Equality

Gillian MacNaughton

INTRODUCTION

Over the past two decades, a growing number of human rights scholars and practitioners have focused on defining the content of the economic and social rights guaranteed in the Universal Declaration of Human Rights (UDHR) and the International Covenant on Economic, Social and Cultural Rights (ICESCR), as well as other international human rights instruments. Numerous works now elaborate on the "minimum core content" of these rights, which grouped together form an international human rights-based poverty line (CESCR 2001; Chapman & Russell 2002; Vizard 2006; Bilchitz 2007). Some works also explore the idea of an "adequate" level of social rights, as explicitly guaranteed in the UDHR and the ICESCR (UDHR Article 25; ICESCR Article 11). Both of these approaches to defining economic and social rights describe the content of the rights in terms of a minimum threshold to which a person is entitled without much, if any, regard for the overall equality in the enjoyment of these rights by the people within a society.

Yet, today there is mounting evidence indicating that economic and social inequality adversely affect many dimensions of people's lives (Commission on the Social Determinants of Health [CSDH] 2008; Wilkinson 2005). Indeed, a growing number of studies show that more unequal societies have higher homicide rates; lower life expectancies; lower average standards of health; greater discrimination against women, racial minorities, and other marginalized groups; and lower participation in elections (Wilkinson 2005). These dimensions correlate strikingly closely to human rights recognized in international human rights legal instruments, including the rights to life, health, nondiscrimination, personal security, and political participation. Thus, the research suggests that economic and social inequality adversely affects the enjoyment of human rights. In view of this evidence, it is timely to consider the extent to which the International Bill of Human Rights encompasses a guarantee of some level of economic and social equality – just as it guarantees some level of civil and political equality.[1]

An inquiry into the relationship of equality to economic and social rights is also timely due to the recent change in the global distribution of people living in poverty. Until recently, most poor people in the world lived in low-income countries. In 1998, for example, 93% of poor people lived in low-income countries and only 7% lived in middle-income countries (Sumner 2010). A decade later, the picture had changed dramatically. By 2008, 72% of people living in poverty lived in middle-income countries and only 28% lived in low-income countries[2] (ibid.). In contrast to the picture just over a decade ago, the majority of poor people – almost 1 billion – now live in middle-income countries (ibid.). This shift in the global distribution of poverty means that poverty is increasingly turning from an international to a national problem, calling for more attention – by human rights scholars and practitioners among others – to domestic taxation and redistribution policies (ibid.). It also raises questions about the role of inequality in our understanding of and hence response to poverty.

Anglo-American governments – and sadly, many human rights scholars and practitioners as well – have traditionally focused on individual civil and political human rights and ignored or even denied the existence of economic and social rights as well as collective rights (Neier 2006; Alston 2008). Nonetheless, a cursory examination of the UDHR reveals a full range of rights. The UDHR encompasses (1) individual rights – such as the right to freedom of opinion and the right to be free from hunger; (2) family rights – such as the right to protection of the family as the fundamental unit of society and the right to an adequate standard of

---

[1] The International Bill of Human Rights includes the UDHR, the ICESCR, and the International Covenant on Civil and Political Rights (ICCPR).

[2] Sumner calculated the global distribution of people living in poverty using five different measures of poverty: (1) US$1.25; (2) child malnutrition measured by height for age; (3) child malnutrition measured by weight for age; (4) the UNDP multidimensional poverty index; and (5) percentage of children out of school. Using the first four measures, the results were the same: 70%–72% of poor people live in middle-income countries and 28%–30% live in low-income countries. Using the percentage of children out of school, he calculated that 56% of poor people live in middle-income countries, whereas 39% live in low-income countries. Under all five measures of poverty, the majority of poor people live in middle-income countries.

living for a family; (3) community rights – such as the rights to form trade unions and to participate in cultural life; and (4) the rights of peoples – such as the rights to self-determination and to freely dispose of their natural wealth. Article 28 of the UDHR then proclaims that "[e]veryone is entitled to a social and international order," in which the rights in the Declaration can be fully realized, creating a collective "umbrella" right (Eide 1999, 597; Morsink 1999, 226).

In the context of this holistic human rights framework, this chapter examines the relationships between poverty, inequality, and international economic and social rights within the domestic social order. In contrast to the chapter in this book by Mark Gibney, which addresses the international order in UDHR Article 28, this chapter focuses on the domestic social order to which everyone is entitled under that article. The justification for this domestic focus is threefold. First, poverty social indicators correlate to economic and social inequality within a society, usually determined within a national framework, rather than across countries (Wilkinson 2005). Second, the global redistribution of poor people from low-income to middle-income countries means that most poor people now live in high- or middle-income countries, which have resources to address poverty within their jurisdictions.[3] Finally, international human rights law places the primary responsibility for securing the realization of human rights on national governments as members of the United Nations and parties to the human rights treaties. Thus, recent evidence on poverty and inequality as well as the legal framework of international human rights law suggests that it is timely to re-examine the domestic dimension of the right to a social order in UDHR Article 28.

Following this introduction, the chapter proceeds in four parts. Part I considers definitions of poverty in terms of income, capabilities, and human rights. Part II examines the minimum threshold definitions of economic and social rights, including the "minimum core content" and the "adequacy" standard. Part III presents the research on the correlation between economic and social inequalities and the length and quality of life, and links this research to specific human rights standards. Drawing on the holistic human rights framework, it proposes that economic and social inequality prevents the full enjoyment of human rights as envisioned in the International Bill of Rights and explicitly set forth in UDHR Article 28. Part IV responds by proposing that the Bill encompasses a right to economic and social equality just as it encompasses the rights to civil and

---

[3] Middle-income countries are also the most unequal (Ortiz and Cummins 2011).

political equality. Part V briefly explores developing the content of the right to social equality in international law. Ultimately, the argument in this chapter is that the right to a social order in Article 28 enshrines a collective right to economic and social equality because such equality is essential to fully realize the other rights in the International Bill of Human Rights.

I. DEFINITIONS OF POVERTY

At the turn of the millennium, poverty eradication became a global priority. Notably, in 2000, the United Nations General Assembly (UNGA) adopted the Millennium Declaration – signed by 189 countries, including 147 heads of state – in which it committed to creating an environment, at national and global levels, conducive to development and the elimination of poverty (UNGA 2000). Although there is now widespread agreement that poverty is a critical global problem that requires global efforts to effectively address it, there is no consensus on how to define poverty or how to eliminate it (Riddell 2004). For purposes of this chapter, three types of definitions of poverty are important: monetary, capability, and human rights-based definitions.

1. Monetary Thresholds

The most common method of defining poverty is in monetary terms (Laderchi, Saith, and Stewart 2003). Generally, monetary approaches use poverty lines based on an estimate of the income required to purchase a minimum basket of goods and services (CESCR 2001). This basket usually includes basic food, clothing, shelter, education, and health needs. People with incomes below the required amount to purchase this minimum basket fall below the poverty line and are therefore deemed to be living in poverty. Monetary approaches to poverty provide a convenient shorthand method – based on widely available data – of identifying those who are poor (Laderchi et al. 2003).

Several monetary measures of poverty are used in public policy circles (Sachs 2005). Extreme poverty and severe poverty are measures generally used in developing countries. The World Bank, for example, defines extreme poverty as living below US$1.25 per day, measured in purchasing-power parity, and severe poverty as living between US$1.25 and US$2 per day. It found that in 2005, almost half of the world's population – 2.5 billion people – lived on less than US$2 per day, and one-quarter of the population – 1.38 billion people – lived on less than US$1.25 per day (Chen and Ravillion 2009). Moreover, whereas the proportion of people living on less than US$2 per day decreased between 1981 and 2005 from about 70% to just less than 50% of the total world population, the total number of people living on less than US$2 per day actually increased by more than 25 million people (ibid.).

Absolute poverty lines are also used in developed countries, but the minimum threshold is defined substantially higher (Riddell 2004). For example, in the United States, the 2009 poverty threshold for a single person less than sixty-five years of age and living alone was $10,956 (U.S. Census Bureau 2011). In that year, the U.S. Census found that 43.6 million people were living in poverty, 14.3% of the total population (ibid.). Relative poverty lines, used more frequently in developed countries, are generally defined "as a household income level below a given proportion of average national income" (Sachs 2005, 20). In the European Union (EU), the Eurostat definition sets the poverty line at an income level equal to 60% or less of the median income in the specific country (Eurostat 2005). Based on this definition, about 72 million people in the EU were living in poverty in 2005, which was about 16% of the total population (ibid.).

Although monetary indicators of poverty are used frequently in policy circles, today, poverty is generally understood to be a multidimensional concept, encompassing "broader features, such as hunger, poor education, discrimination, vulnerability and social exclusion" (CESCR 2001, para. 7). There are several concepts of multidimensional poverty, including capability- and human rights-based definitions.

2. Capability Deprivation

In contrast to monetary definitions, a capability-based definition focuses on the substantive freedoms people have to lead the lives and pursue the objectives they have reason to value (Sen 1999). The concept of "capability" refers to a person's real opportunities – coined "substantive freedoms" – to achieve well-being. Basic capabilities include, for example, being adequately nourished, clothed, and sheltered; avoiding premature morbidity; and being able to take part in the community (Office of the High Commissioner for Human Rights [OHCHR] 2004). From this perspective, poverty is a deprivation of basic capabilities (Sen 1999).

Although low income is clearly one of the major causes of capability deprivation, it is not the only criterion for identifying poverty from a capability perspective (ibid.).

There are three key differences between monetary and capability approaches to poverty. First, from a capability perspective, low income is only instrumentally significant in that low income will predispose a person to an impoverished life, lacking in real opportunities (ibid.). Second, from a capability perspective, poverty is a multidimensional concept, involving many features such as the lack of opportunities to be well nourished, to lead a healthy life of full life span, to read and write, and to participate in society (ibid.). Third, the capability perspective recognizes that people have different abilities to convert income into opportunities for well-being (ibid.). For example, people of different ages or abilities might require different resources to achieve the same real opportunities.

The capability approach has been embraced by the United Nations Development Program (UNDP) and has had significant influence on development discourse in many international organizations, including the World Bank[4] (UNDP 2000; World Bank 2005). Additionally, the OHCHR has drawn on the capability approach in developing a human rights-based definition of poverty (OHCHR 2004). The importance of the capabilities discourse in current public policy circles is reflected in the shift in recent years from an emphasis on development as economic growth – without concern for the quality of life of the people involved – to development as expanding people's capabilities – with the central concern for what people can actually do and be (World Bank 2005).

3. Human Rights-Based Definitions

Poverty has also been defined in terms of human rights. Although the term "poverty" does not appear in the International Bill of Human Rights, it is a central concern of the CESCR, which is responsible for monitoring implementation of the ICESCR by the state parties. The CESCR deems the rights to work, an adequate standard of living, housing, food, health, and education – all enumerated in the Covenant – to have a direct

---

[4] UNDP has attempted to capture the capabilities approach in its composite Human Development Index, which includes three dimensions: a long and healthy life, education and access to knowledge, and a decent standard of living.

bearing on the eradication of poverty (CESCR 2001). The Committee defines poverty as a deprivation of the resources, capabilities, and power necessary to enjoy an adequate standard of living and other civil, cultural, economic, political and social rights (ibid.). Thus, in the view of the CESCR, "poverty constitutes a denial of human rights" (ibid., para. 1).

The human rights-based definition of poverty draws significantly on the capability definition of poverty, and consequently has many common features (OHCHR 2004). Like the capability definition, poverty in terms of human rights is a multidimensional concept. The OHCHR considers a person to be living in poverty when a lack of command over economic resources results in the non-realization of a number of rights, such as the rights to food, health, education, and political participation (OHCHR 2006). Although economic resources are key in this definition, as in the capability definition, a human rights-based definition of poverty views economic resources primarily as instrumental to realizing human rights (OHCHR 2004). Additionally, these two definitions also have in common the understanding that living in poverty means lacking the basic capabilities or human rights necessary to live in dignity (ibid.).

Although the capability and human rights-based definitions have much in common, there are also significant differences. First, there is no consensus on identifying the specific capabilities relevant to poverty or even on the method to do so (Alkire 2007). In terms of human rights, however, the definition of poverty draws on the normative framework set out in international law, and the strategies for eliminating poverty seek to support people in advancing their human rights. Indeed, "[f]undamentally, a human rights approach to poverty is about the empowerment of the poor" (OHCHR 2004, 13). A second difference is that by drawing on the international legal framework, the human rights-based definition of poverty gives rise to legally binding obligations on all branches of the government (ibid.). Accordingly, a human rights-based approach requires governments to establish effective mechanisms of accountability, which allow people to hold their governments to account for their human rights obligations (ibid.).

In view of the added value of using the human rights framework to define multidimensional poverty, some scholars have urged that the controversy over the indeterminate nature of the capabilities definition be settled by drawing on international human rights treaties (Vizard 2006; Woodward 2010). Polly Vizard, for example, argues that international human rights treaties provide a selection of capability dimensions developed by public consensus at the international level, thus providing a morally and legally legitimate enumeration of basic capabilities coupled with a system of accountability (Vizard 2006). As a result, the two approaches may be converging, if not at the theoretical level, at least at the practical level. Indeed, Martha Nussbaum, one of the pioneers of the capabilities approach, has characterized it as a "species of human rights approach" (Nussbaum 2007a, 21). This convergence makes possible, as Vizard states, "an integrated cross-disciplinary framework for analyzing global poverty as a human rights issue that bridges ethics, economics and international law" (Vizard 2006, 246).

4. *Other Definitions of Poverty*

Poverty is also defined from several other perspectives. Drawing on John Rawls's notion of "primary social goods," a basic needs approach also takes a multidimensional view of poverty (Stewart 1989). In this approach, the core basic needs include food, water, health, education, and shelter, as well as nonmaterial aspects such as access to work and participation in decision making (ibid.). *Social exclusion* is a concept of poverty originally developed in Europe to describe the process of marginalization and deprivation in wealthy countries (Laderchi et al. 2003). A basic definition of social exclusion is the processes by which people, individually or in groups, are excluded from full participation in the society in which they live (Riddell 2004). A participatory definition of poverty involves poor people themselves in articulating what poverty means to them (ibid.). The World Bank, for example, undertook a worldwide consultation with poor people, which led to its publication *Crying Out for Change: Voices of the Poor* in 2000 (World Bank 2000).

Definitions matter in at least two respects. First, who is identified as poor depends on how poverty is defined (Laderchi et al. 2003). A number of studies have shown that there are large discrepancies in those identified as poor according to the different definitions (ibid.). Thus, programs for poor people will address different populations depending on the definition employed. Second, policy implications differ depending on the perspective of poverty adopted (ibid.). Based on a monetary definition, economic growth may provide adequate solutions. Capability approaches, however, tend toward emphasis on providing public goods, and social exclusion perspectives tend toward redistribution and nondiscrimination policies (ibid.). Human rights-based approaches focus on empowering people to claim their rights and hold duty bearers to account (Khan 2009).

II. TWO MINIMUM THRESHOLD APPROACHES TO ECONOMIC AND SOCIAL RIGHTS

Common to many of these definitions of poverty is the notion of a minimum threshold defined in terms of basic rights, capabilities, or needs. Over the past couple of decades, the idea of such a minimum threshold has received considerable attention in human rights circles. There are two prevailing manners of defining a minimum threshold for economic and social rights: (1) minimum core obligations and (2) adequate levels of social rights.

1. Minimum Core Obligations

As early as 1990, the CESCR introduced the concept of the "minimum core obligation" of state parties "to ensure the satisfaction of, at the very least, minimum essential levels of each of the rights" in the Covenant (CESCR 1990, para. 10). Audrey Chapman and Sage Russell explain that the "'[m]inimum core content is often defined as the nature or essence of a right, that is, the essential elements without which it loses its substantive significance as a human right and in the absence of which a State party should be considered to be in violation of its international obligations" (2002, 9). For the CESCR, the rights in the Covenant must be construed to establish a minimum core obligation; otherwise "it would be largely deprived of its *raison d'être*" (CESCR 1990, para. 10). The minimum core content and the minimum core obligation are closely related concepts; however, the CESCR has chosen the formulation of obligations (Chapman and Russell 2002). By focusing on obligations, the CESCR avoids creating a hierarchy of components of the rights – core versus noncore – and rather seeks to guide state action and signal violations of the Covenant (ibid; Young 2008).

Since 1990, the minimum core obligation has been further defined by the CESCR as well as debated by courts and scholars. A number of key features are now well established. The minimum core obligations apply to every state party to the ICESCR regardless of its level of development (Vizard 2006). They are immediate obligations and must be prioritized before the state "moves into the territory of progressive realization" (Chapman and Russell 2002, 14). Core obligations are binding constraints on the allocation of resources, meaning that they cannot be traded off in favor of spending outside the core (OHCHR 2006).

Moreover, a lack of resources does not justify a state in failing to meet this minimum obligation. The state must "demonstrate that every effort has been made to use all resources that are at its disposition in an effort, to satisfy, as a matter of priority, those minimum obligations" (CESCR 1990, para. 10).

As the CESCR defines it, the minimum core obligation requires ensuring, at the very least, minimum essential levels of rights, such as essential food, primary health care, basic shelter, and the most basic forms of education (CESCR 1990). It also includes other measures such as ensuring nondiscrimination in the enjoyment of rights, adopting and implementing a national strategy and plan of action for the realization of rights, and establishing and maintaining a system of indicators and benchmarks necessary to monitor the progress in the realization of rights (CESCR 1990 and 2000). In its *General Comments* subsequent to 1990, the CESCR has defined the minimum core obligations for many of the rights enumerated in the ICESCR, including the rights to food, education, health, water, work, and social security. For the CESCR, poverty-reduction strategies that do not reflect this minimum threshold are inconsistent with the legal obligations of the state party (CESCR 2001).

In addition to the state party's legal obligation to ensure the minimum core, the CESCR also recognizes the obligations of other states, as well as international organizations, in a position to assist, to provide economic and technical support to enable developing states to meet this obligation (OHCHR 2006). In its *Statement on Poverty*, the CESCR establishes that the core obligations for economic, social, and cultural rights play a crucial role in national and international development policies, including poverty-reduction strategies (CESCR 2001). Together, these core obligations establish an international minimum threshold for all development policy and practice (ibid.). "In short, core obligations give rise to national responsibilities for all States and international responsibilities for developed States, as well as others that are in a 'a position to assist'" (ibid., 16). According to Vizard, the minimum core threshold can be understood to establish a legal basis for an international human rights poverty line (Vizard 2006).

Although the CESCR has devoted considerable efforts to define the minimum core content of economic and social rights, courts and policy makers have generally not looked upon it favorably. In *Government of the Republic of South Africa v Grootboom*, for example, the Constitutional Court of South Africa considered but declined to adopt a minimum core approach to the right to adequate housing. The Court ruled that the real question under the South African Constitution "is whether the measures taken by the state to realize the right afforded by section 26 [right to adequate housing] are reasonable" (2001, para. 33). In the Court's view, determining the minimum core of the right to housing would be difficult given that needs are diverse; "[T]here are some who need land; others need both land and houses; yet others need financial assistance" (ibid.). Although it noted that there may be cases where it is appropriate to consider the minimum core in determining whether the state's actions are reasonable, it left open the question of whether it would be appropriate for the Court to determine the minimum core content of a right in the first instance (ibid.).

In terms of policy guidance, the OHCHR produced *Principles and Guidelines for a Human Rights Approach to Poverty Reduction Strategies*, which refer briefly to the concept of the minimum core obligation but does not focus on ensuring that everyone achieves this threshold (OHCHR 2006). On the contrary, the *Principles and Guidelines* go far beyond the CESCR's concept of an international minimum threshold for development policy, describing the full content of each of the rights determined to be most relevant in the context of poverty, including the rights to work; adequate food, health, education, personal security, and privacy; equal access to justice; and political rights and freedoms. The concept of the minimum core obligation does not feature prominently in the discussion of these rights or in the principles for implementing a human rights-based approach to poverty reduction.

The minimum core is also difficult to reconcile with the language of the Bill, which does not indicate that the guarantees it encompasses are minimal. For example, parties to the ICESCR "agree that education shall be directed to the *full development* of the human personality and the sense of its dignity" (ICESCR Article 13(1), emphasis added). Further, everyone has a right "to the enjoyment of the *highest attainable* standard of physical and mental health" (ICESCR Article 12(1), emphasis added). Additionally, everyone has the right to an adequate standard of living and "to *continuous improvement* in living conditions" (ICESCR Article 11(1), emphasis added). Overarching all these rights, a state party has the obligation to use "the *maximum* of its available resources" to achieve "the *full realization* of the rights" (ICESCR Article 2(1), emphasis added). On its face, the ICESCR does not guarantee minimal rights. Indeed, the International Bill of Rights guarantees the rights deemed by the members of the UN to be necessary to human dignity, not to survival (ICESCR preamble, ICCPR preamble). It is therefore difficult to sustain a threshold of core rights that are by definition less than what the Bill proclaims is necessary to human dignity. Doing so also creates a hierarchy of rights, which is inconsistent with the UN's position that all rights are equal.[5] The idea of a minimum core of rights is therefore inconsistent with both human dignity and the holistic framework of the International Bill of Human Rights.

On the other hand, the minimum core obligation has been supported by the CESCR and several scholars as a practical obligation for international cooperation and assistance (CESCR 2001; Young 2008; Phillips 2001). In the context of defining international obligations for ensuring the enjoyment of economic and social rights, the minimum core obligation is less controversial. As Katherine Young states, "A minimalist definition of economic and social rights is needed to mediate the legal, as well as political and philosophical, challenges of holding states accountable for the socioeconomic deprivations experienced by citizens in other states" (Young 2008, 123). As a domestic standard, however, it simply regulates timing by setting out what states must accomplish first in moving toward full implementation of the rights (Chapman and Russell 2002).

Notably, capabilities approaches, often accepted as providing the underlying theoretical basis for human rights-based approaches to poverty, likewise focus on ensuring a basic minimum threshold of capabilities for all. According to Martha Nussbaum, "The capabilities approach is a doctrine concerning a social minimum, deliberately agnostic about how we treat inequalities above a rather ample threshold" (Nussbaum 2007b, 125). Nussbaum's notion of a basic social minimum of central capabilities to be secured to everyone is, as she illustrates, closer to the full enjoyment of the rights enumerated in the UDHR and implemented in the international human rights treaties than to the CESCR minimum core obligation (Nussbaum 2000). This basic social minimum is informed by the "idea of a life that is worthy of the dignity of the human being," and therefore, equates more accurately to the notion of "adequate" rights (ibid., 5).

2. Adequate Economic and Social Rights

"Adequacy" in international human rights derives from Article 25 of the Universal Declaration of Human Rights, which states that "[e]veryone

---

[5] Phillip Alston pressed a similar criticism against the 1998 ILO Declaration on the Fundamental Principles and Rights at Work because it prioritized four Core Labour Standards, thus creating a hierarchy of rights (Alston 2004).

has the right to a standard of living *adequate* for the health and well-being of himself and his family, including food, clothing, housing and medical care and necessary social services, and the right to social security" (emphasis added). ICESCR Article 11 then guarantees the right to an adequate standard of living, which includes adequate food, clothing, and housing. Further, CESCR *General Comment 19* recognizes the right to social security, adequate in amount and duration (CESCR 2008). CESCR *General Comment 14* on the right to health includes the right to an adequate food supply, adequate nutrition, an adequate supply of safe and potable water, adequate sanitation, adequate housing and living conditions, and adequate medicines and medical equipment (CESCR 2000). Thus, adequacy sets another minimum threshold for these rights distinct from the minimum core obligation.

David Bilchitz explains that these two thresholds of interest differ in their degree of urgency to people (Bilchitz 2007). The first is the most urgent as it is the interest in being free from threats to survival (ibid.). He refers to this minimal interest in survival, or meeting absolute needs, as "the first threshold of provision" (ibid., 187). Meeting this threshold would require, for example, having at least minimum shelter from the elements such that one's health and ability to survive are not at risk due to exposure to cold or wet conditions. It may also include access to basic services such as safe water and sanitation. According to Bilchitz, the minimal interest correlates to the CESCR minimum core obligations of states to meet, as a matter of priority, the minimum essential levels of each of the rights in the ICESCR (ibid., 188).

For the second threshold of provision, Bilchitz explains, "It is not only survival that matters: we need protection of our interest in the general conditions that are necessary for the fulfillment of a wide range of purposes" (2007, 188). Thus, adequate housing, for example, is more than just minimal shelter from the weather; it must also provide security and privacy, as well as serve social functions. This second threshold of provision must enable people to fully develop their personalities and achieve their goals. Defining this higher threshold is relative to a particular society in which people live, including the level of development of the society. To live in dignity, people in a richer society may need more goods and services than people in a poorer society. This higher standard, Bilchitz notes, corresponds to the requirements of adequacy identified by the CESCR (ibid.).

In this respect, adequacy, unlike the minimum core obligation, is relative. To the extent that the definition of what is adequate with respect to social rights – such as the right to an adequate standard of living – depends upon comparators, it begins to approach the idea of equality. A number of judicial decisions illustrate this point. For example, in *Rose v. Council for a Better Education* (1989), the Kentucky Supreme Court's ruling on the meaning of the constitutional right to an adequate education relied upon comparisons of state educational efforts and achievements nationally as well as in the region. The court defined a constitutionally adequate education as one that provides, among other factors, "sufficient levels of academic or vocational skills to enable public school students to compete favorably with their counterparts in surrounding states, in academics or in the job market" (ibid., 212). As a result, what is adequate education in Kentucky turns out to be surprisingly close to what is equal to the education offered in nearby states.[6] Indeed, when adequacy is defined in comparison to the society in which one lives, as in *Rose*, it may not be logically distinct from equality (Phillips 1999).

To summarize, international human rights law establishes two minimum thresholds for economic and social rights: the minimum core obligation, which the CESCR has linked to the human rights-based definition of poverty; and the higher adequacy standard, which is explicitly set out in the UDHR and the ICESCR as the level of enjoyment of these rights necessary to live in dignity. Neither approach is specifically concerned with the level of economic and social equality in society. Rather, they both focus on identifying those who are poor and aim to ensure that they have a minimum threshold of rights or capabilities – moving everyone above this poverty line – without regard to the economic and social inequalities that exist now and would continue to exist to a large extent under minimum-threshold formulations for social rights. Minimum-threshold approaches, thereby, ignore a key condition necessary to fully realizing social rights and thus eliminating multidimensional poverty: social equality.

III. THE IMPORTANCE OF EQUALITY TO INDIVIDUAL AND COMMUNITY WELL-BEING

Over the last several decades, a growing number of human rights scholars and practitioners have advocated for economic and social rights to

---

[6] Similarly, in *Campaign for Fiscal Equity v. State of New York* (2003), the Court of Appeals of New York relies in part on comparisons of state and national high school completion rates as well as comparisons of the educational materials and supplies in city schools compared to schools across the state to determine the meaning of the state constitutional right to a "sound basic education." In this case, adequacy does not require equality; however, the court's reasoning suggests that some level of inequality implies inadequacy too.

be recognized as equally important as civil and political rights. Although the importance of a minimum guarantee of economic and social rights to well-being is now broadly accepted, with few exceptions, human rights scholars and practitioners have given considerably less attention to the relationship of equality to economic and social rights. Mounting research, however, suggests that addressing economic and social inequalities may be necessary to fully realizing social rights, as well as other human rights. If this is so, minimum threshold approaches to economic and social rights are simply insufficient to establish a social order, as required by UDHR Article 28, in which all rights in the UDHR can be fully realized. Equality with respect to economic and social rights is necessary, as well. Among the reasons to recognize a right to social equality are the following: (1) equality is intrinsically important to people; (2) inequality adversely affects many dimensions of people's lives, including life expectancy, health, and political participation; and (3) a focus on poverty tends to ignore the problems of wealth and privilege.

1. The Intrinsic Value of Equality

At an intuitive level, we know that equality – in some form – is important to most people. Indeed, research shows that most people feel that great social and economic inequalities violate a sense of fairness (World Bank 2005). Not surprisingly, the importance of equality to people is reflected in many major religions and philosophies, as well as in international human rights law, which recognizes the inherent equality of all human beings (ibid.). Indeed, being regarded as an equal member of society is central to the notion of human dignity. Consequently, these ideas are tied together in Article 1 of the UDHR: "All human beings are born free and equal in dignity and rights." This close relationship between equality, dignity, and fairness, in international human rights law as well as in religions and philosophies around the world, indicates the intrinsic value of equality to people.

Although there is some debate on the kinds of equality that dignity demands, there is also general agreement on the importance of some kinds of equality. The prohibition against discrimination on the basis of race, for example, is considered a fundamental principle of international law from which no derogation is permitted (Brownlie 2008). Thus, a worldwide movement condemned the system of apartheid in South Africa. Other forms of discrimination – on the basis of sex, religion, or language, for example – are also regarded as fundamentally unfair and as violations of human dignity. The adoption by the UNGA and ratification by most countries in the world of international human rights instruments addressing such inequalities show the widespread support for eliminating discrimination on such grounds.

Inequality, however, need not be on the grounds of any particular status, such as race or sex, to feel intrinsically unfair. Arbitrary inequality also raises a sense of injustice. For example, when the government distributes health benefits unequally across health districts, the press in the United Kingdom has highlighted the unfairness of the so-called post-code lottery. In one case, a woman was denied potentially lifesaving medication that was available to all women with her condition in other districts simply because she lived in the wrong district (*Rogers v Swindon* 2006). The arbitrary distinction in this case also raised a sense of unfairness. Similarly, other disparities in government resource distribution across districts strike us as unjust. Parents and students in several states in the United States have sued state governments for such disparities in education funding. Indeed, injustice appears greatest when the government, responsible for ensuring equal respect and dignity of all of its people, treats them unequally. Thus, inequalities in public education, health care, and water and sanitation services seem particularly unfair (World Bank 2003).

Economic inequality may also raise a sense of injustice. The *World Development Report 2006: Equity and Development* compiled research on equity and well-being and concluded that income inequality is generally associated with lower levels of subjective well-being (World Bank 2005). One study indicated that people in the United States and Europe at all income levels have a higher tendency to report that they are unhappy when income levels are more unequal (ibid.). The World Bank suggests, "One reason that inequality might make people less happy, even when controlling for absolute income levels, is that it violates their sense of fairness" (ibid., 82). Another cross-national study on attitudes toward income inequality examined several developed countries and similarly found that people in these countries, on average, believe that less well-paid professionals should be paid more and better-paid professionals should be paid less (ibid.). Likewise, in an opinion survey carried out in eighteen Latin American countries, 89% of respondents considered the income distribution in their countries either "unfair" or "very unfair" (ibid., 82–83).

A recent study in the United States, examining Americans' attitudes on wealth inequality, also found that respondents preferred a comparatively more equal distribution of wealth (Norton and Ariely 2011).

Researchers asked respondents to indicate what percent of wealth each quintile in the United States owned, and then what an ideal distribution would be. Respondents vastly underestimated the wealth inequality in the United States and "constructed ideal distributions far more equitable than even their erroneously low estimates of the actual distribution" of wealth (ibid., 10). Overall, researchers concluded that Americans prefer a more equal distribution than currently present in the United States. In fact, the study showed that Americans prefer a distribution somewhere between the distribution in Sweden – one of the most equal countries in the world – and perfect equality between quintiles. Americans, like people in the rest of the world, intuitively consider wealth inequality, especially vast inequality, undesirable. Indeed, the greater the inequalities the more unfair they appear and the more difficult they are to justify (Sen 1999). In short, economic and social equality – to some extent – is intrinsically valuable to most people.

2. The Adverse Impacts of Inequality on the Length and Quality of Life

Equality is also instrumentally valuable to people. Recent research shows that it is not just absolute poverty that has an adverse impact on the quality of life. Inequality – or relative poverty – also has devastating impacts on the length and quality of life of individuals as well as on the social fabric of society (Wilkinson 2005). The CSDH, established by the World Health Organization (WHO), issued the 2008 report *Closing the Gap in a Generation: Health Equity through Action on the Social Determinants of Health*, in which it explains the close relationship between socioeconomic level and health. The report concludes that in countries at all levels of development, health and illness follow a social gradient; the lower the socioeconomic position people hold, the worse their health. According to the Commission, this "health inequity is caused by the unequal distribution of income, goods, and services" (CSDH, 31). As a result, the Commission contends that "[w]e need to be concerned with both material deprivation – the poor material conditions of the 40% of the world's population that live on US$2/day or less" but also with "the social gradient in health that affects people in rich and poor countries alike" (ibid.).

Likewise, in *The Impact of Inequality: How to Make Sick Societies Healthier*, Richard Wilkinson maintains that in developed countries, where basic subsistence conditions are usually met, health inequalities are not related to absolute levels of income or standards of living (Wilkinson

2005). Instead, health inequalities are related to relative income and social status. In Wilkinson's words, "The higher people's status, the longer they live" (ibid., 15). In numbers, this means that the average person in the wealthiest community may have as much as 25% more life expectancy than the average person in the poorest community in the same country. For example, the difference in life expectancy between whites in rich areas and blacks in poor areas of the United States is close to sixteen years (ibid).

Income equality is also associated with other poor social indicators. According to Wilkinson, there are now more than fifty studies showing that societies with greater income inequality are more violent (Wilkinson 2005). This holds true in comparisons of homicide rates, for example, across countries, developing and developed, as well as across states in the United States and provinces in Canada. Studies also show that there is greater discrimination against women, racial minorities, and other vulnerable groups in societies with greater income inequality. Additionally, a smaller proportion of people actually vote in elections in societies with greater inequality. Based on his research on income inequality, Wilkinson concluded that "more unequal places are marked by a more conflictual character of social relationships – so that they suffer not only more homicide, but also more violent crimes, less trust, less involvement in community life, and more racism" (ibid., 55). In sum, this research shows that income inequality has profoundly adverse impacts on the health of both individuals and societies.

In *The Spirit Level: Why More Equal Societies Do Better* (2009), Wilkinson and Pickett document further the adverse impacts of inequality. They present evidence that more unequal societies are associated with lower life expectancy, higher rates of infant mortality, lower birth weight, and greater rates of depression, among other poor health indicators. The evidence and arguments on the impact of inequality presented by Wilkinson and Pickett have been critiqued (Saunders 2010). On the other hand, the WHO Commission on the Social Determinants of Health, as well as a recent report prepared for UNICEF by Isabel Oritz and Matthew Cummins, reached conclusions similar to Wilkinson and Pickett (CSDH 2008; Oritz and Cummins 2011).[7] Additionally, a comprehensive review of the literature by the Joseph Rowntree Foundation

---

[7] Michael Marmot, chair of the WHO Commission on the Social Determinants of Health, and Richard Wilkinson also published a comprehensive compilation of research on health inequalities and the social determinants of health, providing additional support for their assertions on the adverse impacts of inequality (Marmot and Wilkinson 2006).

concluded that there is indeed a correlation between income inequality and health and social problems (Rowlingson 2011). Although there is less agreement about whether income inequality causes ill health and social problems, the Rowntree study concluded that the explanation presented by Wilkinson and Pickett – that income inequality is harmful because it places people in a hierarchy causing status anxiety leading to poor health and other negative outcomes – is the most plausible explanation for the adverse impacts of income inequality (ibid.).

The findings of the WHO Commission on the Social Determinants of Health, Wilkinson and Pickett, and others on the adverse impacts of inequality – in terms of violence, discrimination, nonparticipation in elections, ill health, and premature mortality – correlate closely to provisions in international human rights law on the rights to security of the person, nondiscrimination, participation, health, and life. This suggests that economic and social inequality has profoundly adverse impacts on the enjoyment of human rights, which in turn indicates that achieving a minimum threshold of economic and social rights will not allow full realization of the human rights in the UDHR without addressing economic and social inequality, as well.

3. The Problems with Wealth and Privilege

Minimum threshold approaches also fail to consider the problems associated with great wealth and privilege, including the adverse impacts on the exercise of political rights by those less privileged, on the functioning of governmental institutions, and on the economic and political stability of the society. In contrast, invoking a right to social equality involves examining the top of the economic and social hierarchy in addition to the bottom, questioning the human rights impacts of the vast accumulation of wealth in the hands of the few, and comparing the actual enjoyment of human rights in light of the central tenant of UDHR that all human beings are equal in dignity and rights (UDHR, Article 1). In short, a focus on equality instead of poverty sheds light on situations where the wealth and privilege of some may prevent the full enjoyment of human rights by others.

In the first place, economic inequality and political inequality are often intertwined, and when economic inequalities are great, political inequality is likely to be great, as well. According to the World Bank, "In societies with large inequalities of assets and incomes, the rich will tend to have more influence and an advantage in adopting and distorting institutions to their benefit" (World Bank 2005, 108). The unequal distribution of wealth creates an unequal distribution of power and thus an unequal influence on institutions. As a result, the rich are in a position to ensure that institutions continue to favor them and their accumulation of wealth and power. In this way, inequality creates further inequality in a vicious cycle (ibid.). As the World Bank reports:

> A society with greater equality of control over assets and income will tend to have institutions that generate equality of opportunity for the broad mass of citizens. This will tend to spread rewards and incomes widely, thereby reinforcing the initial distribution of incomes. In contrast, a society with greater inequality of assets and income will tend to have a less egalitarian distribution of power and worse institutions, which tend to reproduce the initial conditions (ibid., 108).

In this way, economic and social inequality have an impact on the exercise of civil and political rights, including the rights to take part in the government (UDHR, Article 21) and to equality before the law (UDHR, Articles 7 and 10). It is not simply that wealthy people are able to enjoy their human rights to a fuller extent than other people. The problem is that their wealth, power, and influence actually diminish the power of others and their real opportunities to influence the policymaking institutions that have an impact on their lives. In this way, economic and social inequality adversely affects political participation – in the real sense of having opportunities to influence policy making – and prevents people who are not part of this elite from full enjoyment of their human rights in contradiction to the social order envisioned in UDHR Article 28.

At its most extreme, economic and social inequality causes political and economic instability (Oritz and Cummins 2011). Ortiz and Cummins report, "While the sources of political conflict vary from country to country, conflict generally originates from severe social grievances, including class conflict and the perception of inequality among ethnic, religious or other groups" (ibid., 35). Political destabilization, conflict, and violence often lead to further denial of the enjoyment of human rights. Ortiz and Cummins assert that inequality is dysfunctional because it "slows economic growth, results in health and social problems and generates political instability" (ibid., vii). For these reasons, they maintain that equality should be at the center of the development agenda. For the same reasons, a right to social equality should be at the center of the human rights agenda.

Defining the minimum content of economic and social rights – whether in terms of a minimum core or an adequate level – was, and continues to be, important to setting out state obligations in order to monitor the steps states parties are taking and hold them accountable for progressively realizing these rights. On the other hand, these thresholds are insufficient to ensure that the rights set out in the UDHR and the International Covenants can be fully realized because they do not take into account the importance of equality to people or the adverse impacts of inequality on individuals and societies. Moreover, minimum threshold approaches do not reflect the central idea in the holistic framework of the International Bill of Human Rights that everyone is born equal in dignity and rights (UDHR, Article 1). The content of the rights in the International Bill of Human Rights should reflect this fundamental idea captured in the holistic framework. Economic and social equality are crucial components of the holistic framework reinforced by the right to a social order – the umbrella right – enshrined in UDHR Article 28.

IV. THE RIGHT TO A SOCIAL ORDER UNDER UDHR ARTICLE 28

Article 1 of the UDHR sets out the foundation for human rights, the equality of all human beings, which is followed by Articles 2–27, enumerating a full range of civil, cultural, economic, political, and social rights. After these individual, family, community, and peoples' rights, Article 28 encompasses the full panoply of rights, providing that, "Everyone is entitled to a social and international order in which the rights and freedoms set forth in this Declaration can be fully realized." According to Stephen Marks, Article 28 requires no less than "the transformation of human rights from their legitimate status of morally justified entitlements to rights that are legally enforced and enjoyed in practice" (Marks 2009, 238). Similarly, Asbjørn Eide maintains that Article 28 calls for "nothing less than a structural adjustment of the existing social and international order to create the conditions under which human rights can in fact be enjoyed by all" (Eide 1999, 602). This broad understanding of Article 28 has been affirmed repeatedly by the UNGA, for example in the Declaration on Social Progress and Development in 1969 and the Declaration on the Right to Development in 1986.

Although there have been many such general pronouncements, the content of Article 28 remains unspecified, and therefore Article 28 appears merely aspirational – as it was when it was adopted in 1948. Nonetheless,

Article 28, importantly, sets forth the intention for the rights in the UDHR to be implemented, as they have been through subsequent international human rights treaties. Additionally, there are several important points to note about Article 28.

First, Article 28 refers to both the social order and the international order, implying that structures must be changed at both the domestic and the international level for all the rights in the UDHR to be enjoyed by all the people in the world (Eide 1999). Although there is no doubt that the international order plays an increasingly important role in the economic arena, the state retains the primary responsibility under international human rights law for ensuring enjoyment of these rights. Second, human rights scholars have described Article 28 as taking a structural approach that implies the need to actively alter power relations within society as well as the social structures so that they are conducive to realizing the full range of human rights (Eide 1999; Marks 2009). According to Eide, the UDHR was formulated in abstract terms to provide states with flexibility in transforming their internal systems; however, this broad policy space would be gradually reduced as rights were given more substance over time (Eide 1999).

Third, Article 28 implies, as does the preamble to the UDHR, that the rights in Articles 2–27 compose a package of integrated and interdependent rights. In this respect, Article 28 embraces a holistic human rights framework in which each of the rights is necessary to the whole (Morsink 1999). According to Morsink, the drafters of the UDHR believed in the fundamental equality and unity of all human rights, and intended that each article in the UDHR be interpreted in view of the other rights in the framework. This is the essence of the holistic approach over which Article 28 serves as the umbrella right, requiring a social order in which all the rights in the UDHR can be fully realized.

The CESCR acknowledges this holistic approach to human rights. This is evident in its definition of poverty, which it sees as a multidimensional concept that implicates a full range of civil and political rights as well as economic, social, and cultural rights (CESCR 2001). The CESCR also recommends that the rights in the human rights treaties be interpreted in light of each other. Significantly, in *General Comment 9* on the domestic application of the Covenant, the CESCR states that "Guarantees of equality and nondiscrimination should be interpreted, to the greatest extent possible, in ways which facilitate the full protection of economic, social and cultural rights" (CESCR 1998, 15). To guide states in doing so, the CESCR could take a holistic approach and reinterpret the rights to equality and nondiscrimination in light of the other rights in the International Bill of Human Rights. In this manner, it could construe equality and nondiscrimination to require a domestic social order that supports the full realization of social rights for all as envisioned by Article 28.

One step the CESCR could take in this direction is to elaborate on the meaning of the prohibition of discrimination on the basis of economic status under Article 2 of the ICESCR. Article 2(2) states that the parties to the Covenant undertake to guarantee the rights in the Covenant "without discrimination of any kind as to race, colour, sex, language, religion, political or other opinion, national or social origin, property, birth or other status." In this context, "property" means economic or wealth status. This is evident in the official Spanish version of the ICESCR, which states *"posición económico"* in the place of "property." Indeed, human rights scholars have generally recognized that "property" in Article 2 means economic status (Morsink 1999; Nowak 1993; Skogley 1999).[8]

Although the CESCR has recognized economic status in its country reports, it asserts in *General Comment 20* that economic status falls under "other status" in ICESCR Article 2. By doing so, the CESCR weakens the nondiscrimination protection for poor people, as state parties are less likely to follow the CESCR in recognizing grounds that are not explicitly enumerated. Moreover, a lower level of scrutiny often applies to "other" statuses (Vandenhole 2005). Additionally, the CESCR has not determined with any clarity the measures that states must take to ensure that they do not discriminate on the basis of economic status with respect to social rights. According to Morsink, the drafters of the UDHR, who first adopted this nondiscrimination provision, understood that it attached to the economic and social rights in the UDHR and therefore that it called for far-reaching egalitarianism (1999).

Another step the CESCR might consider is how the right to equality – or the idea of human beings equal in dignity and rights – could be construed to advance economic and social rights (UDHR, Articles 1 and 7). One possibility is to infer a right to equality in the substantive economic and social rights as it is implied with respect to civil and political rights. Just as the right to vote implies a right to a vote of equal weight to the votes of others (HRC 1996), some courts have concluded that the right

[8] The American Convention on Human Rights, which contains a similar nondiscrimination provision enumerating the same list of prohibited statuses, also uses "economic position" in the place of "property" in the English version (ACHR, article 1.1).

to education implies the right to an equal education (*Brigham* 1997). Indeed, the CESCR has asserted a right to "equality of access to health care and health services" and that health resource allocations should not favor the privileged part of the population (CESCR 2000, para. 19). Such rulings and recommendations provide initial parameters for the right to equality with respect to economic and social rights – as redistribution – and set out a foundation for further elaboration of state obligations for a domestic social order in which all human rights may be realized.

In effect, it is now necessary to recognize the right to social equality just as we have recognized the rights to civil and political equality. The holistic human rights framework set out in the International Bill of Human Rights demands nothing less than a full integration of the panoply of human rights it encompasses. Further, Article 28 of the UDHR compels states to establish a social order to actively "restructure society, at the national and international levels, in such a way that the equality and dignity of the human being can be transformed from rhetoric to reality" (Eide 1999, 602). In this sense, Article 28 necessarily implies a right to social equality.

V. THE RIGHT TO SOCIAL EQUALITY

The UDHR clearly reflects the efforts of the UN Commission on Human Rights, as well as John Humphrey, who prepared the initial draft, to steer a course between the liberal West and the Communist states (Glendon 2002). As a result, it draws heavily on the Latin American and Continental European constitutional traditions and presents a framework that is primarily a social democratic vision for realizing human rights (ibid.). This vision is not apparent yet in the work of the CESCR, and not prominent among human rights scholars. With the debate on the judiciability of economic and social rights now largely settled by the adoption of the Optional Protocol to the ICESCR, human rights scholars and practitioners may now focus more attention on the relationship of equality to economic and social rights.

Scholars engaged in discussions on substantive equality have begun this work. Sandra Fredman, for example, proposes that a social democratic paradigm best promotes substantive equality because it embraces social rights as integral to the state system (Fredman 2008). Fredman explains:

> Instead of the isolated individual in the "lonely market," the social democratic model views individuals as essentially social. This is not at the expense of individual autonomy but instead a way of achieving individual

autonomy: social progress is viewed as the best way to achieve individual well-being (ibid., 235).

In such a system, the social democratic state ensures universal access to quality "public goods such as health, education, childcare, leisure and public spaces" (ibid.). The aim is a comprehensive socialization of risk, such as that exemplified by the National Health Service in the United Kingdom or the comprehensive child care services in Scandinavian countries. This universal approach to public goods promotes quality services because everyone is invested in them (ibid.). It also promotes the right to equality with respect to social rights.

Similarly, Martha Fineman proposes the *responsive state*, which focuses on ensuring that societal institutions reduce rather than exacerbate individual vulnerability (Fineman 2008). From her perspective, individual autonomy is aided by the support of the state and societal institutions. In her words, "Autonomy is not an inherent characteristic, but must be cultivated by a society that pays attention to the needs of its members, the operation of its institutions, and the implications of human fragility and vulnerability" (Fineman 2010, 260). Consequently, she maintains that the state has the responsibility to structure conditions such that "individuals can aspire to meaningfully realize their individual capabilities as fully as possible" (ibid., 274). Moreover, the state must be held accountable for promoting substantive equality through its institutions and those it regulates in the private sector (Fineman 2008). Her vision of the responsive state might be characterized as a domestic social order in which all the rights and freedoms set forth in the UDHR can be fully realized. It also entails a right to social equality.

The parameters of the right to social equality, as a component of the UDHR Article 28 domestic social order, must develop over time as empirical evidence is produced – such as that on the adverse health impacts of inequality – and is subsequently incorporated into human rights standards by the decision-making bodies. Nonetheless, some initial thoughts with respect to equality and the rights to education and health may contribute to the discussion. Some level of equality with respect to all economic and social rights is necessary; however, the state plays a particularly important role in fulfilling the rights to education and health, which in turn are important means for achieving a right to social equality (Fineman 2008).[9]

---

[9] Education and health indicators are often used, as for example in the Human Development Index, to provide a multidimensional picture of poverty.

1. The Obligation to Respect

The obligation to respect requires states to refrain from interfering directly or indirectly with the right to social equality; in other words, the right to equality with respect to social rights. Moreover, the state must repeal laws and reform institutional structures that perpetuate social inequality. For example, states must refrain from establishing or perpetuating parallel systems of public education, such as the public school system in *Brown v. Board of Education* (1954), which was segregated on the basis of race, or the "two schools under one roof" school system in Bosnia and Herzegovina, in which children from different ethnic groups are separated on the premises or attend at different times and learn separate curricula (CESCR 2005). Similarly, states must refrain from establishing school financing systems that result in significant disparities in the resources per child across schools or school districts or between rural and urban areas (*Brigham* 1997; CESCR 1999). States have an immediate obligation to ensure that their school systems do not discriminate on the basis of race, ethnicity, or economic status.

Similarly, states should refrain from establishing or maintaining health care systems that are segregated on prohibited grounds (ICESCR, Article 2). In particular, tiered systems based on economic or employment status, which usually reflect the economic disparities in the society, reinforce such disparities rather than mitigating against them. For example, in 2008, the Constitutional Court of Colombia ordered the government to unify a two-tiered health care system that provided different benefit packages based on employment status (T-760/2008, para. 2.2.3). In reaching this decision, the Court relied upon ICESCR Article 12, and the CESCR's General Comment elaborating on that right, noting that the right to health included the right to a system of health protection that provides equal opportunity for all to enjoy the highest attainable level of health (ibid., para. 3.4.2.3). The Court's decision enforces the right to health, the right to equality in health care implied in the right to health, and the right to social equality. A unified and universal health care system with equal benefits for all is one step toward realizing the right to social equality.

Indeed, targeted programs for disadvantaged individuals and groups tend to be stigmatizing and often do not reach the most marginalized people. Thus, for example, a study found that only 37% of eligible high school students in San Francisco take advantage of the subsidized meal program because of the stigma of accepting a government lunch

(Pogash 2008). Katharine Young contends, "By invoking universal programs which only implicitly target particular groups, redistributive claims have had greater success in the United States" (Young 2009, 193). According to Young, "Universalism within redistributive politics is an innovation of the Universal Declaration, shared with other emancipatory agendas, but settled within the powerful discourse of rights" (ibid.). Thus, states should refrain from creating schemes for redistribution that are targeted and stigmatizing when universal systems may serve toward realizing the right to social equality.

Additionally, courts must refrain from dismantling health care and education systems that the legislature has established to ensure the right to equal and adequate health care services for all. In *Chaoulli v. Quebec Attorney General* (2005), the Canadian Supreme Court attempted to do so. The Court ruled that the Quebec statutes that prohibited private insurance, for services that were available in the public system, violated the claimants' rights to life and security under the Quebec Charter because the statutes prevented them from seeking services in the private sector to avoid the long waiting lines in the public sector. As the government had prohibited the parallel private system in order to ensure the equality and adequacy of public health care for all, the Court's direct interference and attempt to require the government to create a two-tiered public-private system implicate the right to social equality in international human rights law (Jackman 2006).

2. The Obligation to Protect

The obligation to protect requires the state to take measures to prevent third parties from interfering with the right to social equality. For the rights to education and health, the state must ensure there are systems to provide universal education and health care, whether through public or private institutions or, as is more often the case, through a combination of public and private institutional arrangements. In any scenario, the state must regulate the institutions as well as professionals to ensure that they respect human rights and promote the right to social equality in the work that they do. The state must therefore ensure that these institutions and professionals do not discriminate on any prohibited ground (CESCR 1999; CESCR 2000).

In the case of education, parents have a right to choose schools other than those established by the state (ICESCR, Article 13.3). Nonetheless, the state has an obligation to ensure that these schools provide an education that is equal to that provided in the public schools in terms of preparing students for employment and participation in democratic institutions of the society. Moreover, the state must ensure that the content of education in such private schools is "directed to the full development of the human personality and the sense of its dignity," strengthens "respect for human rights and fundamental freedoms," and promotes understanding among all racial, ethnic, and religious groups (ICESCR, Article 13.1). Just as the public schools must be directed to promote the right to social equality, so the state must ensure, through regulation and other appropriate means, that private schools are as well. Education is understood to be one of the primary means of escaping poverty and achieving social equality (CESCR 1999), and thus, the state must ensure that children and adults – especially of marginalized groups – are not prevented by third parties, including parents, spouses, and grandparents, from attending school (ibid.).

In the case of health care, the state must ensure that private health care facilities and providers do not discriminate on any prohibited ground, including economic status, by, for example, refusing to admit or treat people who are on welfare, unemployed, or uninsured. "Payment for health-care services, as well as services related to the underlying determinants of health, has to be based on the principles of equity, ensuring that these services, whether privately or publicly provided, are affordable for all, including socially disadvantaged groups" (CESCR 2000, para. 12[b][iii]). Additionally, the state must ensure that adolescents and women are not prevented by their families from obtaining health services and information, particularly in the area of sexual and reproductive health, by ensuring, among other measures, that such services are widely available and accessible to all, including in rural areas, and that they are delivered in a manner appropriate to cultural context (ibid.).

Privatization of health care, in particular, poses significant challenges to realizing the right to social equality. In recent years, the World Bank has encouraged countries with public health care systems to establish private health care financing for the wealthier segments of society to allow the diminished public sector to concentrate on providing low-income groups with a minimum package of services. Such segmentation, however, generally results in unequal systems for rich and poor people (McCoy 2006) Further, multiple insurance pools are less efficient than a single pool, and make it more difficult to plan and coordinate health care as well as to ensure equity (McCoy 2006; WHO 2010). The CESCR has warned that states have an obligation to ensure that privatization does not threaten the availability, accessibility, acceptability, and quality of health facilities, goods, and services (CESCR 2000). In short, Article 28 demands a strong role for the state in regulating the private sector to ensure a social order in which all the rights in the UDHR, including the right to social equality, may be realized.

3. The Obligation to Fulfill

The obligation to fulfill requires states to take all appropriate means, including legislative, administrative, budgetary, judicial, and promotional, to ensure the progressive realization of the right to social equality. Although the CESCR indicates that it is neutral about the economic system and the particular measures states adopt to implement social rights, state parties must use "all appropriate means" to "move as expeditiously and effectively as possible" toward realizing these rights (ICESCR Article 2; CESCR 1990, paras 4 and 9). The state also has an immediate obligation to adopt a national plan to progressively realize the right to social equality including full equality in the rights to health care and education. Progress toward this goal must be monitored via indicators and benchmarks with opportunities for people to participate in developing the plan and to provide feedback as it is implemented.

To fulfill the right to social equality with respect to education and health care, the state must establish a school system and a health system, and it must ensure that these systems do not discriminate or increase inequality on the basis of any prohibited ground – including economic status (ICESCR Article 13(2)(e); Hunt 2008). The state must also take steps to promote social equality in education and health care by ensuring that the facilities and services are available, accessible, acceptable, of good quality, and equal for all. To equalize health care and education, the state may not equalize down due to the presumption against retrogression. It must therefore equalize up, progressively realizing the equal rights to the education and health system for all. Further, the state must use maximum available resources, taking into account that realizing equality with respect to these rights depends upon building systems that promote social equality – a key ingredient to fully realizing social rights. To do so, the state must consider the research on the most effective means to support realization of the right to social equality and ensure that best practices are integrated into its systems.

When gearing up the health care and education sectors to provide services to those previously underserved or without any service at all, states may establish temporary second-tier education or health services, provided there is a detailed plan to equalize these services within a reasonable period of time. For example, the health care system in Colombia established in 1993 initially introduced a two-tier system of health care benefits; however, the same law that established the two tiers required the system to be unified by 2001 (Yamin, Parra-Vera, and Gianella 2011). Similarly, a two-tiered system of education was established in India to expand primary education to areas where there was none. States may establish such second-track measures provided they are temporary and do not perpetuate social inequalities, but rather are concrete and targeted steps toward full implementation of social rights and the right to social equality.

In the case of the right to education, states have the "principal responsibility for the direct provision of education in most circumstances" (CESCR 1999, para. 48). As education is an empowerment right, it is an essential means through which the state may promote the right to social equality. Indeed, state parties "have an enhanced obligation to fulfill" the right to education by actively developing a system of schools" (ibid.). Moreover, the state must actively promote social equality in the content of the education by including in the curriculum human rights education (ICESCR, Article 13[1]). In the case of the right to health care, there are public models, such as that in the United Kingdom, as well as public-private, such as that in Canada or France, that are successful in terms of health outcomes and costs. Regardless of the type of system the state maintains, it must regulate it to ensure that it is advancing the enjoyment of the right to health. In sum, the obligation to fulfill the right to social equality requires the state to take positive measures to assist individuals and communities in realizing this right and to maintain a social order in which all human rights may be realized.

CONCLUSION

In 2001, the CESCR issued a *Statement on Poverty*, explicitly asserting that "poverty constitutes a denial of human rights" (CESCR 2001, para. 1). Today, scholars and practitioners generally view poverty as a major human rights issue. Moreover, they have begun to conceptualize and apply human rights-based approaches to poverty eradication. Current approaches focus on identifying poor people and ensuring them a minimum core content or adequate level of social rights. Yet, minimum thresholds do not address the importance of economic and social equality to people and societies. Economic and social equality is important to people because intuitively they link it to fairness, and because it has an impact on other aspects of quality of life, including health, longevity, personal security, participation, and nondiscrimination. As a result, the right to equality – well beyond a right to civil and political equality – must play a critical role in eradicating multidimensional poverty.

Historically, Anglo-American states have emphasized civil and political equality at the expense of economic and social equality, and individual rights at the expense of collective rights. Article 28 of the UDHR, however, demands a social order in which all human rights may be realized, thus embracing a holistic human rights framework that includes a full spectrum of interdependent human rights. In this framework, the intrinsic and instrumental importance of economic and social equality to individual and societal well-being makes it essential to realizing economic and social rights as well as other human rights. In short, economic and social equality is necessary to the equal enjoyment of human rights. As a result, the right to equality with respect to economic and social rights – the right to social equality – must be implied in the social order required under Article 28 of the UDHR.

REFERENCES

Alkire, Sabina, 2007. "Multidimensional Poverty: How to Choose Dimensions," *Maitreyee* 7: 2–4.

Alston, Philip, 2004. "Core Labour Standards and the Transformation of the International Labour Rights Regime," *European Journal of International Law* 15: 457–521.

Alston, Philip, 2008. "Putting Economic, Social and Cultural Rights Back on the Agenda of the United States," in William F. Schultz (Ed.) *The Future of Human Rights: U.S. Policy for a New Era*, 120–138, Philadelphia: University of Pennsylvania Press.

Bilchitz, David, 2007. *Poverty and Fundamental Rights: The Justification and Enforcement of Socio-Economic Rights*, Oxford: Oxford University Press.

Brigham v. State of Vermont, 1997. 692 A.2d 384, Vt.

Brown v. Board of Education, 1954. 347 U.S. 483.

Brownlie, Ian, 2008. *Principles of Public Law*, 7th edition, Oxford: Oxford University Press.

Campaign for Fiscal Equity v. State of New York, 2003. 801 N.E.2d 326, NY App. Div.

Chaoulli v. Quebec Attorney General, 2005. 1 SCR 791.

Chapman, Audrey and Sage Russell (Eds.), 2002. *Core Obligations: Building a Framework for Economic, Social and Cultural Rights*, Antwerp and Oxford: Intersentia.

Chen, Shaohua and Martin Ravillion, 2009. "The Developing World is Poorer Than We Thought, But No Less Successful in the Fight Against Poverty." The World Bank Development Research Group, Policy Research Working Paper 4703.

CESCR (Committee on Economic, Social and Cultural Rights), 1990. *General Comment No. 3*, The nature of the States parties obligations, Article 2(1), UN Doc. HRI/GEN/1/Rev.1, December 14.

CESCR, 1998. *General Comment No. 9*, The domestic application of the Covenant, UN Doc. E/C.12/1998/24, December 3.

CESCR, 1999. *General Comment No. 13*, The right to education, Article 13, UN Doc. E/C.12/1999/10, December 8.

CESCR, 2000. *General Comment No. 14*, The right to the highest attainable standard of health, Article 12, UN Doc. E/C.12/2000/4, August 11.

CESCR, 2001. *Poverty and the International Covenant on Economic, Social and Cultural Rights*. UN Doc. E/C.12/2001/10, May 10.

CESCR, 2005. *Concluding Observations* of the Committee on Economic, Social and Cultural Rights: Bosnia and Herzegovina. UN Doc. E/C.12/BIH/CO/1, November 25.

CESCR, 2008. *General Comment No. 19*, The right to social security, Article 9, UN Doc. E/C.12/GC/19, January 30.

CESCR, 2009. *General Comment No. 20*, Non-discrimination in economic, social and cultural rights, Article 2.2, UN Doc. E/C.12/GC/20, July 2.

Corte Constitucional de la República de Colombia (Constitutional Court of Colombia), Sentencia (Judgment) No. T-760/2008 (2008).

Craven, Matthew, 1995. *The International Covenant on Economic, Social and Cutural Rights: A Perspective on its Development*, Oxford: Clarendon Press.

CSDH (Commission on the Social Determinants of Health), 2008. *Closing the Gap in a Generation: Health Equity through Action on the Social Determinants of Health*, Geneva: World Health Organization.

Eide, Asbjørn, 1999. "Article 28," in Gudmundur Alfredsson and Asbjørn Eide (Eds.) *The Universal Declaration of Human Rights: A Common Standard of Achievement*, 567–635, The Hague: Martinus NijHoff Publishers.

Eurostat, 2005. "Income Poverty and Social Exclusion in the EU25," *Statistics in Focus* 13: 1–2.

Fineman, Martha Albertson, 2008. "The Vulnerable Subject: Anchoring Equality in the Human Condition," *Yale Journal of Law and Feminism* 20: 1–24.

Fineman, Martha Albertson, 2010. "The Vulnerable Subject and the Responsive State," *Emory Law Journal* 60: 251–275.

Fredman, Sandra, 2008. *Human Rights Transformed: Positive Rights and Positive Duties*, Oxford: Oxford University Press.

Fredman, Sandra, 2009. "Engendering Socio-Economic Rights," *South African Journal of Human Rights* 25(3): 410–441.

Glendon, Mary Ann, 2002. *A World Made New: Eleanor Roosevelt and the Universal Declaration of Human Rights*. New York: Random House Trade Paperbacks.

Government of the Republic of South Africa v Grootboom, 2001. (1) SA 46 (CC).

HRC (Human Rights Committee), 1996. *General Comment No. 25*, The right to participate in public affairs, voting rights and the equal right to public service, Article 25, UN Doc. CCPR/C/21/Rev.1/Add.7, July 12.

Hunt, Paul, 2008. "Annual Report of the Special Rapporeur on the Right to Health to the UN Human Rights Council," UN Doc. A/HRC/7/11, January 31.

Hunt, Paul, 2009. "Missed Opportunities: Human Rights and the Commission on Social Determinants of Health," *Global Health Promotion* 16: 36–41.

Jackman, Martha, 2006. "'The Last Line of Defense for [Which] Citizens': Accountability, Equality, and the Right to Health in *Chaoulli*," *Osgoode Hall Law Journal* 44: 349–375.

Khan, Irene, 2009. *The Unheard Truth: Poverty and Human Rights*, New York: W.W. Norton & Company.

Laderchi, Caterina Ruggeri, Ruhi Saith, and Frances Stewart, 2003. "*Does it matter that we don't agree on the definition of poverty? A comparison of four approaches*," Working Paper Number 107, Queen Elizabeth House, University of Oxford.

Marks, Stephen, 2009. "The Past and Future of the Separation of Human Rights into Categories," *Maryland Journal of International Law* 24: 209–243.

Marmot, Michael and Richard G. Wilkinson. 2006. *Social Determinants of Health*, Oxford: Oxford University Press.

McCoy, David, 2006. "Financing Health Care: For All, for Some, for Patients or for Profits?" in Lois L. Ross, Maureen Johnson and William Meyer (Eds.), *The Global Rights to Health: Canadian Development Report 2007*, pp. 59-83, Ottawa: Renouf Publishing.

Morsink, Johannes, 1999. *The Universal Declaration of Human Rights: Origins, Drafting and Intent*, Philadelphia: University of Pennsylvania Press.

Neier, Areyeh, 2006. "Social and Economic Rights: A Critique," *Human Rights Brief* 13(2): 1–3.

Norton, Michael I. and Dan Ariely, 2011. "Building America – One Wealth Quintile at a Time," *Perspectives on Psychological Science* 6(1): 9–12.

Nowak, Manfred, 1993. *U.N. Covenant on Civil and Political Rights: CCPR Commentary*, Kehl, Germany: N.P. Engel.

Nussbaum, Martha, 2000. *Women and Human Development: The Capabilities Approach*, Cambridge: Cambridge University Press.

Nussbaum, Martha, 2007a. "Human Rights and Human Capabilities," *Harvard Human Rights Journal* 20: 21–24.

Nussbaum, Martha, 2007b. "The Capabilities Approach and Ethical Cosmopolitanism: A Response to Noah Feldman," *Yale Law Journal Pocket Part* 117: 123–129.

OHCHR (Office of the High Commissioner for Human Rights), 2004. *Human Rights and Poverty Reduction: A Conceptual Framework*, HR/PUB/04/1, Geneva: OHCHR.

OHCHR, 2006. *Principles and Guidelines for a Human Rights Approach to Poverty Reduction Strategies*, HR/PUB/06/12, Geneva: OHCHR.

Oritz, Isabel and Matthew Cummins, 2011. "Global Inequality: Beyond the Bottom Billion: A Rapid Review of Income Distribution in 141 Countries," New York: UNICEF Division of Policy and Practice.

Phillips, Anne, 1999. *Which Equalities Matter?*, Cambridge: Polity Press.

Phillips, Anne, 2001. "Feminism and Liberalism Revisted: Has Martha Nussbaum Got it Right?" *Constellations* 8(2): 249–266.

Pogash, Carol, 2008. "Free Lunch Isn't so Cool, So Some Students Go Hungry." *The New York Times*. Retrieved from http://www.nytimes.com/2008/03/01/education/01lunch.html?pagewanted=all.

Riddell, Roger, 2004. "Approaches to Poverty: A Note from the 'Development' Perspective," International Council on Human Rights Policy, Researchers' Meeting on Poverty, Development, Rights, Geneva, November 24–25.

Rogers v. Swindon NHS Primary Care Trust, 2006. EWA Civ 392.

Rose v. Council for Better Education, 1989. 790 S.W.2d 186, Ky.

Rowlingson, Karen, 2011. "Does Income Inequality Cause Health and Social Problems?" London: Joseph Rowntree Foundation.

Sachs, Jeffrey, 2005. *The End of Poverty: Economic Possibilities for Our Time*, New York: Penguin.

Saunders, Peter, 2010. "Beware False Prophets: Equality, the Good Society and the Spirit Level," London: Policy Exchange.

Sen, Amartya, 1999. *Development as Freedom*, New York: Anchor Books.

Sen, Amartya, 2005. "Human Rights and Capabilities," *Journal of Human Development* 6(2): 151–166.

Skogley, Sigrun, 1999. "Article 2," in Gudmundar Alfredson and Asbjørn Eide (Eds.) *The Universal Declaration of Human Rights*, 75–87, Alphen aan den Rijn, The Netherlands: Kluwer Law International.

Stewart, Frances, 1989. "Basic Needs Strategies, Human Rights, and the Right to Development," *Human Rights Quarterly* 11: 347–374.

Sumner, Andy, 2010. "Global Poverty and the New Bottom Billion: What If Three-Quarters of the World's Poor Live in Middle-Income Countries?" Brighton, UK: Institute of Development Studies, IDS Working Paper 349.

UNDP (United Nations Development Program), 2000. *Human Rights and Human Development, Human Development Report 2000*, Oxford and New York: Oxford University Press.

UNGA (United Nations General Assembly), 2000. United Nations Millennium Declaration, Res 55/2, UN Doc A/RES/55/2.

United States Census Bureau, 2011. "Poverty." Retrieved from http://www.census.gov/hhes/www/poverty/.

Vandenhole, Wouter, 2005. *Non-Discrimination and Equality iin the View of the UN Human Rights Treaty Bodies*, Antwerp: Intersentia.

Vizard, Polly, 2006. *Poverty and Human Rights: Sen's 'Capability Approach' Explored*, Oxford: Oxford University Press.

WHO (World Health Organization), 2010. *The World Health Report 2010 – Health Systems Financing: The path to universal coverage*, Geneva: World Health Organization.

Wilkinson, Richard, 2005. *The Impact of Inequality: How to Make Sick Societies Healthier*, Abingdon, UK: Routledge Press.

Wilkinson, Richard and Kate Pickett, 2009. *The Spirit Level: Why More Equal Societies Almost Always Do Better*, London: Penguin Books.

Woodward, David, 2010. "How poor is 'poor'? Towards a rights-based poverty line," New Economics Foundation. Retrieved from http://www.neweconomics. org/publications/how-poor-is-poor.

World Bank, 2000. *Crying Out for Change: Voices of the Poor*, Deepa Narayan (Ed)., Oxford: Oxford University Press.

World Bank, 2001. *Attacking Poverty: World Development Report 2001*, New York: Oxford University Press.

World Bank, 2003. *Making Services Work for Poor People*, New York: Oxford University Press and The World Bank.

World Bank, 2005. *Equity and Development: World Development Report 2006*, New York: Oxford University Press.

Yamin, Alicia, Oscar Parra-Vera, and Camila Gianella, 2011. "Colombia – Judicial Protection of the Right to Health: An Elusive Promise?" in Alicia Yamin and Siri Gloppen (Eds.) *Litigating Health Rights: Can Courts Bring More Justice to Health?*, 103–131, Cambridge: Harvard University Press.

Young, Katharine, 2008. "The Minimum Core of Economic and Social Rights: A Concept in Search of Content," *Yale Journal of International Law* 33: 113–175.

Young, Katharine, 2009. "Freedom, Want, and Economic and Social Rights: Frame and Law," *Maryland Journal of International Law* 24:182–208.

12

The Right to Development from a Human Rights Approach: Conceptual Bases, Legal Framework, and Contemporary Challenges

Flavia Piovesan

1. INTRODUCTION

The right to development is the right of individuals and peoples to an enabling environment for development that is equitable, sustainable, participatory, and in accordance with the full range of human rights and fundamental freedoms. Such an environment is free from structural and unfair obstacles to development domestically as well as globally (UN High Level Task Force 2010).

The current scale and severity of global poverty provide a jarring contrast and add urgency to efforts to attain the sought-for enabling environment. In light of this, this chapter discusses the key attributes of the right to development from a human rights perspective, considering its conceptual and legal bases. As such, it particularly examines social justice; participation, accountability, and transparency; and international cooperation. It gives special emphasis to the legal framework of the right to development, examining the extent of the state duties to respect, protect, and fulfill the right to development at a national and international level.

Considering the 1986 Declaration on the Right to Development as a dynamic, living instrument of enduring value in addressing current and emerging challenges central to development, this chapter concludes by highlighting the contemporary challenges and perspectives of the implementation of the right to development, inspired by the human rights-based approach to development and a development approach to human rights.[1]

---

[1] Development from a human rights perspective was also endorsed by the 1993 Vienna Declaration of Human Rights, which stresses that democracy, development, and respect for human rights and fundamental freedoms are interdependent and mutually reinforcing, adding that the international community should support the strengthening and promoting of democracy, development, and respect for human rights in the entire world.

2. CONCEPTUAL BASES AND LEGAL FRAMEWORK OF THE RIGHT TO DEVELOPMENT

Among the extraordinary achievements of the 1986 United Nations Declaration on the Right to Development is the advancement of a human rights-based approach to development. This approach integrates the norms, standards, and principles of the international human rights system into the plans, policies, and processes of development.

Although the topic of development has traditionally been monopolized by economists – with an exclusive emphasis on the Gross Domestic Product – the meaning of development has been revised since the 1980s, and has come to be guided by the human dimension. Article 2 of the Declaration recognizes that, "The human person is the central subject of development and should be the active participant and beneficiary of the right to development."

To Stephen P. Marks:

> The Declaration takes a holistic, human-centred approach to development. It sees development as a comprehensive process aiming to improve the well-being of the entire population and of all individuals on the basis of their active, free, and meaningful participation and in the fair distribution of the resulting process. In other words, recognising development as a human right empowers all people to claim their active participation in decisions that affect them – rather than merely being beneficiaries of charity – and to claim an equitable share of the benefits resulting from the development gains (Marks 2011, 2).

To adopt Amartya Sen's conception, development has to be conceived of as a process of expansion of the true freedoms that people can benefit from.[2] Thinking along similar lines, Arjun K. Sengupta states that the right to development is the "right to a process that expands the capabilities or freedom of individuals to improve their well-being and to realize what they value" (Sengupta 2000).

---

[2] In conceiving of development as freedom, Amartya Sen suggests that the expansion of liberties is both as 1) an end in itself and 2) the main meaning of development. Such ends may be respectively termed the constitutive and the instrumental function of liberty with regard to development. The constitutive function of liberty is related to the importance of substantive liberty for the elevation of human life. Substantive liberties include elementary capacities such as avoiding privation due to hunger, malnutrition, avoidable mortality, premature death and liberties associated with education, political participation, prohibition of censorship, etc. From this constitutive perspective, development involves the expansion of human liberties (Sen 1999). On the right to development, see also Karel Vasak (1977).

Development from a human rights perspective embraces three key attributes:

(a) social justice (through inclusion, equality, and nondiscrimination, taking the human person as the central subject of development and paying special attention to the most deprived and excluded);
(b) participation, accountability, and transparency (through free, meaningful, and active participation, focusing on empowerment); and
(c) international cooperation (as the right to development is a solidarity-based right).

2.1. Social Justice

According to Article 28 of the Universal Declaration of Human Rights, "Everyone is entitled to a social and international order in which the rights and freedoms set forth in this Declaration can be fully realized." Social justice is a central component of the conception of the right to development. The realization of the right to development, inspired by the value of solidarity, must provide equal opportunity to all in the access to basic resources, education, health care, food, housing, work, and wealth distribution (Rosas 1995).

For the Declaration on the Right to Development, development comprises an economic, social, cultural, and political process, aimed at ensuring the constant improvement of the well-being of the population and of individuals, based on their active, free, and significant participation in this process, guided by the fair distribution of the benefits resulting from it. States have the primary responsibility for the creation of national and international conditions conducive to the realization of the right to development, and the duty to cooperate in ensuring development and eliminating obstacles to development (Article 3). However, in promoting development, equal consideration must be given to the implementation, promotion, and protection of civil, political, economic, social, and cultural rights.

Effective measures must also be adopted to provide women with an active role in the process of development. In the contemporary world order, poverty is "feminized," as women constitute 70% of those living in poverty. Guaranteeing the empowerment of women is a condition essential to the furthering of development. Statistics show that the countries with the highest Human Development Index (HDI), which measures a population's quality of life, access to healthcare, education and work, are precisely those with the smallest gender gap; that is, the smallest difference between men and women in the exercise of human rights.[3] In the words of Amartya Sen, "Nothing is as important today in the political economy of development as an adequate recognition of political, economic and social participation and leadership of women. This is indeed a crucial aspect of 'development as freedom'" (Sen 1999).

In addressing the right to development from a human rights approach, Mary Robinson states that, "The great merit of the human rights approach is that it draws attention to discrimination and exclusion. It permits policy makers and observers to identify those who do not benefit from development . . . so many development programmes have caused misery and impoverishment – planners only looked for macro-scale outcomes and did not consider the consequences for particular communities or groups of people" (Robinson 2005, 36).

About 80% of the world's population lives in developing countries, marked by low incomes and educational levels and high rates of poverty and unemployment.[4] Roughly 85% of the world's income goes to the richest 20% of the world's population, whereas 6% goes to the poorest 60% (Hurrell 2009). The World Health Organization emphasizes that, "Poverty is the world's greatest killer. Poverty wields its destructive influence at every stage of human life, from the moment of conception to the grave. It conspires with the most deadly and painful diseases to bring a wretched existence to all those who suffer from it"(WHO 1995, 1).[5]

The Declaration urges that appropriate economic and social reforms should be carried out with a view to eradicating all social injustices. It also adds that states should encourage people's participation in all spheres as an important factor in development and the full realization of all human rights (Article 8).

---

[3] Note that Arab countries (such as Morocco, Saudi Arabia, and Yemen) have the worst performance in gender disparities and inequalities. In these countries, disadvantages facing women and girls are the source of high inequality levels. See Hausman, Tyson, and Zahidi (2011).

[4] Jeffrey Sachs states that, "Eight million people around the world die each year because they are too poor to stay alive" (Sachs 2005, 1). He adds that, "One sixth of the world remains trapped in extreme poverty unrelieved by global economic growth and the poverty trap poses tragic hardships for the poor themselves and great risks for the rest of the world" (Sachs 2008, 6).

[5] See Paul Farmer (2009). To Andrew Hurrell (2009, 296), "It is highly implausible to believe that the 20% of the world's population living in the high-income countries can insulate itself from the instability and insecurity of the rest and from revisionist demands for change."

2.2. *Participation, Accountability, and Transparency*

The principle of participation and the principle of accountability are central to the right to development. According to the 1986 Declaration:

> The human person is the central subject of development and should be the active participant and beneficiary of the right to development.... States have the duty to formulate appropriate national development policies that aim at the constant improvement of the well-being of the entire population and of all individuals, on the basis of their active, free and meaningful participation in development and in the fair distribution of the benefits resulting therefrom.

The 1986 Declaration is the only international instrument that makes the nature of participation in development so explicit, emphasizing that states should encourage, promote, and ensure free, meaningful, and active participation of all individuals and groups in the design, implementation, and monitoring of development policies.

Political liberties and democratic rights are among the constituent components of development, as spelled out by Amartya Sen.[6] Democracy demands access to information, alternative sources of information, freedom of expression, freedom of association, political participation, dialogue, and public interaction.[7] Based on public reasoning, democracy is conditioned not just by the institutions that formally exist but by the extent to which different voices can be heard. The concept of participation and its relevance as a core element to a rights-based approach to development require that democracy be addressed at both a procedural and substantive level. At a procedural level, there are diverse forms of participation by populations in development through mechanisms such as public consultation, information, and decision-making, with special consideration given to the participation of vulnerable groups, and particularly taking the gender, race, and ethnicity perspectives, thus giving voice to the deprived and vulnerable.

Civil and political rights are cornerstones of empowerment, strengthening democracy and improving accountability. Democracy enriches

---

[6] "Democracy is assessed in terms of public reasoning, which leads to an understanding of democracy as "government by discussion" (Sen 2009, XIII).

[7] Every kind of democracy should meet a few basic requirements. To Robert Dahl, democracy will meet these seven requirements: 1) elected authorities; 2) free and fair elections; 3) inclusive suffrage; 4) the right to be elected; 5) freedom of expression; 6) alternative sources of information; and 7) freedom of association (Dahl 1989). See also Dahl, Shapiro, and Cheibub (2003); Dahl (2005,2000).

reasoned engagement through the enhancement of informational availability and the feasibility of interactive discussions. The fact that "no famine has ever taken place in the history of the world in a functioning democracy" (Sen 2009, 343) is revealing of the protective power of political liberty. Having an effective voice requires material capacities and the material conditions on which meaningful political participation depends (Hurrell 2009).

In the light of the principle of participation,[8] it is essential to promote participatory rights in national-level policy making, as well as in the decision-making processes of global institutions. At a national level, the right to free, active, and meaningful participation demands the expansion of the universe of those entitled to participate in the democratic game, inspired by the clause of equality and nondiscrimination based on gender,[9] race, ethnicity, and other criteria, and paying special attention to the most vulnerable.[10]

On the other hand, it demands the expansion of participatory arenas, strengthening democratic density – which can no longer be limited to who participates in the democratic game, but must also include how to participate[11] – based on the principles of transparency and accountability, highlighting human beings as agents for democracy. The rise of local participatory processes has taken different forms, fostering citizen participation. People should be active participants in development, and implement development projects rather than being treated as passive beneficiaries. Every democracy entails agents and their consequent dignity as moral beings that deserve to be treated with full consideration and respect.

In addition to being active and free, participation should be meaningful as an effective expression of popular sovereignty in the adoption of

---

[8] Participatory rights are also enshrined by international human rights instruments that give universal protection to political rights, including Article 21 of the Universal Declaration of Human Rights, Article 25 of the International Covenant on Civil and Political Rights, and Article 7 of the Convention on the Elimination of All Forms of Discrimination against Women, among others.

[9] Regarding the participation of women, according to the United Nations Development Program (UNDP), about one in five countries has a quota imposed by law or the constitution reserving a percentage of parliamentary seats for women, contributing to a rise in women's share from 11% in 1975 to 19% in 2010 (UNDP 2010).

[10] The lack of a voice is a problem afflicting refugees and migrants who no longer live in their countries of origin and are unable to participate politically in their countries of residence.

[11] See Bobbio (1989). Formal processes of democracy have proliferated at a national level, as illustrated by pioneering initiatives in Brazil, such as the participatory budget formulation process.

development programs and policies. Meaningful participation and empowerment are reflected by the people's ability to voice their opinions in institutions that enable the exercise of power, recognizing the citizenry as the origin and the justification of public authority.

According to Freedom House, nearly forty years ago more than half of the world was ruled by one form of autocracy or another, and many millions lived under outright totalitarianism;[12] the majority now lives in democratic states. In 2010, the number of electoral democracies stood at 115. However, a total of forty-seven countries are deemed not free, representing 24% of the world's polities and 35% of the global population. Using regional criteria, in Western Europe 96% of the countries are considered free, whereas in the Middle East and North Africa just 6% of countries are considered free and 78% not free. A free country is one where there is open political competition, a climate of respect for civil liberties, significant independent civic life, and independent media. A not-free country is one where basic liberties are widely and systematically denied (Freedom House, 2011).

At a global level, the principle of participation demands an increase in the role of civil society organizations in policy discussion and decision-making processes. In addition, there is a pressing need to strengthen the participation of developing countries in international economic decision-making and norm-setting (UN Economic and Social Council 2004). As stated by Joseph E. Stiglitz:

> We have a system that might be called global governance without global government, one in which a few institutions – the World Bank, the IMF, the WTO – and a few players – the finance, commerce, and trade ministries, closely linked to certain financial and commercial interests – dominate the scene, but in which many of those affected by their decisions are left almost voiceless. It's time to change some of the rules governing the international economic order (Stiglitz 2003, 21–22).

In this context, the struggle for a new multilateralism is urgent. This would involve reforms in the global financial architecture in order to achieve a new political balance of power, democratizing financial institutions and enhancing their transparency and accountability.[13] The

---

[12] The share of countries designated as free increased from 31% in 1980 to 45% in 2000, and the proportion of countries designated as not free declined from 37% in 1980 to 25% in 2000. A free country demands free institutions, free minds, civil liberties, and law-based societies (Freedom House 2011).

[13] According to Joseph Stiglitz, "We have a chaotic, uncoordinated system of global governance without global government." The author defends a "reform package," including,

establishment of the G20 (shifting global politics from the old G7 to a new group of emerging powers), demands for reform of the voting structures of Bretton Woods institutions (International Monetary Fund and World Bank), as well as other initiatives aimed at broadening global governance, democratizing international decision-making arenas, and strengthening the voice of the South are worthy of mention. Global challenges cannot be faced without adequate representation for a large proportion of humankind – Africa, Latin America, and Asia – at major international forums and decision-making bodies. International order has to be reconceived and reconceptualized. As observed by Andrew Hurrell, "Today's new emerging and regional powers are indispensable members of any viable global order. But the cost of this change is both a far greater degree of heterogeneity in the interests of the major states, as well as an enormous increase in the number of voices demanding to be heard" (Hurrell 2009, 7). Due to the lack of democracy in global governance, it is essential to promote good governance at an international level and effective participation of all countries in international decision-making processes (UN High Level Task Force, 2010).

2.3. International Cooperation

Besides social justice and participation, the right to development requires international cooperation as a key dimension. The right to development is a solidarity-based right presenting both national and international dimensions.

If the human rights grammar – as it was conceived by the 1948 Universal Declaration – is mostly inspired by the value of human dignity from an individualistic approach, the right to development is mostly inspired by the value of solidarity from a collectivist approach embracing the local, regional, and international levels. The right to development demands that globalization be ethical and incorporate the principle of solidarity. In the understanding of Mohammed Bedjaqui:

> In reality, the international dimension of the right to development is nothing more than an equitable distribution with regard to global social and economic well being. This reflects a crucial question of our age, in so far as

among other measures: 1) changes in voting structure at the IMF and World Bank, giving more weight to developing countries; 2) changes in representations (who represents each country); 3) adopting principles of representation; 4) increasing transparency (as there is no direct democratic accountability for these institutions); 5) improving accountability; and 6) ensuring better enforcement of the international rule of law (Stiglitz 2007, 21).

four fifths of the world's population no longer accept the fact that a fifth of the world's population continues to build its wealth on the basis of the remainder's poverty (Bedjaqui 1991, 1182).

As already mentioned, according to the 1986 Declaration, states have the primary responsibility for the creation of national and international conditions favorable to the realization of the right to development and the duty to cooperate in ensuring development and eliminating obstacles to development. States also have the duty to take steps, individually and collectively, to formulate international development policies with a view to facilitating the full realization of the right to development.

Considering that the right to development has both national and international dimensions, it is essential to focus on the joint and external responsibilities of states in the realization of the right to development as a solidarity-based right. It is also important to note that the policies of international financial institutions are determined by the same states that have legally binding obligations under the International Covenant on Economic, Social and Cultural Rights (ICESCR).[14]

In dealing with the responsibilities of states acting collectively at the global and regional levels for the implementation of the right to development, the following criteria should be considered[15]: a) a stable global economic and financial system; b) a rule-based, open, predictable and nondiscriminatory international trading system; c) access to adequate human and financial resources; d) access to the benefits of science and technology; e) environment of peace and security; f) environmental sustainability; g) constant improvement in human well-being; h) incorporating relevant international human rights standards in formulating development goals; i) integrating norms of nondiscrimination, participation, access to information, and effective complaint and remedy into their policies, systems, and programming right across the board, including in project assessment, planning, implementation, and evaluation; j) promoting good governance at an international level, including promoting the

---

[14] It is also notable that the Maastricht Guidelines on Violations of Economic, Social and Cultural Rights deem a human rights violation of omission "the failure of a State to take into account its international legal obligations in the field of economic, social and cultural rights when entering into bilateral or multilateral agreements with other States, international organizations or multinational corporations."

[15] See the report of the High Level Task Force on the implementation of the right to development for the April 2010 session of the Working Group, including the list of criteria, sub-criteria, and indicators (UN High Level Task Force 2010).

democratization of the system of international governance and promoting effective participation of all countries in international decision-making; k) providing for a fair and equitable distribution of the benefits and burdens of development; and l) strengthening of global financial institutions, improving democratization, transparency, and accountability of international financial institutions.

In the light of the international rule of law,[16] it is important to identify the extent and degree of the international responsibilities of states in the realization of the right to development, reviewing the traditional human rights doctrine, which endorses as state obligations the duty to respect, protect, and fulfill human rights, in order to include the duty to cooperate. The duty of international cooperation is based on the value of solidarity as the moral component of the right to development. Considering that the 1986 Declaration should be perceived as a dynamic and living instrument, there emerges the contemporary challenge of how to strengthen the states' duty to cooperate for the implementation of the right to development in the global arena.

3. RIGHT TO DEVELOPMENT: THE EXTENT OF STATE DUTIES

Classical doctrine identifies three state obligations in the field of human rights: to respect, protect, and implement human rights. The obligation to respect impedes the state from violating such rights. Regarding the obligation to protect, the state must avoid and prevent third parties (non-state actors) from violating these rights. Finally, the obligation to implement demands that the state adopt measures for the realization of these rights.[17]

Katarina Tomasevski feels:

> The obligations to respect, protect and fulfil each contain elements of obligation of conduct and obligation of result. The obligation of conduct requires action reasonably calculated to realize the enjoyment of a particular right. The obligation of result requires States to achieve specific targets to satisfy a detailed substantive standard.... The obligation to protect includes the State's responsibility to ensure that private entities or

---

[16] For Tom Bingham, "The rule of law requires compliance by the State with its obligations in international law as in national law" (2010, 110).

[17] In General Comment No. 12, the Committee of Economic, Social and Cultural Rights highlights that the obligation to fulfill can be broken down into the obligation to facilitate, promote, and provide.

individuals, including transnational corporations over which they exercise jurisdiction, do not deprive individuals of their economic, social and cultural rights. States are responsible for violations of economic, social and cultural rights that result from their failure to exercise due diligence in controlling the behaviour of such non-state actors"[18] (Tomasevski 2001, 729, 732).

With reference to the right to development, as well as the traditional obligations to respect, protect, and implement, the obligation to cooperate also stands out. This is because the right to development has solidarity as a founding value, which, in an increasingly global order, invokes the duty of international cooperation. In Article 22, the 1948 Universal Declaration itself enshrines "the right to social security through national effort and international co-operation and, of the economic, social and cultural rights indispensable for his dignity and the free development of his personality." The principle of international cooperation is also enshrined in Article 2 of the ICESCR: "Each State Party to the present Covenant undertakes to take steps, individually and through *international assistance and co-operation*, especially economic and technical, to the maximum of its available resources, with a view to achieving progressively the full realization of the rights recognized in the present Covenant." The duty of international cooperation is therefore essential as far as the right to development is concerned.

As well as the obligation to respect, protect, implement, and cooperate, the international jurisprudence promoted by the Committee on Economic, Social and Cultural Rights (CESCR) has endorsed the duty of the states to observe a minimum core obligation as far as economic and social rights are concerned. For the Committee, "Minimum core obligations are those obligations to meet the 'minimum essential levels of a right.'" The duty to observe the bare minimum economic and social rights has its source in the greater principle of human dignity, which is a founding, nuclear principle of human rights law, and demands absolute urgency and priority.

---

[18] As David Bilchitz points out, "The UN Committee has provided various categorizations of the obligations imposed by socio-economic rights on state parties. In General Comment 3, it recognized the distinction between obligations of conduct and obligations of result. Obligations of conduct require the taking of action 'reasonably calculated to realize the enjoyment of a particular right.' Obligations of result require states to achieve specific targets to satisfy a detailed substantive standard... socio-economic rights typically impose both obligations of conduct and obligations of result" (Bilchitz 2007, 183–184).

Regarding the implementation of economic and social rights, the Committee adopts the following criteria: accessibility; availability; adequateness; quality; and cultural acceptability. The Committee has also developed the legal content of economic and social rights (housing – *General Comment No. 4*; adequate food – *General Comment No. 12*; health – *General Comment No. 14*; and education – *General Comment No. 13*). Lastly, the reach of the legal obligations resulting from the right to development also includes the principle of the progressive application of economic and social rights. From this results the principles of non-regression and the prohibition of government inaction.

General Comment No. 3 by the CESCR states the obligation of states to adopt measures for the implementation of economic and social rights by means of concrete, deliberate, and focused actions in the most effective way possible. Therefore, states have the duty to avoid measures of social regression. For the Committee, "Any retrogressive measures would involve the most careful consideration and would need to be fully justified by reference to the totality of the rights provided for in the Covenant in the context of the full use of the maximum available resources."

It must be mentioned that the ICESCR sets the obligation of the states to recognize and progressively implement the rights declared by it, utilizing the maximum amount of resources possible. From the progressive application of economic, social, and cultural rights results the clause of prohibition of social regression in terms of economic and social rights, as well as the prohibition of government inaction or omission.

Note that there are immediate application measures concerning economic and social rights, as in the case of the prohibition of discrimination clause. As the Limburg principles highlight:

> Some obligations under the Covenant require immediate implementation in full by the State parties, such as the prohibition of discrimination in article 2(2) of the Covenant.... Although the full realization of the rights recognized in the Covenant is to be attained progressively, the application of some rights can be made justiciable immediately while other rights can become justiciable over time[19] (UN Commission on Human Rights, 1987).

---

[19] As Asbørn Eide observes, "State obligations for economic and social rights were elaborated by a group of experts, convened by the International Commission of Jurists, in Limburg (the Netherlands) in June 1986. The outcome of the meeting is the so-called Limburg Principles, which is the best guide available to state obligations under the ICESCR. A decade later, experts on economic, social and cultural rights met in Maastricht to adopt a set of guidelines on violations of human rights (The Maastricht

4. CONTEMPORARY CHALLENGES OF THE RIGHT TO DEVELOPMENT

Considering the key attributes of the right to development from a human rights perspective, its conceptual, legal bases, and the extent of state duties, the main challenges to its implementation in the contemporary world order stand out.

1) Adoption of Indicators to Measure the Implementation of the Right to Development

One of the main weaknesses of the international human rights system is related to the difficulty in implementing rights – the so-called implementation gap. Thus, the challenge of the implementation of the right to development is clear.

The UN High Level Task Force on the implementation of the right to development has made significant efforts to produce indicators and criteria for evaluating and measuring the implementation of the right to development. It recognizes that it is imperative to develop criteria, standards, and guidelines for the implementation of the right to development based on a rigorous conceptual and methodological foundation.[20]

For Katarina Tomasevski:

> The creation of indicators provides an opportunity to extend the rule of law, and thereby international human rights obligations, to the realm of economics which has thus far remained by and large immune from demands of democratization, accountability and full application of human rights standards. Indicators can be conceptualized on the basis of international human rights treaties because these lay down obligations for governments (Tomasevski 2001, 531–532).

The use of indicators allows the human rights impact assessment to be carried out in relation to the policies, programs, and measures adopted by the state. This allows for accountability in relation to the obligations contracted by the state resulting from the right to development in the international and domestic arena. It also promotes the generation of data,

Guidelines on Violations of Economic, Social and Cultural Rights)" (Eide, Krause, and Rosas 2001, 25).
[20] See the report by the UN High Level Task Force on the implementation of the right to development for the April 2010 session of the Working Group, including the attributes of the right to development and the list of criteria, sub-criteria, and indicators (UN High Level Task Force 2010).

statistics, and information, which make up a solid base for carrying out a precise diagnosis of the implementation of the right to development.

Adopting indicators means that it is possible to identify advances, steps backward, and inaction by public powers in terms of the right to development. It is a precondition for making a precise diagnosis of how public action and inaction are framed in the field of the right to development. It is from a precise diagnosis that it is also possible to identify priorities and strategies aimed at improving the realization of the right to development.

The creation of indicators to measure the implementation of the right to development will allow the strengthening of the states' responsibility to respect, protect, and implement the right to development. It will stimulate information by the state, which will allow more precise formulation and evaluation of public policies, thus favoring the incorporation of the human rights perspective into the formulation of such policies.

2) Adoption of an International Treaty for the Protection of the Right to Development

This proposal has caused politico-ideological polarity and tension among states that favor only the Declaration on the Right to Development and states that desire the strengthening of legal protection of the right to development through the adoption of a legally binding instrument (in the form of an international treaty). This debate involves the controversy between the national and international dimension of the right to development.

In general, developed countries emphasize the national dimension of this right, defending that the tutelage of the right to development should be maintained by means of soft law (in this case, with the 1986 Declaration only), without the need to adopt a treaty to this end; whereas developing countries emphasize the international dimension of the right to development, and defend the adoption of a treaty to better protect it.

In this context, those who favor the adoption of a treaty for the protection of the right to development are essentially the member-states of the Non-Aligned Movement, which includes the G77 countries and China. Those are the actors that most actively defend a legally binding Convention for the Protection of the Right to Development. However, Canada, the EU, and Australia have expressed their resistance and opposition to the proposal. Note that fifty-three states voted against the Convention proposal, including developed countries (all of the members of the Organization for Economic Cooperation and Development and the EU), whose effort is essential for international cooperation.

However, developing countries emphasize that the majority of member-states of the UN General Assembly favor the adoption of a legally binding instrument, which would strengthen the international dimension of the right to development. They argue that a binding instrument would signify the crystallization and consolidation of a legal-rights regime applicable to the right to development, adding that in the history of the affirmation of human rights at an international level, the first step toward protection has involved the adoption of a declaration and later the adoption of a treaty, which perfects the degree of legal protection of a right. They add that the existence of an international treaty can even have a high impact in the domestic sphere, providing a special opportunity for setting parameters for the implementation of the right.[21]

3) Ratification of the Optional Protocol to the International Covenant on Economic, Social and Cultural Rights

One of the greatest gaps in the legal apparatus hindering the monitoring of the right to development by the treaty bodies is that there is not a mechanism through which to petition the protection of economic, social, and cultural rights.[22] Only on December 10, 2008, was the Optional

---

[21] Note that in Article 22, the African Charter on Human and Peoples' Rights (1986) establishes that, "All peoples shall have the right to their economic, social and cultural development with due regard to their freedom and identity and in the equal enjoyment of the common heritage of mankind." In 2010, the African Commission on Human and Peoples' Rights condemned the State of Kenya for the violation of the right to development of the Endorois community, comprising around 60,000 individuals, who had lived for centuries in the region of Lake Bogoria, from which they were removed without any previous consultation or later compensation. For the Commission:

> Arguments recognizing the right to development requires fulfilling five main criteria: it must be equitable, non-discriminatory, participatory, accountable, and transparent, with equity and choice as important, over-arching themes in the right to development.... The result of development should be the empowerment of the Endorois community. It is not sufficient for the Kenyan Authorities to merely give food aid to the Endorois. The capabilities and choices of the Endorois must improve in order for the right to development to be realized (Endorois Community v Kenya).

[22] In the perception of Asbjørn Eide, "Social rights refer to rights whose function is to protect and to advance the enjoyment of basic human needs and to ensure the material conditions for a life in dignity" (Eide 2005, 234).

Protocol to the ICESCR[23] finally adopted. It introduced a system of individual petitions, interim measures, inter-state communication, and *in locum* investigations in cases of grave and systematic violations of economic and social rights by a member-state. In 1996, the CESCR adopted a Protocol project, counting the support of countries from Latin America, Africa, and Eastern Europe, and facing resistance from the UK, United States, Canada, and Australia, among others.

Since 1966, civil and political rights have counted on the mechanism of individual petitions through the adoption of the Optional Protocol to the ICESCR, which has strengthened the justiciability of these rights in the global, regional, and local spheres. As for social rights, only in 2008 were they able to count on this system, which will positively affect the degree of justiciability of these rights. Thus, the Optional Protocol is an important initiative to break the unequal protection assigned to civil and political rights and economic, social, and cultural rights in the international sphere.

In the regional systems of human rights protection, the same ambivalence can be observed regarding the diverse manner of treating civil and political rights and economic, social, and cultural rights. In the inter-American system, although civil and political rights were exhaustively enshrined by the 1969 American Convention on Human Rights (which in 2010 comprised twenty-five member-states), economic, social, and cultural rights only came to be enshrined by the San Salvador Protocol in 1988, which comprised only fourteen member-states. The same ambivalence is present in the European system. The European Convention on Human Rights, which only considers civil and political rights, had forty-seven member-states in 2010, whereas the European Social Charter only had twenty-seven.

4) International Financial Institutions Reform

Action by international financial institutions – especially with regard to trade, debt, and technology transfer – is crucial to the realization of the right to development. The UN High Level Task Force has considered a heavy debt burden as a major obstacle for poor developing countries

---

[23]   The Optional Protocol to the International Covenant on Economic, Social and Cultural Rights was approved by General Assembly Resolution A/RES/63/117 on December, 10, 2008.

in meeting their obligations under the ICESCR,[24] jeopardizing the right
to development. The Task Force observes that the poverty afflicting the
least-developed countries is exacerbated by an unsustainable debt burden,
and that the billions of dollars those countries pay in their debt-servicing
obligations divert a large part of the scarce resources from crucial programs of education, health care, and infrastructure, severely limiting the
prospects for the realization of the right to development. It endorses that
a state's obligation to debt take national priorities of human development
and poverty reduction sufficiently into account, consistent with its human
rights obligations and the need to maintain trust in the financing system.
A human rights approach would imply that, under any circumstance,
expenditure should not be restricted to the extent that it amounts to
violations of the rights to food, health, education, an adequate standard
of living, and social security. It should also highlight the heavy burden
that the current financial and economic crisis is putting on developing
countries, especially the poor.

The World Bank and the International Monetary Fund have operated
with diligence to reduce the impact of this debt, and have introduced
innovative programs.[25] The debt-relief initiative is contributing in a significant way to the right to development. However, debt cancelation alone
will not be enough for affected developing countries to benefit from the
right to development. It must be accompanied by enhanced state capacity, improved governance and respect for human rights, and promotion
of equitable growth and the sharing of benefits thereof. An important
connection between the right to development and debt-relief initiatives
is constituted by noneconomic challenges, particularly those relating to
issues of political instability, armed conflict, and governance, all of which
are impediments to the right to development.

The strengthening of global financial institutions, giving developing
countries greater voice and representation, improving democratization,
transparency, and accountability of international financial institutions
would also be essential for the realization of the right to development.

---

[24] In its General Comment No. 2, in Article 22 of the ICESCR, the CESCR has indicated
that "international measures to deal with the debt crisis should take full account of the
need to protect economic, social and cultural rights through, inter alia, international
cooperation. In many situations, this might point to the need for major debt relief
initiatives."

[25] See the Heavily Indebted Poor Countries Initiative, launched in 1996 by the World Bank
and International Monetary Fund, and the Multilateral Debt Relief Initiative, launched
in 2005, to assist heavily indebted poor countries reach the Millennium Development
Goals.

The policies of the international financial institutions are determined by the same states that have legally binding obligations under the ICESCR.[26] The principle of the shared responsibility of debtors and creditors is at the heart of an equitable global financial system. Principles of participation, inclusion, transparency, accountability, the rule of law, equality, and nondiscrimination must be upheld by both the lender and the borrower.

5) Promoting International Cooperation

Thomas Pogge observes that:

> In 2000, the rich countries spent about US$4.650 billion on development assistance for meeting basic needs abroad while also selling the developing countries an estimated US$25.438 million in conventional weapons. This represents 69 percent of the entire international trade in conventional weapons. The main sellers of arms are the US, with over 50 percent of sales, then Russia, France, Germany, and the UK (Pogge 2002).[27]

In this context, it is vital that developed countries invest 0.7% of their GDP in a "vulnerability fund" to aid developing countries, thus meeting the commitments made in the Monterrey Conference on Financing for Development – "Monterrey Consensus," 2002.

Currently, around 80% of the world's population live in developing countries. It is estimated that more than 1.7 billion people live in poverty (Fitoussi, Sen, and Sitglitz 2011). A vicious cycle is set in place, in which economic inequality feeds political inequality in the exercise of power at an international level and vice versa. It is essential that international cooperation be conceived of not as mere charity or generosity, but as solidarity, in the sphere of the principle of shared responsibilities in the global order.

6) Stimulating Action by Private Actors in the Promotion of Human Rights

Regarding the private sector, there is also a need to accentuate its social responsibility, especially that of multinational companies, inasmuch as they constitute the great beneficiaries of the globalization process. It suffices to mention that out of the world's 100 greatest economies, 51 are multinational companies and 49 are nation-states. For example, it is

---

[26] See the Maastricht Guidelines on Violations of Economic, Social and Cultural Rights.
[27] See also Sen (2006).

important to encourage companies to adopt human rights codes relative to commercial activities; to demand commercial sanctions on companies that violate social rights; and to adopt the "Tobin tax" on international financial investments, among other measures.

The panorama of deep financial collapse is demanding the reinvention of the role of the state, greater responsibility by the markets, and a new international financial architecture. It is therefore crucial that the private sector, especially transnational corporations, widen its responsibility in the promotion of human rights, strengthening social, environmental, and ethical responsibility.

5. CONCLUSION

The implementation of the right to development involves challenges of a legal, cultural, political, and economic nature. In the legal and cultural sphere, we can envisage that the right to development encompasses a multiplicity of actors that transcends the actors involved in the realization of other human rights.

The right to development requires a rupture with the traditional view inspiring the protective international architecture, in which human rights violations point, on one hand, to the state (as the violator) and on the other, to the singularly considered individual (as the victim). In its complexity, the right to development, in both its national and international dimension, does not only consider the state as violator (but also international institutions and non-state actors) and the individual as victim (but also communities and groups). It is worth saying that the right to development invokes a pattern of conflict different from the classical and traditional pattern that inspires the system of international human rights protection.

In addition, the right to development is inspired by the value of solidarity from a collectivist approach embracing the local, regional, and international levels. The traditional human rights grammar – as it was conceived by the 1948 Universal Declaration – is mostly inspired by the value of human dignity from an individualistic approach.

If the struggle for social justice has been the core of the social and economic rights (through inclusion, equality, and nondiscrimination, giving special attention to the most deprived and excluded), the right to development adds the attributes of participation, accountability, and transparency (through free, meaningful, and active participation, focusing on empowerment) and international cooperation (as the right to development is a solidarity-based right). Participation and solidarity at the national, regional, and global levels constitute key components of the right to development. In its essence, the right to development embodies the right to a national and international environment that ensures the exercise and expansion of individuals' and peoples' human rights, as well as their basic freedoms.

As if such a legal and cultural challenge were not daunting enough, there is still a challenge of a more political nature. The process of implementation of the right to development has been characterized by ideological tensions and political ambivalence. The refusal by states to assign the same treatment to economic, social, and cultural rights as to civil and economic rights stands out. In this sense, the resistance by states to ratify the Optional Protocol to the ICESCR and to adopt a Convention on the Right to Development must be mentioned.

A challenge of an economic nature adds to these challenges, considering that the global economic and financial crisis primarily affects the poorer and more vulnerable. Thus, states face the challenge of adopting individual and collective measures and actions for implementing the right to development in the national and international spheres.

In an increasingly complex arena, it is crucial to advance the affirmation of the right to development and global justice in the social, economic, and political fields; to compose a new architecture able to respond to the challenges of the current agenda, of the new power dynamics in the international sphere and in a growing landscape of shared responsibilities.

Demonstrations in different geographical locations – from the Arab Spring to *los indignados* in Spain, and also including the demonstrators in Italy and the Occupy Wall Street movement in the United States – denounce a setting of extreme inequality and yearn for the same cause: social justice. They reveal the importance of respecting the right to development, focusing on how human beings live and what substantive freedoms they enjoy in each society. These movements have the violation of the right to development as their major cause and their implementation as their major claim, based on active, free, and meaningful participation. They reflect how the 1986 Declaration on the Right to Development shall be perceived as a dynamic and living instrument capable of addressing the contemporary challenge of advancing global democracy and global justice based on international cooperation and the creativity of civil society, considering development as an empowering process.

REFERENCES

African Charter on Human and Peoples' Rights, 1986. Adopted by the Organization of African Unity, October 1986.

Alston, Philip and Mary Robinson (Eds.), 2005. *Human Rights and Development: Towards mutual reinforcement*, Oxford: Oxford University Press.

Bedjaqui, Mohammed, 1991. "The Right to Development," in M. Bedjaqui (Ed.) *International Law: Achievements and Prospects*, 1177–1204, Dordrecht, The Netherlands: Martinus Nijhoff Publishers.

Bilchitz, David, 2007. *Poverty and Fundamental Rights: The Justification and Enforcement of Socio-Economic Rights*, Oxford: Oxford University Press.

Bingham, Tom, 2010. *The Rule of Law*, London: Penguin books.

Bobbio, Norberto, 1989. *Democracy and Dictatorship: The nature and limits of state power*, translated by Peter Kennealy, Minneapolis: University of Minnesota Press.

CESCR (UN Committee on Economic, Social and Cultural Rights), 1990. *General Comment 3:* The Nature of States Parties' Obligations, Fifth Session, UN Doc. E/1991/23, annex III at 86 (1991), reprinted in Compilation of General Comments and General Recommendations Adopted by Human Rights Treaty Bodies, UN Doc. HRI/GEN/1/Rev.6 at 14 (2003).

CESCR, 1999. *General Comment 12:* Right to Adequate Food, Twentieth Session, UN Doc. E/C.12/1999/5 (1999), reprinted in Compilation of General Comments and General Recommendations Adopted by Human Rights Treaty Bodies, UN Doc. HRI/GEN/1/Rev.6 at 62 (2003).

Dahl, Robert, 1989. *Democracy and Its Critics*, New Haven: Yale University Press.

Dahl, Robert, 2000. "A democratic paradox?" *Political Science Quarterly* 115(1): 35–40.

Dahl, Robert, 2005. "What political institutions does large-scale democracy require?" *Political Science Quarterly* 120(2): 187–197.

Dahl Robert, Ian Shapiro, and José Antonio Cheibub (Eds.), 2003. *The Democracy Sourcebook*, Cambridge, MA: The MIT Press.

Eide, A., C. Krause, and A. Rosas (Eds), 2001. *Economic, Social and Cultural Rights: a textbook*, 2nd revised edition, Dordrecht: The Netherlands: Martinus Nijhoff Publishers.

Eide, Asbjørn, 2005. "Social Rights," in Rhona K.M. Smith and Christien van den Anker (Eds.) *The Essentials of Human Rights*, 234, London: Hodder Arnold.

Endorois Community v Kenya. Centre for Minority Rights Development and Minority Rights Group International on behalf of Endorois Community v the Republic of Kenya, Case number 276/2003.

Farmer, Paul, 2009. *Pathologies of Power*, Berkeley: University of California Press.

Fitoussi, Jean-Paul, Amartya Sen, and Joseph Stiglitz, 2011. *Mismeasuring our Lives*, New York: Perseo Books.

Freedom House, 2011. *Freedom in the World 2011 – Annual survey of political rights and civic liberties – The authoritarian challenge to democracy.* Washington, D.C.

Hausman, Ricardo, Laura Tyson, and Saadia Zahidi, 2011. *The Global Gender Gap Report – 2010*, Harvard University, University of California, Berkeley and World Economic Forum.

Hurrell, Andrew, 2009. *On Global Order: power, values and the Constitution of International Society*, Oxford: Oxford University Press.

International Covenant on Economic, Social and Cultural Rights, Adopted by the United Nations General Assembly, 1976. ICESCR, paragraph 22, UN doc.E/CN.4/1987/17.

Marks, Stephen P., 2011. *The Politics of the Possible: The Way Ahead for the Right to Development*, Berlin, Germany: Friedrich Ebert Stiftung.

Pogge, Thomas, 2002. *World Poverty and Human Rights*, Cambridge: Polity.

Robinson, Mary, 2005. "What rights can add to good development practice," in Philip Alston and Mary Robinson (Eds.) *Human Rights and Development: Towards mutual reinforcement*, 25–44, Oxford: Oxford University Press.

Rosas, Allan, 1995. "The Right to Development," in Asbjørn Eide, Catarina Krause, and Allan Rosas (Eds.) *Economic, Social and Cultural Rights*, 254–255, Dordrecht: Martinus Nijhoff Publishers.

Sachs, Jeffrey, 2005. *The End of Poverty: Economic Possibilities for Our Time*, New York: Penguin Press.

Sachs, Jeffrey, 2008. *Common Wealth: Economics for a crowed planet*, London: Penguin Books.

Sen, Amartya, 1999. *Development as Freedom*, New York: Alfred A. Knopf.

Sen, Amartya, 2006. *Identity and Violence: The illusion of destiny*, New York: W.W. Norton & Company.

Sen, Amartya, 2009. *The Idea of Justice*, Cambridge: Harvard University Press.

Sengupta, Arjun, 2000. Report by the Independent Expert on the Right to Development, The General Assembly of the UN, A/55/306, August 17, 2000, para. 22.

Smith, Rhona K.M. and Christien van den Anker, 2005. *The Essentials of Human Rights*, London: Hodder Arnold.

Steiner, Henry and Philip Alston, 2000. *International Human Rights in Context: Law, Politics and Morals*, 2nd edition, Oxford: Oxford University Press.

Stiglitz, Joseph, 2003. *Globalization and Its Discontents*, New York: W.W. Norton Company.

Stiglitz, Joseph, 2007. *Making Globalization Work*, London: Penguin Books.

Tomasevski, Katarina, 2001. "Indicators," in A. Eide, C. Krause, and A. Rosas (Eds.) *Economic, Social and Cultural Rights: a textbook*, 2nd revised edition, Dordrecht, The Netherlands: Martinus Nijhoff Publishers.

UN Commission on Human Rights, *Note verbale dated 86/12/05 from the Permanent Mission of the Netherlands to the United Nations Office at Geneva addressed to the Centre for Human Rights ("Limburg Principles")*, 8 January 1987, E/CN.4/1987/17, available at: http://www.unhcr.org/refworld/docid/48abd5790.html [accessed 9 August 2012].

UN Economic and Social Council, Commission on Human Rights, Office of the High Commissioner for Human Rights, 2004. *Analytical study of the High Commissioner for Human Rights on the fundamental principle of participation and its application in the context of globalization*, E/CN.4/2005/41. http://daccess-dds-ny.un.org/doc/UNDOC/GEN/G04/169/72/PDF/G0416972.pdf?OpenElement.

UN General Assembly, 2008. *Optional Protocol of the International Covenant on Economic, Social and Cultural Rights*, General Assembly Res. A/RES/63/117.

UN High Level Task Force, 2010. Right to Development: Report on the implementation of the right to development on its Sixth Session, A/HRC/15/WG.2/TF/2, Add 2, Geneva: UN High Level Task Force.

UNDP (United Nations Development Programme), 2010. Human Development Report 2010, *The Real Wealth of Nations: Pathways to human development*, New York: UNDP.

Vasak, Karel, "Human Rights: A Thirty-Year Struggle: The Sustained Efforts to Give Force of law to the Universal Declaration of Human Rights," *UNESCO Courier* 30:11, Paris: United Nations Educational, Scientific, and Cultural Organization, November 1977.

World Health Report, 1995. Bridging the Gaps, Report of the Director-General, World Health Organization, Retrieved from http://www.who.int/whr/1995/en/whr95_en.pdf.

13

Constitutional Environmental Human Rights: A Descriptive Analysis of 142 National Constitutions

Christopher Jeffords

I. INTRODUCTION

Environmental human rights, succinctly defined as entitlements to clean air, water, and soil for present and future generations (Hiskes 2009), have both conceptual and legal foundations (Sax 1990).[1] These rights fit within the basic rights framework outlined by Shue (1996), most notably subsistence rights. Without clean air, water, and soil, humans will be unable to enjoy other rights and life activities (Collins-Chobanian 2000). Because pollution does not respect geographic and, especially, temporal borders, environmental human rights necessitate a deeper concern for the rights of future generations. Recognizing these unique characteristics of environmental degradation, the first principle of The Stockholm Declaration of 1972 notes the responsibility humans have to protect the environment for both present and future generations. Although its signatories are not legally bound to uphold its principles, much of the language of the declaration forms the basis for modern binding and nonbinding instruments and declarations concerning the environment including, but not limited to, The African Charter of Human and People's Rights, the Brundtland Report, and the Ksentini Report (Hiskes 2011). Given these foundations, environmental human rights impose specific duties and obligations on governments, and have vast implications for government efforts to

[1] For similar definitions see, generally, Sax 1990, Shelton 1991, Weiss 1992, Collins-Chobanian 2000, and Lercher 2007.

I thank Amy Jeffords for her love and support, and for helpful editing. I thank Lanse Minkler and Shareen Hertel for helpful comments and suggestions that led to improvements in this chapter. I also thank Joshua Berning and participants in the 2011 Economics and Social Rights Group Workshop for thoughtful discussions. I gratefully acknowledge funding support from the Association for Social Economics through the William R. Waters Research Grant. Of course, any errors are my own.

respect, protect, and fulfill said rights, including the nature of interference and definition of rights violations.[2]

Governments seem to take these obligations seriously, as the world has seen a significant increase in the number of multinational and bilateral treaties and declarations concerned with recognizing a human right to a safe, healthy, or clean environment (Herz 2000; Hiskes 2011). This is also true for the human right to water (Scanlon, Cassar, and Nemes 1999). However, the question remains to what extent governments are trying to formalize and institutionalize these rights in national policy and law. Evidence of government effort can be found by looking closely at national constitutions, the topic of this chapter.

As of 2010, out of 198 national constitutions of developed and developing countries across every continent, 142 include at least one reference to the environment, in a broad sense. Of these 142, 125 have a specific environmental human rights provision or at least the makings of one, and 10 include a direct human right to water. These findings may already surprise many, but to further explore the nature of constitutional environmental human rights this chapter employs a keyword analysis to provide deeper insight into each provision and the nature of justiciability. Furthermore, the keyword analysis is used to form a simple additive index of provision strength based on six to seven specific categories of language. The index is offered as an alternative approach to interpreting the language of constitutional environmental human rights provisions as either directive principles or enforceable law (Jung and Rosevear 2011).

Minkler (2009) offers an explanation of the differences between directive principles and enforceable law within the context of economic rights. *Directive principles* are "important goals meant to guide policy action" (381). Policy makers who fail to incorporate these goals into actual policy face potential reelection repercussions, at least to the extent that the policy makers' constituency is truly concerned with the underlying claims associated with these directive principles. Including a constitutional provision as enforceable law, on the other hand, creates a legal entitlement that acts to "tie policymakers' hands because it would force

---

[2]   Collins-Chobanian (2000) notes that interference with environmental rights can only be for an overriding justification. This includes, for example, adding a harmful chemical to a water supply to eradicate an even more harmful bacteria. It does not include, however, "harms to be imposed in pursuit of goals that do not outweigh the harms" (146). Thoroughly defining interference, and a subsequent rights violation, is a practical difficulty. For example, water can be physically limited in supply and has various industrial, agricultural, and recreational uses that complicate government efforts to respect, protect, and fulfill the human right to water.

them to concoct policies and devote resources for that purpose" (382). Enforceable law thus provides legal action and penalties for rights violations. Whether or not a constitutional provision is interpreted as a directive principle or enforceable law is important for environmental rights outcomes. The nature of the provision imposes different constraints on government efforts to respect, protect, and fulfill the right, where the constraints are often expressed as duties and obligations. Because the distinction between directive principles and enforceable law is not always clear, empirical analyses linking provisions to rights outcomes are complicated by potential measurement error stemming from subjective interpretation of constitutional language.

Further complicating the nature of justiciability is the presence of negating statements or provisions before or after an existing constitutional environmental human rights provision. These statements, which either directly negate the scale and scope of the environmental rights provisions, or refer the responsibility of the environment to the domain of law, are important caveats to government duties and obligations. As of 2010, these exist in twenty constitutions, thereby relinquishing some degree of government responsibility for environmental human rights violations.

Interpreting the justiciability of a constitutional environmental human rights provision based solely on keywords and phrases is clearly a cumbersome task, but this burden is also faced by all constitutional human rights. Furthermore, government efforts to respect, protect, and fulfill economic and social rights are hampered by resource constraints, as evidenced in the language of Article 2 of the International Covenant on Economic, Social, and Cultural Rights (ICESCR). For environmental human rights, however, these resource constraints arguably include the physical parameters of the world, in addition to the economic, political, and financial ones. Such physical constraints make environmental human rights fundamentally different from other human rights.[3] Take, for example, the human right to water. Gleick (1998) notes that the human right to water entails access to a basic minimum consumption requirement of roughly 13 gallons per person per day. This includes drinking water (10%), sanitation services (40%), bathing (30%), and food preparation (20%), but excludes the amount of water required to grow the daily food needs of

---

[3] I recognize that the increased costs associated with procuring scarce natural resources could be capitalized into a country's financial and economic constraints; however, by separately breaking them out, the vagueness of the language of the ICESCR is further exposed.

an individual, which is an additional 713 gallons. For an enforceable human right to water, is the minimum requirement 13 or 726 gallons? The difference between the two is clearly nontrivial from a pure quantity perspective, to say nothing of quality differences, but a minimum requirement is only part of the story. Recognizing a human right to water presents interesting legal questions for the current water-consumption habits of households with pets, pools, jacuzzis, lawns and gardens, bird baths, water pistols, and so on. Would these households be grandfathered into a new legal structure or be forced to pay, financially and/or legally, for their possible overconsumption? In this sense, the problem becomes strikingly similar to the tragedy of the commons, where the unregulated use of water could ultimately lead to resource exhaustion, and regressively affect poorer households unable to afford more expensive stocks of water.[4]

Despite these practical difficulties, since the middle of the twentieth century the human right to water has gained significant traction in many international, national, and regional legally binding and non-legally binding instruments (Scanlon et al. 1999). This has happened directly in that the right is explicitly delineated and recognized separately from broader environmental human rights, and indirectly, or implicitly, through some broader concern such as the right to an adequate amount of food or standard of living.[5] This is also the case within national constitutions. In fact, as of 2010, only ten explicitly recognize the human right to water in a

[4] See Hardin (1968) and Ostrom (1990) for a discussion of the tragedy of the commons. In a theoretical model of the human right to water embedded in a standard nonrenewable resources framework with a backstop technology, Jeffords and Shah (forthcoming) find that fulfilling the human right to water through government fiscal policy (i.e., tax and subsidy policy) is a difficult task, often requiring a certain degree of income inequality among poor and rich households. They also find that policies aimed at reducing the price of the backstop, increasing water conservation efforts, spurring income growth, including firm tax proceeds, or extraterritorial assistance can mitigate the need for the government to enact its human rights fiscal policy.

[5] From 1945 through 1989, nine legally binding international instruments were developed, starting with the United Nations Charter and ending with The Convention on the Rights of the Child. From 1948 through 2002, twenty-one non-legally binding international instruments were created beginning with The Universal Declaration of Human Rights through the World Summit on Sustainable Development – 71% of these instruments were formed over 1990–2002. With varying dates, forty-nine national instruments (i.e., constitutions) include environmental human rights language as of the date of publication of their article. In addition, eight state constitutions in the United States recognize the right to a healthy environment. Lastly, from 1981 to 2002, eight regional instruments were formed, starting with the African Charter on Human and People's Rights (Scanlon et al., 1999).

separate provision or as a section of an overall environmental human rights provision. If, however, environmental human rights imply the human right to water, then ten might be an underestimate of the true number of countries that have recognized this right, albeit indirectly and to varying degrees of justiciability.[6]

As populations grow and countries transition from developing to developed, the role of constitutional environmental human rights in potentially driving positive environmental outcomes will become increasingly important. Therefore, this chapter not only looks at whether or not a country has constitutionalized environmental human rights, but also how these provisions can be characterized by strength and number. This analysis is important because researchers need to know how constitutional provisions differ before they can assess whether or not they matter in affecting environmental human rights outcomes. The method I offer here has the attractive feature that it counts fundamental keywords in constitutions, which thereby avoids the potential measurement error of interpreting the meaning of specific language found in alternative approaches, such as that employed by Jung and Rosevear (2011).

To characterize the nature of constitutional environmental human rights provisions and develop the index of provision strength, the descriptive analysis proceeds in the following way. First, the main data-generating process is described, including a summary of the findings and a note on the 17 countries that are ultimately excluded from the set of 142. This is followed by a broad summary of the environmental human rights provisions in the remaining 125 constitutions and a brief description of the secondary data-generating process. The categories of language used in the secondary analysis are then outlined inclusive of the descriptive findings. Using the keyword categories, the index of provision strength is developed and discussed in detail. The data, including the strength index, are then briefly compared to a subset of data from the Toronto Initiative for Social and Economic Rights (TIESR). Interpreting the language of constitutional provisions for a broad class of human rights, the TIESR data include the right to a safe or healthy environment (HENV), duty of the state to protect the environment (ENVP), and the right to access to

---

[6] Perhaps the biggest step toward recognizing a human right to water occurred in 2010. Following the framework of *General Comment 15* (The Right to Water), the United Nations General Assembly declared "the right to safe and clean drinking water and sanitation as a human right that is essential for the full enjoyment of life and all human rights." For more on this, see the General Assembly document A/64L.63/Rev.1.

food and/or water (FOWA).[7] The final section concludes and provides recommendations for future research.

2. MAIN DATA-GENERATING PROCESS

The data are derived primarily from Constitution Finder, a Web site run by the T.C. Williams School of Law at the University of Richmond.[8] The site provides direct links to the constitutions of most countries, including the year of the constitution and notes about the most recent set of included amendments. For constitutions that were in English, the primary task was to determine if there was a provision referencing the environment. To do so, a keyword search was conducted for the following words, including relevant variations and combinations: "environment, "natur" (to capture nature and natural), "physical," "resource," and "water." If the word was found, the entire provision was extracted and placed in a separate document, no matter the context in which the word was placed. For the twenty-three constitutions that were not posted in English, the task of extracting keywords was slightly more difficult. In some cases, the full constitution was translated from the native language to English and the procedure outlined above was followed. For other cases, the main keywords were converted to the native language and the search proceeded in the native language. When a keyword was found, the entire article was extracted, translated to English, and placed in a separate document.[9] Once all of the data were in English and in a single document, irrelevant articles that referenced some other non-physical environment were noted and discarded.

2.1. At Least One Reference to the Environment

Tables 13.1 and 13.2 display the number of national constitutions, by level of development and continent, that include at least one reference to the environment based on the keywords discussed above. In total, out of the 198 constitutions, 142 include a single reference to the environment

---

7 The entire TIESR dataset covers 136 developing countries in every continent but Australia. Each right in the data is coded as absent, an aspirational directive principle, or enforceable law. Of these 136, there are 95 countries that can be directly compared to the data described in this chapter.

8 Additional data, when unavailable via Constitution Finder, were gathered from the International Constitutional Law Project at http://www.servat.unibe.ch/icl/info.html.

9 This was a tedious process, as there tended to be more than one translation for the main keywords into the native languages. For example, the word "environment" in English has five French translations (at least according to Google Translate).

TABLE 13.1. *Mention or not, with age of the constitution, by country type*
(N = 198)

	Developed	Developing	OECD	Non–OECD	All countries
MENTION	22	120	24	118	142
Average Age	48.09	21.38	44.13	21.73	25.51
Median Age	36.00	18.00	31.00	18.00	18.00
Std. Dev.	42.71	19.87	42.08	20.22	26.44
NO MENTION	12	44	8	48	56
Average Age	92.00	36.73	114.13	37.65	49.43
Median Age	77.50	32.00	117.50	33.00	37.00
Std. Dev.	63.70	29.19	64.94	29.34	45.33
TOTAL	34	164	32	166	198
Average Age	63.59	25.49	61.63	26.33	32.04
Median Age	50.00	19.00	44.00	19.00	19.50
Std. Dev.	54.47	23.65	56.70	24.24	34.17
% MENTION	65%	73%	75%	71%	72%

Source: Author's calculations.

and 56 do not. For example, Article 50 of Ukraine's Constitution (1996) states, "Everyone has the right to an environment that is safe for life and health," whereas Article 145 of Honduras's Constitution (1982) states, "The State shall retain the right environment to protect the health of people."

Before continuing with the descriptive analysis, there is an important caveat to note regarding the age of the constitutions and the age of the environmental human rights provisions, which are not necessarily the same. In fact, the environmental human rights provision is likely considerably younger than the constitution itself. As an extreme example, consider the constitution of Norway. This document was created in 1814, following independence from Denmark and through a peaceful separation from Sweden in 1905, thereby making it 196 years old. However, the environmental human rights provision was actually added in 1992, making it only eighteen years old. To the extent that this systematically occurs in forming constitutions, the age data presented here likely overstate the average age of environmental human rights provisions.[10]

---

[10] This is important not only for the present descriptive analysis but also for any empirical analysis using this data. The effect of constitutional environmental human rights

TABLE 13.2. *Mention or not, with age of the constitution, by continent*
(N = 198)

	Africa	Asia	Europe	Australia	North America	South America	All countries
MENTION	38	37	35	7	13	12	142
Average Age	16.21	24.11	31.31	41.00	27.62	31.08	25.51
Median Age	17.00	18.00	18.00	31.00	27.00	20.50	18.00
Std. Dev.	9.70	20.24	36.10	31.54	19.57	41.36	26.44
NO MENTION	13	12	7	9	15	N/A	56
Average Age	28.31	36.77	75.00	46.00	62.33	N/A	49.43
Median Age	26.00	38.00	66.00	35.00	34.00	N/A	37.00
Std. Dev.	14.14	24.78	59.91	34.27	63.70	N/A	45.33
TOTAL	51	49	42	16	28	12	198
Average Age	19.06	28.13	38.60	43.81	46.21	31.08	32.04
Median Age	18.00	19.00	19.00	33.50	31.50	20.50	19.50
Std. Dev.	12.09	22.03	43.33	32.11	50.84	41.36	34.17
% MENTION	75%	76%	83%	44%	46%	100%	72%

Source: Author's calculations.

With this caveat in mind, on average, the constitutions that mention the environment tend to be considerably younger than those that do not, as noted in Table 13.1. Furthermore, the constitutions of developing and non–Organization for Economic Co-operation and Development (OECD) countries that mention the environment are relatively younger compared to their developed and OECD-member counterparts.[11] The average age of constitutions that reference the environment from developing countries is 21.38 years compared to 48.09 years for developed countries. For developing countries, the average age of constitutions that do not reference the environment is 36.73 years compared to 92 for developed countries. Table 13.1 also illustrates that anywhere between 65% and 75% of countries reference the environment in the constitution depending on development/membership status.

Table 13.2 shows that within continents, constitutions with at least one reference to the environment are also younger compared to those without a reference. On average, the youngest constitutions that reference the environment are from Africa, and the oldest, Australia. The percentage

provisions on environmental rights outcomes cannot be properly identified without controlling for the age of the provisions versus the age of the constitution.
[11] The classification of countries as developed or developing is from the Central Intelligence Agency (CIA) World Factbook.

of constitutions that reference the environment is lowest in Australia (44%) and highest in South America (100%).

Although interesting, simply mentioning the environment does not necessarily indicate the presence of an environmental human right. In order to determine the strength of each provision, as well as the nature of the language, an extended keyword analysis was conducted, the results of which follow. First, however, a note on the countries that are excluded from the secondary analysis.

2.2. *Excluded Countries*

Owing to the way in which the environment was referenced, seventeen countries are excluded from the analysis.[12] The five examples provided illustrate the reason for these countries being included in the original set of 142, as well as for being currently excluded:

- Equatorial Guinea (1991), Sections 28a and 28b: The resources and services reserved to the public sector shall be: mines and hydrocarbons; and services in charge of distributing water and electricity.
- Fiji (1997), Article 186, Section 4c: A law fixing amounts under sub-section (3) must require that account be taken of: the risk of environmental damage.
- France (1958), Article 70: The Economic, Social and Environmental Council may also be consulted by the Government or Parliament on any economic, social or environmental issue. The Government may also consult it on Programming Bills setting down the multi-annual guidelines for public finances. Any plan or Programming Bill of an economic, social or environmental nature shall be submitted to it for its opinion.
- Honduras (1982), Article 145: The State shall retain the right environment to protect the health of people.
- Mauritania (1991), Article 57: The following are the domain of the law: general regulation of water, mines, and hydro-carbons, fishing and the merchant marine, fauna, flora, and the environment.

These five articles, and the remaining twelve, mention the environment or natural resources in some way, but it is not clear if they form any kind

---

[12] These seventeen countries are: Australia, Austria, Cyprus, Equatorial Guinea, Fiji, France, Gabon, Honduras, Ireland, Jamaica, Mauritania, Philippines, Puerto Rico, Saint Lucia, Tanzania, Thailand, and Tuvalu.

of meaningful basis for environmental human rights. As noted earlier, an environmental human right is an entitlement to some clean natural resource for present and future generations. None of these articles seem to impose duties or obligations, whether interpreted as enforceable law or directive principles, on the state. Rather, each provision seems to simply note that the government is in charge of the environment, in a very broad sense, and that any action that affects the environment must be accompanied by some sort of governmental oversight. Perhaps these are relevant from a pure policy perspective, outside of the scope of a directive principle, but the focus of this chapter is to examine the nature of constitutional environmental human rights.

2.3. Negating Statements

Before examining constitutional environmental human rights proper, it is necessary to quickly discuss the presence of negating statements. Occurring in twenty constitutions, these statements mitigate the legal strength of constitutional environmental human rights and leave citizens with little recourse to address rights violations.[13] As an example, consider the following excerpt taken from Article 59.1.e of Albania's Constitution (1998), which is part of a broader social objectives chapter:

> The state, within its constitutional powers and the means at its disposal, aims to supplement private initiative and responsibility with a healthy and ecologically adequate environment for the present and future generations.... Fulfillment of social objectives may not be claimed directly in court. The law defines the conditions and extent to which the realization of these objectives can be claimed.

Failing to account for statements like these could positively bias the estimate of constitutional environmental human rights provisions on rights outcomes. This sort of equivocating discounts government efforts to respect, protect, and fulfill environmental human rights.

2.4. Constitutional Environmental Human Rights Provisions

Tables 13.3 and 13.4 display the number of national constitutions, by level of development and continent, that include an environmental human

---

[13]   The twenty countries are: Albania, Burkina Faso, Central African Republic, Chad, Chile, Comoros, Congo (Brazzaville), Cook Islands, Costa Rica, Estonia, India, Italy, Madagascar, Niger, Paraguay, Sierra Leone, South Korea, Sri Lanka, Togo, and Vanuatu.

TABLE 13.3. *Included and excluded/absent, with age of the constitution, by country type (N = 198)*

	Developed	Developing	OECD	Non–OECD	All countries
INCLUDED	18	107	20	105	125
Average Age	41.28	20.52	37.20	20.90	23.51
Median Age	33.00	18.00	23.50	18.00	18.00
Std. Dev.	43.42	20.21	41.86	20.62	25.71
EXCLUDED	16	57	12	61	73
Average Age	88.69	34.82	102.33	35.67	47.23
Median Age	77.00	31.00	87.00	32.00	36.00
Std. Dev.	55.88	26.82	56.03	27.17	41.81
TOTAL	34	164	32	166	198
Average Age	63.59	25.49	61.63	26.33	32.04
Median Age	50.00	19.00	44.00	19.00	19.50
Std. Dev.	54.47	23.65	56.70	24.24	34.17
% MENTION	53%	65%	63%	63%	63%

Source: Author's calculations.

right directly, regardless of degree of justiciability. After dropping the 17 countries noted earlier, 125 countries remain. In other words, 63% of national constitutions as of 2010 include some form of an environmental human right of a varying degree of justiciability.

TABLE 13.4. *Included and excluded/absent, with age of the constitution, by continent (N = 198)*

	Africa	Asia	Europe	Australia	North America	South America	All countries
INCLUDED	34	33	33	4	9	12	125
Average Age	15.47	22.52	29.18	35.25	21.44	31.08	23.51
Median Age	15.50	18.00	18.00	33.00	23.00	20.50	18.00
Std. Dev.	9.78	18.67	35.91	6.85	19.03	41.36	25.71
EXCLUDED	17	16	9	12	19	N/A	73
Average Age	26.94	36.88	65.80	46.67	57.95	N/A	47.23
Median Age	24.00	38.00	59.00	33.50	34.00	N/A	36.00
Std. Dev.	12.87	25.23	54.65	36.84	57.14	N/A	41.81
TOTAL	51	49	42	16	28	12	198
Average Age	19.06	28.13	38.60	43.81	46.21	31.08	32.04
Median Age	18.00	19.00	19.00	33.50	31.50	20.50	19.50
Std. Dev.	12.09	22.03	43.33	32.11	50.84	41.36	34.17
%INCLUDED	67%	67%	79%	25%	32%	100%	63%

Source: Author's calculations.

Out of 164 developing countries, 107 include an environmental human right compared to 18 out of 34 developed countries. Perhaps not surprisingly, the constitutions that include a right are also younger than those that do not include (i.e., exclude) a right. Furthermore, comparing the "included" group of Tables 13.3 and 13.4 to the "mention" group of Tables 13.1 and 13.2, the average age of the constitutions that include a right has fallen across each growth classification, as well as by continent.[14] This is also true for the "excluded" group compared to the "no mention" group, with the exceptions of Asia and Australia.

This analysis so far does not take into consideration the strength of each provision, which is perhaps the most important aspect for driving rights outcomes. To do so, a secondary keyword analysis was performed on each provision, the explanation and results of which follow.

3. SECONDARY DATA-GENERATING PROCESS

Once each constitutional environmental human right was sorted out, an extended keyword analysis was conducted to further examine the strength of each provision. The presence of a single word from a group of seven categories of language was coded as one and zero otherwise. That is, if a single word occurred more than once within a provision, all that was coded was the presence or absence, not the total count. The seven language categories are described here.

3.1. Category Descriptions and Justifications

Category One (1) includes keywords and phrases associated with state duties, obligations, protections, and so on. The language of Category Two (2) is generally weaker, but is also associated with the state. It includes such language as "shall ensure," "take measures," "must see to," and "fundamental objective." Thus, the major difference between these two categories is the strength of the language.[15]

Category Three (3) includes language regarding a citizen's right to be informed about the status of the environment and provides citizens

---

[14] It is possible that constitutions with environmental human rights provisions tend to be younger within developing and non–OECD countries could simply be a definitional artifact or an issue of selection.

[15] Citing Sunstein (2004), who argues for constitutionalizing certain economic rights, Minkler (2009) notes a similar distinction with respect to economic rights provisions. Category One, independently, could be considered the language of enforceable law; the language of Category Two is similar to directive principles.

with an avenue to seek information. The right to information is noted in Section 12.c.iv of *General Comment 15*, although with respect to the human right to water. Extending this right to environmental human rights in general necessitates information about (at least) air, water, and soil that should be readily and freely available and accessible to all. The right to information alone, however, is not necessarily an environmental human right. For example, an environment could be excessively polluted leading to an environmental human rights violation in theory, yet in practice the right to information would at most provide citizens with knowledge about the nature of the pollution. Without the relevant legal mechanisms in place to address the harm caused from excessive pollution, the right to information may be an important precursor to defining, defending, and securing a practical environmental human right. Therefore its relevance as a singular provision or for adding potential legal strength to an existing constitutional environmental human right cannot be ignored.

Category Four (4) refers directly to a citizen's right to a clean or healthy environment, separate from the duties and obligations of the state to provide a clean or healthy environment as outlined in Categories One and Two. This distinction is also noted by Jung and Rosevear (2011) in HENV and ENVP, respectively. However, it is not clear that the two are independent provisions rather than jointly forming the basis of an environmental human right. Explicitly including both types of language likely acts to form a stronger (in a legal sense), more explicit environmental human right. Otherwise, this type of double counting begs the question of why other economic and social rights are not also delineated in this way in the TIESR data (and within national constitutions) – the right to social security and duty of the state to protect social security; the right to rest or leisure and duty of the state to protect rest or leisure; and so on.

Category Five (5) denotes the explicit concern for future generations as written into the environmental human rights provision. Hiskes's (2009) definition of human rights is carefully derived to include a concern for future generations. Channeling Rawls (1999), Hiskes (2011) further outlines environmental human rights as not only expanding geographical borders, but also temporal boundaries in an intergenerational justice sense. Within the context of sustainability, Weiss (1992) argues that each generation holds the planet in trust for other generations, placing obligations on current generations to protect and preserve the environment for future generations. Economists have also tackled the notion of sustainability from an intergenerational perspective. Citing Howarth (1997) and Barrett (1996), Padilla (2002) argues that present generations have the ability to augment the conditions of nature that the future will inherit and, because of this, present generations have a direct responsibility to the future.[16] Whether the concern is for some future, unborn generation, or for the myriad living generations of humans that vary in degree of autonomous decision-making capacity (i.e., children), individuals know their own preferences best and can only guess at the preferences of others. In other words, it is not clear if future generations will have the same preferences for environmental human rights as the current generations do. Governments can only guess these preferences, thus further complicating national instantiation of constitutional environmental human rights.

Category Six (6) includes language about duties and obligations as applying to citizens and (the royal) everyone.[17] A noted conceptual problem with such language is that by making everyone responsible, that is, a duty-bearing addressee of environmental human rights, no one may feel the burden of any responsibility.[18] Nevertheless, even if there are practical difficulties in legally enforcing such a provision (at least the duties to protect and fulfill), its real power may come from its persuasiveness as a directive principle.

Category Seven (7) denotes the constitutions that explicitly include a human right to water. As noted earlier, the human right to access to clean water (and sanitation) has received increasing national and international attention over the last sixty-plus years, most notably in 2010. With the seven categories explicitly defined, the next section discusses the results of the secondary keyword analysis.

4. KEYWORD SUMMARY AND CATEGORY ANALYSIS

Figure 13.1 shows the frequency of reference to the seven categories of language discussed above. Tables 13.5, 13.6, and 13.7 display the instance of a specific word or phrase from each category for each country

---

[16] Based on a contractarian premise, Howarth (1997) argues for sustainability, or sustainable development, through property rights whereby the present endows the future with a "structured bequest package" that provides at least undiminished stocks of natural resources and environmental quality. See Beckerman (1997) for a critique of the link between intergenerational equity or justice and sustainability.

[17] Shrader-Frechette (2007) offers a discussion about citizens' ethical responsibility to stop environmental injustice, broadly defined as the disproportionate burden of environmental harm regressively affecting children, poor people, minorities, or other subgroups. Based on the benefits that some citizens may have received or currently receive from environmental injustice, these citizens therefore have a duty to stop doing so. Second, citizens have a democratic responsibility to stop environmental injustice.

[18] See Hiskes (2010) for a discussion of the addressee within the context of environmental human rights.

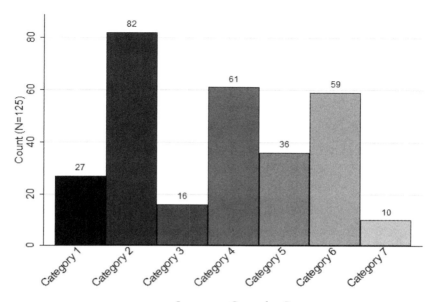

FIGURE 13.1. Language Count by Category.

with an environmental human rights provision (n = 125). A 1 indicates the presence of the word(s) and/or phrase(s), and 0 indicates otherwise. Examples of the language of each of the seven categories included in Figure 13.1, and Tables 13.5, 13.6, and 13.7, are discussed later.

4.1. Category One (1) – State Duties

Category One is comprised of keywords and phrases associated with the state. The language is generally strong and, independently, might be interpreted as enforceable law. The keywords include, but are not limited to, the following: "duty," "will protect," "obliged," and "incumbent upon." These keywords and phrases occurred in twenty-seven constitutions and five examples are provided below[19]:

- Afghanistan (2004), Article 15: The state is obliged to adopt necessary measures for safeguarding forests and the environment.

---

[19] The 27 countries are: Afghanistan, Azerbaijan, Brazil, Central African Republic, Chile, Columbia, Congo (Kinshasa), Costa Rica, El Salvador, Greece, Guyana, Iran, Latvia, Maldives, Mali, Mozambique, Nicaragua, Niger, Panama, Peru, Portugal, Senegal, Seychelles, South Africa, Sudan, Turkey, and Vietnam.

TABLE 13.5. *Categories by country (1 of 3)*

Country	Continent	Age	Categories Developed (1)(2)(3)(4) (5)(6)(7)	Total (1–6)	Total (1–7)	JR Age	FOWA	HENV	ENVP
Afghanistan	Asia	6	0100000 0	1	1	6	0	1	1
Albania	Europe	12	0001010 0	2	2	22	0	1	1
Andorra	Europe	17	1010010 0	2	2	N/A	N/A	N/A	N/A
Angola	Africa	18	0010100 0	2	2	18	0	2	2
Argentina	South America	157	0011110 0	4	4	16	0	2	2
Armenia	Asia	5	0010010 0	2	2	15	0	2	2
Azerbaijan	Asia	32	0101010 0	4	4	15	0	2	2
Bahrain	Asia	37	0010000 0	1	1	8	0	0	1
Belarus	Europe	6	0001010 0	3	3	14	2	2	2
Belgium	Europe	16	1000100 0	1	1	N/A	N/A	N/A	N/A
Benin	Africa	20	0010010 0	3	3	20	0	2	2
Bolivia	South America	1	0010110 0	3	3	1	2	2	2
Brazil	South America	22	0100011 0	3	3	22	0	2	2
British Virgin Islands	North America	3	0000110 0	2	2	N/A	N/A	N/A	N/A
Bulgaria	Europe	19	0010010 0	3	3	19	0	1	1
Burkina Faso	Africa	19	0000010 0	2	2	19	0	1	0
Cambodia	Asia	17	0010000 0	1	1	17	0	0	1
Cameroon	Africa	38	0010010 0	3	3	38	0	1	1
Cape Verde	Africa	18	0011010 0	4	4	18	0	2	2

Country	Region									
Cayman Islands	North America	1	0010010 0	2	2	N/A	N/A	N/A	N/A	N/A
Central African Republic	Africa6	6	0100100 0	2	2	6	0	2	2	0
Chad	Africa	14	0010100	3	3	14	0	2	2	2
Chile	South America	30	0100100 0	2	2	30	0	2	2	2
China	Asia	28	0010000 0	1	1	28	0	1	1	1
Colombia	South America	19	0100110	4	4	19	1	1	1	1
Comoros	Africa	9	0000101 0	2	2	9	0	2	2	0
Congo (Brazzaville)	Africa	9	0010010	3	3	N/A	N/A	N/A	N/A	N/A
Congo (Kinshasa)	Africa	5	0110101 0	4	4	N/A	N/A	N/A	N/A	N/A
Cook Islands	Australia	45	0011100 0	3	3	N/A	N/A	N/A	N/A	N/A
Costa Rica	North America	61	0110100 0	3	3	61	2	2	2	2
Côte d'Ivoire	Africa	10	0000101 0	2	2	10	0	1	1	0
Croatia	Europe	20	0010100 0	2	2	20	0	1	1	1
Cuba	North America	34	0010010 0	2	2	18	1	0	0	0
Czech Republic	Europe	18	0100000	1	1	18	0	1	1	0
East Timor	Asia	8	0010111 0	3	3	8	0	0	2	2
Ecuador	South America	2	0010111 1	4	5	12	2	2	2	2
El Salvador	North America	27	0100110 0	3	3	27	0	2	2	2
Eritrea	Africa	14	0010010 0	2	2	13	0	0	0	1
Estonia	Europe	18	0000001 0	1	1	18	0	0	0	0
Ethiopia	Africa	55	0010010 1	2	3	16	1	0	2	1
Finland	Europe	11	1010010 0	2	2	N/A	N/A	N/A	N/A	N/A
Gambia	Africa	13	0010001 1	2	3	N/A	N/A	N/A	N/A	N/A
Total			3 9 27 6261519 3							

Note: Jung & Rosevear (2011) data coded as absent (0), directive principle (1), and enforceable law (2).

Source: Author's calculations.

TABLE 13.6. *Categories by country (2 of 3)*

Country	Continent	Developed Age	(1)(2)(3)(4)(5)(6)(7)	Categories Total (1–6)	Categories Total (1–7)	Age	JR FOWA	JR HENV	JR ENVP
Georgia	Asia	15	0011110	5	5	15	0	2	2
Germany	Europe	61	1010010	2	2	N/A	N/A	N/A	N/A
Ghana	Africa	18	0010010	2	2	18	0	0	1
Greece	Europe	9	1100000	1	1	N/A	N/A	N/A	N/A
Guatemala	North America	25	0010000	1	1	25	2	0	2
Guyana	South America	30	0100110	3	3	30	0	0	1
Haiti	North America	23	0010010	2	2	23	1	0	1
Hungary	Europe	61	0010100	2	2	61	0	2	2
India	Asia	61	0010010	2	2	61	1	0	1
Indonesia	Asia	65	0000100	1	1	65	0	1	0
Iran	Asia	31	0100010	2	2	31	2	0	0
Iraq	Asia	5	0010010	2	2	5	0	1	1
Italy	Europe	63	1010100	2	2	N/A	N/A	N/A	N/A
Kazakhstan	Asia	15	0010010	2	2	15	0	0	2
Kenya	Africa	0	00001101	2	3	47	0	0	0
Kosovo	Europe	2	00000010	1	3	N/A	N/A	N/A	N/A
Kuwait	Asia	48	0010000	1	1	48	0	0	0
Kyrgyzstan	Asia	0	0010100	3	3	N/A	N/A	N/A	N/A
Laos	Asia	19	00000010	1	1	19	0	0	0

Latvia	Europe	88	0101100 0	3	3	88	0	2	2
Lesotho	Africa	17	0010010 0	2	2	17	0	1	1
Lithuania	Europe	18	0010001 0	2	2	18	0	0	2
Macedonia	Europe	19	0010101 0	3	3	N/A	N/A	N/A	N/A
Madagascar	Africa	18	0010010 0	2	2	12	0	0	1
Malawi	Africa	16	0010010 0	2	2	16	2	1	1
Maldives	Asia	4	0100111 1	4	5	N/A	N/A	N/A	N/A
Mali	Africa	18	0100101 0	3	3	18	0	1	1
Malta	Europe	46	1010101 0	1	1	N/A	N/A	N/A	N/A
Moldova	Europe	16	0001101 0	3	3	16	2	2	0
Mongolia	Asia	18	0010101 0	3	3	18	0	2	2
Montenegro	Europe	3	0011101 0	4	4	N/A	N/A	N/A	N/A
Mozambique	Africa	20	0110111 0	5	5	20	0	2	1
Myanmar	Asia	2	0000001 0	1	1	2	0	0	1
Namibia	Africa	20	0010010 0	2	2	20	1	0	1
Nepal	Asia	3	0010100 0	2	2	3	2	0	1
Netherlands	Europe	8	1010000 0	1	1	N/A	N/A	N/A	N/A
Nicaragua	North America	3	0100100 0	2	2	24	2	2	2
Niger	Africa	11	0110101 0	4	4	11	0	1	1
Nigeria	Africa	11	0010000 0	1	1	11	1	0	1
North Korea	Asia	12	0010010 0	2	2	38	1	1	1
Norway	Europe	196	1001110 0	3	3	N/A	N/A	N/A	N/A
Oman	Asia	14	0010000 0	1	1	14	0	0	1
Total			6 9 28 5 18 11 22 2						

Note: Jung & Rosevear (2011) data coded as absent (0), directive principle (1), and enforceable law (2).
Source: Author's calculations.

TABLE 13.7. Categories by country (3 of 3)

Country	Continent	Age	Developed (1)(2)(3)(4)(5)(6)(7)	Categories Total (1–6)	Total (1–7)	Age	JR FOWA	HENV	ENVP
Palau	Australia	31	0010000 0	1	1	N/A	N/A	N/A	N/A
Panama	North America	16	0100001 1	2	3	38	2	2	2
Papua New Guinea	Australia	35	0000011 0	2	2	N/A	N/A	N/A	N/A
Paraguay	South America	18	0001000 0	1	1	18	2	2	2
Peru	South America	17	0110110 0	4	4	17	0	2	1
Poland	Europe	13	0011010 0	4	4	N/A	N/A	N/A	N/A
Portugal	Europe	34	1100100 0	3	3	N/A	N/A	N/A	N/A
Qatar	Asia	7	0010010 0	2	2	7	0	0	1
Romania	Europe	19	0010000 0	1	1	19	0	2	0
Russia	Asia	17	0001101 0	3	3	17	0	2	0
San Marino	Europe	36	1010000 0	1	1	N/A	N/A	N/A	N/A
Sao Tome and Principe	Africa	7	0010100 0	2	2	35	0	2	1
Saudi Arabia	Asia	18	0010000 0	1	1	18	0	0	1
Senegal	Africa	9	0100100 0	2	2	9	0	1	0
Serbia	Europe	4	0011010 0	4	4	4	0	2	2
Seychelles	Africa	17	0100101 0	3	3	17	0	2	2
Sierra Leone	Africa	19	0010000 0	1	1	19	0	0	0
Slovakia	Europe	18	0011101 0	4	4	18	0	1	1
Slovenia	Europe	19	0010100 0	2	2	19	0	1	1

Country	Region								
South Africa	Africa	14	11001001	2	3	14	2	2	2
South Korea	Asia	62	10101010	3	3	62	0	1	1
Spain	Europe	32	10101010	3	3	N/A	N/A	N/A	N/A
Sri Lanka	Asia	32	00100000	1	1	32	1	0	1
Sudan	Africa	5	01001010	3	3	5	0	1	1
Suriname	South America	23	00100000	1	1	N/A	N/A	N/A	N/A
Swaziland	Africa	5	00100010	2	2	6	0	0	1
Sweden	Europe	36	10100000	1	1	N/A	N/A	N/A	N/A
Switzerland	Europe	11	10100100	2	2	N/A	N/A	N/A	N/A
Taiwan	Asia	63	10100000	1	1	64	0	0	0
Tajikistan	Asia	16	00100010	2	2	16	0	0	2
Togo	Africa	19	00101000	2	2	18	0	1	0
Turkey	Asia	28	11001010	3	3	8	0	2	2
Turkmenistan	Asia	18	00100000	1	1	18	0	2	2
Uganda	Africa	15	00000111	2	3	15	1	2	1
Ukraine	Europe	14	00011000	2	2	44	2	2	0
Uruguay	South America	43	00100101	2	3	44	0	0	0
Uzbekistan	Asia	19	00100010	2	2	19	0	0	0
Vanuatu	Australia	30	00000110	2	2	N/A	N/A	N/A	N/A
Venezuela	South America	11	00100110	3	3	11	2	2	2
Vietnam	Asia	18	01000000	1	1	18	0	0	1
Zambia	Africa	19	00100101	2	3	18	1	1	1
Total			9 9 27 5 17 10 18 5						

Note: Jung & Rosevear (2011) data coded as absent (0), directive principle (1), and enforceable law (2).
Source: Author's calculations.

349

- Chile (1980), Article 8: The right to live in an environment free from contamination. It is the duty of the State to watch over the protection of this right and the preservation of nature.
- El Salvador (1983), Article 117: It is the duty of the State to protect natural resources and the diversity and integrity of the environment, to ensure sustainable development.
- Mali (1992), Article 15: Every person has a right to a healthy environment. The protection and defense of the environment and the promotion of the quality of life is a duty of everyone and of the State.
- Turkey (1982), Article 56: It is the duty of the state and citizens to improve the natural environment, and to prevent environmental pollution.

4.2. *Category Two (2) – State Objectives*

Category Two is comprised of keywords and phrases also associated with the state but with weaker language compared to Category One, and could independently be viewed as directive principles. These include, but are not limited to, the following: "fundamental objective," "must see to," "manage," "shall ensure," and "take measures." These keywords and phrases occurred in eighty-two constitutions and five examples are provided here[20]:

- Angola (1992), Article 12, Section 2: The State shall promote the protection and conservation of natural resources guiding the exploitation and use thereof for the benefit of the community as a whole.
- Bulgaria (1991), Article 15: The Republic of Bulgaria shall ensure the protection and reproduction of the environment, the conservation of living Nature in all its variety, and the sensible utilization of the country's natural and other resources.

---

[20] The eighty-two countries are: Andorra, Angola, Argentina, Armenia, Bahrain, Benin, Bolivia, Bulgaria, Cambodia, Cameroon, Cape Verde, Cayman Islands, Chad, China, Congo (Brazzaville), Congo (Kinshasa), Cook Islands, Costa Rica, Croatia, Cuba, Czech Republic, East Timor (Timor-Leste), Ecuador, Eritrea, Ethiopia, Finland, Gambia, Georgia, Germany, Ghana, Guatemala, Haiti, Hungary, India, Iraq, Italy, Kazakhstan, Kuwait, Kyrgyzstan, Lesotho, Lithuania, Macedonia, Madagascar, Malawi, Malta, Mongolia, Montenegro, Mozambique, Nepal, Netherlands, Niger, Nigeria, North Korea, Oman, Palau, Peru, Poland, Qatar, Romania, San Marino, Sao Tome and Principe, Saudi Arabia, Serbia, Sierra Leone, Slovakia, Slovenia, South Korea, Spain, Sri Lanka, Suriname, Swaziland, Sweden, Switzerland, Taiwan, Tajikistan, Togo, Turkmenistan, Uruguay, Uzbekistan, and Venezuela.

- Ghana (1992), Article 36, Section 9: The State shall take appropriate measures needed to protect and safeguard the national environment for posterity; and shall seek co-operation with other states and bodies for purposes of protecting the wider international environment for mankind.
- Kazakhstan (1995), Article 31, Section 1: The state shall set an objective to protect the environment favorable for the life and health of the person.
- Poland (1997), Article 5: The Republic of Poland shall safeguard the independence and integrity of its territory and ensure the freedoms and rights of persons and citizens, the security of the citizens, safeguard the national heritage and shall ensure the protection of the natural environment pursuant to the principles of sustainable development.

4.3. Category Three (3) – Right to Information

Category Three refers to a citizens' right to be informed about the status of the environment. The main keyword was "information," or some variation of it. The keywords or phrases occurred in sixteen constitutions and five examples are provided here[21]:

- Azerbaijan (1978), Article 39, Section 2: Everyone has the right to obtain information about the real condition of the environment and to receive compensation for the health or property damage caused by the violation of ecological law.
- Belarus (1994), Article 34: Citizens of the Republic of Belarus shall be guaranteed the right to receive, store, and disseminate complete, reliable, and timely information on the activities of state bodies and public associations, on political, economic, and international life, and on the state of the environment.
- Georgia (1995), Article 37, Section 5: A person shall have the right to receive complete, objective and timely information as to a state of his/her working and living environment.
- Moldova (1994), Article 37, Section 2: The State guarantees every citizen the right of free access to truthful information regarding the state of the natural environment, the living and working conditions, and the quality of food products and household appliances.

---

[21] The sixteen countries are: Albania, Argentina, Azerbaijan, Belarus, Cape Verde, Cook Islands, Georgia, Latvia, Moldova, Montenegro, Norway, Poland, Russia, Serbia, Slovakia, and Ukraine.

- Poland (1997), Article 74, Section 3: Everyone shall have the right to be informed of the quality of the environment and its protection.

4.4. CATEGORY FOUR (4) – RIGHT TO A HEALTHY ENVIRONMENT

Category Four refers explicitly to a citizen's right to a healthy or clean environment. The language is generally strong and includes, but is not limited to, the following: "right to a healthy environment," "right to a clean environment," "safe," "healthy," and "favorable" (all within the context of the natural environment). These keywords and phrases occurred in sixty-one constitutions and five examples are provided here[22]:

- Benin (1990), Article 27: Every person has the right to a healthy, satisfying and lasting environment and has the duty to defend it. The state shall watch over the protection of the environment.
- Chad (1996), Article 47: Every person has the right to a healthy environment.
- Macedonia (1991), Article 43, Section 1: Everyone has the right to a healthy environment to live in.
- Russia (1993), Article 42: Everyone shall have the right to a favorable environment, reliable information about its condition and to compensation for the damage caused to his or her health or property by ecological violations.
- Ukraine (1996), Article 50, Section 3: Everyone has the right to an environment that is safe for life and health, and to compensation for damages inflicted through the violation of this right. Everyone is guaranteed the right of free access to information about the environmental situation, the quality of food and consumer goods, and also the right to disseminate such information. No one shall make such information secret.

---

[22] The 61 countries are: Angola, Argentina, Azerbaijan, Belarus, Belgium, Benin, Bolivia, British Virgin Islands, Bulgaria, Burkina Faso, Cameroon, Cape Verde, Chad, Central African Republic, Chile, Colombia, Comoros, Congo (Brazzaville), Congo (Kinshasa), Cook Islands, Costa Rica, Cote d'Ivoire, Croatia, East Timor (Timor-Leste), Ecuador, El Salvador, Georgia, Hungary, Indonesia, Italy, Kenya, Kyrgyzstan, Latvia, Macedonia, Maldives, Mali, Moldova, Mongolia, Montenegro, Mozambique, Nepal, Nicaragua, Niger, Norway, Paraguay, Peru, Portugal, Russia, Sao Tome and Principe, Senegal, Serbia, Seychelles, Slovakia, Slovenia, South Africa, South Korea, Spain, Sudan, Togo, Turkey, and Ukraine.

4.5. *Category Five (5) – Future Generations*

Category Five refers to the concern for future generations as explicitly written into some constitutional environmental human rights provision. The main keywords were "future," "generation," and "sustainable development." These occurred in thirty-six constitutions and five examples are provided here[23]:

- Albania (1998), Article 59, Section 1, Subsection E: The state, within its constitutional powers and the means at its disposal, aims to supplement private initiative and responsibility with: a healthy and ecologically adequate environment for the present and future generations.
- Eritrea (1996), Article 10, Section 3: The State shall have the responsibility to regulate all land, water and natural resources and to ensure their management in a balanced and sustainable manner and in the interest of the present and future generations; and to create the right conditions for securing the participation of the people to safeguard the environment.
- Lesotho (1993), Article 36: Lesotho shall adopt policies designed to protect and enhance the natural and cultural environment of Lesotho for the benefit of both present and future generations and shall endeavor to assure to all citizens a sound and safe environment adequate for their health and well-being.
- Qatar (1993), Article 33: The State shall preserve the environment and its natural balance in order to achieve comprehensive and sustainable development for all generations.
- Uganda (1995), Article 27: This is to promote development and awareness for proper management of land, air and water resources for the present and future generations.

4.6. *Category Six (6) – A General Duty to Respect*

Category Six refers to duty, in a general sense. This includes the duty of citizens and a catch-all category, "everyone," to "respect," "defend,"

---

[23] The 36 countries are: Albania, Andorra, Argentina, Armenia, Bolivia, Brazil, British Virgin Islands, Cayman Islands, Columbia, Cuba, East Timor (Timor-Leste), Ecuador, El Salvador, Eritrea, Ethiopia, Georgia, Germany, Guyana, Iran, Kenya, Lesotho, Malawi, Maldives, Mozambique, Norway, Papua New Guinea, Peru, Poland, Qatar, Switzerland, Uganda, Uruguay, Vanuatu, and Venezuela.

"conserve," and so forth the environment or nature. These keywords and phrases occurred in fifty-nine constitutions and five examples are provided here[24]:

- Cape Verde (1992), Article 7, Section 1, Subsection E: Everyone shall have the right to a healthy life and ecologically balanced environment and the duty to defend and conserve it.
- Estonia (1992), Article 53: Everyone has a duty to preserve the human and natural environment and to compensate for damage caused to the environment by him or her. The procedure for compensation shall be provided by law.
- Kyrgyzstan (2007), Article 48, Section 3: Everyone must take care of the environment, flora, and fauna.
- Mongolia (1992), Article 17, Section 2: It is a sacred duty for every citizen to work, protect his or her health, bring up and educate his or her children and to protect nature and the environment.
- Seychelles (1993), Article 40, Section E: It shall be the duty of every citizen of Seychelles to protect, preserve, and improve the environment.

4.7. Category Seven (7) – Right to Water

There are ten constitutions containing a specific human right to water: Ecuador, Ethiopia, Gambia, Kenya, Maldives, Panama, South Africa, Uganda, Uruguay, and Zambia. The specific articles are listed here:

- Ecuador (2008), Section 2.15: Energy sovereignty will not be achieved at the expense of food sovereignty, nor affect the right to water. Article 67, Section 2: The right to a dignified life, to ensure the health, food and nutrition, drinking water, housing, sanitation, education, labor, employment, and leisure.
- Ethiopia (1998), Article 90: Every Ethiopian is entitled, within the limits of the country's resources to . . . clean water.
- Gambia (1997), Social Objectives 216, Section 4: The State shall endeavor to facilitate equal access to clean and safe water, adequate

---

[24] The 59 countries are: Azerbaijan, Belarus, Benin, Brazil, Bulgaria, Burkina Faso, Cameroon, Cape Verde, Chad, Colombia, Comoros, Congo (Brazzaville), Congo (Kinshasa), Cote d'Ivoire, East Timor (Timor-Leste), Ecuador, Estonia, Finland, Gambia, Georgia, Ghana, Guyana, Haiti, India, Iraq, Kazakhstan, Kosovo, Kyrgyzstan, Laos, Lithuania, Macedonia, Madagascar, Maldives, Mali, Moldova, Mongolia, Montenegro, Mozambique, Myanmar, Niger, North Korea, Panama, Papua New Guinea, Poland, Portugal, Russia, Serbia, Seychelles, Slovakia, South Korea, Spain, Sudan, Swaziland, Tajikistan, Turkey, Uganda, Uzbekistan, Vanuatu, and Venezuela.

health and medical services, habitable shelter, sufficient food and security to all persons.

- Kenya (2010), Article 43: Every person has the right – to clean and safe water in adequate quantities.
- Maldives (2008), Section 23a: Every citizen has the following rights pursuant to this Constitution, and the State undertakes to achieve the progressive realization of these rights by reasonable measures within its ability and resources: adequate and nutritious food and clean water.
- Panama (1994), Chapter 7, Article 114: The basic duty of the State to ensure that people are living in a healthy environment free of pollution, where air, water and food meet requirements of the proper development of human life.
- South Africa (1996), Article 14: Everyone has the right to have access to sufficient food and water.
- Uganda (1995), Article 27b: The State shall endeavor to fulfill the fundamental rights of all Ugandans to social justice and economic development and shall, in particular, ensure that...all Ugandans enjoy rights and opportunities and access to education, health services, clean and safe water, decent shelter, adequate clothing, food, security and pension and retirements benefits.
- Uruguay (1967), Article 47: The protection of the environment is of general interest. People should refrain from any act causing depredation, destruction or serious environmental pollution. Law shall regulate this provision and may provide penalties for violators. Water is a natural resource essential to life. Access to safe water and access to sanitation are basic human rights.
- Zambia (1998), Article 112: The state shall endeavor to provide clean and safe water.

5. A SIMPLE INDEX OF PROVISION STRENGTH

Summing across each of the categories provides an indication of the legal strength of a constitutional environmental human rights provision. Treating the entire set of language surrounding the natural environment as forming the basis of an environmental human right is fundamentally different from defining the nature of the provision as a directive principle or enforceable law. However, it is unclear if this sum should be across Categories 1–6 or 1–7. The human right to water is arguably legally nested within constitutional environmental human rights in general, but the converse is not necessarily true. Having an explicit human

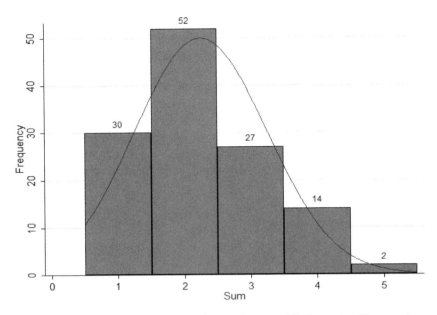

FIGURE 13.2. Summation across Categories 1–6, All Countries (N = 125).

right to water says nothing of air and soil, whereas a general environmental human right, based on the definition provided in the introduction, covers air, soil, and water. Further research should consider this distinction, both empirically and theoretically. Empirically, the two are highly correlated, and thus might serve the same purpose for the sake of inference. Theoretically or conceptually, however, the distinction is important because the legal duties and obligations imposed on the government could be drastically different if the constitution includes solely an environmental human right versus a direct human right to water. For the latter case, the government might never be held responsible for polluted air and soil. Without taking a stand on which summation is empirically and theoretically robust, the following analysis considers both.

Table 13.8 and Figures 13.2 and 13.3 illustrate the distribution of countries across the category summations by average age and development status. For Categories 1–6, the majority of countries have a score of 2, and the average score (not included in the table) is 2.248. Only one country has a score of 0 (Kenya) and two have a score of 5 (Georgia and Mozambique); none score the maximum of 6. There seems to be no discernible pattern between the category summation and the average

TABLE 13.8. *Language category count by age and development status*
(N = 125)

Category sum	Count % of total	Count average	Age	Count Developed	Developing
		For Categories 1–6			
0	0	0.00%	N/A	0	0
1	30	24.00%	24.00	7	23
2	52	41.60%	19.62	6	46
3	27	21.60%	31.59	5	22
4	14	11.20%	22.21	0	14
5	2	1.60%	17.50	0	2
6	0	0.00%	N/A	0	0
Total/ Average	125	100%	23.512	18	107
		For Categories 1–7			
0	0	0.00%	N/A	0	0
1	30	24.00%	24.00	7	23
2	44	35.20%	19.20	5	39
3	35	28.00%	29.37	6	29
4	12	9.60%	25.42	0	12
5	4	3.20%	10.25	0	4
6	0	0.00%	N/A	0	0
7	0	0.00%	N/A	0	0
Total/ Average	125	100%	23.51	18	107

Source: Author's calculations.

age of constitutions, although those countries with a score of 4 or 5 are both under the aggregate average age of the 125 constitutions (23.51). The majority of developing countries have a score of 2, whereas developed countries are almost evenly spread across scores 1, 2, and 3, with a majority having only 1.

For Categories 1–7, the majority of countries also have a score of 2, and the average score is slightly higher at 2.328. Based on this summation, no countries have a score of 0, 6, or 7. The average age of the countries with a score of 5 has dropped considerably to 10.25. In fact, across all scores with the exception of 1 and 4, the average age of constitutions has fallen. The distribution of developed countries has changed slightly, with one country moving from a score of 2 to 3 (South Africa). Comparing Figures 13.2 and 13.3, the summation across Categories 1–6 and 1–7

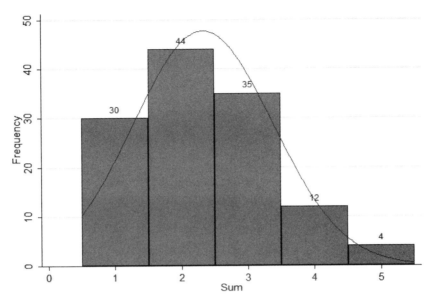

FIGURE 13.3. Summation across Categories 1–7, All Countries (N = 125).

yields distributions that are slightly more right or positively skewed (i.e., the right tail of the distribution is longer than the left tail) than a standard normal distribution.

Table 13.9 illustrates the correlation matrix for the seven keyword categories and a total across the first six and all seven. The correlation coefficients between the totals and Category 1 are positive at 0.300 and 0.301, respectively, and significant at the 1% level. These correlations are much weaker with respect to Category 2, and not statistically significant. In other words, although positively related to both the strong and weak language of Categories One and Two, respectively, having a larger total count across the keywords is more strongly (and positively) associated with the language of Category One. Perhaps this lends credence to coding these specific provisions as enforceable law. However, for the variety of language within each constitutional environmental human rights provision, subjectively coding the provision may not be as robust of an explanatory variable in an empirical analysis as the finer keyword approach offered in this chapter. Only validity tests in further research will tell. Both coding schemes are prone to measurement error; however, a subjective interpretation is likely more so because of the potential coding bias of the researcher.

TABLE 13.9. *Linear correlations across categories*

	(1)	(2)	(3)	(4)	(5)	(6)	(7)	Total (1–6)	Total (1–7)
(1)	1.0000								
(2)	(0.520)***	1.0000							
(3)	(0.085)	(0.126)	1.000						
(4)	0.265***	(0.236)***	0.297***	1.000					
(5)	0.010	0.023	0.021	(0.161)*	1.000				
(6)	0.049	0.125	0.117	0.167	(0.141)	1.000			
(7)	0.060	(0.097)	(0.113)	(0.052)	0.268***	0.017	1.000		
Total (1–6)	0.300***	0.028	0.459***	0.610***	0.304***	0.522***	0.045	1.000	
Total (1–7)	0.301***	0.002	0.408***	0.569***	0.360***	0.502***	0.304***	0.966***	1.000

Numbers in parentheses are negative.
* Significant at the 10% level;
** , 5%; and
*** , 1%.

Source: Author's calculations.

6. A BRIEF COMPARISON TO TIESR DATA

For environmental human rights, the TIESR data include ninety-five constitutions, thirty fewer than the set used here. This can be seen by the presence of "N/A" in the last three columns of Tables 13.5, 13.6, and 13.7. Age discrepancies between TIESR and this data, such as for Albania and Argentina, are either due to using a constitution from a different year (Albania) or considering the age based on the most recent amendment (Argentina). For an empirical analysis, the year in which the constitution was written is important to consider because it could be different from the year in which the environmental human rights provision was included. Nonetheless, there are few age discrepancies between the two sets of data.

In the TIESR data, there are twenty-six constitutions that include the right to access to FOWA, eleven of which are coded as directive principles; the other fifteen are enforceable law. There are sixty-three constitutions that include the right to an HENV, split between directive principles (twenty-four) and enforceable law (thirty-nine). Lastly, there are seventy-three constitutions that include the duty of the state to ENVP, forty-one of which are coded as directive principles and thirty-two as enforceable law.

Table 13.10 displays correlation coefficients between the categories discussed earlier and FOWA, HENV, and ENVP.[25] For the full sample comparison of ninety-five countries, FOWA, HENV, and ENVP are, in general, positively correlated with most of the keyword categories, with the exception of a few arguably independent correlations and a negative correlation between Category Two and FOWA and HENV, Category Six and FOWA, and Total (1–6) and FOWA. HENV and ENVP are positively and statistically significantly correlated with the index totals from this data, indicating that the presence of more categories of language is positively related to coding the provisions as directive principles or enforceable law. As the correlations are not equal to 1, the remaining variation in the TIESR coding could likely be attributed to the subjective coding of the data. In other words, if these correlations were statistically no different from 1, then the positive and subjective coding methods would arguably be perfect substitutes (empirically speaking). This is not the case based on the coefficient values resulting from the simple linear or pairwise correlations. In fact, the positive association is dampened using pairwise correlations.

---

[25] Comparing FOWA to this data may be misleading because it includes food, not just water.

TABLE 13.10. *Linear and pairwise correlations with TIESR data*

	N	(1)	(2)	(3)	(4)	(5)	(6)	(7)	Total (1–6)	Total (1–7)	FOWA	HBW	BWP
						Linear Correlation							
FOWA	95	0.035	(0.098)	0.035	0.008	0.151	(0.124)	0.281***	(0.011)	0.065	1.000		
HENV	95	0.266***	(0.217)**	0.335***	0.622***	0.085	0.090	0.106	0.522***	0.532***	0.147	1.000	
ENVP	95	0.184*	0.135	0.116	0.196*	0.072	0.149	0.008	0.391***	0.379***	0.164	0.446***	1.000
						Pairwise Correlation							
FOWA	26	0.284	(0.357)*	0.309	0.576***	(0.212)	(0.123)	(0.085)	0.210	0.139	1.000		
HENV	63	0.114	0.085	0.214*	0.186	0.134	0.013	0.143	0.248**	0.286**	0.555**	1.000	
ENVP	73	0.138	0.170	0.257**	0.374***	(0.039)	0.098	0.037	0.282**	0.284	0.833***	0.815***	1.000

Note: Linear Correlation uses listwise or casewise deletion of observations; Pairwise Correlation uses pairwise. Numbers in parentheses are negative.
* Significant at the 10% level;
**, 5%; and
***, 1%. The pairwise correlations between the TIESR data yield the following observations: FOWA and HENV, N = 17; FOWA and ENVP, N = 22; and HENV and ENVP, N = 51.

Source: Author's calculations.

The last three rows of Table 13.10 display the pairwise correlation coefficients between this data and the data from TIESR.[26] The pairwise correlations between FOWA, HENV, and ENVP are considerably strong, positive, and statistically significant. It seems that constitutions that have one tend to have the other, which from a multicollinearity perspective could seriously complicate any empirical analysis using this subset of TIESR data to explain environmental human rights outcomes. Furthermore, that there are a variety of both positive and negative, as well as statistically significant and otherwise, correlations with the language categories proposed in this analysis could lead one to question the methodology behind coding these rights as directive principles versus enforceable law.

7. CONCLUSION

This analysis provides insight into the extent to which countries are taking environmental human rights seriously as evidenced through a keyword analysis of constitutional provisions. Out of 142 national constitutions that mention the environment, 125 contain a direct environmental human right or at least the basis of one, and 10 include a direct human right to water. The provisions were further broken down into seven keyword categories and a novel additive index of the legal strength of constitutional environmental human rights was created. One problem with this index, however, is that it treats all seven keyword categories as equally important, whereas certain categories are likely more important than others in giving the provision actual legal strength. Going forward, it is important to design a more intuitively and empirically robust index, perhaps through variance-based or regression-based weights.

Although many constitutions are sympathetic to environmental human rights, no two provisions are worded the same across countries. This is both a blessing and a curse. On the one hand, this allows for a direct positive interpretation of the provisions based solely on language. On the other hand, it complicates any systematic attempt at a subjective interpretation of justiciability across countries. This is the primary difference between this data and that of TIESR. The second major difference is that TIESR explicitly delineates two general environmental human rights in HENV and ENVP, whereas this chapter does not take such a stand.

---

[26] The pairwise correlation coefficient uses a different method to handle missing observations, notably the pairwise deletion of observations compared to the listwise or casewise deletion of missing observations using the simple linear correlation.

Instead, the data in this analysis are treated like a single provision where the presence of more categories of language indicates a stronger (in a legal sense) constitutional environmental human rights provision.

Further research is necessary to determine if constitutions matter, specifically if constitutional environmental human rights provisions have any appreciable effect on environmental rights outcomes. Taking into consideration the strength of these provisions, which is typically static across time, is an important first step in this direction. However, time-varying measures of government effort to respect, protect, and fulfill environmental human rights are arguably more robust indicators of the effects of constitutional provisions on outcomes.

REFERENCES

Barrett, C., 1996. "Fairness, Stewardship and Sustainable Development," *Ecological Economics*, 19(1): 11–17.

Beckerman, W., 1997. "Debate: Intergenerational Equity and the Environment," *Journal of Political Philosophy*, 5(4): 392–405.

Collins-Chobanian, S., 2000. "Beyond Sax and Welfare Interests," *Environmental Ethics*, 22: 133–148.

Gleick, P., 1998. "The Human Right to Water," *Water Policy*, 1–5: 487–503.

Hardin, G., 1968. "The Tragedy of the Commons," *Science*, 162: 1243–1248.

Herz, R., 2000. "Litigating Environmental Abuses Under the Alien Tort Claims Act: A Practical Assessment," *Virginia Journal of International Law* 40: 545–632.

Hiskes, R., 2009. *The Human Right to a Green Future*, Cambridge: Cambridge University Press.

Hiskes, R., 2011. "Environmental Human Rights," in Tom Cushman (Ed.), *Handbook of Human Rights*, 399–409, New York: Routledge International Handbooks.

Howarth, R., 1997. "Sustainability as Opportunity," *Land Economics* 73(4): 569–579.

Jeffords, C., and F. Shah, forthcoming. "On the Natural and Economic Difficulties to Fulfilling the Human Right to Water Within a Neoclassical Economics Framework," *Review of Social Economy*.

Jung, C., and E. Rosevear, 2011. "Economic and Social Rights in Developing Country Constitutions: Preliminary Report on the TIESR Dataset," http://www.tiesr.org/TIESR%20Report%20v%203.1.pdf .

Lercher, A., 2007. "Are There Any Environmental Rights?" *Environmental Values* 16(3): 355–368.

Minkler, L., 2009. "Economic Rights and Political Decision Making," *Human Rights Quarterly* 31(2): 368–393.

Ostrom, E., 1990. *Governing the Commons: The Evolution of Institutions for Collective Action*, Cambridge: Cambridge University Press.

Padilla, E., 2002. "Intergenerational Equity and Sustainability," *Ecological Economics* 41(1): 69–83.

Rawls, J., 1999. *A Theory of Justice*, Cambridge, MA: Belknap Press.

Sax, J., 1990. "The Search for Environmental Rights," *Journal of Land Use and Environmental Law* 6: 93–105.

Scanlon, J., A. Cassar, and N. Nemes, 1999. "Water as a Human Right?" *UNESCO Courier*.

Shelton, D., 1991. "Human Rights, Environmental Rights, and the Right to Environment," *Stanford Journal of International Law* 28: 103–138.

Shrader-Frechette, K., 2007. "Human Rights and Duties to Alleviate Environmental Injustice: The Domestic Case," *Journal of Human Rights* 6(1): 107–130.

Shue, H., 1996. *Basic Rights: Subsistence, Affluence, and US Foreign Policy*, Princeton, NJ: Princeton University Press.

Sunstein, C., 2004. *The Second Bill of Rights: FDR's Unfinished Revolution and Why We Need it More Than Ever*, New York: Basic Books.

United Nations, 2002. Economic and Social Council Committee on Economic, Social, and Cultural Rights, *General Comment No. 15*, Geneva: UN.

United Nations, 2010. General Assembly Document A/64/L.63/Rev. 1, (7/26/2010).

Weiss, E., 1992. "In Fairness to Future Generations and Sustainable Development," *American University Journal of International Law and Policy* 8: 19.

14

Conclusion: Reflections on the Theory and Practice of Economic and Social Rights

Michael Freeman

A THEORETICAL FRAMEWORK

Human rights scholars and advocates now usually take for granted that economic and social rights are valid human rights. These rights were included in the Universal Declaration of Human Rights (UDHR). The International Covenant on Economic, Social and Cultural Rights (ICESCR) is part of the International Bill of Rights, and has been ratified (as of February 29, 2012) by 160 out of 193, or 82.9%, of all United Nations member-states. For many, the moral argument for recognizing these rights as human rights is at least as compelling as the legal argument: the rights to food, health, housing, social security, work, and education have great intuitive appeal. Economic and social rights have been more acceptable to non–Western governments than civil and political rights, and, whereas Western governments have been reluctant to acknowledge legally binding obligations to fulfill economic and social rights for noncitizens, they have generally recognized them for their own citizens and accept a moral obligation to fulfill them to some extent for noncitizens.

Yet, the contributors to this volume express considerable frustration at the failure of the international community, and even some of its richest states, to implement economic and social rights adequately. An explanation for this failure may be obvious: powerful interests oppose the implementation of these rights. In this, the practical status of economic and social rights is not very different from that of civil and political rights, which are also seriously violated in many countries where powerful interests trample on international law. The truth in this explanation raises practical rather than theoretical problems. However, a law is not a bad law just because it is imperfectly implemented. The fact that there are murders in a country does not entail that the laws prohibiting murder are ill considered.

Nevertheless, the validity of economic and social rights is not settled in political philosophy. Because this discipline is underrepresented in the contributions to this volume, it may be worthwhile to summarize the state of debate among philosophers about economic and social rights as human rights, even though some of the arguments are familiar. It is possible that the causes of the failure to implement these rights lie in part with defects in the very idea of such rights.

Among the possible defects that might concern philosophers are the following: the rights are impractical; they are seriously unclear; if implemented, they might sometimes do more harm than good; they are "incompossible" (the implementation of some is conceptually or empirically incompatible with the implementation of others)[1]; they have uncertain or implausible theoretical justifications; the obligations they entail are either unclear or unreasonable; they are not (universal) human rights, even though they may be desirable social goals, or even legal rights, in some societies. These concerns are distinct, but not completely so. For example, the claim that economic and social rights are impractical may overlap with the claim that they entail unreasonable obligations, for the latter claim may underlie the former. The two claims are not identical, however, for a right may be impractical, not because it entails unreasonable obligations, but because the resources necessary to fulfill the right are unavailable, so that there would be no obligations. Even if all these arguments are unsound, their critical examination should clarify the theoretical basis of these rights, and this may illuminate the prospects for their further implementation. The philosophical controversies about economic and social rights also provide a systematic framework for evaluating the contributions to this volume.

SKEPTICAL ARGUMENTS

Cranston

One of the earliest critics of economic and social rights was Maurice Cranston, and he remains perhaps the best known. Human rights, Cranston maintained, were moral rights that were universal in the sense that they were the rights of all people at all times and in all situations.

---

[1]   On the problem of incompossibility in the theory of rights, see Steiner 1994.

Economic and social rights were not, however, human rights for the following reasons. Firstly, if it was impossible to achieve a certain state of affairs, there could be no right that such a state of affairs be achieved. It was possible for governments to secure civil and political rights easily by legislation. Many governments were, however, too poor to provide all their citizens with the enjoyment of all their economic and social rights. Secondly, economic and social rights, unlike civil and political rights, imposed no universal duties. There was, for example, a universal duty not to torture, but no universal duty to fulfill the right to social security. Because there was no universal duty to fulfill supposed economic and social rights, these rights were not universal human rights. Members of some particular societies might justifiably claim these rights, but a beggar in India could not be equal in such rights to a worker in the United States, whereas each could be equal in civil and political rights. Article 2, paragraph 3, of the ICESCR recognized this by allowing developing countries to determine to what extent they would guarantee economic rights to nonnationals. Thirdly, the holders of economic and social rights were not universal. The rights of employees, for example, were not human rights, because not all humans were employees. Fourthly, economic and social rights lacked the moral urgency of civil and political rights: the right to holidays with pay, for example, lacked the moral urgency of the right not to be tortured (Cranston 1973).

Jack Donnelly has been a leading critic of Cranston. He rejects Cranston's first argument on the ground that all human rights – civil, political, economic, and social – can be difficult to implement in certain circumstances; political rights are harder to implement in North Korea, for example, than economic rights in Sweden. Thus, the difficulty of implementing a right does not mean that it is not a human right. (The right not to be murdered is difficult to implement for everyone, everywhere, at all times). It is true that the resources for the fulfillment of economic and social rights may not be available in particular countries at particular times, but this raises a problem also for the fulfillment of civil and political rights. Lack of resources is not a fact of nature, but a product of various social causes, including the failure to fulfill civil and political rights: corrupt and undemocratic governments are generally less successful in producing the resources for the fulfillment of economic and social rights.[2] This objection to Cranston's first argument undermines

---

[2] This claim is supported by systematic empirical evidence in Halperin, Siegle, and Weinstein (2010).

his second, also. There is no obligation to do what is impossible, but the obligation to fulfill economic and social rights is impossible only if it is interpreted as utopian; there is an obligation to employ all available resources to implement economic and social rights progressively. The duties corresponding to economic and social rights are indeed not universal in the sense that they must be fulfilled by appropriate institutions. However, this is as true of the right not to be tortured as the right to social security, for both require appropriate institutions if they are to be adequately fulfilled.

Cranston's third argument – that the rights-holders are not universal – does not distinguish economic and social rights from civil and political rights, because not all humans have the political right to vote; only adult citizens have this right. Donnelly rejects Cranston's fourth argument on the ground that it relies on a biased comparison. Some economic and social rights, such as the right to food, are as morally urgent as some civil and political rights, such as the right to vote, if not more urgent. Thus, Cranston's arguments demonstrate only the difficulty of implementing all types of human rights in situations of scarce resources or of an unfavorable political, social, and/or economic environment. He fails to demonstrate any radical difference between civil and political rights, on the one hand, and economic and social rights, on the other. This leaves him with little more than an argument that civil and political rights are relatively easy to implement. This argument, Donnelly suggests, is empirically dubious, and, even if it were empirically plausible, it is doubtful that ease or expense of implementation has any conceptual or moral significance (Donnelly 2003). This last point is questionable. The difficulty or cost of implementing a right may be morally relevant because, if the difficulty or cost is very great, it may impose unjustifiable burdens on others. The cost of implementing one right may divert resources from the implementation of other rights or from other legitimate social goals. It is surely morally significant if a society pays the costs of holidays with pay at the expense of lifesaving health care or investment in infrastructure that may improve the fulfillment of human rights in the long-term.

O'Neill

Onora O'Neill has expressed skepticism about economic and social human rights in various contexts, but particularly in that of world hunger and the right to food. She cites Philip Alston's complaint that the right to food has been endorsed more often, and with greater unanimity and urgency, than most other human rights, but has also been violated more comprehensively and systematically than any other right (O'Neill 1986).

Rights-holders can press their claims only when the obligations to meet these claims have been allocated to specified obligation-bearers. An obligation that is neither owed to everyone nor based on a special relationship is *unallocated*, and so cannot be claimed, because it is not specified against whom the claim should be made. When supposed rights are promulgated without allocation to obligation-bearers, they are empty, "manifesto" rights. No one can feed all the hungry, and so the obligation to feed the hungry cannot be a universal obligation, and most of those who are hungry have no special relationship in virtue of which others should feed them, so special obligations will not be sufficient to remedy world hunger. The obligations that correspond to the right to food are imperfect duties of charity or optional beneficence; their performance cannot be claimed by the hungry (O'Neill 1986).

Human rights scholars who start with international human rights law, as many of the contributors to this volume do, may be puzzled by O'Neill's allocation problem. Surely, they may say, international law allocates the obligations that correspond to economic and social rights fairly clearly. States have the obligations to fulfill these rights progressively, according to available resources, and also have the obligation to fulfill the minimum core of the rights immediately. Insofar as states lack the resources to fulfill the rights, they have the obligation to seek assistance from states that have resources to spare, and these states have the obligation to assist the resource-poor states.[3] O'Neill objects that this locates the solution precisely where the problem lies. The concept of human rights is weak precisely because states fail to fulfill the obligations that international law imposes on them. "When no available state agency," O'Neill writes, "can carry significant obligations of justice it can be destructive, even deluded, to assume that they will do so" (O'Neill 2004, 254–255). To proclaim human rights without taking seriously who has the obligation to do what, O'Neill maintains, is morally irresponsible.

O'Neill's concern is that the obligations that correspond to supposed economic and social rights are unallocated to agents that can fulfill them. When obligations have not been so allocated, there can be no rights. It is possible to allocate the obligations that correspond to economic

---

[3] For the argument that the legal obligations of states to fulfill human rights beyond their borders are fairly stringent, see the contribution of Mark Gibney to this volume.

and social rights, but, if this were done, the obligations would have to be allocated to particular institutions, and the resulting rights would be particular not universal rights. Thus, according to her argument, there is no universal human right to health, but citizens of the United Kingdom have the right to health care under the National Health Service. There may also be imperfect obligations of the well-off to assist the poor, but no one has the right that others perform their imperfect obligations in a particular way; that is part of what it means to say that an obligation is imperfect. Thus, the rich may well have imperfect obligations to help the poor, but no poor individual has a human right that any particular rich persons provide them with assistance.

Liberty rights can be universal because they require universal noninterference by others, but economic and social rights cannot be universal because the corresponding obligations cannot be universal. Universal economic and social rights could be fulfilled by distributed obligations that ensured that the rights were fulfilled. Since distributed universal rights presuppose particular institutions, they are typically established in restricted forms, for example, for citizens of certain states. When a liberty right has been violated, it is clear in principle, although not always in practice, who has violated it. This is not so in the case of economic and social rights. Proclamations of universal economic and social rights without attention to the need to justify and establish institutions that identify corresponding obligation-bearers is but bitter mockery to the poor, for whom these rights matter most. A premature rhetoric of rights can inflate expectations while masking a lack of claimable entitlements. Without institutions, supposedly universal economic and social rights are radically incomplete. To institutionalize them is not just to secure the backing of the law, but to define and allocate obligations to provide the relevant goods and services, and so fix the very shape of these rights and obligations. The fact that economic and social rights impose substantial burdens on duty-bearers explains why they are controversial even in rich societies, whereas liberty rights are not. Obligations have less rhetorical appeal than rights, but they have the advantage that they require us to be more realistic, clear, and honest about burdens, their justification and their allocation (O'Neill 1996).

The discourse of human rights, O'Neill maintains, pretends to solve the problem of hunger, but fails to do so because it leaves it to the inadequate response of optional beneficence. If the discourse of human rights were replaced by that of obligations, remedies for world hunger might be required partly by justice and partly by beneficence, and neither would be optional. O'Neill is skeptical of the discourse of economic and social rights, because it lacks a plausible discourse of corresponding obligations. Consequently, it fails to guide action. The discourse of obligations is better able to guide action because it allows for imperfect obligations without corresponding rights. O'Neill acknowledges that neither rights nor obligations offer an algorithm for identifying an optimal action for each context (O'Neill 1986).

Human rights requiring positive action will be in conflict in all sorts of circumstances and will consequently be incompossible. Rights that are incompossible logically cannot be universal. To be universal, the discourse of human rights must remain abstract. The most important audience for the discourse of human rights is that of those whose actions can institutionalize and secure respect for rights. Because the discourse of human rights speaks first to those who claim their rights, and not to those who have the power to fulfill or fail to fulfill their obligations, it often sends only a vague message to those whose action is needed to secure respect for rights. Consequently, widespread acceptance of the abstract rhetoric of rights coexists with widespread failure to respect rights. It is easy to promulgate rights, and the discourse of rights can be attractive to those who have an interest in claiming them, but the abstraction of human rights discourse often leaves indeterminate who is obliged to do what to fulfill them (O'Neill 1986).

However, if proclaiming the right to food does not, as O'Neill argues, feed the hungry, neither does allocating the obligation to feed the hungry to non-state actors, as she recommends. These actors lack the capacity to solve the problem of world hunger, and also lack the legal and political accountability of states (Miller 2009). The problem of fulfilling the right to food is not that we use the discourse of human rights rather than O'Neill's preferred discourse of obligations, but that no one has both the will and the capacity to solve the problem. O'Neill is, however, correct on one important point: asking not who has the right to what but rather who has the obligation to do what (to fulfill human rights) has the advantage of compelling us to be more realistic, clear, and honest about the costs, their justification, and their allocation. This is not – contrary to what O'Neill suggests – a reason to be skeptical about economic and social rights. Rather, it is a reason to combine an emphasis on rights with a serious consideration of where the corresponding obligations should lie, not merely in rhetoric or in law, but in the real political and economic worlds where feasible institutions, strategies, and policies could be developed, and appropriate agents motivated to fulfill these rights.

O'Neill complains that economic and social rights lack specified, effective institutions with the obligations to fulfill these rights. James Nickel counters that this does not support the conclusion that the supposed human rights are not genuine rights, but rather the conclusion that the institutions should be reformed. Institutions do not provide the justification of human rights, but rather the potential means of their fulfillment. The justification of a human right derives from its moral importance, which may be based on the basic needs of human beings (e.g., the right to clean water), the good of society (e.g., the right to freedom of expression), and/or the wrongfulness of a violation (e.g., the right not to be tortured) (Nickel 1993).[4]

Amartya Sen has pointed out that all human rights can be difficult to fulfill, and all human rights entail imperfect obligations to work for the establishment of institutions that will have the obligation to do everything reasonably possible to fulfill the rights. Even the right not to be tortured entails not only the universal perfect obligation not to torture but also the imperfect obligation to do what one can to prevent torture. Thus, the fact that the obligations corresponding to economic and social rights are now imperfectly allocated does not mean that they are not genuine rights, nor does it distinguish them from liberty rights. The tragedy of 9/11 shows that the institutions charged with the obligation to fulfill the right to security are imperfect (Sen 2006).

Thomas Pogge argues that O'Neill is mistaken to believe that human rights require allocated duties. On O'Neill's account slaves would have no right to be free because the obligation to free them is unallocated; no one has a perfect obligation to free slaves in a slave society. The right of slaves to be liberated from slavery entails the imperfect obligation of free persons to do what they reasonably can to abolish slavery. Such imperfect obligations may be quite stringent (Pogge 1992).

---

[4] Donnelly objects to what he calls the "pseudoscientific dodge of needs," and goes on to suggest that it is "positively dangerous" to insist that rights are rooted in need but then be unable to come up with a list of needs adequate to produce an attractive set of human rights (Donnelly 2003, 13–14). No reasonable person can disagree with Donnelly's rejection of pseudoscientific dodges. However, Nickel's example of the right to clean water surely shows that some human rights are indeed rooted in need. To agree with Nickel it is not necessary to undertake the highly problematic task of coming up with "a list of needs adequate to produce an attractive set of human rights." One might riposte to Donnelly that it is positively dangerous to deny that some human rights – especially those discussed in this volume – are rooted in human needs. This claim is not undermined by the fact that claims about which needs are basic can be reasonably contested; this entails only that some of the grounds of human rights are not immune from reasonable contestation.

The argument from the incompossibility of rights may also apply to all human rights: the right to freedom of expression may, for example, conflict with the right to privacy. All human rights require the specification of obligation-bearers; all require institutionalization; all may raise the problem of conflicts of rights. "Manifesto rights" leave many difficult theoretical and practical problems unsolved. This applies, however, to liberty rights as well as to economic and social rights. We ought indeed to be realistic, clear, and honest about burdens, their justification, and their allocation for all human rights.[5]

Nickel

James Nickel emphasizes that human rights may require only burdens that are feasible, and that feasibility is often difficult to estimate.[6] To determine that fulfilling an obligation is feasible is to show that the obligation-bearer not only can fulfill it but also can do so without failing to fulfill a more important obligation. The question as to whether an obligation is feasible therefore always raises questions of priorities. To show that there is a right to social security requires the reasonable belief that there is an obligation-bearer who can fulfill this right without the sacrifice of a more important obligation, such as the obligation to provide physical security. The feasibility requirement means that there are human rights only where there are obligations that can be fulfilled with sustainable, rather than counterproductive, economic and social strategies and policies. Nickel maintains that human rights theorists and activists are reluctant to think carefully about the costs of fulfilling human rights for two reasons: firstly, they involve consideration of economic and social theories that are not within their competence; secondly, they entail priorities that challenge the apparently absolutist rhetoric of human rights. Nickel partly agrees with O'Neill that the emphasis on obligation has the practical merit that it clarifies how human rights ought to be and could be implemented by identifying the primary obligation-bearers and those who have secondary obligations when the primary obligation-bearers cannot or will not fulfill

---

[5] The burden of paying the considerable cost of fair access to legal justice is currently controversial in the United Kingdom. The justification of the right to ridicule religion is controversial at the Human Rights Council and elsewhere.

[6] The question of feasibility permeates the work of Thomas Pogge on the rights to health, to an adequate standard of living and to an international order that protects all human rights (discussed in Mark Gibney's contribution to this volume). See Pogge 2007, 2008, 2010.

their obligations. The emphasis on obligations also highlights the question of priorities among incompossible obligations. However, as we have seen, Nickel rejects O'Neill's conclusion that the moral and practical value of focusing on obligations calls into question the validity of economic and social human rights (Nickel 1993).

Rawls

Among the eminent political philosophers skeptical of economic and social rights was John Rawls. He distinguished "human rights proper," such as those in Articles 3–18 of the Universal Declaration, from international declarations that "appear to presuppose specific kinds of institutions, such as the right to social security, in Article 22, and the right to equal pay for equal work, in Article 23" (Rawls 1999, 80). Rawls rejected the claim that economic and social rights were human rights proper because they presupposed specific kinds of institutions. He seemed to assume that human rights must be "natural" – that is, pre-institutional – rights, such as those found in the work of the classic, natural-law theorists, such as John Locke. However, although debate about the distinctive nature of human rights continues, many human rights theorists would agree with Nickel that institutions do not provide the justification of, but rather the means to implement, human rights. Rawls's reference to presuppositions is ambiguous; it could refer either to the justification or to the means of implementing human rights. Rawls's distinction fails anyway, because several of the rights in Articles 3–18 presuppose specific kinds of institution: for example, the right to "a fair and public hearing by an independent and impartial tribunal" in the determination of rights and obligations, and of any criminal charge in Article 10.

Some eminent political philosophers have, therefore, expressed skepticism about the validity of economic and social rights either on the ground that there are insufficient resources to fulfill them or that the obligations to fulfill them are too indeterminate. The responses to these skeptical objections have acknowledged that the fulfillment of human rights often requires resources that are not currently available, and may be very difficult to mobilize. They point out, however, that these are problems for the fulfillment of all human rights, and that they call into question, not the justification of economic and social rights, but rather the means for their implementation. The most searching questions raised for defenders of economic and social human rights by these philosophers are, firstly, O'Neill's requirement that we need to specify who is obliged to do what in order to fulfill the rights, and, secondly, Nickel's demand that, for any human rights to be plausible, we must show that their fulfillment is feasible. Geoffrey Brennan and Philip Pettit have argued that normative theory has little value if it does not offer plausible motivations and incentives for those who have the capacity and obligation to fulfill rights to carry out their obligations (Brennan and Pettit 2005). The challenge for advocates of economic and social rights, therefore, is not only to clarify and justify the rights, but to clarify who has the obligation to fulfill them, and how those who have this obligation might be motivated to carry it out.

CORE RIGHTS

What are regarded as the "core" economic and social rights derive from Articles 23–26 of the UDHR. They are the rights to food, health, housing, social security, work, and education, which together constitute the right to an adequate standard of living.[7]

The Right to Food

The ICESCR imposes on states parties the obligation to realize the right to food progressively; to devote the maximum of their available resources to this end; and to take measures individually and through international cooperation to ensure the right to adequate food. There is, however, an absolute right to be free from hunger that must be fulfilled immediately, because freedom from hunger constitutes the minimum core content of the right to food.

Randolph and Hertel maintain that there are sufficient resources globally to solve the problem of world hunger, yet the right remains seriously unfulfilled. O'Neill attributed this to the emphasis on rights and the neglect of obligations and effective institutions. However, international law does allocate the obligations, and the world has many institutions that seek to fulfill the right. The problem is not the neglect of obligations or institutions, but the lack of political will, and perhaps of the relevant knowledge, to fulfill the right. This problem is one of perverse political and economic incentives, not of law or philosophy. States are not simply

---

[7] It was not possible to include the right to education in this volume. Here I would say only that some scholars have considered that it has a special place in the configuration of human rights in that the fulfillment of the right to education, although not necessary for the fulfillment of other rights, greatly empowers those who need to claim other rights. This is particularly important for women and, of course, children.

too poor – as skeptics such as Cranston argued – but governed corruptly. The international community does not fail to recognize its obligations – contrary to what O'Neill suggests – but fails to take its obligations sufficiently seriously.[8] Randolph and Hertel complain that the right to food is too state-centric, and consequently ignores the role of non-state actors and the obligations of the well-off. This echoes O'Neill's concern, but, although state-centrism may sometimes be an obstacle to the fulfillment of this right, Nickel's argument that human rights advocates underestimate the importance of supporting their recommendations with feasible economic strategies and policies applies here.

A strong merit of the chapter by Randolph and Hertel is that it draws our attention to large-scale forces that might prevent the fulfillment of the right to food. For example, global supply and demand for food may cause shortages and consequent increases in prices that aggravate world hunger. Also, trade liberalization and the imposition of structural adjustment programs may make it difficult for states to meet even their minimal obligations to implement the right to food. The main lesson to be drawn from this chapter is that economic forces may be major obstacles to the fulfillment of legal human rights obligations. The capacity to fulfill the legal obligation of states to implement economic and social rights, even in their minimal form, is only partly in the power of the obligation-holders. Both states and the international community have to grapple with a global economic order that recognizes, at best only in a weak form, a collective obligation to fulfill the human right to food, and that, often unintentionally, operates to deny this fundamental right to many millions. The institutional structure of the international order is a barrier to the fulfillment of this right, and, within this structure, it is very difficult to develop the motivations and incentives to carry out the necessary institutional reforms.[9]

The Right to Health

Audrey Chapman and Salil Benegal, writing about the right to health, also emphasize that core obligations are independent of resources. They agree with Randolph and Hertel that economic globalization and the ideology of neoliberalism have obstructed the fulfillment of economic and social

---

[8] Pogge 2008.

[9] Pogge 2008 offers a powerful analysis of these issues. For critical debates about Pogge's contribution, see *Ethics & International Affairs* 2005 and Jaggar 2010.

rights, especially by the demand for privatization of public services, the reduction of state expenditures, and the consequent increase in inequality. International financial institutions, especially the World Bank and International Monetary Fund, in combination with transnational corporations, have subjected the provision of health-related services to market forces indifferent to human rights. The liberalization of trade undermines access to water and food security, and encourages health workers to migrate from poor to rich countries. Structural adjustment programs and poverty-reduction strategy papers weaken the protection of economic and social rights. The World Trade Organization, and especially the Agreement on Trade-Related Aspects of Intellectual Property Rights (TRIPS), have hindered efforts to fulfill the right to health for the global poor. They maintain that, if a state makes a trade agreement that foreseeably leads to regress in the fulfillment of the right to health, it has committed a human rights violation. This may be correct within the discourse of international human rights law, but it gives rise to two problems: 1) trade law and human rights law are very poorly integrated at the legal level; and 2) trade law tends to trump human rights law at the political and economic levels. Strengthening the will of states to take human rights seriously in relation to trade is a challenge that governments have barely begun to meet. Taking up this challenge will require careful analysis of the human rights benefits and costs of trade agreements, analysis that human rights scholars are not yet well placed to offer.[10]

The Right to Housing

Cathy Albisa, Brittany Scott, and Kate Tissington are also concerned with the impact of neoliberalism and market economics on human rights, in particular the human right to housing. People often lose their homes to make way for "development," which may be supported by the World Bank. Legal strategies to defend the right to housing have often proved ineffective for various reasons, including the lack of an independent judiciary or the lack of capacity among the poor to have effective access to legal remedies. In some places, popular movements have had some success in limiting violations of this human right.[11] The right to housing has a strong moral basis, and is protected in principle by international human

---

[10] See, however, Leader 2005.
[11] For an excellent account of a campaign to protect the right to housing against a development project in Nigeria supported by the World Bank, see Morka 2011.

rights law, but the economics and politics of housing are complex, and the right to housing may apparently fall victim to the problem of incompossibility in that it may be trumped by "the right to development." However, it is not obviously necessary that development requires that the vulnerable become homeless, and this chapter suggests the desirability of the comparative study of housing policies in the light of this human right. It shows also that failure to fulfill economic and social rights cannot be explained solely by the state's lack of resources, as rich states with inadequately regulated housing markets fail to fulfill the right to housing. Homelessness may be caused by market-based governmental policies, driven by ideology and indifference to the victims of such policies, but it may also be caused by complex social factors, such as changing family and employment patterns, with the result that even well-intentioned governmental policies may face resistance from social and economic structures and dynamics that are recalcitrant to control. Insofar as these factors may be subject to cultural variability, the need for comparative research is strengthened. This chapter does well to open up this field.

The Right to Social Security

Lyle Scruggs, Christian Zimmermann, and Christopher Jeffords maintain that the human right to social security is poorly implemented, and there is consequently a need for more effective monitoring and reporting of progress, or lack of progress, in the fulfillment of this right. They report that, although there has been significant legal progress, there has been less actual progress. There is, however, a lack of data on actual progress, and the need for more research. They find that states that have ratified the ICESCR; have a higher per capita income; are liberal democracies; have a civil law system; have a socialist legal tradition; have low ethnolinguistic diversity; have more social security laws. The lines of causation are, however, uncertain. It is, for example, not clear whether countries that ratify the Covenant go on to enact more social security laws or countries that have more such laws are more likely to ratify the Covenant. Surprisingly, democracy has little impact on the number of social security laws once controls for other factors are taken into account, although this does not mean that democracies do not provide better social security de facto. Ethnic diversity has some negative effect on social security laws, but it is not great. These authors emphasize that their analysis is preliminary in a seriously under-researched field, and the most important unanswered question is the relation between social security laws and the actual fulfillment of the right to social security. As other chapters in this section, this chapter demonstrates very clearly the need to supplement human rights law with well-designed social, economic, and political research on the conditions that are favorable and unfavorable to the fulfillment of the right. It does seem plausible that scarce resources limit the extent to which this right could be fulfilled, but, without further research we can know neither which other factors may be significant nor what the relative weights of these factors are.

The Right to Work

Philip Harvey argues that the right to work has quantitative and qualitative dimensions, but the fulfillment of the latter is dependent on the fulfillment of the former. Thus, reducing the quantity of unemployment is necessary to the fulfillment of the right to work. Since the time of the New Deal, he says, there has been a policy shift from direct job creation to the Keynesian management of demand. This has failed because Keynesian policies came to be associated with unacceptable levels of inflation. Harvey argues that direct job creation is a better policy to fulfill the human right to work. He maintains that the equivalents of the economic and social rights recognized in the UDHR were implemented by the U.S. Congress in 1935 "to some degree or another." Even with the limited funding it was given, the direct job-creation program implemented by the Roosevelt administration during this period "made a far greater dent in the nation's unemployment problem than is generally recognized," providing jobs for an average of about one-third of all unemployed individuals during the second half of the 1930s.

Harvey's chapter makes a valuable contribution to expounding the normative content of the human right to work. He is surely correct to claim that this is a neglected human right. His analysis of the New Deal makes an empirical claim about the governmental policies that would fulfill this right. This raises complex and controversial issues in labor economics. The very richness of Harvey's normative conceptualization of this right might prompt some political philosophers to conclude that it is an aspiration rather than a right. The application of Harvey's empirical claims needs to be tested with further cross-national research.

What emerges from these analyses of core economic and social rights is that the concern of political philosophers with lack of available resources or unallocated obligations is at least partially misplaced. Globally, the resources are available, and, legally, the obligations are fairly clear.

Economic and social rights are not fulfilled as a result of two main causes: 1) those with surplus resources are not willing to pay the price of fulfilling their obligations; and 2) even if they were willing to pay this price, we lack the empirical knowledge of the best strategies and policies to implement economic and social rights.

NONDISCRIMINATION

The right not to be subject to discrimination in the enjoyment of one's human rights is widely considered to be among the most fundamental of human rights. The Committee on Economic, Social and Cultural Rights includes this among the core obligations of states that are not permitted to implement it progressively. However, where discrimination is deeply embedded in society, which is the case almost everywhere in the world, it is hard to see how there could be a realistic alternative to progressive realization, even if it is reasonable to demand that progress be an urgent policy priority.

The Rights of Children

Kathryn Libal and Ken Neubeck maintain that the full range of human rights that states are obliged to respect, protect, and fulfill for adult citizens they are also obliged to accord to children. Yet child poverty is widespread, thereby denying children the right to an adequate standard of living. This is true even of the rich countries, including the United States. Similar to other contributors, Libal and Neubeck attribute to the economic policy fashion for privatization the failure to relieve child poverty. In the United States child poverty is worse than general poverty; it is increasing; it is more common when single mothers are caring for children; and it is worse among racial minorities. The United States has a worse record than that of other rich states. The United States has failed to fulfill the right of children to health and an adequate standard of living. If it were to ratify the Convention on the Rights of the Child, there would be a legal basis for a potentially effective campaign to remedy this policy failure. The failure of the United States to ratify this convention is obviously regrettable from the perspective of children's rights, but its causal role in the problems that these authors identify is uncertain. Again, a comparative study of successes and failures in securing children's rights would be helpful, and one might conjecture that social movements bring about the necessary laws that, under favorable political and social conditions, improve the enjoyment of rights. Ratifying international covenants itself is at most a weak causal factor.[12]

The Rights of Women

Catherine Buerger argues that the economic and social human rights of women have been neglected even by activists for the human rights of women. There is a considerable gap in many countries between the de jure and de facto status of women, especially in relation to poverty and economic empowerment. Although many countries systematically refer to the principle of equality in their constitutions and laws, women still earn less, are more concentrated in informal and vulnerable employment, and lack power in economic decision making. The lack of disaggregated data means that governments do not know the extent to which their equality laws are implemented. Context-specific barriers to the fulfillment of women's rights and the historical prioritization of civil and political rights have hindered the process of translating legal respect for women's economic rights into their fulfillment. To implement human rights, it is essential to obtain local information about the ways that individuals engage with the law on an everyday basis. Legal reforms must be combined with programs that take into account the social, political, and cultural barriers to the implementation of legal rights. Buerger illustrates these generalizations with a case study of women's rights to work and property in Ghana, where the law purports to protect women's rights, but cultural barriers prevent the implementation of the law. Buerger may have identified one of the most important areas in which social forces create strong barriers to the fulfillment of rights that exist in both international and national laws.

The Rights of Stateless Persons

Kristy Belton takes up the surprisingly neglected topic of statelessness in relation to economic and social rights. It is estimated that between 12 and 15 million people in the world lack citizenship. They are consequently vulnerable to human rights violations. This problem has been neglected in the human rights field; the economic and social rights of stateless persons

---

[12] Empirical studies of the causal efficacy of ratifying international human rights treaties have produced results varying from the bleakly pessimistic to the cautiously optimistic, depending on the methodology employed (Landman 2005; Hafner-Burton and Tsutsui 2007; Simmons 2009).

have been especially neglected. There is a human right to a nationality, but this is an empty right, because there is no corresponding obligation. Only states can grant citizenship, and states have no obligations to do so if they choose not to. This is an example of a supposed human right with no allocated obligation that has been overlooked even by those who have been concerned with the allocation of obligations corresponding to human rights.

There are various international instruments that might either restrict the creation of statelessness or fulfill the economic and social rights of stateless persons, but all these provide escape clauses that enable states not to fulfill the obligations apparently envisaged by the conventions.

Solutions to these problems might include taking the right to nationality seriously; paying more attention to the problem by the Committee on Economic, Social and Cultural Rights; a right to petition by the stateless; the appointment of a special rapporteur; and improved recognition of the problem within the UN. It is difficult to estimate the likely effectiveness of these proposals. There might be a hopeful precedent in the movement for the rights of indigenous peoples, who were also effectively excluded from the international legal community of states, but two cautionary thoughts are in order. First, the success of the indigenous peoples' movement is still an open question. Second, it may be that mobilization on behalf of stateless persons will prove even more difficult than that on behalf of indigenous peoples. However, Belton points to one significant possible lever for progress: the very commitment of the international community to both statism and human rights suggests that it has a strong obligation to take seriously the human rights of the stateless.

META RIGHTS

The concept of meta rights is novel, and requires careful analysis. It appears to refer to umbrella rights that are considered to bring other rights together or to be general necessary conditions for the enjoyment of such rights. Some object to meta rights on the grounds that they are redundant or even a distraction from efforts to fulfill established rights. The contributors to the third section of this volume reject such objections.

The Right to an International Order (Article 28)

Mark Gibney draws our attention to Article 28 of the UDHR, which states that everyone has the right to a social and international order in which

the rights set forth in the Declaration can be fully realized. He pc
uncertainties in the meaning of this right. There is a human right
adequate standard of living, and states have some sort of obligation to
assist other states in fulfilling this right, but the nature of this obligation
is unclear and is almost never acknowledged in practice. Thomas Pogge
has appealed to Article 28 to argue that the rich states commit massive
human rights violations by their imposition on the global poor of unjust
economic conditions, and that they have strong obligations to remedy
this injustice (Pogge 2008). Gibney seeks to go beyond morality to argue
that Article 28 imposes legal obligations on states to respect, protect,
and fulfill human rights beyond their borders. Yet states generally do not
recognize that they have such obligations. The concept of human rights,
notwithstanding numerous affirmations of its universality, is still closely
associated with political democracy and the rights of citizens. This is
a serious limitation on the potential to fulfill human rights worldwide.
The recent doctrine of the responsibility to protect seems to envisage
extraterritorial human rights obligations, but at present it seems unlikely
that this doctrine will have more than a marginal impact, and it is not
even intended to protect economic and social rights. The UN Charter, the
ICESCR, comments by the Committee on Economic, Social and Cultural
Rights, the Convention on the Rights of the Child, and the Millennium
Declaration all support the proposition that states have extraterritorial
obligations with respect to all types of human rights. As with all legal
arguments about the obligations of states, the question arises as to how
we might motivate states to practice what they sign up to do.

The Right to Equality (Article 28)

Gillian MacNaughton offers an original interpretation of Article 28 as
proclaiming the right to a social order within national societies in which
human rights can be fully realized. She wants to go beyond the "minimum
content" approach to human rights to social equality. She argues that
human rights advocates have ignored the extent to which social inequality
leads to human rights violations. She argues that Article 28 enshrines a
collective right to economic and social equality because such equality is
essential to fully realize the other rights in the International Bill of Rights.
The common emphasis on a minimum core of rights is complicit with
a denial of human dignity and the requirements of international human
rights law. The minimum threshold of international human rights practice
ignores the inequality that leads to human rights deficits. Equality is

required by both dignity and fairness. To accept inequality is to accept the discrimination prohibited by international human rights law. The right to social equality should be at the center of the human rights agenda. Articles 1 and 28 of the UDHR proclaim the right to equal rights, including the equal right to economic and social rights. The UDHR entails a far-reaching egalitarianism and the politics of social democracy.

MacNaughton's argument raises a number of fundamental questions about international human rights. Is this conception of human rights, as is often said, neutral between the principal religions, philosophies, and ideologies in the world, or does it entail a highly egalitarian form of social democracy? Is MacNaughton's interpretation of international human rights law that intended by its framers, and is it consistent with the best current legal interpretations? Would the implementation of her egalitarianism have costs that she has overlooked? Are her prescriptions feasible? The answers to these questions will be complex and contested. There is a prima facie case that large social inequalities undermine the value of human rights, but there are complex normative and empirical questions about both the meaning of equality and its relations to other values.

The Right to Development

Flavia Piovesan locates the right to development in the field of human rights. This putative right is perhaps the most controversial legally, politically, and economically. On the one hand, it is strongly supported by the governments of developing countries, and it has been included in numerous UN texts. Arguments that might support such a right are the following: 1) development is a necessary condition for the fulfillment of all human rights; and 2) the right to development articulates the obligations of developed countries to assist the developing countries. On the other hand, the claim that there is such a right and a set of corresponding obligations has not been accepted by the developed countries and has never been made the subject of a binding treaty. It is very doubtful that it can be considered part of customary international law. It has been criticized on the ground that it adds nothing to the pre-existing set of human rights and could, in practice, be used as cover for violations of those rights (Donnelly 1985). Tom Sorell and Todd Landman have also argued that there is no (universal) human right to development, because the rich do not have a human right to become even richer, and may have an obligation to become poorer in order to help the poor (Sorell and Landman 2006). The right to development has considerable rhetorical appeal at the

UN, but is generally ignored in the theory and practice of development economics (Salomon 2007). The right to development is sometimes confused with the human rights approach to development. The former claims to have identified a new, universal human right, whereas the latter emphasizes the importance of including respect for (pre-existing) human rights in development strategies. "Development" is a very politically potent term, so that both its meaning and relation to human rights require the most careful conceptual and empirical analysis.

Environmental Rights

Christopher Jeffords is concerned with environmental human rights. He offers a keyword analysis of 142 national constitutions. He finds that 63% of the constitutions that he examined included some environmental human rights. This provides a framework within which we could systematically address the question of whether constitutions tell us whether countries are taking environmental human rights seriously. Jeffords himself believes that further research is needed to answer this question. This research presumably would have to be designed to identify the relative causal weight of constitutional provisions and other possible causal factors.

Meta rights are problematic, because the precise meaning of "meta" may be unclear. Is a meta right a universal, individual human right; if so, what work is the term "meta" doing? Is it something more than a familiar type of human right; if so, precisely what meaning is added to that of human right by the prefix "meta"? The strongest case for meta rights has perhaps been made by Pogge and Gibney, because they appeal to a right enshrined in the Universal Declaration, so that its legal status is established, and because they insist on the institutional framework that they claim is empirically necessary for the fulfillment of the other human rights. The chapters on meta rights present interesting challenges to clarify the conceptual and empirical value of this concept.

CONCLUSIONS

Some philosophers have been skeptical about economic and social human rights on the grounds that they are impossible, incompossible, or unallocated (there are no corresponding obligations). The contributions to this volume show that these objections can be met, because the necessary resources are available, globally; conflicts of rights are not specific to economic and social rights, but raise problems for the most uncontroversial human rights; and international law allocates obligations. One theme that emerges from this volume, however, is that of the limitations of law – international and national – in fulfilling economic and social rights. The causes of failures to fulfill economic and social rights are neither lack of resources nor failure to allocate obligations, but the power of political and economic forces – some intended, others unintended – to block the fulfillment of human rights. There may well be conflicts among human rights, but these apply to all human rights, and are not in principle irresolvable – human rights courts resolve them almost every day. Human rights – all human rights – are ideals based on various fundamental values, such as respect for human dignity, the requirements of a minimally decent life, and so forth. There is no agreed philosophical foundation of human rights, and consequently no perfect agreement on the list or interpretation of human rights. In this, human rights do not differ from other fundamental moral and political values. International human rights law provides guidance for what we ought to do, but it fails to give us the capacity to achieve the aims that it sets for the international community. The struggle for human rights is essentially political; that is to say, it is a struggle for power. This is the final message of this volume.

REFERENCES

Brennan, Geoffrey and Philip Pettit, 2005. "The Feasibility Issue," in Frank Jackson and Michael Smith (Eds.) *The Oxford Handbook of Contemporary Philosophy*, 258–279, Oxford: Oxford University Press.

Cranston, Maurice, 1973. *What Are Human Rights?* London: Bodley Head.

Donnelly, Jack, 1985. "In Search of the Unicorn: The Jurisprudence and Politics of the Right to Development," *California Western International Law Journal* 15(3): 473–509.

Donnelly, Jack, 2003. *Universal Human Rights in Theory & Practice*, 2nd edition, Ithaca: Cornell University Press.

Ethics & International Affairs, 2005. "Symposium on World Poverty and Human Rights" 19(1): 1–83.

Hafner-Burton, Emilie M. and Kiyoteru Tsutsui, 2007. "Justice Lost! The Failure of International Human Rights Law to Matter Where Needed Most," *Journal of Peace Research* 44(4): 407–425.

Halperin, Morton H., Joseph T. Siegle, and Michael M. Weinstein, 2010. *The Democracy Advantage: How Democracies Promote Prosperity and Peace*, revised edition, London: Routledge.

Jaggar, Alison M. (Ed.), 2010. *Thomas Pogge and His Critics*, Cambridge: Polity.

Landman, Todd, 2005. *Protecting Human Rights: A Comparative Study*, Washington, DC: Georgetown University Press.

Leader, Sheldon, 2005. "Trade and Human Rights II," in Patrick F.J. Macrory, Arthur E. Appleton, and Michael G. Plummer (Eds) *The World Trade Organization: Legal, Economic and Political Analysis*, 663–696, New York: Springer.

Miller, David, 2009. "The responsibility to protect human rights," in Lukas H. Meyer (Ed.) *Legitimacy, Justice and Public International Law*, 232–251, Cambridge: Cambridge University Press.

Morka, Felix, 2011. "A Place to Live: Resisting Evictions in Ijora-Badia, Nigeria," in Lucie E. White and Jeremy Perelman (Eds.) *Stones of Hope: How African Activists Reclaim Human Rights to Challenge Global Poverty*, 17–41, Stanford: Stanford University Press.

Nickel, James W., 1993. "How human rights generate duties to provide and protect," *Human Rights Quarterly* 15(1): 77–86.

O'Neill, Onora, 1986. *Faces of Hunger: An Essay on Poverty, Justice and Development*, London: Allen & Unwin.

O'Neill, Onora, 1996. *Towards Justice and Virtue: A Constructive Account of Practical Reasoning*, Cambridge: Cambridge University Press.

O'Neill, Onora, 2004. "Global Justice: Whose Obligations?" in Deen K. Chatterjee (Ed.) *The Ethics of Assistance: Morality and the Distant Needy*, 242–259, Cambridge: Cambridge University Press.

Pogge, Thomas, 1992. "O'Neill on Rights and Duties," *Grazer Philosophische Studien* 43: 233–247.

Pogge, Thomas, 2007. "Severe Poverty as a Human Rights Violation," in Thomas Pogge (Ed.) *Freedom from Poverty as a Human Right: Who Owes What to the Very Poor?*, 11–53, Oxford: UNESCO and Oxford University Press.

Pogge, Thomas, 2008. *World Poverty and Human Rights: Cosmopolitan Responsibilities and Reforms*, 2nd edition, Cambridge: Polity Press.

Pogge, Thomas, 2010. *Politics as Usual: What Lies Behind the Pro-poor Rhetoric*, Cambridge: Polity Press.

Rawls, John, 1999. *The Law of Peoples*, Cambridge, MA: Harvard University Press.

Salomon, Margot E., 2007. *Global Responsibility for Human Rights: World Poverty and the Development of International Law*, Oxford: Oxford University Press.

Sen, Amartya, 2006. "Human Rights and the Limits of Law," *Cardozo Law Review* 27(6): 2913–2927.

Simmons, Beth A., 2009. *Mobilizing for Human Rights: International Law in Domestic Politics*, New York: Cambridge University Press.

Sorell, Tom and Todd Landman, 2006. "Justifying Human Rights: The Roles of Domain, Audience, and Constituency," *Journal of Human Rights* 5(4): 383–400.

Steiner, Hillel, 1994. *An Essay on Rights*, Oxford: Blackwell.

Index